Nations Unbound

Nations Unbound

Transnational Projects, Postcolonial Predicaments, and Deterritorialized Nation-States

Linda Basch

Nina Glick Schiller

Cristina Szanton Blanc

GORDON AND BREACH SCIENCE PUBLISHERS
Australia • Canada • France • Germany • India • Japan • Luxembourg
Malaysia • The Netherlands • Russia • Singapore • Switzerland

First published 1994
Fifth printing 2000

Amsteldijk 166
1st Floor
1079 LH Amsterdam
The Netherlands

Library of Congress Cataloging-in-Publication Data

Basch, Linda G. (Linda Green)
    Nations unbound : transnational projects, postcolonial predicaments, and deterritorialized nation-states / by Linda Basch, Nina Glick Schiller, and Cristina Szanton Blanc.
        p. cm.
    Includes bibliographical references (p.   ) and index.
    ISBN 2-88124-607-9 (hardcover). -- ISBN 2-88124-630-3 (softcover)
    1. Emigration and immigration--Social aspects. 2. Ethnicity.
3. International economic relations. 4. International cooperation.
5. Internationalism. I. Schiller, Nina Glick. II. Szanton Blanc, Cristina. III. Title.
JV6225.B37 1993
304.8--dc20   93-28765
                                                                  CIP

CONTENTS

ACKNOWLEDGMENTS

This book is the product of an intensely collaborative process, conducted across the boundaries of nation-states, geographic spaces, job descriptions, and women's kin work. During the six years it took to develop and complete this project, children have been educated, some marriages have been dissolved, and jobs have changed, but friendship has remained. We have been assisted in our efforts to understand transnational cultural practices that stand outside formal structures by the fact that this book was written without the formal support of sabbaticals or grant-funding beyond the research.

The book represents an interweave of our various data, which we worked together to analyze, and benefits from the interpretations we all brought to the transnational projects and postcolonial predicaments we observed. Nonetheless, in the later stages, with the demands of Linda's deaning and Cristina's position with UNICEF, we profited from the time and resources Nina had as a faculty member at the University of New Hampshire to do the additional work that enabled this project to reach fruition. We wish to acknowledge this contribution.

We also are appreciative of the contributions of our various co-researchers, who helped us both conduct and conceptualize the research: Marie Lucie Brutus, Carolle Charles, Josh DeWind, George Fouron, Lourdes Franco, Martial Pierre, Shirley Seward, Antoine Thomas, Joyce Toney, Nora Villanueva, Rosina Wiltshire, and Winston Wiltshire. We wish to thank all the transmigrants who shared their life stories with us. In addition, we acknowledge the scholarly reading of the text provided by Richard Downs and Les Field, the skillful word processing of the final manuscript by Valerie Jo Brown and of earlier drafts by Aline McGrail, and the assistance of Iching Wu, who worked as bibliographer through many drafts, and of Ancil Etienne, David Karjanen, and Peter Szanton, who aided with this task.

We save the most important for last. We dedicate this book to our families — to our spouse, partners, children, and parents. To Sam, Ethan, Arielle, and Abigail Basch; Cecile and Harold Green; Rachel and Naomi Schiller; Stephen Reyna; Evelyn Barnett; Blanche Schiller; Julia and Peter Szanton; and Elena Blanc; we give special thanks for your faith in this project and for your unending support.

Chapter ONE

Transnational Projects: A New Perspective[1]

The Presidential Palace in Haiti, for decades under the Duvalier regime a location rumored to be the site of terrible tortures and beatings, was eagerly entered in January 1991 by over one hundred visitors from the Haitian diaspora. While many were U.S. citizens, most had been born in Haiti. Some had fled Haiti into exile and struggled to rebuild their lives, while others had grown up abroad and obtained educations, professional careers, and social standing in the United States and Canada. Both men and women, they were a prosperous group, well incorporated into their new societies. But their visit to Haiti was more than a sentimental journey. Their special invitation to the palace to witness and celebrate the inauguration of Father Aristide, Haitians' new and freely elected President, marked them as active participants in efforts to rebuild the Haitian nation-state. This became clear when the newly inaugurated President greeted them as members of *Dizyèm Depatman-an*, "the 10th Department," although the territory of the country of Haiti is divided into nine administrative districts, each called *"Depatman."* In this pronouncement, which had no legal substance, Aristide was directly

1

articulating what many Haitians had long maintained. No matter where they settle, or what passport they carry, people of Haitian ancestry remain an integral part of Haiti.

* * *

Approximately 200 well-dressed Grenadian immigrants, mostly from urban areas in Grenada and presently employed in white collar jobs in New York, gathered in 1984 in a Grenadian-owned catering hall in Brooklyn to hear the Grenadian Minister of Agriculture and Development. The Minister shared with Grenada's "constituency in New York" his plans for agricultural development in Grenada and encouraged the immigrants to become part of this effort. Addressing the immigrants as nationals of Grenada, even though many were U.S. citizens, the Minister asked the audience to encourage their relatives at home to become engaged in agricultural production, and to convince them that this generally demeaned activity was worthwhile and important. Further, treating the immigrants as national leaders and as people who could wield influence at home and even help develop an entire industry, the Minister implored the immigrants to assist in developing an exotic fruit industry for export. But in asking the immigrants to "do what they could" to introduce Grenadian agricultural goods to the U.S. market, including lobbying U.S. government agencies to obtain approval to import the fruits, the Minister was also addressing the immigrants as ethnics in the United States.

Several of the immigrants in the audience were in a position to provide some assistance with these tasks. Some of the immigrants had recently formed a Caribbean–American Chamber of Commerce, both to assist Caribbean immigrants in establishing businesses in the United States and to market West Indian goods. And some, including the organizers of this meeting, had been in the United States a minimum of ten years and were as involved in the local politics of New York City as they were in the political life of Grenada. Grenada's ambassador to the United Nations, for example, had been a leader in the New York West Indian community for over forty years and had spearheaded support groups to elect mayors of New York City.

* * *

In one of the offices of a company in New Jersey in 1988, an employee at a desk is helping a customer close the box of goods she is shipping "home" to her family in the Philippines and complete the listing of items it contains. A regular flow of such boxes leaves every day from seven to eight major Filipino shipping companies. Anything — appliances, electronic equipment and the like — can be sent or carried back as long as these goods fit the weight, size and other prescriptions defining a *balikbayan* box; they can be admitted into the Philippines almost tax free.

President Marcos had first used the term *"balikbayan"* (Homecomers) during a major national speech in which he encouraged Filipino migrants overseas to visit their home country and announced new regulations to facilitate their return. Mrs. Aquino extended the *balikbayan* regulations and stated her concern for the numerous silent "heroes and heroines of the Philippines" working overseas. The Filipino returnees could purchase up to $1,000 in duty-free gifts upon entering the Philippines. The Filipino transnational social field, built on family networks and sustained through economic exchanges and gift-giving, has thus been further structured and officially sanctioned by the Philippine state.

* * *

Faced with the long-term and probably permanent settlement abroad of substantial sectors of their populations, the political leaderships of Grenada, St. Vincent, the Philippines, and Haiti, are engaged in a new form of nation-state building. Sometimes through specific public policies, as in the case of the *balikbayan* regulations, but often through the use of symbols, language, and political rituals, migrants and political leaders in the country of origin are engaged in constructing an ideology that envisions migrants as loyal citizens of their ancestral nation-state. This ideology recognizes and encourages the continuing and multiple ties that immigrants maintain with their society of origin. Ignored in this construction, however, is the ongoing incorporation of these immigrants into the society and polity of the country in which they have settled. Yet the significance of transmigrants to their country of origin in many ways rests on the extent of their incorporation into the national economy and political processes of their country of settlement.

Neither the representations nor the practices of these immigrants in relationship to their "home" nation-states are encompassed within the analytical paradigms that predominate in migration studies, focusing as they do on immigrant incorporation within the country of settlement. The time has come for all of us — social scientists and immigrants — to rethink our conceptions of the migration process, immigrant incorporation, and identity.

I. STATEMENT OF THE PROBLEM

The word "immigrant" evokes images of permanent rupture, of the abandonment of old patterns of life and the painful learning of a new culture and often a new language (Handlin 1973). The popular image of immigrant is one of people who have come to stay, having uprooted themselves from their old society in order to make for themselves a new home and adopt a new country to which they will pledge allegiance. Migrants, on the other hand, are conceived of as transients who have come only to work; their stay is temporary and eventually they will return home or move on. Yet it has become increasingly obvious that our present conceptions of "immigrant" and "migrant," anchored in the circumstances of earlier historic moments, no longer suffice. Today, immigrants develop networks, activities, patterns of living, and ideologies that span their home and the host society.

At first glance the problem seems to be a straightforward one of revamping our vocabulary to come to terms with this new kind of migrant flow. Consequently, increasing numbers of social scientists have begun calling the emergent migration process in which people live lives stretched across national borders "transnational" (Georges 1990; Kearney 1991a; Sutton 1992a), but the term is often used loosely and without specificity. Frequently the phenomenon of transnationalism is thought to be the outcome of transformations in the technology of communication and transportation, a product of accessible air travel and telecommunications (Wakeman 1988). Language is, however, part and parcel of the manner in which we understand and experience the world; the need to change or extend our language is driven by broader political and economic transformations (Asad 1986).

To come to terms adequately with the experience and consciousness of this new immigrant population, we believe that new conceptualizations and a new analytical framework are in order. The development of a transnational analytical framework is the task of this book.

A. Transnationalism "Discovered"

Before writing the book, each of us had been separately grappling with the problem of how to understand the migrations we were seeing and experiencing all around us. Linda Basch had been working with several Caribbean colleagues in a comparative study of the patterns of organization and self-identification adopted by residents of Grenada and St. Vincent who had migrated to Trinidad or to the United States. As an initial step in their research agenda, they sought to identify immigrants in both New York and Trinidad who had relatives on these two small eastern Caribbean islands and to trace the interconnections sustained between those who stayed at home and those who settled abroad. However, the research team soon discovered that the lives of their "subjects" did not fit into the expected research categories of "immigrants" and those "remaining behind." Their experiences and lives were not sharply segmented between host and home societies.

Rather, the migrants in the study sample moved so frequently and were seemingly so at home in either New York or Trinidad as well as their societies of origin, that it at times became difficult to identify where they "belonged." This same complexity characterized the lives and subjectivities of several members of the research team whose households, activities, and identities stretched across national borders and included both Trinidad and St. Vincent. For a long time these researchers, most of whom were themselves transmigrants, as well as many persons in the study sample, lived lives at variance with the language both immigrants and social scientists were using to describe the migrant experience.

In grappling with the contradictions of their research, Basch, not herself a migrant but influenced by immigrant experiences of rupture and adaptation still alive in her family history, and Rosina Wiltshire, Winston Wiltshire, and Joyce Toney, three West Indian scholars who were her co-researchers and who themselves were transmigrants, recognized that the dichotomized social science categories used to analyze migration experiences could not explain the simultaneous involvements of Vincentian and Grenadian migrants in the social and political life of more than one nation-state. Rather than fragmented social and political experiences, these activities, spread across state boundaries, seemed to constitute a single field of social relations. These researchers began to use the terms "transnationalism" and "transnational social field" to describe this interconnected social experience. Moreover, they found that transnationalism characterized the migrations to both Trinidad and New York, although their intensities and emphases varied.

At about this time, Nina Glick Schiller sat with Josh DeWind, with whom she had designed a research project to study Haitian immigrant identity. They both stared at a blackboard on which Josh had arranged two columns, one labeled "ethnic" for persons who were oriented towards the incorporation of Haitian immigrants into the United States, and the other "national" for individuals in New York who sought to galvanize Haitian immigrants into political activities designed to obtain political change in Haiti. Some Haitian leaders they readily saw as "U.S. ethnics," while others could be identified as "Haitian nationalists." But many leaders ended up in both columns. Schiller and DeWind, both born in the United States, carried with them into their ethnographic encounters family stories of the uprooting and resettlement of immigrant ancestors. When they began to work as a research team with several Haitian scholars who had immigrated to the United States, these colleagues, although they themselves were migrants, brought much similar baggage. Mary Lucie Brutus, Carolle Charles, Georges Fouron, and Antoine Thomas, using the reading of immigrant history that predominated in the United States, also tended to see an antinomy between identification with political struggles in Haiti or settlement in the United States (Fouron 1983, 1984).

However, it was only when Glick Schiller began to compare her field observations with Basch's conceptualization of transnationalism that it became clear to both her and her colleagues, Haitian and non-Haitian alike, that the two poles they were examining were not opposite orientations but part of a single social experience. They were witnessing an emergent Haitian transnationalism. Neither the categories of social science that they had brought to the study, nor the categories that had meaning for the Haitian migrants, were adequate to articulate the nature of daily life for a large section of the Haitian immigrant population throughout the United States.

Meanwhile, Cristina Szanton Blanc was having transnationalism thrust upon her. She had spent a number of years conducting research in the rural Philippines among people who two decades ago had, for the most part, not even been to Manila. She had not set out to study Filipino migration per se, but found that increasing numbers of the people she had known in small Filipino towns were showing up at her doorstep in the United States in the early 1980s. These old friends and acquaintances had first obtained an education in the Philippines and then migrated to the United States where they worked as health professionals and white-collar workers, bought houses, and established themselves. Now they were working to build houses or to supplement the material resources of their family households in the Philippines. At the same time a growing number of Filipino organizations made presentations on Philippine national issues in public forums she organized at Columbia University. Drawing comparisons between Cristina's Filipino example and Linda's and Nina's Caribbean cases enabled us to more fully develop the concept of transnationalism. Cristina could readily identify with the juggling of life, identities, and social worlds that was the daily practice of transmigrants. Born in Italy and settled in the United States, with networks and activities located in both countries, she discovered that she herself was a transnational migrant.

Clearly the concept of "transnationalism" is an "idea whose time has come." Our "discovery" of transnationalism happened as several other scholars were independently beginning to move in the same direction (Appadurai and Breckenridge 1988; Gupta 1992; Kearney 1991a; Rouse 1991, 1992). Even before the term transnational became popular, students of migration had observed the circulation of populations between home and host societies. For example, Elsa Chaney talked about "people with feet in two societies" (1979:209). Others, such as Jorge Dandler and Carmen Medeiros, who observed the same processes of migration while analyzing Bolivian highland migration to Argentina, became preoccupied with how to distinguish methodologically between "temporary" and "permanent" migrants because of the constant back and forth movements that characterized the lives of the Bolivian migrants (Dandler and Medeiros 1988).

B. Definitions

We define "transnationalism" as the processes by which immigrants forge and sustain multi-stranded social relations that link together their societies of origin and settlement. We call these processes transnationalism to emphasize that many immigrants today build social fields that cross geographic, cultural, and political borders. Immigrants who develop and maintain multiple relationships — familial, economic, social, organizational, religious, and political — that span borders we call "transmigrants." An essential element of transnationalism is the multiplicity of involvements that transmigrants' sustain in both home and host societies. We are still groping for a language to describe these social locations. Transmigrants use the term "home" for their society of origin, even when they clearly have also made a home in their country of settlement. The migration literature describes the country of settlement as the "host," but such a term, though compact and convenient, carries the often unwarranted connotations that the immigrant is both "welcome" and a "visitor." Transmigrants take actions, make decisions, and develop subjectivities and identities embedded in networks of relationships that connect them simultaneously to two or more nation-states.

Our definition of transnationalism allows us to analyze the "lived" and fluid experiences of individuals who act in ways that challenge our previous conflation of geographic space and social identity. This definition also will enable us to see the ways transmigrants are transformed by their transnational practices and how these practices affect the nation-nation-states of the transmigrants' origin and settlement.

While we speak a great deal in this book about transnationalism as processes and of the construction of identities that reflect transnational experience, individuals, communities, or states rarely identify themselves as transnational. It is only in contemporary fiction (see Anzaldua 1987; Ghosh 1988; Marshall 1991; Rushdie 1988) that this state of "in-betweenness," has been fully voiced. Living in a world in which discourses about identity continue to be framed in terms of loyalty to nations and nation-states, most transmigrants have neither fully conceptualized nor articulated a form of transnational identity. Nations-states, as "hegemonic representations of ... spatial identity," continue to be primary in "an increasingly postmodern world" (Gupta 1992:75).

Although the current period of capitalism is marked by new diasporas, identities of migrant populations continue to be rooted in nation-states. As part of this "reinscription of space" (Gupta 1992:63), both the political leaderships of sending nations and immigrants from these nations are coming to perceive these states as "deterritorialized." In contrast to the past, when nation-states were defined in terms of a people sharing a common culture within a bounded territory, this new conception of nation-state includes as citizens those who live physically dispersed within the boundaries of many other states, but who remain socially, politically, culturally, and often economically part of the nation-state of their ancestors. In the case of the Haitian "Tenth Department," the Grenadian "constituency" in New York, and the Filipino *balikbayan*, transnational ties are taken as evidence that migrants continue to be members of the state from which they originated.

Such reconstructions of nation-states and national loyalties are discrepant with the complexity of the lives of transmigrants. As transmigrants operate in the national arena of both their country of origin and country (or countries) of settlement, they develop new spheres of experience and new fields of social relations. In their daily activities transmigrants connect nation-states and then live in a world shaped by the interconnections that they themselves have forged. There is currently a gap between the daily practices of transmigrants and the ways both transmigrants and academics represent these practices.

C. Variables and Constants

To explore transnationalism this book will compare the migrations of Caribbean and Filipino populations into the New York metropolitan area. First, we will explore transnational processes in depth through two case studies, one of immigrants from the eastern Caribbean islands of St. Vincent and Grenada, and one of immigrants from Haiti. The two case studies will be used to develop insights into transnational processes based on the concrete historical experiences of these populations. Particular attention will be given to the ways these migrants are both identified and identify themselves in terms of race, ethnicity, and nation. The findings from these case studies will then be highlighted by contrasting Caribbean transnationalism to that of the Philippines.

The populations we are examining share both the experience of settling in the same region of the United States and certain crucial aspects of their political and economic histories. In each case the immigrants have been shaped by the political geography of the United States, and more particularly still, by that of the New York area. The countries from which each of these populations originated share a history of massive economic, political, and cultural penetration by the United States.[2] In all cases, immigrants have multiple and complex networks that encompass more than just the United States. Family members, for example, often settle in several different countries and move between them. However, in all four cases, the relaxation of immigration restrictions in the United States after 1965 and the concurrent restructuring of aspects of the global economy resulted in increased immigration to the United States, which became a major country of long-term settlement for both Caribbean and Filipino immigrants. We leave for other analyses an exploration of the manner in which variations among the different regions of the United States, as well as differences among countries of settlement, affect the dynamics of transnationalism.[3]

Although the transnationalism of each of these populations is shaped by many factors, the racial structuring of the United States is a particularly potent force. The elaboration of identities by these populations includes a process by which members of each try to avoid U.S. racial categorizations. The growth of nationalism at home, combined with the changing size and composition of these populations in New York, has also been important. For Caribbean and Filipino peoples, the ability to live transnationally is an accommodation both to the controlling forces of global capitalism and to their place within the global racial order. For them, transnationalism is a creative response to these forces.

II. PLACING OURSELVES THEORETICALLY: ON THE GLOBAL ECONOMY, SUBJECTIVITIES, AND HEGEMONIES

As soon as we began to write this book it became apparent that to rethink the manner in which we understand migration is to embark on a journey that takes us away from the bounded thinking of much of social science and into a terrain which is only now being explored (see John Comaroff 1982). Our journey is timely, but it is also complicated by the moment of our departure. It occurs during a period in the formation of the social sciences in which post-modern ethnographers are arguing for a world of multiple paths in which no course can be clearly charted and no direction affirmed (Tyler 1986). By even proposing the term "analytical framework" we run the risk of being dismissed as being in the sway of 19th century Western positivism.[4]

Our purpose in raising these issues is not to reiterate what has been elaborated and critiqued elsewhere (see, for example, Rebel 1989; Roseberry 1989), but to place ourselves theoretically. Marxist-influenced scholars over the past few years have responded to the challenge of reflexive and postmodernist thrusts in anthropology by developing a dialectical anthropology that brings together the study of structure, cultural process, and human agency (Roseberry 1989; J. and J. Comaroff 1991; B. Williams 1991). This developing dialectical anthropology explicitly seeks to span the "series of stubborn dichotomies in the legacy of modern social analysis — the division between global and local perspectives, between materialist and semantic interpretations, between structuralist and processual models and between subjectivist and normative methodologies" (Jean Comaroff 1985:3). Our interest in this book is to bring this dialectical approach into the study of migration in order to explicate some of the forces that shape the cultural practices and subjectivities of transmigrants.

A. The Development of a Global Perspective

In theorizing transnationalism we need to build on the global perspective of world systems theory as well as on the writings of those whose subsequent critiques and clarifications (Laclau 1977; Bach 1980) have enhanced the broad generality of this theory with a more particularistic historiography (C. Smith 1984; John Comaroff 1982). Wallerstein defines the "world system" as a social system comprised of geographic regions which perform different and unequal functions in a global division of labor (Wallerstein 1974:229–231). While Wallerstein emphasized exchange as the fundamental relationship between the units of the system (Wallerstein 1979), an approach that sees the world as integrated by a global mode of production seems more insightful in explicating the current international division of labor (Laclau 1977; Portes 1978; Portes and Walton 1981; Sassen 1988).

Wallerstein perceives the world as divided into a "core," those areas which dominate and profit from the international division of labor, and a "periphery," those regions whose production is expropriated and whose people are subordinated within the system. According to Wallerstein and other world systems theorists, the past several decades have experienced new levels of capital penetration in post-colonial Third World economies (Stavrianos 1981; Nash and Fernandez Kelly 1983; Bossen 1984), the development of export processing as a major economic strategy of capital, which moves readily around the globe (Nash and Fernandez Kelly 1983), and the migration of third world peoples to capitalist centers (Bryce-LaPorte 1980; Sassen-Koob 1981).

When we join a global level of analysis with a scrutiny of particular histories of peoples (Portes and Walton 1981) we can better understand the movements of labor at specific points in time. We are able to link the wave of migration into the advanced capitalist countries in the last twenty-five years to new forms of capital concentration and global investment (Kritz, Keely, and Tomasi 1983; Sassen-Koob 1981). Although conditions of labor and production processes in core areas are in certain respects coming to resemble those in the peripheries, in developing an overview of the dynamics of global political processes, the terms "core" and "peripheral" still have a great deal of analytic power. It is important to heed those who remind us that these flows of capital are still structured by the regulatory mechanisms of nation-states (Zolberg 1983) and backed by the force of arms. Some nation-states, such as the United States, have greater power to shape the identity and parameters of actions of other states.

However, world systems theorists have tended to reduce migration to labor migration and immigrants to workers, eliminating all discussion of the many different racial, ethnic, or national identities which shape people's actions and consciousness. Migrants are indeed providers of labor power for capitalist production in a world economy, but they are at the same time political and social actors.

The development of transnationalism within the past several decades is part of a long-term process of global capitalist penetration. The development of an international division of labor and the integration of the world by transnational corporations that develop worldwide systems of production, distribution, and marketing affect both the flow of immigrants and the manner in which they come to understand who they are and what they are doing.

B. Hegemonies, Subjectivities, and Ideologies

We define culture as all human practice, understood to include both thought and action, since all human action is symbolically structured and representation is part and parcel of all human behavior. However, in treating culture, the "empowering, authoritative dimensions" must be specified (J. and J. Comaroff 1991:20). Hence our analytical framework must address the link between "culture and relations of power and domination" (Roseberry 1989:25).

The concept of "hegemony," articulated by Gramsci (1971) and explicated by R. Williams (1977), has been recently introduced into anthropological discourse (Brow 1988; J. and J. Comaroff 1991; B. Williams 1991) and has been extremely helpful in this regard. Raymond Williams in his definition of hegemony emphasized that relations of power structure systems of meaning. Insisting that hegemony is "the lived dominance and subordination of particular classes," he defined hegemony as a "system of meanings and values — constitutive and constituting — which as they are experienced as practices appear as reciprocally confirming" (R. Williams 1977:110). Building on this definition the Comaroffs have defined hegemony as an

> order of signs and practices, relations and distinctions, images and epistemologies — drawn from a historically situated cultural field — that come to be taken-for-granted as the natural and received shape of the world and everything that inhabits it... This is why its power has so often been seen to lie in what it silences, what it prevents

people from thinking and saying, what it puts beyond the limits of the rational and credible. In a quite literal sense hegemony is habit forming. For these reasons, it is rarely contested directly (J. and J. Comaroff 1991:23).

When we talk about hegemony we are talking about only one aspect of the relationship between those who dominate within the state and those who are dominated. While relations of domination are ultimately maintained by force, the social order is sustained by daily practice, habit, and common sense.

The Comaroffs distinguish between hegemony and ideology in order to delineate two different cultural processes by which the dominant class obtains and maintains consent.[5] They follow Raymond Williams in specifying that, as compared to hegemony, ideology is a "relatively formal and articulated system of meanings, values, and beliefs of a kind that can be abstracted as a 'worldview'" (R. Williams 1977:109). Distinguishing between hegemony and ideology allows the Comaroffs to make it clear that while hegemony is the province of the dominant class, many social groupings can create ways of seeing and analyzing the world which may challenge current hegemonic constructions. The sources of these variant ideologies lie in the fact that despite the domination of hegemonic practice and ruling ideas, each group has its own social location, cultural history, and thus discrete experiences. While as Marx and Engels specified, "the ideas of the ruling class are in every epoch the ruling ideas" (1964 [1846]:60), each social grouping within a political community tends to produce its own ideology as it contends for position and self-identification.

We also think that arenas of contention must be mapped and the social locations from which subaltern groupings challenge aspects of their subordination must be specified. However, we do not find it helpful to distinguish between ideological and hegemonic processes. While the definition of ideology as systematized and publicized systems of meanings proves analytically useful, it should not be placed in counterdistinction to hegemony. In our reading, hegemonic processes include all the dynamics of consent, both the "taken for granted" practices, the commonsensical and customary representations, as well as the formal ideologies that both engender consent and undermine it. We concur with Hall that "hegemony never has only one character ... or predominant tendency ... it is always 'destruction *and* reconstruction'" (Hall 1988:54).

As Chatterjee (1986), Fox (1990a), Rafael (1988), and Sider (1985) have demonstrated, oppositional ideologies are never constructed on virgin soil. The dominated struggle within a medium of formulations shaped by the dominators. Whether people plead for remediation, organize for reform, or rise up in revolution, the thoughts they think, the words they speak, and the practices they follow are never free of hegemonic construction. We use the term "hegemonic construct" to describe both consciously articulated statements and embedded perceptions that are used and reappropriated by transmigrants, and which serve ultimately to empower and legitimate dominant forces in both the migrants' societies of origin and of settlement.

Our inclination to draw no hard and fast lines between formal ideologies and embedded meanings derives from three analytic concerns arising from our ethnographic findings. These analytic concerns are underdeveloped in the literature on hegemony and will be explored and clarified in this book. First of all, a conception of hegemonic construct must encompass concepts of race, ethnicity, and nation which simultaneously make up the scaffolding of formal idea systems of both subalterns and dominant sectors and remain rooted in the "common sense" categories with which we all experience the daily structuring of our lives (Centre for Contemporary Cultural Studies 1982).

Furthermore, not all differentiated social locations become publicly voiced. For example, whatever their class origins, most immigrants experience incorporation into U.S. society as workers. Together with their fellow workers, they are disciplined by the organization and rhythms of the work place (Rouse 1992). Yet immigrants, as most other workers in the United States, most often articulate their identities in terms of entirely different sets of references — those of nation of origin, race, and ethnicity (Katznelson 1981). A goal of this book is to clarify the manner in which hegemonic constructions shape the manner in which immigrants identify themselves.

Finally, we need a language of analysis that can clearly explicate the relationship between the political unit of the state and hegemonic processes. The existence of the state often is assumed rather than specified. Gramsci, in his formulations of hegemony, sometimes argued that hegemonic control was the sphere of "civil society," while force was the domain of the state (1971:243). However, his location of hegemonic processes is inconsistent. In contrast, we have not found the state and "civil" institutions such as foundations, churches, and schools to operate in different domains but rather to work together in the processes of hegemonic construction, contention, and reformulation.

As we explicate the contradictory processes that transnationalism engenders, we will endeavor to place the hegemonic contentions and incorporations of transmigrant populations located in specific nation-states within a global perspective. Our global perspective includes the systematic historicization of our most basic analytical categories (Trouillot 1990, 1991). Rather than conceptualizing nation-states and the global political economy as two different levels of analysis (Gupta 1992), we see them as integrally related. Here we build on the work of those who have examined hegemonic contention between the colonizer and the colonized, between the core and periphery, or between Europe and regions of the third world in the colonial and post-colonial periods (Fox 1990a; Blanc-Szanton 1990; Cooper and Stoler 1989).

A global perspective must explicate the role and dynamic tensions generated by global capitalist hegemony, the hegemonic forces within each of the competing core capitalist states, the hegemonic constructions generated by dominant forces within peripheral states, and the active agency of the world's people as they live lives stretched across national borders. In this book we will see how transmigrants, by living their lives straddling several nation-states, are affected by, pose special challenges to, and contribute to hegemonic processes in several separate states.

C. The Positioned Observer

Each generation, with a new vocabulary but with a continuity of concerns, continues to debate the position of social science vis-à-vis its subjects. Underlying the differing positions are fundamental questions of phenomenology and epistemology. While it is not our purpose to address this debate directly, we must say something about the positioning of our observations. Implied by the term hegemony and necessary to any discussion about the role of social science in contributing to or in deconstructing hegemonic models, is a position about positioning, about the subject/object divide, and about objectivity and reflexivity.

The hegemonic constructs of race, ethnicity, and nation, for example, have powerfully shaped the ways social scientists have described migrations to the United States. These constructs have determined what variables were included or excluded in the collection and categorization of data. They have also structured the ways in which the "observers" and the persons they have categorized have come to experience, represent, and think about these populations.

However, the importance of these constructs in the exercise of domination has rarely been acknowledged because race, ethnicity, and nation were reified as bounded social and cultural phenomena rather than analyzed as aspects of the hegemonic control of subordinated populations. In order to be able to conceptualize the dynamics of global capitalism and of transnational migration, analysts must include their own concepts, social position, and discipline in their analysis.

Transmigrants simultaneously are affected by, incorporate, and participate in hegemonic contentions "back home" as they learn new meanings and forms of representation in their new settings. They respond to and resist these constructions, and by so doing progressively transform them. We think that it is only by focusing on both social scientists and transmigrants as agents and as subjects that we can understand something about the ways migrants have been influenced by local hegemonic contentions and global contexts, while at the same time influencing them. Social scientists, in their relationship to their subjects, contribute directly to the practices and subjectivities of immigrants, and in turn are influenced by them.

When we indicated that social scientists are consumers of and contributors to hegemonic concepts, we obviously are taking a stand. As social scientists, we see ourselves dialectically as both observers and the observed. At the same time, those about whom we write are both the subjects of our inquiry and subjects who, in relationship to what is being said and done around them, including the work of social scientists, and in relation to their own varying motivations, act upon and change the world of our inquiry. We, in turn, observe these actions and are influenced by them. What is more, we evaluate the actions, the beliefs, and the stance of our subjects. We are, as are all social scientists, whether or not it is acknowledged, positioned observers. Our perceptions, whether we objectify them by identifying them as "data" or as "texts," are influenced by our position in the world and our positions about the state of the world.

That is to say, we see the position described as "essentialist" and that described as "reflexive" as fundamentally the same. There is no discourse of identity that flows from the subjectivity of actors that is not, at one and the same time, a development of the conditions and social positions within which those actors become and continue to be conscient human beings.

When we began to speak and write about transnationalism in 1987, the transmigrants among whom we worked had developed transnational practices that did not fit the vocabulary of social science. Living within a hegemonic context that did not acknowledge home ties, transmigrants themselves rarely acknowledged that they lived in both places. For the eastern Caribbean countries of St. Vincent and Grenada, the movement into a discourse about transnationalism was early and gradual, a continuation, as we shall see, of their historic sense of belonging to partial societies that looked outward and elsewhere for part of their definitions of self. For the Filipinos and Haitians it was the upheaval of political crisis that drew them into more open discussions of their home ties. In all cases, their new discourse was part of a reconstitution of their identification with their home nation-states.

As for us, we began as observers, but once we began to speak publicly about transnationalism we also became participants. Our efforts to popularize the term 'transnationalism' as part of a larger project to rethink migration has made us actors — together with transmigrants — in the discourse about transmigrant identity. We are finding that we have become participants whose discourse about transnationalism both offers a critique and is inserted within intense political discussion about ways in which immigrants can challenge the domination that structures their daily lives. For example, in 1985 Linda was discussing transnationalism in a research setting with her West Indian colleagues. By 1991 Nina found herself invited by Haitian Students at Cornell to be a speaker at a conference dedicated entirely to Haitian transnationalism.

These developments bring home the need continually to critique our position as observers, turning the discussion of agency into an examination of our role in the processes of social construction, domination, and resistance. We will return to these matters in the conclusion of the book.

III. THE STRUCTURE AND CONTENT OF THIS BOOK

In this first introductory chapter we have argued that three analytical approaches needed to be brought together into a single framework in order to speak to the paradoxes presented by transnationalism: (1) the emerging global relations of capital; (2) the relationship between power and hegemonic constructions of culture and practice; and (3) the position and outlook of the social scientist. In a second introductory chapter we will offer four premises that taken together compose an analytical framework for the study of transnationalism. These premises historically locate transnationalism within the current conjuncture of global capitalism. The chapter argues against the bounded, categorical thinking that has kept us from being able to describe or theorize about the transnational practices that surround us. It offers a critique of the hegemonic constructs of race, ethnicity, and nation that shape transmigrant subjectivities and social science analysis.

Part Two contains two ethnographic case studies of Caribbean transnational migration to the United States. Chapters Three and Four describe the eastern Caribbean migration from St Vincent and Grenada and Chapters Five and Six that from Haiti. In the course of these case studies we develop and explore the analytical framework proposed in this first chapter. The case studies examine the historical development of two variants of Caribbean transnationalism. They describe the practices through which transmigrants transform geographic distance into the close social connections of family, business, and organizational activities. The case studies end with an examination of the hegemonic contention over the identities and loyalties of transmigrants who at different times have been identified and who identify themselves in terms of race, ethnicity, and nation. Organizational activities are a focus of this study, because they have provided an arena of hegemonic contention in which dominant forces in both home and host societies compete over the manner in which immigrant populations come to understand their identities and formulate their course of political action.

In Section Three, the concluding section of the book, Chapter Seven contrasts the transnational migration of Filipinos to the United States with that of the Caribbeans in order to underscore the global nature of the transnational processes we have been exploring. Having demonstrated the similarities between the Caribbean and Filipino cases, as well as having located the manner in which particularities of culture and history lead to certain variations in the dynamics of transnationalism, we draw some conclusions in Chapter Eight. This final chapter explores more fully the contradictions that transnational populations pose to efforts of both core capitalist and capital dependent states to control populations and legitimate their positioning. The constructions of deterritorialized nation-states and global racial constructions also are examined. Both of these forms of identification provide vehicles through which transmigrants contribute to the perpetuation of their subordination as labor, at the same time that they challenge the continuity of the current "new world order."

NOTES

1. Portions of an earlier draft of this chapter appeared in Glick Schiller, Basch, and Blanc-Szanton (1992a, 1992b).

2. The four countries of origin for these immigrants are also experiencing the investments and cultural influences of other countries as well: Japan in the Philippines, Britain and Canada in the English-speaking Caribbean, and France and Germany in Haiti.

3. That constructions of an immigrant identity are influenced by variations in the local political culture and economic history is documented for the United States by Di Leonardi (1984).

4. See for example the discussion of "blurred genres" in Geertz (1983:20) and "the erosion of classic norms" in Rosaldo (1989:25).

5. Marx's famous explication of commodity fetishism is for the Comaroffs a study of hegemonic processes. The worker, as he enters into the process of selling his labor power, experiences the domination of the capitalist class as an abstract impersonal force propelled by natural laws.

Chapter
TWO

Theoretical Premises[1]

We are sitting in Cristina's living room on the top floor of a Renaissance palace trying to concentrate on our text, with the red roofs of Florence and the golden hills of Tuscany providing a backdrop for our discussion of transnationalism. Cristina's identity as both Italian and American had led her from the Bronx, New York, where we started the book and where she maintains a home, to Florence, where she was then coordinating a research project for UNICEF.

Our discussion is intense as we try to "theorize" our complex ethnographic findings and figure out, after more than a year of writing, what we are writing about. Is the book about transnational practices of immigrants to the United States and a study that challenges us to rethink our understanding of migration? Or is our focus the effect of transnational processes on the racial, ethnic, and national identities of transmigrants?

The discussion becomes heated. How much does Linda's and Nina's constant discussion of identities reflect the fact that they both had worked with Caribbean immigrant organizations in the United States that play a role in the public presentation of immigrant populations to the larger society? How much does Cristina's emphasis on transnational practices reflect her awareness of the importance of the *balikbayan* concept, of the role of the state in constructing that concept, and of her own experience of having simultaneous ties to the United States and Italy?

Out of the heat emerges a new synthesis. To arrive at a theory of transnationalism we will develop a framework that could encompass both transnational practices and the contention about the identities of the transmigrants taking place within the United States and post-colonial nation-states. The introduction of the book will have to bring together disparate literatures about world systems, migration, nation, race, and ethnicity. The very disparateness of these literatures will be shown to reflect the manner in which intellectuals participate in the construction of bounded categories that preclude alternate visions. The conclusion of the book will examine contradictions between the transnational practices of transmigrants and the manner in which their identities are being forged in contexts framed by the nation building projects of the United States and their "home" nation-states. Our framework for the study of transnationalism will consist of four interrelated premises that situate transnational processes within global history, make central the agency of transmigrants, and contextualize ongoing contention over the loyalty and identity of immigrants.

I. OUR FOUR PREMISES:

1. Transnational migration is inextricably linked to the changing conditions of global capitalism and must be analyzed within the context of global relations between capital and labor.

2. Transnationalism is a process by which migrants, through their daily life activities and social, economic, and political relations, create social fields that cross national boundaries.

3. Bounded social science concepts that conflate physical location, culture, and identity can limit the ability of researchers first to perceive and then to analyze the phenomenon of transnationalism.

4. By living their lives across borders, transmigrants find themselves confronted with and engaged in the nation building processes of two or more nation-states. Their identities and practices are configured by hegemonic categories, such as race and ethnicity, that are deeply embedded in the nation building processes of these nation-states.

II. A FRAMEWORK FOR THE STUDY OF TRANSNATIONALISM

A. Premise One: Transnational Migration is Inextricably Linked to the Changing Conditions of Global Capitalism and Must be Analyzed Within the Context of Global Relations Between Capital and Labor

Transnational migration is actuated by the relationship between classes that is at the core of capitalism as a mode of production. We understand capitalism to be a historically constituted mode of production centered around the relationship between a capitalist class that possesses the means of production and a working class that produces surplus value or makes possible such production of value (Mohun 1983; Wolf 1982). Class is defined as a set of people whose positioning within the process of production is similar. Because class is about positioning, class is a description of social relationships. As a mode of production, capitalism also includes an array of other classes ranging from peasants, who own small bits of land, to professionals, who control some special knowledge or skill. While the capitalist class is increasingly global in the manner in which it incorporates all areas of the world into a single system of production, political processes that maintain the inequities between classes remain structured within separate states. The exercise of state power is normally central to the maintenance of class relations, since control of the productive forces is ultimately protected by force, and force is generally the province of the state. This summary statement is not meant to encompass the complexity of class relations and capitalist processes, but rather to serve as a grounding for our discussion of why the current historical conjuncture is a moment of widespread transnational migration. Inevitably issues of class will be interwoven into all of our analyses.

Some observers have pointed to advances in technology as a primary explanation for the fact that current immigrants seem to maintain much more intimate and enduring relations with their home countries than did earlier generations (Wakeman 1988). Jet planes, coupled with low cost fares, make it possible almost literally to have a foot in two countries, while telephones, fax machines, money transfer companies, and rapid freight shipments facilitate the movement of material goods and ideas. Today's electronic technology lends a sense of immediacy to the social relations of people who are geographically distant. According to this logic, the explanation

for transnationalism is to be found within the elision of time and
space made possible by modern technology.

The presence of technological innovations, however, explains
neither why immigrants invest so much time, energy, and resources
in maintaining home ties, nor why transportation and communication systems bridge distances between particular geographic locations and not others. Technological explanations for the emergence of
more transnational patterns of migration prove to be incomplete
when divorced from an analysis of the social relations of production.[2]
Rather it is the current moment of capitalism as a global mode of
production that has necessitated the maintenance of family ties and
political allegiances among persons spread across the globe.

It is also possible to argue that transnationalism is not a new
phenomenon and that although recent technological advances have
facilitated communication, previous waves of migrants to countries
such as the United States also maintained home ties. Certainly, a
reading of immigrant history that argues that current transnational
migration represents a continuity with past immigrant behavior
would be resonant with recent efforts to build a global history. Wolf
argues, for example, that the circulation of labor has been part of the
entire expansion of capitalism (Wolf 1982). Both a barely remem-
bered historiography and a recent reexamination of U.S. ethnic history provide evidence that the image of the "uprooted" may be as
questionable a portrait of many earlier immigrant populations as it is
of recent migrants (Takaki 1989). Many European immigrants of the
19th and early 20th century remained in communication with their
home countries and participated in those countries' nationalist
movements (Vassady 1982; Portes and Rumbaut 1990). Czech and
Slovak immigrants in the United States provided propaganda and
funds to wrest a Czechoslovakian state out of the Austro-Hungarian
empire (Wittke 1940). Irish immigrants in the United States have
been noted for their continuing involvement with Ireland, but many
other immigrants, including those from Italy, Germany, and central
Europe have also maintained links to their countries of origin (Glazer
1954; di Leonardi 1984; Portes and Bach 1985).[3] Latin American
immigrants also engaged in nation building movements from the
shores of the United States. It was from the United States, for example that Cubans organized the struggle against Spain (Portes and
Rumbaut 1990).

We believe, however, that current transnationalism marks a new
type of migrant experience, reflecting an increased and more pervasive global penetration of capital. We also argue that only a global

perspective of migration processes will enable social scientists to understand the similarities and differences between past and present migrations.

The multi-stranded transnationalism that has been gaining shape and intensity over the past two decades parallels the slide of the world economy into "sustained economic crisis" (Gordon, Edwards, and Reich 1982:215) and the trend toward an increased internationalization of capital. By the first half of the 1970s, corporations owned and controlled by interests in core capitalist states found it more profitable to set up industrial production in areas previously peripheral to industrial capitalist development, where labor was cheap and politically repressive regimes "guaranteed" labor peace.[4] The consequent reduction of industrial production in "core" economies such as the United States and the establishment of capital intensive industries in "the periphery," including Caribbean countries and the Philippines, led to dramatic changes in the labor markets of these nation-states.

By the 1980s, the structure of employment in the United States had undergone transformations often called "deindustrialization" (Block 1987:156), or "post-Fordism" (Navarro 1991). In many large urban areas, well-paying, unionized, industrial employment was replaced by service sector and clerical employment. Plants closed, wages and benefits declined, and underemployment and unemployment grew, especially among African-Americans, Puerto Ricans, and other Hispanics (Wilson 1987). White workers often were forced into the ranks of the peripherally employed, frequently at low wages. Changes in the immigration law in 1987 made it more difficult for undocumented workers, who had been a key factor in secondary sector jobs, to obtain this employment. The "underground economy" of sweat shops, street vendors, child labor, and piece work in the home grew rapidly, all characterized by low pay, an absence of benefits, and insecurity (Sassen 1988).

The global restructuring of capital also disrupted the local economies of the third world. Large loans made to third world countries by the International Monetary Fund (IMF), the World Bank, and the international banking establishment led to an increasing level of debt service. While in 1980 these countries were the net recipients of capital at the level of 39.6 billion dollars, by 1986 the amount of capital that flowed into these countries through private investment and foreign aid was exceeded by a net outflow of 24 billion dollars (Knight 1989:32).

The loans and investments were supposed to create, according to donor agencies, development and growth in the "less developed countries." However, even in their most optimistic projections, development agencies acknowledged that dislocation, unemployment, and pressures to emigrate would occur in the early stages of investment (DeWind and McKinney 1986). Disruption of local economies indeed did accompany the most recent wave of intense capital penetration and resulted in an increased pool of available labor as whole families often migrated to urban areas. This displaced and underemployed labor could not be easily absorbed by the growing but still relatively small manufacturing sector often dominated by multinationals. The stay of these foreign-capitalized companies has often been short-lived, as firms have moved from country to country in search of even lower labor costs, creating a further displacement of workers. And when workers in locations such as the Caribbean and the Philippines have taken to the streets in various political actions, the export processing industries have taken off to other countries. This under- and unemployed labor force has then been available for further international migration (Rothstein and Blim 1992).

The economic dislocations in both capital dependent and core capitalist countries have increased migration to the latter. However, as the urban sectors of core country economies have slipped into decline, it has become increasingly difficult for migrants to construct secure social or economic bases within their new settings. The current conjuncture of global capitalism contributes to the insecurity of international migrants, because global economic dislocations, long-term economic retrenchment and recession, and the restructuring of production processes throughout the world have either reduced or unexpectedly altered demands for labor. In a discussion of "the political economy of migration" Roger Ballard points out that "migrants often find themselves socially, politically and economically vulnerable, no less in the society they have left than in the one they have joined" (1987:23).

> Doing better ... than they would have done had they stayed at home, they are nevertheless disadvantaged in comparison with members of the indigenous population among whom they live and work, and with whom they are, as newcomers, in unequal competition for jobs and other scarce resources. ... As long as they remain identifiable, they will always be in danger. In times of adversity, outsiders make ideal scapegoats. So it is that some of the most explosive popular movements in the contemporary world are directed against

minorities which can be identified as 'immigrant' ... And such hostility is usually not just directed at immigrants themselves, but also at their locally born offspring (Ballard 1987:18).

Both U.S. social scientists (Sowell 1981) and Caribbean immigrants often say, in contrast to African Americans, that people from the Caribbean are "making it in America." An analysis of the 1980 earnings of African-Americans, Afro-Caribbeans, native-born and foreign-born whites, however, found that Caribbean populations did not have higher earnings than native born blacks.[5] Foreign-born whites, on the other hand, earn significantly more than Caribbean immigrants, but less than native born whites (Model 1991). Economic and political vulnerability, magnified by the factor of race, augment the likelihood that migrants will construct a transnational existence.

B. Premise Two: Transnationalism is a Process by Which Migrants, through Their Daily Life Activities and Social, Economic, and Political Relations, Create Social Fields that Cross National Boundaries

Our conceptualization of transnationalism calls attention to connections between people as well as to the movement of ideas and objects. This approach to transnationalism differs from, but does not contradict, the recent explorations of what is being described as "transnational cultural studies" (Appadurai and Breckenridge 1988). Work on transnational culture "moves away from unified representations of culture and toward more multiply inflected cultural objects" (Society for Cultural Anthropology 1993). The term "transnational" is used to signal the fluidity with which ideas, objects, capital, and people now move across borders and boundaries. Scholars of transnational culture speak in the vocabulary of postmodernism and make reference to hybridity, hyperspace, displacement, disjuncture, decentering, and diaspora (Diaspora 1991; Appadurai 1990). Examining the production of "public culture" in postcolonial settings, they note that despite a "global cultural economy" the world remains filled with "disjuncture and difference" (Appadurai 1990:1). Calling such cultural production "creolization," Hannerz (1989) has noted that peripheries do indeed respond in various ways to transnational flows from the center, in the process generating their own counterflows and reformulating what is handed to them. Power centers define and peripheries constantly try to redefine the terms of the debate and thus gain control over them. And as the peripheries develop their own definitions, the centers of power coopt, reformulate, and again disseminate these definitions in order to continue their hegemony.

Productive of a new imagery, much of this discourse on transnationalism has remained evocative rather than analytical. By linking our definition of transnationalism to migration and rooting our analysis in social relations, we are engaged in a somewhat different, although connected, effort. Our focus becomes the manner in which migrants, through their life ways and daily practices, reconfigure space so that their lives are lived simultaneously within two or more nation-states. We wish to examine the flow of material goods as they are embedded in social relations, because we think that, while it is interesting to talk about the manner in which imported items become "multiply inflected," something more needs to be said.

If someone sends a barbecue grill home to Port-au-Prince, the grill does not stand in and of itself as an item of material culture reflecting and producing hybrid cultural constructions. The grill is a statement about social success in the United States and an effort to build and advance social position in Haiti. The grill will be used in a fashionable round of party going in which status is defined and redeemed in the context of consumption. When someone from a small town in St. Vincent, Grenada, or the Philippines who now lives in New York sends home a cassette player, how are we to interpret this flow? The player can be used along with imported cassettes to bring the latest musical forms and themes from around the world into these rural countrysides. But on this same cassette those sitting on a mountain side in Grenada, in a rural village in the Philippines, or on a family veranda in St. Vincent send messages, warnings, or information about kith and kin "at home" that shape and influence how people behave and what they think in New York, Miami, or Los Angeles. Connections are continued, and a wider system of social relations is maintained and reinforced.

Observing the propensity of migrants to maintain home ties even as they settle in new societies, some scholars of migration have begun to apply network analysis (Barnes 1954; Mitchell 1969) to the study of the social relations of international migrants. Eades has conceptualized the outcome of contemporary chain migration as "an international network ... more like a 'spider's web' than the conventional bipolar model of migration" (1987:8). Examining the circulatory migration that they see as a product of the capitalist world system, Portes and Walton have argued that networks "tie-in groups distributed across different places, maximizing their economic opportunities through mutual aid and multiple displacements" (1981: 60).

Providing us with a clear statement of the ongoing connectedness of migrant ties to "different places," the call for network analysis focuses our attention on migrants as actors. These formulations, however, do not look at the implications of these networks for the formation of migrant political and social identity, or the complexities of nationalist identifications within transnational social fields. The "spider-web" networks of transmigrants must be located within the hegemonic processes of multiple nation-states, and we must move beyond descriptions of networks to a view of migrants as active agents in a process of hegemonic construction.

To understand what "social relations" mean in the flow and fabric of daily life we must explore how linkages are maintained, renewed, and reconstituted in the context of families, of institutions, of political organizations, of political structures, and of economic investments, business, and finance. The case studies in the next section of the book will explore in four different settings the manner in which these connections have been forged, elaborated, and maintained over time. Each case study will also focus on the historical global context out of which these linkages arise as well as on the particular manifestations in that specific nation-state.

Our focus is on migrants as builders of social fields (see Basch, Wiltshire, Wiltshire, and Toney 1990) that provide the staging grounds for the construction and reappropriation of practices and identities. A handful of studies have examined transnational migration from this perspective. In 1975, in describing the migration of Barbadian immigrants, Sutton and Makiesky-Barrow (1992:114 [1975]) spoke of a "transnational sociocultural and political system." They linked such a system to "the bidirectional flow of ideas such that political events at home (e.g., independence) had an impact on the migrant communities abroad while migrant experiences were relayed in the opposite direction" (1992 [1975]:113). Rouse (1991:15) has used the term 'transnational migrant circuits' to describe dense social networks that link residents of a small town in Mexico with family and friends who have settled in Redwood City, California. "Through the continuous circulation of people, money, goods and information, the various settlements have become so closely woven together that, in an important sense they have come to constitute a single community spread across a variety of sites" (1991:15). Kearney notes that "transnational labor migration has now become a major structural feature of communities which have themselves become truly transnational" (1991:53).

Noting the constant penetration of borders, Kearney suggests that we have entered the age of transnationalism, a post-national age in which "members of transnational communities ... escape the power of the nation-state to inform their sense of collective identity" (1991a:59). In contrast, we think that the current period, in which the construct of the deterritorialized nation-state is being forcefully articulated, can best be conceived as the moment of a new nationalism. While transmigrants cannot be contained or restrained by national boundaries, the world is still very much divided politically into nation-states that are unequal in their power and that serve differentially as base areas of international capital.

C. Premise Three: Bounded Social Science Concepts such as 'Ethnic Group,' 'Race,' and 'Nation' Can Limit the Ability of Researchers First to Perceive and then to Analyze the Phenomenon of Transnationalism

Previous to the development of a concept of transnationalism, anthropologists had developed a rather large body of literature in anthropology to describe how people move between various social locations.[6] Descriptions of the movement of labor — often in rich detail — in which ties have been maintained in two settings can be found in the literature of both internal and international migration. This is not to say that there are no differences between internal and international migration. The use of political borders to categorize migrants as "guests," temporary or illegal, does shape migrant behavior and consciousness as well as influence the demand for such labor (Sassen-Koob 1981). However, in many ways these seemingly different movements of people can be seen as similar responses to worldwide deployments of capital and labor. What was lacking was a way to conceptualize and emphasize the interconnectedness that enabled migrants to remain actors in several disparate locations.

The early African Copperbelt studies (Epstein 1958; Mitchell 1956; Mayer 1971) and more recent studies in Africa, Latin America, and the Caribbean (Pessar 1988; Roberts 1978) contain accounts of migrants who enter into the social system of the distant city or country yet continue to maintain their identification and social ties with their region and group of origin. Epstein, in attempting to capture the total experience of migrants to the Copperbelt of Northern Rhodesia (now Zambia), described this context as a "wider field which embraces both the rural and the urban areas of Northern Rhodesia. Developments in the towns reach back and have a profound influence on the life of the villages: but the rural influence on the towns is also continuous and very strong" (1958:238).

Until recently, much of this literature has portrayed the maintenance of ongoing linkages and the following of social practices of both rural and urban settings as a temporary first phase of adjustment to industrialization or urbanization. "The continuing importance of kinship ties, customary ritual activities, 'peasant' modes of production in the city" (Roberts 1976:99) were seen as transitional, and therefore the implications of the continuing linkages between home and area of settlement were not fully explored. Even when long-term patterns of migration and continuing linkages with home societies were documented, the implications of these patterns for immigration dynamics and identity formation were not analyzed (Basch 1982). Caribbean migrants, for example, were described as belonging to "remittance societies" in which generations of migrants spent long periods away from home, supporting their families and often family landholdings or small enterprises with the money they sent home (Rubenstein 1983; Thomas-Hope 1985; Wood and McCoy 1985). The Caribbean experience was seen as a special case rather than as a growing global pattern that challenged our conceptualizations of migration and "the immigrant."

Yet studies of the "new immigrants" of the post-World War II era were replete with descriptions of the propensity of the newcomers to plant firm roots in their new world while maintaining vital ties to the old. In 1971 Fitzpatrick, noting the circulation of Puerto Ricans between their island and mainland homes, suggested that they are best understood as commuters rather than migrants (1971).[7] Richardson, writing about the seemingly circular movements of Caribbean migrants, pointed to the existence of this phenomenon elsewhere as well. He reported that "students of the movements of Pacific islanders have found human mobility there so routine that they now employ the term circulation rather than migration" (1983:176). Georges (1990) documented the vital economic links between Dominican migration and a small Dominican town. Pessar (1988) used the title *When Borders Don't Divide* for a volume of articles on labor migration and refugee movements in the Americas. And in his book *Double Passage*, Gmelch (1992) describes Barbadian immigrants in England and the United States who sustained ties with Barbados that led to their eventual return.

Gonzalez specially turned her attention to the question of how these "individual segments of a transnational ethnic group can sustain a sense of unity" (1988:10). She observed that although many Garifuna, whom she labeled "sojourners," have "become U.S. citizens," they think of themselves as members of two (or more) societies." Gonzalez spoke of the Garifuna forming 'part societies' within several countries" (1988:10). However, none of these studies addressed the implications of the maintenance of multiple ties across political borders nor did they develop a concept of transnationalism.

The inability to conceptualize transnationalism fully reflects the limitations of the conceptual tool kit that all of us have been using. In the face of a crisis in conceptualization, some have reconfigured the entire ethnographic project (Tyler 1986), while others speak of a postmodern world in which the neat social fabric of bygone times has unraveled into the current *bricolage* of cultures and identities. Appadurai, for example, has argued that there is a need to reconceptualize the "landscapes of group identity," a need that flows from the current world conjuncture in which "groups are no longer tightly territorialized, spatially bounded, historically unselfconscious, or culturally homogeneous" (1991:191). Clifford reports that "'cultural' difference is no longer a stable, exotic otherness; self-other relations are matters of power and rhetoric rather than of essence. A whole structure of expectations about authenticity in culture and art is thrown in doubt" (1988:14).

However, the epistemological problem is more fundamental. Bounded concepts of culture, whether signaled by the rubric of tribe, ethnic group, race, or nation, are social constructions. They are reflective not of the stable boundaries of cultural difference but of relations of culture and power. Moreover, while at any one time, culturally constructed boundaries — be they those of nations, ethnicities, or races — may seem fixed, timeless, or primordial, dynamic processes of reformulation underlie the apparent fixity. The current conflations of time and space bought about by global communications and transnational social relations only serve to highlight more deepseated contradictions in the way in which we think about culture and society (Wolf 1988).

The people of the world have long been interconnected, populations often have been mobile, and their identities have long been fluid, multiple, and contextualized. It is possible to argue that since the beginning of state societies "the world of humankind constitutes a manifold, a totality of interconnected process" (Fried 1975:3), with identities of differentiation constructed by dominant powers or in resistance to them. Certainly since the expansion of Europe, the history of the people of the world has been tightly interwoven (Wolf 1982; Worsley 1984).

When we examine the historical record rather than our contemporary political landscapes, the relationships between struggles for political domination and the differentiation of sectors of the population through the construction of cultural categories are easier to perceive. We know, for example, that early states in their encounters with populations beyond their boundaries created tribes, both on the basis of some existing unifying elements or at times without them, and gave them a politicized boundedness (Fried 1975). The relationship between European colonial expansion and the designation of tribal demarcations also has been documented (Helm 1975 [1968]; Vail 1989). Since the time they were the chroniclers of early state conquest, intellectuals have spun webs of mystification within which the subordinated have found themselves trapped in a narrative detailing the particulars of their cultural difference (Fried 1975).

A global perspective on history, as well as the contingencies of the current historical conjuncture, challenge us to move beyond bounded visions of culture and society. However, we are often confined by our analytical tool kit of concepts like nation, ethnic group, and tribe that divide the world into autonomous, geographically rooted, and culturally distinct units (Van Binsbergen 1981). These units have been treated as bounded entities, endowed with given, "natural," and "group-specific" properties.

To develop a perspective that emphasizes the constructed nature of bounded units is not to deny the significance of boundaries once they are constructed. Whether or not they share unspoken lifeways or distinctive and celebrated customs, once people find themselves conceptualized and come to conceptualize themselves as bound together with a common situation or identity, distinctiveness does indeed arise. Boundaries, whether legally created borders, as in the case of nation-states (Sahlins 1989), or socially forged created boundaries, as in instances of group ethnicities (Keesing 1989; Roosens 1989), once conceptualized, are given meaning and sentiment by those who reside within them. They acquire a life of their own. Conceived as culturally distinct, these social constructions persist and therefore shape and influence people's behavior and daily practices (Friedman 1992). They are also available to be reformulated and/or politicized according to specific politically and economically generated circumstances.

In order to problematize these categories that are "implicated in the texture of everyday life and ... thoroughly presupposed in academic discourse on 'culture' and 'society'" (Gupta 1992:63), we need a global perspective and a sense of the processual and historical.

> On the one side, we need to investigate processes of place making, of how feelings of belonging to an imagined community bind identity to spatial location such that differences between communities and places are created. At the same time, we also need to situate those processes within a systematic development that reinscribes and reterritorializes space in the global political economy (Gupta 1992:62).

A major task of this book is to delineate the processes through which transmigrants, living lives stretched across borders, reterritorialize their practices as well as their identities. We also look for moments, locations, and cultural practices in which such reinscriptions become undone or fail to encapsulate experience.

D. Premise Four: By Living their Lives Across Borders, Transmigrants Find themselves Confronted with and Engaged in the Nation Building Processes of Two or More Nation-States. Their Identities and Practices Are Configured by Hegemonic Categories Such As Race and Ethnicity that are Deeply Embedded in the Nation Building Processes of these Nation-States

The paradox of the current world conjuncture is the increased production of cultural and political boundaries at the very time when the world has become tightly bound together in a single economic system with instantaneous communication between different sectors of the globe. In order to disentangle these contradictory trends, it is necessary to place the construction of cultural demarcations and political boundaries being erected between groupings of people within the context of contention for political power and control of productive resources, including labor power.

However, it has been difficult for social science to acknowledge that there is a relationship between the growth of capitalism, nation building processes, and the categories of race and ethnicity. The fact that discussions of race, ethnicity, and nation have been separate areas of social science discourse both reflects the lack of a critical perspective on the relationship between race, culture, and power and contributes to a failure to develop such a perspective. Part of the task of this book is to understand the manner in which the conceptual

categories of race, ethnicity. and nation are hegemonic constructions
and are all part of the historical exercise of state power and domination. With such a perspective, we can see the manner in which the
emerging transnational populations are shaped by and participate in
the shaping of such hegemonic constructions.

1. Nation Building and Constructions of Race and Ethnicity

Recent scholarship has made it clear that the legitimacy of political
units defined as nation-states to exercise power over territory was
established in the 18th and 19th century by invoking and inventing a
historical past shared by a unified people (Anderson 1991; Gellner
1983; Herzfeld 1985; Kapferer 1988; Hobsbawm 1990). Classes and
elite strata striving to maintain or contend for state power constructed memories of a shared past and used this historical narrative
to authenticate and validate a commonality of purpose and national
interests. At first, the study of "nation" as a cultural construction
sparked a debate over whether nations were built on primordial
cultural roots (A. Smith 1981) or "invented traditions" (Hobsbawm
and Ranger 1983). Increasingly we have come to understand that
nation-states, whether they were "imagined" (Anderson 1991) in
Western Europe, in postcolonial settings or as part of socialist
projects, were not totally new visions. Rather they have been built
out of historically grounded culture, including the religious and
philosophical concepts that have been pervasive in particular regions
(Herzfeld 1985; Kapferer 1988; Sahlins 1989; Verdery 1991).

While documenting the novelty and recent vintage of the concept
of the nation-state and linking it to the rise of capitalism, the new
scholarship has given us few insights into the manner in which
nation building processes simultaneously include and exclude. Not
adequately addressed by present approaches to nationalism are the
multiple voices that contend and are differentially incorporated
within the hegemonic processes of nation-states. Still to be explained
are the processes by which national identity and nationalism spring
up in opposition to state power. That such explanations are overdue
became obvious when the resurgence of nationalism in various sectors of the globe in the 1990s, including its dramatic and often violent
manifestations in Eastern Europe and former Soviet Asia, took social
scientists by surprise.

In calling our attention to a social dynamic in which unity may be
secured "in and through (not despite) differences" Hall (1977) helps
us to conceptualize the relationship between nation building and the

categorization of populations as racially or ethnically different. According to Hall,

Most societies with complex social structures achieve their 'unity' via the relations of domination/subordination between culturally different and differential strata. What we are required to 'think' is the nature of the difference which constitutes the specific 'unity' and complexity of any social formation. The 'unity' of a social formation is never a simple, undifferentiated unity. Once we grasp the two ends, so to speak, of this chain — differentiated specificity/complex unity — we see that we are required to account, not simply for the existence of culturally distinct institutions and patterns, but also for that which secures the unity, cohesion and stability of this social order in and through (not despite) its differences... [T]he focus on ... complexity-and-unity requires us to concentrate on the mechanisms of power, legitimation and domination: of *hegemony* (Hall 1977:158).

Similarly, Kearney has theorized that

The fundamental project of the state — the inward task of the modern nation-state — is to elaborate and resolve the contradiction of differentiation and unity. The disciplinary power of the state must facilitate the reproduction of social and cultural differentiation within the nation while at the same time perpetuating national unity ... [T]he state must also insure the reproduction of difference as social inequality (Kearney 1991a:55).

The dialectic of simultaneous inclusivity and exclusivity of the nation-state can be understood in relationship to two processes of domination: (1) the mechanisms by which all state societies legitimate structures of power; and (2) the relationship between capital and labor that is at the historical core of nation building projects.

Nation-states differ from other forms of the state by legitimating the power of the dominant class in terms of a shared culture and history that unite the populations contained within them. This unity is constructed without reference to any divisions that continue to persist, including, but not limited to, divisions of class. We call nation building the hegemonic processes, structures, and daily practices by which subordinated classes within a state consent to their domination. The dominant class within a nation-state forges legitimacy by claiming to represent a unity among sectors of the population that may be culturally diverse and are always hierarchically stratified. When the dominant class is itself a cultural minority, it may actively obfuscate these differences in order to reinforce subordination (Blanc-Szanton 1982b, 1985b).

Nation building processes are interwoven into the very matrix of the nation-state, embedded in its institutions, manifested in its policies and practices, and organized through state bureaucracies. As with any hegemonic process, specific representations of the nation emerge through active contention in which a country's leaders and populations both play an active role. Part of nation building is nationalism, the politicized language or ideology of national unity used by those participating in projects of identity construction that focus on the nation. Nationalism is an ideology of identity; part of the ideology is the belief that national identity is fundamental and natural.

In previous generations, social scientists contributed to the hegemony of nationalist ideologies by assuming that nation-states were a necessary and natural product of history. (See, for example, such modernization theorists as Apter 1965; Parsons 1951; and Pye 1966.) As Malkki has noted, "That the world should be composed of sovereign, spatially discontinuous units is a sometimes implicit, sometimes a stated premise in much of the literature on nations and nationalism" (1992:26). In envisioning the nation as natural, nationalism must be understood as a legitimization of state power though concepts of biology and destiny.

To talk about nation, therefore, is to talk about race. We are coming to understand that concepts of nation and race can be usefully understood to be two poles of a single historical discourse (B. Williams 1989; Takaki 1990). If at its core the concept of nation is oppositional and hierarchical, the nation stands in opposition to those defined as biologically different only by envisioning the nation as composed of those who are biologically similar.[8] The equation of race and nation was somewhat more obvious in the 19th century, when race was used as a gloss for 'nation' and national culture was thought to be rooted in biology. This usage was carried into the 20th century and articulated not only by such infamous authors as Gobineau, but in every day speech in expressions like "the British race."

The designation of race differs from that of nation in that racial designations highlight biological rather than cultural or political differences (Berreman 1972; Harris 1964; Montagu 1974).[9] Racial categories have contributed to the differential treatment of whole populations within the development and dynamics of capitalist processes of extracting surplus value produced by labor (E. Williams 1964 [1944]). As Wolf has pointed out, in their origins

> Racial designations, such as 'Indian' or 'Negro,' are the outcome of
> the subjugation of populations in the course of European mercantile

expansion... The two terms thus single out for primary attention the historic fact that these populations were made to labor in servitude to support a new class of overlords (1982:380).

Wolf's analysis of the construction of global categories of race within the development of capitalism highlights the economic relationships that underlie racial categorization. However, the processes of race-making are simultaneously political. The development of capitalism, although it occurred on a global landscape, both contributed to and strengthened a division of the world into nation-states and colonies. Concepts of both nation and race, honed and developed within the context of the expansion of Europe and the development of colonialism, developed as ways to speak about (1) the imagining of the national identity of the colonizer in relationship to the racially differentiated colonial population (Centre for Contemporary Cultural Studies 1982) and (2) the positioning of different sectors of the work force within the colonizing state. These two processes of differentiation are related but not identical.

In this book our focus of discussion will be on the way in which race is constructed within the nation building processes of the United States and the postcolonial states of St. Vincent, Grenada, Haiti, and the Philippines. Forged as they were out of a fabric of European conquest and movements of resistance and empowerment, postcolonial nation-states carry within them their own readings of race. Their nation building processes both reject and reinscribe the global meanings of race developed in the course of European conquest and colonialism. In the succeeding chapters, dominant classes within St. Vincent, Grenada, Haiti, and the Philippines will be shown to have shaped their hegemonic constructs of nation in response to and cognizant of the global racial constructions according to which their populations were defined as racially different and hence inferior and without history or culture.

Those who have written about the international division of labor tend to focus on the global economic and military dominance of core capitalist states (Wallerstein 1979; Portes 1978; Portes and Walton 1981; Sassen 1988). It is important to note that this dominance is accompanied by and legitimated by cultural influences that are ever more pervasive, as cinema, television, and other forms of media penetrate the post-colonial world. Within this cultural penetration, furthermore, racial categorizations continue to be used to differentiate and justify domination. Subordinated nation-states continue to be categorized in racial terms, so that civilization continues to be implicitly white.

The term "ethnic" has its own oppositionality and historical relationship to both nation and race (B. Williams 1989). In the current U.S. context, concepts of race and ethnicity have come to have different meanings; they are tropes for two different relationships between dominant and subordinate populations. It should be noted that in the past, populations that today would be defined in the United States as "ethnic" — for example, Irish or Italian immigrants — were both seen as biologically distinct groups and as persons of distinctive national origin.

This situation pertains in many nation-states of Europe at the current time. In nation building projects in Eastern Europe, for example, concepts of biological difference, referred to in a language of ethnicity, have become salient in the efforts to define by force and legitimate the relationships between populations within territories claimed by particular states. The Serbian campaign of 'ethnic cleansing,' rather than being an aberration of nationalism, illustrates all too well the racial logic embedded in the concept of nation-state.

As in the case of other hegemonic processes, we can see that ethnic identification emerges from daily, embedded, habitual, familiar, and often familial, cultural practices (Bentley 1987). As the dominant sectors within the nation-state seek to incorporate populations in ways that subordinate them economically and politically, these daily practices can become the material out of which identity and differentiation are constituted. As the terms of this incorporation are imposed, negotiated, and contested, the dominant strata use culture to justify differential incorporation (di Leonardo 1984; Roosens 1989).

Ethnic processes then, as they establish hierarchy and diversity, contribute to the building and maintenance of a nation-state. At the very same time, however, these processes create the conditions for and contribute to the formation of a leadership that can challenge the domination by a nation-state from within, often without challenging the very concept of "nation-state." Subordinated populations may utilize their differentiation as a rallying point or even as a battle cry, but the challenge continues to be made within the language of nationalism (Gilroy 1992).

In summarizing the process in which resistance is mediated by the language of domination, we must conclude with something about gender. We are aware that both colonialist and nationalist discourses are gendered (Comaroff and Comaroff 1991; Gilman 1986; Stoler 1989; Blanc Szanton 1990). When women have joined struggles for national liberation they have found themselves calling on representations that contributed to their own disempowerment (Enloe

1990). As in the case of class, the hegemonic categories of race, ethnicity, and nation leave unspoken the divisions and inequalities that accompany the structure of gender differentiations. Throughout this book gender often remains an unmarked category, although it is a "lived experience" in the lives of the transmigrants being discussed and of the authors. In our conclusions, we point to gender as a location from which to construct identities that allow us to think beyond the nation building processes of particular nation-states.

2. Race and Identity in U.S. Nation-Building Projects

At the core of the U.S. concept of nation has been a concept of whiteness (Lieberson 1980; B. Williams 1989). First developed during the initial genocidal encounters with Native Americans, whiteness became a thread of commonality used by the emerging capitalist class to meld together a population of diverse origins. Takaki (1990) traces the embedding of race-making constructions within the concept of the American people to the crisis of legitimacy faced by the founding fathers. No longer joined together as subjects of the king, the free population of the newly independent country differed in their histories, language, and religion, but they shared skin color (Hobsbawm 1990). Throughout U.S. history, national identity has been built by distancing the body politic from the racially different other. The construction of the "American people" as white has served to justify and perpetuate the subordination of the African-American population as well as to assimilate certain immigrant populations and exclude others. In the course of this nation building process, class and race were conflated (B. Williams 1989). In such a conflation, populations said to be black were assumed to be on the bottom and distant from those who truly belonged to the nation. As they distanced themselves from blackness, European immigrant workers came to identify with America and positioned themselves on the side of its dominant class.

The social location of blackness as a marker of the bottom of society has been frequently noted by African-American writers (Baldwin 1971; Hurston 1979). James Baldwin described the meaning of blackness in America through the imagery of social location.

> In a way, the Negro tells us where the bottom is: because he is there, and where he is, beneath us, we know where the limits are and how far we must not fall. We must not fall beneath him. We must never allow ourselves to fall that low (1971:22).

All other persons categorized as racially distinct — that is non-white — find their place above blacks but also outside of the white nation. At times this assumption of whiteness as a diacritic of citizenship has been made explicit in immigration laws that forbade the naturalization of people of color and in the court cases that upheld those laws (Takaki 1990). However, this "racial order" (Greenberg 1980) is usually not directly acknowledged. Because the United States is a nation of immigrants, the task of imagining an American people has been especially problematic. In addition to their multiple cultural and linguistic histories, immigrants have brought their political histories and commitments to political processes within other states (Glazer 1954). Consequently, the government of the United States and the hegemonic forces of U.S. civil society have long been concerned both with issues of assimilation and of loyalty and patriotism. The loyalty of U.S. immigrants has been won by material incentives, both real and imagined. The Horatio Alger myth of the poor man who works hard and makes millions is retold to new generations of immigrants. U.S. hegemonic forces have also worked to win the loyalty of white immigrants by continuing to reinvigorate a national construction of the American people as a white people. U.S. hegemonic forces always have feared having populations living within the United States whose political allegiance is elsewhere. Such a population could serve to challenge the legitimacy of the U.S. class system at home and the role of the United States abroad.[10]

U.S. social science, since its founding, has played an important role in shaping the manner in which immigrant populations were understood to relate to the U.S. nation. What analysts felt to be politically and socially necessary was presented as a description of both the current and presumably inevitable historical process. Confronted with the cultural diversity that the influx of immigrants from Southern and Eastern Europe brought to U.S. urban centers at the beginning of the 20th century, the Chicago school of Sociology, led by Park and Burgess, defined their problematic as one of "maintaining political order ... in a community that has no common culture" (Park and Burgess 1969:734). Their emphasis was not on the study of differences but on the necessity of assimilation. Migrants were viewed as "peoples who have abandoned the *political allegiances* of the old country, and are gradually acquiring the culture of the new" (Park and Burgess 1969:734, emphasis added).[11]

The process of "Americanizing" differentiated the newcomers from the mainstream, even as it mandated their incorporation into the body politic. For example, in the 1920s at the same time that

immigrant populations were subject to intense acculturative pressures and all out efforts were made to insure their political loyalty to
the "American nation," these populations were widely referred to as
"nationalities" and thus as hyphenated Americans, distinguishing
them from Americans, who were by inference white Protestant descendants of early English settlers. Although the drive to acculturate
European immigrants has often been described by historians and
sociologists as "assimilationist" (Higham and Brooks 1978; Steinberg
1981), the Americanization campaigns, from the flag waving parades
to the introduction of immigrant school children to Thanksgiving
turkey and stuffing (Siskind 1992), can be seen as efforts to obtain
consent from the newly incorporated. Much of this project, while it
was articulated in an idiom of citizenship, focused on the making of
subjects rather on the facilitation of access to the political process. In
sorting out the contradictions between a rhetoric of assimilation on
the one hand and the continuing emphasis on the diverse cultural
origins of immigrants that led to the particularization and perpetuation of ethnicities on the other, it is helpful to see these contradictions
as stemming from hegemonic processes in which dominant strata
strive to maintain their control.

The political response of the immigrants to this forceful and often
forced recruitment into the "American" national polity seems to
have been similar to the reaction of subordinated populations to
nation building efforts throughout the world. They both
"Americanized" and turned to their hyphenated American identities
as a base area for political organizing for empowerment. Intellectuals
and professional strata among U.S. immigrant populations played a
leading role in the development of ethnic institutions and the articulation of ethnic identities (Higham and Brooks 1978; Tomasi and
Engel 1970).[12] Finding their own aspirations blocked, emergent "ethnic leaders" organized forms of resistance and encouraged the
development of ethnic institutions such as churches, schools,
newspapers, and voluntary organizations in the United States. To
some extent these "ethnic" institutions contributed to national movements in the immigrants' home countries, but the disruption caused
by two world wars and intermittent Americanization drives left most
ties to home as affective, romanticized memories.

Hegemonic processes often legitimate not with a single vision but
by defining the boundaries of thinkable possibilities and the range of
alternative visions (Hall 1988). Confronted with the unrest of the civil
rights movement of the 1960s, which quickly began to escalate into
demands for empowerment "by any means necessary" (Malcolm X,

cited in Cone 1991) there was some effort by hegemonic forces to move toward a culturally more plural definition of the "American nation." The influx in the 1960s of a large number of immigrants of color posed additional challenges to hegemonic strategies of immigrant assimilation and led to the generation of alternative constructions of the "American nation" and the popularization of a model of cultural pluralism. When in 1963 Glazer and Moynihan called to "look beyond the melting pot" (1970), their call marked an effort to develop a form of "cultural pluralism that ... would be in the interests of both individual groups and the entire nation" because the emphasis would be on how "distinctive histories and cultures [are] integrated into a larger sense of American history and the American experience" (Glazer 1983:115).

In this alternative vision of the United States, the nation was composed of multiple ethnic populations that compete equally within the U.S. nation-state. Populations conceived of as racially different, such as African-Americans or Puerto Ricans, were equated with non-WASP Europeans, such as Italians or Jews. The image projected by the cultural pluralists was of a nation composed of bounded, persisting ethnic groups that each had its own shared cultural beliefs and practices (Greeley 1971; Novak 1973; Sowell 1981).[13] The new paradigm also drew on the pluralist model developed in American political science that portrayed the United States not as class stratified but as a politically plural and open society (Dahl 1961).

The concept of "ethnic group" was a central aspect of the new construction of immigrant populations. As popularized within U.S. social science, the term "ethnic" refers to a set of cultural practices, beliefs, and values that are imputed to have originated in the shared tradition of a nation, territory, or language grouping outside of the territorial United States. It is this use and conceptualization of ethnicity that pervaded the popular press and remains enshrined in today's descriptions of American social structure. Cultural pluralists have viewed the culture of immigrants in terms of a metaphor of roots that could be transplanted rather than as tendrils that maintain living vital links. Just as much a political ideology as the assimilationist theory that it replaced, cultural pluralism represented a new agenda with which to construct a U.S. nationality that incorporated, and yet kept subordinated, people of color.

The pluralist model did not put aside an ideology of individual mobility or address the political economy of the United States or the structure of global capitalism. Maurice Stans, who headed the U.S. Chamber of Commerce, made clear how racial oppression was being addressed when he said in 1969 "what the black people, the minority people, need more than anything else today is a modern Horatio Alger, the kind of guy who will tell the story of how he succeeded and let everyone else believe that they can accomplish the same result. As time goes on, we are going to do everything we can to publicize the stories... This is the way we will build the pride of these people, and this is the way we will convince the young fellows coming up that they have a chance to do the same thing" (cited in Blaustein and Faux 1972:155).

At the same time, the cultural pluralist model contained new explanations of inequalities within the U.S. population. Ethnic cultures themselves allowed some groups to compete and succeed while other ethnic groups failed miserably. Hence Glazer and Moynihan (1970:xi) could posit that "a significant check to the economic rise of the Negroes might be found in the values of American Negroes themselves." Ethnic groups whose members had achieved some modicum of success were posed as models for other groups as well as competitors whose very success stood as barriers to those less successful in obtaining "a piece of the pie" — in the most widely used pluralist idiom of the 1970s. In recent years Asians have been given a prominence in this model and set up as a contrasting category to blackness. Against the backdrop of "deindustrialization," which was accompanied by declining labor force participation among young blacks (Wilson 1987), Asian-Americans have been held up as exemplars of the upward mobility minorities could obtain in the United States if only they made the effort. For example, in a speech to a group of Asian and Pacific Americans in the White House, February 23, 1984 (Asian Week, March 2, 1984 cited in Takaki 1990:304), President Reagan heralded these populations as models of the values of self-reliance and industriousness.

By the 1990s, scholars, educators, and politicians began to talk about "multiculturalism," but the current political struggle contains many of the same demands made by the earlier advocates of cultural pluralism.[14] The call for multiculturalism also contains many of the same limitations. As did the cultural pluralists, the multiculturalists call for the validation of the contributions of various cultures to the fabric of U.S. national culture. However, while cultural pluralists initially gave no place to the racial structuring of the United States in their model, so that Caribbeans and Filipinos were equated with Italians as competing ethnic groups, multiculturalism often is specifically understood as a national reconstruction incorporating previously subaltern people into representations of the American nation (Asante 1992; Gordon and Lubiano 1992). Takaki, for example, argues passionately that "we need to re-vision" history because

> Eurocentric history serves no one. It only shrouds the pluralism that is America and makes our nation so unique, and thus the possibility of appreciating our rich racial and cultural diversity remains a dream deferred. Actually, as Americans, we come originally from many different shores — Europe, the Americas, Africa, and also Asia (Takaki 1989:7)

The renewed calls for the recognition of cultural diversity have highlighted the continuing privileging of a Eurocentric canon (Gates 1986). Some scholars and educators have used the term multiculturalism to raise political agendas that speak to issues of class inequalities and that extend political identifications beyond the boundaries of nation-states (Turner 1992). However, despite important differences in approaches to multiculturalism, by and large, those who have been leading the struggle for multiculturalism do not look beyond the borders of the United States (see, for example, Winkler 1990). The history they seek to rectify and the culture they see themselves as building is bounded by the borders of the United States (see Gilroy 1991 and 1992 for a critique of "ethnic absolutism" in Great Britain). Their commitment, as Takaki makes clear, is "America," defined as unique from, and by implication, superior to, other nations. Moreover, as did the cultural pluralists before them, they imply that when cultural and political representation is obtained, people of color will be empowered in the United States. Increasingly, advocates of multiculturalism speak of "cultural citizenship" (Rosaldo 1993). The horizons of the political struggle remain on the level of symbolic representation within the nation-state. While it may open new realms of discourse, the acceptance of multiculturalism does not in itself signal the empowerment of subordinated populations. "Minorities by any other name — people of color, or whatever — will still bear a huge burden of poverty, discrimination, and racial harassment. Verbal uplift is not the revolution" (Ehrenreich 1992:336).

CONCLUSIONS

As this book will demonstrate, transmigrants of all classes live a complex existence that forces them to confront, draw upon, and rework different hegemonic constructions of identity developed in their home or new nation-state(s). Transmigrants simultaneously participate in nation building in their home country and in processes of nation building in the United States that are ordinarily subsumed under the rubric "ethnicity." At the same time, the racial structuring in the United States and in post-colonial countries and migrants' experiences of the linkage between race and nation in these various polities shape the nature of their participation in these nation-building processes. Faced with these processes of differentiation and subordination, Caribbean and Filipino immigrants have embraced the nation building processes of newly deterritorialized nation-states newly imagined by their political leadership.

Within the situations of political and economic domination and racial and cultural differentiation, building transnational social fields and imagining a deterritorialized nation-state can be seen as a form of resistance on the part of Caribbean and Filipino immigrants. However, the issue of resistance is a complex one that must be contextualized within the always partial and unfinished construction of identities shaped by the pressures of national hegemonies. Subordinated populations may internalize many of the meanings and representations that pervade their daily surroundings, but that internalization remains partial and incomplete. Meanings are often subverted and there is always, at the level of daily practice, some opening for innovation. Moreover, when hegemonic constructions are more fully internalized, that internalization provides the very basis for the reutilization of meanings in counter-hegemonic arguments against subordination.

In other words, there are many levels of resistance, beginning with the construction of individual identities and personal behaviors, but extending to group responses, organizational initiatives, and counter-hegemonic and revolutionary movements. In the following chapters we will make reference to many of these levels as we discuss transmigrant identities, practices, and struggles across national borders. In our conclusion we will then focus on two hegemonic constructs, race and deterritorialization, by which transmigrants resist and reappropriate nation building processes even as they accommodate to situations of unequal power.

NOTES

1. Portions of the initial sections of this chapter appear in Glick-Schiller, Basch, and Blanc-Szanton (1992a, 1992b). Portions of the sections on race and nation were presented by Glick-Schiller (1992b). The relation-

ship of hegemonic categories and ethnic identities was discussed in Blanc Szanton (1982, 1985b). The concept of transnational social field was set forth in Basch, Wiltshire, Wiltshire, and Toney (1990).

2. See Noble (1977) on technological reductionism.

3. Estimating that two-fifths of the immigrants were returning to Europe, the U.S. Immigration Commission Report of 1911 speculated that many among the returnees actually made multiple trips (cited in Portes and Bach 1985:31).

4. It should be noted that the reported capitalist restructuring has been uneven and that only highly specific and small areas of the world have become recipients of reinvestment (Gordon 1988). It may be that although the past two decades have seen new levels of capitalist control, financial restructuring, and cultural and ideological penetration, these changes do not indicate the tighter consolidation of global capital. Instead they may mark a crisis whose dimensions have shifted to a global level.

5. These figures are influenced, however, by the finding that non-English-speaking migrants, many of whom are from the Caribbean, earn considerably less.

6. Appadurai has noted that since World War II, a concept of place has pervaded the construction of anthropological theory (1986).

7. Chaney suggests that "We must study the strategies involved in such migration variations as 'commuting,' 'trial,' migration, and 'visiting,' and what implications these apparently wide practices have for the receiving societies" (1979:210).

8. The ideologies of nationalism were constructed by coupling concepts of sovereignty and territory to older definitions of nation that referred not to polity but to shared descent of a particular folk or people (Hobsbawm 1990).

9. In the popular imagination as well as in the minds of many scholars in many fields, race refers to biologically distinctive populations. In contrast, there is a widespread understanding among anthropologists and sociologists that "markers of both racial and ethnic difference are subjective, historically and culturally contingent, and tend to overlap contextually with other markers of cultural difference such as regional affiliation, class and gender" (Hegeman 1991:77).

10. In the 1920s, after a large surge in immigration, the pledge of allegiance was changed to make it clear that people were pledging not to any flag but to that of the United States of America.

11. The U.S. racial order was not addressed in this model; rather, groups seen as culturally different were described in the language of race so that the pathways toward assimilation became a "race-relations" cycle (Park 1950).

12. See Higham (1984) on the role of Kallen as an intellectual, who came to identify himself with American Jewry and became an early spokesman for an ideology of cultural pluralism.

13. There were actually two variants of cultural pluralism. As the term has been used in the United States it drew on the writings of Horace Kallen (Higham 1984) and Glazer and Moynihan (1970). A different understanding of pluralism developed in the Caribbean, drawing on an analytic formulation of Furnivall as conceptualized by M. G. Smith (1965b). In contrast to the US version, Smith's model was essentially a conflict model that assumed that societies composed of different racial and cultural groups could be held together only by coercion (Basch 1978).

14. The word "multicultural education" actually was used much earlier in discussions of integrating an appreciation of ethnic cultures into school curricula, but in this earlier usage, as in discussions of cultural pluralism, the histories of racial discrimination faced by people of color were not emphasized. (Herman 1974, cited in Glazer 1983:107).

Chapter THREE

The Making of West Indian Transmigrant Populations: Examples from St. Vincent and Grenada[1]

I. INTRODUCTION

It was April 1984 and Herbert Blaize, a former colonial Chief Minister of Grenada, was addressing a crowd of approximately 600 Grenadians of all ages and seemingly of different class strata in a well appointed catering hall in Brooklyn owned by a Grenadian immigrant. It was only a few months after the assassination of the Grenadian prime minister, Maurice Bishop, and Blaize was seeking the support of the immigrant community in his efforts to become the next prime minister of Grenada.

The meeting had been organized by a support group for Blaize in New York headed by Lamuel Stanislaus, a highly respected political leader in the Grenadian immigrant community and an old friend and political ally of Blaize.[2] Most of the members of the support group had similarly been supporters if not members of Blaize's political party, the Grenada National Party (GNP), even though they lived in New York.

The audience voiced many questions and apprehensions about the direction in which Blaize would move Grenada. Bishop's assassination had been followed by the military occupation of Grenada by American forces and the establishment by these forces of an interim government. Bishop's policies, which in their attempts to lessen the nation's dependence on the United States and steer a more autonomous course, had established close ties with Cuba and the then Soviet Union. Although some Grenadians had applauded this seemingly independent course, others had feared that Grenada's new alliances would facilitate the spread of communism in the Caribbean region.

Some in the middle classes with property interests in Grenada had been worried that their property might have been confiscated by the Bishop government, which had expressed an intention to redistribute idle land to the peasantry. They wondered whether Blaize would develop any safeguards to protect property owned by immigrants abroad. Others, pleased with the large airfield Grenada had been building — even if with Soviet funds and Cuban workers — which would finally enable this nation to receive jets filled hopefully with tourists from abroad, wanted to know if this effort would be completed. Yet others questioned whether there would be an overseas registration, which would enable the immigrants to vote in the upcoming election.

Blaize underscored his party's respect for personal property, at the same time vowing to complete the airport, which he asserted would be essential for the island's industrial development as well as for tourism. Further invoking a rhetoric of autonomy associated with independent nation-states, Blaize asserted that "anyone who gives aid must come with clean hands, with no strings attached." This included all outside interests — Soviet, Cuban, and American. Blaize underscored the importance of the immigrant constituency to Grenada's nation building, pointing out that while there were 90,000 Grenadians living in Grenada, only 32,000 of whom were adults, there were 60,000 adult Grenadians living in North America, many of whom owned property at home.

Stanislaus closed the meeting by asking for contributions for Blaize's campaign and urging those in the audience to encourage their relatives and friends at home to support Blaize. (It was announced that $500 had been collected.) The immigrants were also encouraged to show their support for Grenada by returning home for Carnival the coming summer.

* * *

This vignette provides us with a glimpse of the myriad involvements immigrants living in New York sustain with their home country of Grenada. Many of the immigrants attending this meeting owned property — land and houses — in Grenada, while some had business interests and investments — for example, in hotels, in small shipping companies, in farms, and in transportation. Others had children living in Grenada who were minded by relatives.

However, this vignette also raises important questions about the nature of these immigrants' relationship to Grenada. After all, many of the Grenadians in this audience had been settled in the United States for many years, owned property in New York and were U.S. citizens, as was Stanislaus. Yet others had begun to participate on local community boards and school boards and had started to record their narratives on the social and cultural scapes of New York — through the print media, on radio and television, through music, through churches and cultural festivals, and through the many newly emerging catering establishments.

Why was Blaize addressing this audience and seeking its members' support as part of his election campaign? And why was the audience so concerned with the intricacies of Grenadian policies, as we saw in the questions the immigrants posed to Blaize, and with voting in the then upcoming Grenadian election? What does this vignette tell us about the identifications of present day Grenadian immigrants?

Blaize's statements during this meeting — some of which had a contradictory flavor — carefully addressed the somewhat divergent concerns of the various class segments of this differentiated audience. By underscoring his party's respect for private property, while stressing its concerns with creating jobs through economic development projects such as tourism, the attraction of industrial investments, and completing the airport, and at the same time invoking a rhetoric of autonomy, Blaize was attempting to reach out to Grenadian immigrants of all class strata and age. His aim was to unite them behind an encompassing national ideology. In the wake of the political turbulence of the past decade in Grenada, which had exacerbated Grenadian social divisions, Blaize and Stanislaus were seeking to strengthen the immigrants' identification with the Grenadian nation and make new claims on their loyalty.

At this meeting the immigrants were being addressed and were acting as nationals of Grenada. Both Blaize's and Stanislaus' messages were that even though the immigrants lived abroad and were engaged in the affairs of the United States, perhaps as citizens, they had continuing economic, political, and social responsibilities to Grenada that they were expected to act on. In other words, the immigrants continued to be seen as integral to the nation building efforts of their "home" state.

By treating the immigrants in the audience as members of the Grenadian nation-state, Blaize and Stanislaus were contravening European derived conceptions of the nation-state in which territory and population were seen as coterminous and the nation-state was defined as a geographic entity comprised of a unified people who share cultural practices, a single language, and loyalty to a common government. In contrast, in the nation-state conceptualized by the participants at this meeting, social location, identity, and political loyalty were no longer geographically bounded.

While this vignette focuses on the transnational social and political practices of Grenadian immigrants and their expression of a collective Grenadian national identity, immigrants from St. Vincent engage in almost identical transnational practices and express similar allegiances to the deterritorialized constructions forged by representatives of the St. Vincent nation-state.

It is significant that Blaize, who himself had lived abroad for many years and had, in fact, cut his political teeth as a worker in the U.S. owned oil refinery in Aruba, and Stanislaus and other immigrant leaders in the audience who had maintained transnational networks were challenging geographically bounded definitions of the nation-state. In advancing the construction of the deterritorialized nation-state, they were giving public acknowledgement to the transnationalism that characterized their lives.

Transnationalism, the living of personal and political lives across geographic boundaries, has become for many Grenadians — and the same can be said for Vincentians — woven into the very fabric of their lives. In large measure, their present transnational practices build on a particular migration tradition, the contours of which had been shaped and nourished over the past century and a half. The specific historic circumstances that have constituted the impetus for Grenadians and Vincentians to emigrate since the mid-nineteenth century as both response and resistance to their marginal positioning in the global political economy have led them, as well as other West Indian immigrants, to retain ties to both kin and places at home.

Following the decolonization of the 1960s, the transnational and reciprocal ties immigrants sustained with their kin at home through remittances, property ownership, and child-minding, began to take on a public flavor. Beyond their personal networks, immigrants started to support public projects in their home towns — schools, hospitals, and other philanthropies — often through immigrant organizations. With political independence, these ties mushroomed, becoming even more multi-stranded. Responding to the social, economic, and political marginalization they experienced within the U.S. racial order, immigrants found in their home societies the social validation, and increasingly the political opportunities, that they were denied in the United States.

Although Grenadian and Vincentian immigrants increasingly live lives that cross geographic boundaries and unite social spaces, the world in which they live is defined in terms of discrete, bounded nation-states. The construction of the deterritorialized nation-state articulated by Blaize, for example, did not acknowledge the multi-stranded relationships the immigrants sustain across the borders of Grenada and the United States. Neither they nor their leaders have yet given voice to an identity that reflects their transnationalism. Rather, Blaize's involvement in nation building processes in Grenada — concretized in the construction of the deterritorialized nation-state — led him to emphasize the immigrants' primary loyalty to Grenada and the similarity of the situations of all Grenadians. At other times, Stanislaus and other immigrants on the U.S. support committee for Blaize have encouraged the immigrants to become involved in U.S. political processes to advance the immigrants' situations in the United States.

From their divergent perspectives born of their different class positions in both Grenada and the United States, their different regions of origin in Grenada, their different genders, and their different experiences with settlement in the United States, the Grenadian transmigrants in the audience were not all equally responsive to Blaize's and Stanislaus' construction of the deterritorialized Grenadian state. Nor had Grenadian immigrants been similarly responsive a few years earlier when Bishop, arguing for the same loyalty from immigrants to the home nation-state, had represented Brooklyn as "Grenada's largest constituency." Yet, membership in an independent nation-state, in which color and race are not the primary markers of social position and which does not force a disavowal of ties developing in the United States — in fact, sometimes seeks to build on them — has resonance among all strata of immigrants.

Since the early part of the century both Grenadian and Vincentian immigrants have seen themselves as politically involved populations within the United States. During the earlier years, when they could not identify with their colonial states of origin, they embraced a racial political identity, joining with African-Americans to demand greater access within the U.S. sociopolitical system. At the same time, however, they celebrated their Vincentian, Grenadian, and Caribbean cultural roots. In the more recent postcolonial context, the ethnic and nationalist identities of these immigrant populations have become mutually reinforcing, as Grenadian and Vincentian immigrant populations have begun to identify themselves publicly as part of a "Caribbean" political force.

Yet, although the transnational social relationships that the immigrants construct draw them into the social practices, hegemonic constructions, and ideologies of both their home countries and the United States, the identity constructs of these immigrants do not reflect the complexity that incorporation into several societies brings to their lives. The material of these seemingly dislocating yet interconnected experiences leads Grenadian and Vincentian immigrants in the United States to see themselves variously as black, African, West Indian, Vincentian, or Grenadian and to engage in activities in the name of these discrete identities. The next chapter will probe the contradictions generated by the escalating Vincentian and Grenadian transnational practices, on the other hand, and the nation-bound ways in which these immigrants continue to understand their experiences and articulate their identities, on the other.

First, however, this chapter will outline the development and scope of Vincentian and Grenadian transnationalism. Current transnational processes are shown to build on earlier migration experiences and traditions established within the Caribbean. The transnational practices of Vincentian and Grenadian immigrants are anchored in the familial, social, and economic relationships the immigrants have created, which, as we shall see, span the geographic and social borders of the United States and Grenada or St. Vincent.

II. SOME BACKGROUND NOTES

A. Researchers and Methods

The field research which forms the basis of Chapters Three and Four was conducted from 1982 to 1985 among Vincentian and Grenadian immigrants in New York and Trinidad and their kin living in St.

Vincent and Grenada.[3] The research was built on preliminary observations that Basch made from 1979 to 1982 while developing an overview of Caribbean migration patterns and practices for the United Nations Institute for Training and Research (Basch 1982).[4] Her co-researchers in the study of Caribbean migration included Rosina Wiltshire and Winston Wiltshire and Joyce Toney (see Basch, Wiltshire, Wiltshire, and Toney 1990; Wiltshire, Basch, Wiltshire, and Toney 1990; Toney 1988). Interviews were conducted with 130 Vincentians and Grenadians in New York and 80 in Trinidad; 100 relatives of these immigrants living in St. Vincent and Grenada were also interviewed.[5]

The snowball method used in developing the research samples meant that immigrants' social and political networks were studied. This enabled us to observe the actual ways immigrants forged and acted upon transnational relationships. Attention was also given to encompassing in the samples those of different ages, relatively equal numbers of women and men, and those who came with and without documents. Several of the twenty Vincentian and eighteen Grenadian voluntary organizations in New York were also studied during the course of this research.

B. Terms of Understanding

St. Vincent and Grenada are two of the smallest island nation-states in the chain of English-speaking islands located in the southern part of the Caribbean Sea. These islands, along with Guyana on the South American mainland, constitute the West Indies (known as the British West Indies during colonial times). Although the peoples of this area use the terms West Indian or Caribbean to describe themselves,[6] we will use the term West Indian, reserving the term Caribbean for those peoples from all the islands in the Caribbean Sea and from the countries of Surinam and French Guyana along the northern rim of South America.

The nation-state of Grenada is composed of three islands: the tiny island of Petit Martinique, the slightly larger island of Carriacou, and the main island of Grenada. Although together they house a population of no more than 100,000, each island has a distinct regional identity; however, collectively they identify themselves as Grenadian. Similarly, St. Vincent contains a main island of St. Vincent and a chain of smaller islands known as the Grenadines. People from all these island call themselves Vincentians.

In relative terms, the populations of Vincentians and Grenadians in New York are minuscule. The 1980 census listed roughly 2,700 Vincentians and 5,000 Grenadians living in New York City (City Planning Commission 1985), although the undocumented among these populations probably pushed the combined total closer to 15,000. In many ways Vincentians and Grenadians identify themselves as part of the larger West Indian population in New York, which today is officially more than one quarter million (Basch 1992:148). Although Vincentians and Grenadians constitute only 0.05% of the combined West Indian population, these immigrants, both as prominent individuals and through collective activities, make their presence felt in New York City. Their members include the executive director of the Caribbean American Chamber of Commerce, the president of the New York branch of the Hotel and Hospital Workers Union, the publisher of a major Caribbean monthly, *Everybody's* magazine, and a columnist for the largest African-American weekly, the *Amsterdam News*. Members own and publish immigrant weeklies, produce radio shows, organize dance companies, and own a variety of entrepreneurial establishments in the immigrant community — catering halls, bakeries, shipping companies, and beauty salons, for example. They are calypsonians, steel band players, and cricketers of note; they participate on community and school boards, have spearheaded support groups for mayoral candidates, and have generally been active participants in the political milieu of New York City.

III. GLOBAL CAPITALISM, HISTORIES OF PARTIALNESS, AND MIGRATION

Transnational migration is but one aspect of the processes by which Vincentians and Grenadians have been incorporated into the ever-engulfing structures of global capitalism. The positioning of these societies in the global economic hierarchy has influenced most of their institutions — their economies, class and social structures, family life, their politics and education systems — as well as their cultural practices and hegemonic constructions. Basic to the history of these islands has been capitalism's demand for labor. First, African populations were imported as slaves to work on the islands' sugar plantations. Following emancipation, smaller numbers were brought from India as indentured laborers to do the same work. Then these island populations became sources of migrant labor for capital development elsewhere. Island institutions have been closely interwoven with migration, shaping its character but at the same time being shaped by the various migration trajectories.

The very creations of global capitalism, St. Vincent and Grenada have always been partial societies; they exist only in relation to somewhere else. From their beginnings, the colonial "structures implanted in these societies served the economic requirements of the metropolitan systems which controlled Caribbean territories ... their economies were designed neither for self-sufficiency nor independent growth" (W. Wiltshire 1984:1). All aspects of the histories of St. Vincent and Grenada — their sparse material bases, their rigid social and political structures, welfare and education systems, and their development policies — have underscored this dependence.

While the situation of St. Vincent and Grenada is to some extent that of all the societies of the West Indies, the small size and scale of St. Vincent and Grenada, combined with their meager resource bases and impoverishment, render them extreme examples of dependency. Emigration has been a historic necessity almost from the outset for all classes.

A. Material Resources and Constraints

The physical beauty of St. Vincent and Grenada belie the extreme fragility of their material conditions. St. Vincent, located just west of Barbados and north of Trinidad, is a mere 18 miles long and 11 miles wide and occupies 133 square miles. Although lush in tropical vegetation with fruit trees of almost every imaginable kind, a central mountain range that bisects the island leaves only one-third of the island's land mass available for agriculture. Moreover, St. Vincent's silvery-gray sand beaches, although adding mystery to the island, dissuade tourists (Rubenstein 1987; Colthurst 1977).

Roughly the same size as St. Vincent and located only 70 miles south of St. Vincent and 90 miles northeast of Trinidad, Grenada is similarly endowed with high rainfall, myriad types of lush, tropical vegetation, and fertile volcanic soil. It has a somewhat more arable land mass than St. Vincent, but it, too, has a rugged and mountainous interior that has severely limited the amount of land suitable for cultivation and pasture and the type of crops that can be successfully planted. Some of Grenada's main agricultural products are exotic spices — mace, nutmeg, cloves, and vanilla — which have led to the island's appellation of the "Spice Island." Its long stretches of fine, white sandy beaches have provided more of a potential for tourist development than have St. Vincent's. Both nation-states are highly

vulnerable to natural disasters such as hurricanes, and in the case of
St. Vincent, volcanic eruptions, which are capable of destroying entire annual crops and whole industries.[7]

These islands have not always been backwaters. Prized for their
rich soil at a time when sugar made fortunes in Europe, they were
contested terrains between France and England before 1763, when
British claims were recognized. Both islands easily attracted colonial
planters to develop their sugar industries, and slave importation
began on a large scale on each island to support the industry's
growth. This boom was short-lived in both locations, however. Both
islands were prohibited by parliamentary edict from developing any
indigenous commerce, trade, or manufacture which could compete
with established British home enterprises. These islands became, as
did the other West Indian islands, no more than "one-industry
branch-plants," dependent on the mother country for most of their
foodstuffs, financial capital, shipping, work force, and manufactured
items (E. Williams 1964 [1944]:51–57).

The economic histories of these islands are composed of the short-
lived ascent, followed by severe decline, of a variety of crops — on St.
Vincent, sugar, arrowroot, and cotton, and on Grenada, cocoa, coffee,
and nutmeg. Bananas, more recently, have been a major crop on both
islands. Infrastructure was developed only in relation to the production requirements of the major crops. Roads on St. Vincent and
Grenada, for example, were built to the sugar estates to facilitate the
movement of canes to local factories for boiling down to molasses
and to the docks for easy export from the island. To this day, few
roads exist to the small banana holdings of peasant cultivators on
these islands, and the entire upper half of St. Vincent — largely
inhospitable to agriculture because of its volcanic soil — remains
roadless, its population isolated. The economic problems on both
islands have been exacerbated by this lack of infrastructure, by inef-
ficient production techniques, and by an absence of profits for reinvestment because of their repatriation to metropolitan capitals.

The stagnation on both St. Vincent and Grenada translates into
unemployment and underemployment rates that are among the
highest and per capita incomes that are among the lowest in the
region; it brings other forms of human misery as well. In St. Vincent,
for example, malnutrition and intestinal disease among children
under the age of five accounted for 57% of all deaths prior to 1969
(University of the West Indies Development Mission 1969:4–5, cited
in Rubenstein 1987:23), and it appears that little has occurred since to
improve these conditions.

B. Colonialism, Economic Marginalization, and Emergent Migration Ideologies: 1838–1970

Although Grenada and St. Vincent were sighted by Columbus in 1498, European settlement did not begin until after the defeat of the original Carib inhabitants in Grenada in 1674 and in St. Vincent in 1719. By the early 1800s, the basic contours of plantation society were formed on both islands. Although slavery ended in 1838, the system of class relations and the exploitation this model spawned, together with its supporting ideologies, set the pattern of social relations and color hierarchies that pervaded the long colonial period and that continue to resonate in current class structures and ideologies. Relations within and between each class were rigidly prescribed, supported by the separate cultural practices, world views, and beliefs that each stratum held about itself and each other and that precluded informal mixing (Carmichael 1833; Rubenstein 1987; M. G. Smith 1965a).

Throughout the colonial period these islands were dominated by small upper classes. At the apex were white absentee owners of sugar estates, together with senior government officials, lawyers, merchants, doctors, and clergymen, often linked by kinship to the estate owners. In 1848, only twelve out of a total of 100 estate proprietors were resident on St. Vincent (Davy 1971 [1854] in Nanton 1983:223). The minimal social and cultural development allowed on each island by their scant land, population, and resource bases promoted an outward orientation among the members of the dominant class almost from the outset. Britain was the place children were sent for their educations and to search for mates; it was the source of aesthetic sensibility, knowledge, and style — it was the motherland. Whenever possible, the planters returned to England to live, to visit with relatives, or for cultural renewal, leaving their day-to-day business affairs in the hands of resident managers. Living lives built on familial and economic links that connected St. Vincent or Grenada with England, the members of this stratum practised an incipient transnationalism. The life ways of this stratum set the framework for the sense of partialness that was to pervade the cultures of these islands.

Both colonies had a small intermediate stratum of clerks, accountants, small proprietors, salaried shop attendants, dress makers, and tailors. The descendants of white colonialists and African slaves, members of this stratum were known as "colored" and were socially constructed as brown in skin color. They received a British colonial education and served as the managers of the society. While they became culturally assimilated to the upper classes, they were never socially or politically accepted into them.

Most of the population belonged to the dark skinned, unschooled lower class, who lived primarily by agricultural labor, although there were some rural artisans. After the end of slavery in St. Vincent, with arable land scant, the dominant strata attempted to gain control over agricultural labor by making land available for use only by workers who "donated" their labor to the estates. Over the course of the next century, a small peasantry developed as some laborers fled to the remote interior, where they cultivated steep and rapidly eroded fields, while others were able to acquire richer but minute bits of land. In Grenada, with more ample lands than St. Vincent for agricultural production, a peasantry was created when the decline of sugar led to the sale of small lots, formed from abandoned estates, to former slaves. Those estate owners who remained used various forms of tenancy and sharecropping to harness the labor of the former slaves.

While the nineteenth century played out slightly differently on Grenada and St. Vincent because of their different mixes of agricultural resources, they shared an economic profile. Their economies remained dominated by agriculture, which stagnated under a system of absentee landowners and small scale peasant production. Agricultural profits remained low, although there were fluctuations because of erratic climatic conditions and price competition on world markets. Absentee landlords emphasized short-term profits, which led to generally poor soil management practices on the estates. Moreover, profits were rarely reinvested in production. The constant extraction of surplus from the peasantry and agricultural laborers by the dominant strata served as an additional brake on growth.

After the end of slavery in 1838, migration became a means of resisting colonial domination for the lower and middle strata of the population. Agricultural laborers began to migrate first, beginning at the time of emancipation on St. Vincent, and shortly thereafter on Grenada. Ex-slaves responded to recruitment schemes offered by the late developing, more resource-endowed, and worker-impoverished British colonial territories of Trinidad and Guyana. Later in the century workers also took up the seasonal, short-term, and often back-breaking plantation and construction work available in Cuba, Costa Rica, and Panama. As time went on, skilled and trained artisans as well as smallholders and those in the lower middle stratum also became migrants. They became the more trained and statused policemen, panboilers in sugar factories, bookkeepers, petty civil servants, and school teachers.

From 1888 to 1911, at least 10,000 of the 40,000 inhabitants of St. Vincent were reported to have emigrated (Toney 1986:22) for more favorable wages in other areas, and between 1911 and 1921, migration to Panama, Cuba, and the United States was so heavy that Grenada experienced an actual reduction in population (Singham 1968:68). From the 1930s to the 1950s, the oil refineries in Aruba and Curaçao and the oilfields and refineries in Trinidad became destinations. This emigration, which was male centered because of the nature of the work, furthered the economic downslide of both islands by shrinking the available labor pools. The decline of the arrowroot industry on St. Vincent has been attributed in part to the absence of low cost labor (Toney 1986).

As the economic fortunes of St. Vincent and Grenada further plummeted and resources to provide assistance to the impoverished were in short supply in both locations, emigration — begun as resistance by the island populations to their oppression — became state policy. Emigration eventually came to be viewed by these colonial governments as a safety valve for the populations that their economic policies and practices could not support. Although initially determined to restrict the movement of workers away from the plantation, both countries, as their plantations further deteriorated, began actively to encourage emigration, while they refused to release workable land to the lower strata. When the Soufrière volcano erupted in St. Vincent in 1902, the colonial authorities organized emigration to Jamaica for the dispossessed rather than initiate an equitable land-distribution scheme (Nanton 1983).

Later colonial government policies even more explicitly favored emigration: colonial administrators both welcomed recruiters from foreign countries — for example, from the U.S.-owned oil refinery in Aruba — and approached other governments to recruit their workers. In 1951 the Colonial Administrator of St. Vincent publicly stated that "the employment of workers outside the colony greatly assists the social and economic well-being of the people" (cited in Toney 1986:23–26). The St. Vincent and Grenada governments also supported efforts to recruit their populations as contract farm labor to the United States.

The savings workers gained abroad and the monetary remittances sent back to kin were highly attractive to these capital-poor states. Some recruitment programs, such as U.S. farm schemes, even involved compulsory savings.[8] Migrants' savings provided subsistence in some cases, but also were transformed into house construction and land improvements. Short-term or circular migration, often with returns home for varying periods, and the remittance of savings to kin have constituted the special character of circum-Caribbean migration. This pattern was dictated by the specific terms of incorporation of the Caribbean region into the structure of global capital. Cast as an appendage meant to service the capital needs of the colonial centers, this area historically has been allocated to the margins of capital development. It is these terms of economic and political incorporation, and the kinds of social relations that evolved to support them, that planted the seeds in the early twentieth century for the multi-stranded transnationalism that has emerged to connect West Indian immigrants, their kin at home, and their home states today.

Changing economic conditions and global market factors, which underscored the vulnerability of many of these colonial development projects, shaped the length of migrations. The onset of World War I led to major layoffs of workers in the Panama Canal, while the worldwide slump in sugar prices in 1921 and the depression of the 1930s resulted in restrictive immigration policies and the expulsion of workers from Panama, Costa Rica, Cuba, and the Dominican Republic. Automation in the oil refineries of Aruba and Curaçao in the early 1950s also created massive layoffs, enforced early retirements, and repatriation (Proudfoot 1950:14–19; Rubenstein 1987:72). The absence of pensions, old-age security, or disability benefits further necessitated returns home, as did the hazardous working conditions in many of these locations, which resulted in disease and serious accidents. These shifting and uncertain economic conditions required workers to keep a place for themselves in their societies of origin through continuing their roles in their families, sending remittances to family members, building houses, and purchasing land.

Much ethnography of West Indian village life has a bifurcated quality. Although these studies seem to be describing the timeless, traditional cultural practices of isolated populations (see Blake 1961; Herskovits 1947; Rodman 1971; M.G. Smith 1965; Wilson 1973), most of these ethnographies also report the fact of emigration, and its pervasiveness in many cases. Yet, aside from discussions of the monetary remittances sent home, most of these ethnographies do not recognize the way migration links local village life to world capitalist conditions and cultural contexts. Migrants were forced by economic stagnation and limited opportunities to leave their villages in order to achieve economic stasis as well as advancement back home. In a

Vincentian village studied by Rubenstein in the late 1960s, 48.3% of the men and 35.6% of the women were living outside St. Vincent (Rubenstein 1987:197). These are also the villages the migrants returned to in many cases.

Migration has had a profound impact on many aspects of Vincentian and Grenadian institutional life. Family relations, economic undertakings, ideology and consciousness, while reflecting an interweave between African and European cultural traditions and productions, have all been shaped in the context of migration experiences and the infusion of ideas and practices from elsewhere. Those who were elsewhere have constituted another face of local institutional life for over a century.

While many of these migrations were intended to be short-term, the continuing economic stagnation on both Grenada and St. Vincent often forced migrants to keep moving to new situations. Their extremely sparse resource bases did not provide fertile fields in which migrants could convert their savings into productive activities.

These migration experiences established special migration traditions and ideologies — a "host of beliefs and values about migration" (Rubenstcin 1987:198; see also Philpott 1973; Richardson 1983; Thomas-Hope 1978) — on small West Indian islands. Rubenstein has described the ideologies that evolved on St. Vincent from these migration practices as follows:

> a widespread desire to leave the island, a 'definition' of migration as a temporary phase, an obligation *to have in mind* those left at home, manifested in the requirement to send remittances to and/or sponsor the migration of close relatives and good friends, and a continued involvement with the household from which migration took place (Rubenstein 1987:198).

It is these migration ideologies and traditions that help frame the practices and beliefs of the migrants who have been involved in more long-term migrations to New York.

IV. EARLY MIGRATION TO NEW YORK, 1900–60:
RESISTANCE TO RACIAL CONSTRUCTIONS

During the first two decades of the twentieth century, Vincentians and Grenadians were part of a larger West Indian migration coming to the United States. There they joined the large pool of labor streaming in from various quarters of Europe, the Caribbean, as well as the southern United States to meet the needs of the rapidly industrializing economy. Although no records were kept of the extent of Vincentian and Grenadian migration, the profile available for the West Indies gives us some sense of the timing and ebb and flow of the migration. From 1900 to 1924 some 5,000 to 8,000 West Indian immigrants entered each year. In the 1920s, when the influx from southern and eastern Europe was slowed by immigration restrictions, West Indian immigrants, who were counted as part of the underutilized British quota,[9] entered at an annual rate of over 12,000.

During the Depression and World War II the West Indian migration dropped precipitously. In fact, from 1932 to 1937, the number of West Indians returning home exceeded those entering (Reid 1939, cited in Kasinitz 1992:24). After World War II, immigration climbed slightly, to about 3,000 a year, until 1952, when the restrictive McCarran–Walter Act ended the use of European quotas by colonial subjects. Most of those entering in the 1950s joined families who had come earlier, under family reunification provisions, or entered for higher education and remained after completing their degrees. Until the 1960s, large scale post-World War II West Indian migration went to England. These migration statistics give us a picture of thirty years of relatively open migration that was cut rather dramatically by the next thirty years of economic hard times, war, and reaction. They help explain the continuation, despite a generation of permanent settlement in the United States, of a migration ideology that validated and justified the continuation of ties to home.

This first stage of eastern Caribbean migration to the United States differed from the circum-Caribbean migrations of the same period in the possibilities it offered for longer term jobs and the establishment of a family life. However, the extreme racism that these early immigrants encountered in the United States, one that penetrated all spaces of their lives, played a prominent role in shaping their opportunities and influencing their attitudes toward incorporation into the United States. Because they were products of a British colonial primary education, most of these immigrants were literate, a fact that should have given them a competitive edge in negotiating their new and unfamiliar situations. Yet most worked at menial jobs. Downward mobility was the norm. "Teachers became porters, and shipping clerks were former accountants at home" (Toney 1986:79); West Indians also were employed as janitors, waiters, elevator operators, and longshoremen. The women who began to come, often to join male family members, became maids, seamstresses, and factory workers.

All other aspects of the immigrants' beings — their educations, skill training, cultural bearing, which had provided them some measure of mobility in the West Indies — dimmed in face of the master status of race. Discrimination, poverty, and segregation dominated the experiences of most of the immigrants. A light-skinned Grenadian who came to the United States in 1945 to attend graduate school, but who had experienced the racial segregation of colonialism growing up in Grenada and working in Trinidad at the U.S. base during World War II, recalled to me his initial dismay and outrage at being relegated to a separate "negro only" rail car when he first arrived, being directed to separate drinking facilities, and being addressed as "boy."

Vincentian and Grenadian immigrants entered a context in which no more than 5% of the blacks in the United States in 1930 could be described as middle class, and they were primarily professionals working in segregated institutions or service providers to all-black clienteles (Patterson 1987 in Kasinitz 1992:33). Better educated than many African-Americans, those Vincentians and Grenadians who did come with professional training joined other West Indians in making up an important component of this tiny professional stratum. West Indians constituted 8% of the physicians, 4.5% of the lawyers, 14% of the businessmen, 4.5% of the clergy, 3% of the college faculty, and 4% of the writers and authors among blacks in the United States by 1930. In addition, they were one-fourth of the skilled artisans (Toney 1986:81). West Indians also became small entrepreneurs in the black community, opening tailor shops, restaurants, grocery stores, real estate companies, and bakeries. At one time there were so many small businesses owned by West Indian immigrants that African-Americans joked: "If a West Indian has ten cents above a beggar, he opens a business" ("Negroes of New York," *Writers Program*, Research Studies of the Works Project Administration in New York City, 1936–41, cited in Toney 1986:86).

During the first half of the century, Vincentians and Grenadians were crowded together with other West Indians into segregated residential areas with African-Americans, many of whom had recently migrated north from the U.S. South. Their experience of being black in the United States was shaped by their immersion in the massive settlement of African-Americans in northern cities such as New York. It was during the first three decades of the century that the black population of New York grew two and a half times faster than the total population (Kasinitz 1992:41).

Although many eventually bought homes, raised children, and joined political movements that challenged U.S. racial barriers, most of these immigrants resisted full incorporation into the socio-racial hierarchy of the United States, which positioned them at the bottom. They sent remittances to relatives and helped sponsor the migration of close relations. Many Vincentians and Grenadians retained close connections with kin and communities at home, even if they never returned for a visit, and large numbers, reflecting the migration ideology forged during circum-Caribbean migrations, continued to believe they would return "home" some day. Many of the immigrants among the sample we interviewed, who had come to New York during the earlier migrations, had in fact purchased the land and built the houses to facilitate this return.

The dynamics of continuing these linkages were essentially three-fold: they rested on earlier established migration practices and ideologies that shaped the terms of emigration from St. Vincent and Grenada, the rigid racial structuring of the United States, which allocated the immigrants to the most vulnerable sectors of the U.S. economy regardless of their class origins and skills, and the uneven economic opportunities and sporadic insecurities intrinsic to global capitalism.

Their resistance to incorporation within the United Sates was reflected in their preference for maintaining their colonial status rather than becoming U.S. citizens, even though the majority were literate enough to have passed the examination. Only 4% of the West Indian men and 18% of the women living in the United States in 1920 had become U.S. citizens, compared with 49% of the white male and 53% of the white female immigrants (Toney 1986:112).

V. DECOLONIZATION AND POLITICAL INDEPENDENCE, NEW ECONOMIC CRISES AND TRANSNATIONAL TIES

When St. Vincent, having achieved self-rule in the early 1960s, was well on its way toward political independence, its young Minister of Education and Health addressed a meeting of the St. Vincent Progressive Youth organization in 1972. His theme was the negative implications of the "constant exodus of young people from developing countries such as St. Vincent." Seeming to question the strategy of emigration, the Minister argued that

a country can only develop through the training and experience of its people, but once the youngsters in St. Vincent are trained and experienced, when they should really return to pass on benefits of their training and experience, they [leave] instead for the developed countries where they contribute to the increased imbalance between rich and poor, developed and developing countries (St. Vincent Newsletter 1970, cited in Toney 1986:184).

This young minister, expressing an emerging national Vincentian identity, was trying to counter what one researcher has termed the "obsession with emigration as a solution to the colony's economic problems, ... [an] attitude bred by colonialism of finding solutions to problems outside the society" (Singham 1968:71). He was also challenging what we have termed the construction of partialness — of externality — that had long pervaded Grenada and St. Vincent and filtered throughout the institutions of these societies.

In the course of the next two decades, as St. Vincent and Grenada moved from colonial status to decolonization to the granting of political independence, which St. Vincent achieved in 1979 and Grenada in 1974, the citizens of both these new nation-states developed a new national identity and cultural pride. The drives toward decolonization and independence on both islands led to the public reevaluation of symbols and ideologies and the construction of cultural representations associated with Africa, the peasantry, and Caribbean folk life.

Before their national independence the inhabitants of both countries had seemed eager to emigrate. During the beginning of the decolonization movement, Rubenstein (1987) found that emigration was considered a rite of passage among youths in the Vincentian village where he conducted his research. Of 108 school children Rubenstein interviewed, asking whether they wanted to leave St. Vincent, 107 answered positively. As their pride in and identification with their new nation-states grew, Vincentians and Grenadians seemed less enthusiastic about emigration. Some twelve years later, five years after political independence, our research in St. Vincent conducted among adults, many of whom were young, found that only 33% expressed an interest in emigration, and their reasons for the most part were for jobs and education. But the same survey contained a seemingly contradictory finding that requires explanation. Forty-two percent of the Vincentians and more than half of the Grenadians interviewed (54%) said that they believed people needed to leave home to progress.

The explanation for why considerable numbers of people still see the need to emigrate, and why independence has in fact been accompanied by a massive population exodus and the growth of transnationalism, can be found in developments that have unfolded in the years since independence. Despite the nation building ideologies and practices of Saint Vincent and Grenada, these states have remained subordinated within the context of global capitalism. The result of this intensified capital penetration, often assisted by post-colonial political leaderships, has been that in the years since independence these countries have experienced further dislocations of their economies, continuing economic stagnation, and the outflow of large numbers of migrants from all class strata primarily to New York and Trinidad.

For both St. Vincent and Grenada, the increasing capital investment in postcolonial countries that was part of the global restructuring of capital outlined in Chapter 1, affected export agriculture, the importation of food, and the development of small export manufacturing plants and tourism. The increasing foreign debt and the need to service this debt, plus the tendency of both countries to import more than they export, have led to unfavorable balances of payments for each (Ambursley 1983; Nanton 1983; Toney 1986), which the foreign exchange from migrants' remittances in part helps to offset.

In both states, ownership of the means of production has continued to reside with the planter class, which was transformed into what Hall terms a "bourgeois-aristocracy." Its members were central players in the shift from plantation agriculture to business, commercial activities, and trade (Hall 1977). They forged alliances with both foreign capital and local post-colonial political leaders, which enabled them for the most part to control the surplus produced by the other classes. These alliances have left both islands highly vulnerable to the penetration of foreign capital and to foreign control.

The banana industry on St. Vincent is the apt example. By 1976 this industry accounted for approximately 60% of St. Vincent's exports and 50% of its total economic activity. Produced by some 6,000 peasant farmers, more than half of whom have holdings of under ten acres, the survival of this industry depends on the distribution and pricing of a single trading firm (Nanton 1983:230). The vulnerability of the farmers is underscored by their dependence on this crop alone.

In Grenada as well, a few large trading firms, whose interests are in food importation and export agriculture, dominate the agricultural sector. Here too, the farmer's share of income from export agriculture has been declining.[10] In St. Vincent, the purchase of estates by the government to encourage the diversification of crops and to stabilize prices has not really accomplished either. In the absence of the government's ability to negotiate favorable trade agreements for export crops, because of the control exercised by foreign owned trading firms, both gluts and extreme shortages in sugar and arrowroot have become the norm (Nanton 1983; Toney 1988).

In both countries, the emergent bourgeois class and the "invisible" whites and mulattos who continue to dominate it provide strong financial backing to the major political parties. On St. Vincent, political power since independence has oscillated between two parties, both middle class in composition. The New Democratic Party (NDP), with its roots in the trade union movement, was originally led by E.T. Joshua, who gained his trade union experience working in the American-owned oil refinery in Aruba. The other party, the St. Vincent Labor Party (SVLP), with a largely black middle class leadership led by Milton Cato, a barrister, is one of the few parties in the West Indies without a trade union base. There are other splinter radical parties in St. Vincent, which have been influenced by the Black Power Movement in the United States and the Bishop government in Grenada, and which at various moments have been harassed, especially when the SVLP was in power in the 1970s and early 1980s.

Political change in Grenada has been more contentious. Political power in that decolonizing nation was first captured by Eric Gairy, who had been a worker in the American-owned oil refinery in Aruba and a trade union activist, and who was the island's first prime minister. He was overthrown in 1979 by the New Jewel Movement, a movement that gathered force in the diaspora and was led by Maurice Bishop, a barrister. Murdered in 1983 by a faction of his party, Bishop was succeeded by Herbert Blaize, who had been an accountant in the same American-owned oil refinery in Aruba where Gairy had gained his trade union experience.

Even though labor leaders have headed both countries, the policies of their regimes helped open the door to foreign capital. The governments and bourgeoisie in both St. Vincent and Grenada have advocated national development through foreign investment in manufacturing and tourism as a means to strengthen their economies. Both strategies, however, have led to further economic dislocations without creating adequate numbers of new jobs or high enough wage levels. The advantages offered by St. Vincent to foreign capital included tax holidays for the first ten to fifteen years, duty-free raw materials and machinery, access to land for building, entitlement to full repatriation of profits, and low labor rates (St. Vincent Development Corporation 1977). Yet even these concessions have not been enough for some firms, which have demanded a "training [wage] rate" at thirty percent less than the minimum wage (Nanton

1983:235). In the case of tourism, an industry in which some foreign companies have been able to buy rights to entire small Grenadine islands, the importation of technical staff, low wages, and the repatriation of profits have underscored the weak bargaining positions of both St. Vincent and Grenada and their inability to direct foreign investment.

Another factor dampening productive development has been the large civil services these countries inherited from the British, which have in part encouraged the concurrent tendency among the governments of both countries to continue to swell their state bureaucracies. Because the governments are the largest single employers on both St. Vincent and Grenada, expenditures on salaries have often been at the expense of investment in productive sectors. On both islands unemployment is believed to hover between 15 and 25%. These conditions have provided powerful inducements to emigration to populations for whom this strategy has become institutionalized.

The experience of the New Jewel Movement (NJM) in Grenada demonstrates the difficulty of breaking out of the economic conundrum created by this country's weak global position and extreme foreign penetration. Influenced by the ideology of the Black Power Movement, the Movement's planks were "genuine independence, self-reliance, anti-Gairyism, and anti-imperialism" (Ambursley 1983: 200). The Movement aimed to rid Grenada of the repressive tactics of Eric Gairy and the policies he advanced, which the Movement saw as reinforcing and deepening the penetration of foreign capital and a culture of dependency that fostered foreign investment. The Movement's policies, and in particular Bishop's stance against American domination, which led Grenada to accept aid from both the Soviet Union and Cuba, gained status for Grenada throughout the nonaligned movement. Yet, in the context of Grenada's sparse resource base, the NJM continued to rely on aid from the International Monetary Fund (IMF), the World Bank, and the Caribbean Development Bank (CDB). It allowed the bourgeoisie to retain many of its privileges and sought investments from private investors and tourism operators in the United States. At the same time, the Bishop government was developing strategies to empower the working and peasant classes, whose interests cut across those of the dominant strata.

The demise of the Movement in late 1983 and the related U.S. military intervention were in part consequences of the contradiction posed by ideologies of autonomy and the reapportionment of wealth and privilege in the face of extreme foreign penetration and dependency. Blaize, Bishop's successor, backed away from the latter's anti-imperialist ideology. The foreign penetration in manufacturing, tourism, and agriculture has continued in Grenada; the most recent indicator of deepening dependency is reflected in the 118 off-shore banks that are presently registered in Grenada (M. Roberts 1991:3).

The accession of local Vincentians and Grenadians to political power and the political volatility that has marked both islands' post-colonial experiences, have further contributed to emigration. Because of the scarcity of resources on both islands and the retention of wealth by the dominant strata, access to state power and the attainment of political power have been fiercely contested. The swollen state bureaucracies mean that access to many jobs is controlled through politics. The dominant role of politics in the economic life of the population and the shape this reality gives to local political processes have been described by one social scientist as follows. While this description pertains to St. Vincent, it is also apt for Grenada.

> The scarcity of jobs, the high unemployment, and the meagerness of the economy have made patronage, and its counterpart, victimiza tion, the very foundations of the economic and political life of the vast majority of Vincentians. In short, political support has become synonymous with patronage and affects the very means of subsistence and survival for most Vincentians (Hourihan in Rubenstein 1987:70).

Several immigrants in New York, who were either involved in trade unions or held civil service positions back home, reported leaving St. Vincent and Grenada when their political party lost power.

Labor unrest in the 1970s, linked to St. Vincent's economic crisis, generated large spurts of emigration. The dissatisfaction centered on government delays in agreeing to new contracts with public employees — from 1970 to 1978 there were no salary increases in real terms for public employees — and to the unwillingness of some employers to recognize trade unions (Nanton 1983). Teachers and nurses, as well as sugar workers at a government-owned sugar estate, all struck. Teachers in particular responded to the harsh suppression of their strike by migrating to New York, although a number of Vincentians in the other categories also left for the Unites States or Trinidad.

Emigration spawned by political turmoil and changes in the political fortunes of political leaders has meant that under these countries' conditions of sparse economic opportunities, considerable numbers of the political bases of each party reside abroad. This has contributed to the development of transnational political practices among the immigrants, especially in New York, and to their continuing involvement in the political affairs of St. Vincent or Grenada, as we shall see in the next chapter.

Institutions, such as education, reinforce this orientation and continue to prepare Vincentians and Grenadians for a life elsewhere. Technical schools produce more skilled artisans than can be absorbed by the Vincentian economy. The curriculum contains little about agriculture, other development needs of St. Vincent or Grenada, or about their economic histories. The presentation of all course materials is framed by hegemonic constructions that continue to validate European and metropolitan cultural domination. Moreover, considering that education has been the major route to mobility on both islands, there are still too few secondary schools on either island or state scholarships to the University of the West Indies. This means that many Vincentians and Grenadians emigrate for education. In our interviews with 130 Vincentians in New York, we found that education for themselves or their children was paramount among the reasons the migrants cited for their migration.

VI. IMMIGRANTS IN NEW YORK CITY, POST 1965: INCREASING SOCIAL AND POLITICAL INCORPORATION, EXPANDING TRANSNATIONALISM

The continuing deterioration of the political economies of St.Vincent and Grenada and other Caribbean micro-states led several Vincentians and Grenadians from the middle, lower-middle, and artisan classes to settle in the United States, especially in the New York metropolitan area, in the 1970s and 1980s. Although the U.S. economy was itself entering a period of rapid deindustrialization, most of the immigrants were able to find employment in the expanding service sector, for which their educations had to some extent prepared them.[11] However, the ability of this new wave of immigrants to obtain jobs, and to achieve a degree of incorporation in the United States not possible during earlier migrations, did not lead them to cut their ties to home. The limited opportunities the immigrants encountered in the United States, which they experienced as a ceiling on their mobility, coupled with the racism that continued to haunt their experience, although it no longer posed the absolute barrier it had earlier in the century, created conditions for transnationalism. This impulse was furthered by the immigrants' increasing identification with their politically independent home nation-states.

The immigrants' educations, training, and command of English directed many to positions in white-collar service industries, such as finance, insurance, real estate, educational services, communications, the media, business services, import-export, entertainment, health care, and social work. Although many were employed as domestics (see Colen 1986, 1990) and janitors when they first arrived, especially if they had entered the United States without legal documents, they ultimately found jobs as clerks, bookkeepers, bank tellers, data processors, health care workers, and as low level administrators.

Many immigrants also have become part of the "enclave employment sector" (see Sassen-Koob 1985:321), occupying jobs in professional and entrepreneurial activities generated and controlled by the West Indian immigrant population. Vincentians and Grenadians in New York own small shipping companies, beauty shops, record and music stores, restaurants, catering establishments, and bakeries that employ Vincentians, Grenadians, and other West Indians. They are entertainers and musical arrangers, directors, and producers of musical, dance, and theatrical productions, almost all expressing a West Indian cultural flavor. Some immigrants also write for and own newspapers and magazines that cater to immigrant West Indians, while others serve West Indians and some African Americans as physicians, dentists, accountants, and lawyers.

On the face of it, many West Indian immigrants succeed economically in New York. Of the 130 employed individuals in the Vincentian and Grenadian households we studied in 1984, less than 30% drew annual incomes smaller than $10,000; roughly 33% earned annual incomes between $11,000 and $20,000; 20% brought home between $21,000 and $30,000; and 15% earned between $30,000 and $50,000. This income, however, was usually linked to the participation of two or more household members in the labor force at a given time and from the pooling of family resources. Benefits also derived from immigrants living in immigrant enclaves, where the goods and services produced, such as child care, cooked foods, hair styling, tailoring, repair services, and professional services cost less than in the wider urban environment (Basch 1987a:166–168).

Vincentian and Grenadian immigrants also have been able to advance educationally in New York. Education, an aspiration shared by many of the immigrants, historically has been a major means for the immigrants to improve their social status and economic positions both at home and among other immigrants in New York. Of the immigrants we interviewed, 82% had some secondary schooling prior to emigrating. Yet, taking advantage of educational opportunities in New York, 60% percent went beyond a high school diploma and 27% gained a university or postgraduate degree in New York at night. Armed with this training, several of the immigrants were able to move into supervisory and managerial positions by their second jobs.

At first glance, what strikes the observer is the birth of yet another U.S. ethnic group, carving its niche in New York City. From the 1970s to the 1990s, West Indian immigrants responded to the new terms of their incorporation by transforming urban space, giving parts of New York City a Caribbean face. Writing in 1972, Bryce-Laporte, a Caribbean social scientist assessing the Caribbean experience in the United States, highlighted the "invisibility" of the Caribbean population and its merger, in the mindsets of most Americans, into the larger African American population (Bryce-Laporte 1972). Writing just twelve years later, in 1984, another West Indian observer noted a dramatically transformed urban space and Caribbean place within it:

> In Crown Heights and East Flatbush, American candy stores have given way to Jamaican restaurants, Puerto Rican bodegas and Trinidadian roti shops. In Cambria Heights and Laurelton, the manicured lawns and newly painted homes proclaim the presence of the Caribbean bourgeoisie. On Boston and Gunhill Roads, the record stores belt out the pulsating lyrics of the soca, and the lilting rhythms of reggae (Moore 1984:13, also cited in Basch 1987:160).

What is especially new about the inscription of West Indian cultural representations on New York space is its public dimension. While Vincentians, Grenadians, and other West Indians during the earlier period of settlement in New York looked to their Caribbean cultural roots, these assertions were confined to the more private social domain of kin and friendship networks and the benefit organizations and social clubs the immigrants built. Expressions of West Indian cultural identity today call public attention to distinctive West Indian cultural practices. Vincentians, Grenadians, and other West Indians play reggae, calypso, and steel band music throughout the City — in Central Park, Prospect Park, City concert halls and posh entertainment clubs, and offer up Trinidadian roti and Jamaican Jerk chicken in fashionable as well as local restaurants in all the City's boroughs.

These public expressions of West Indian collective identity are also the statements of a group making claims to political space in the ethnicized structure of New York politics. Within this milieu, as Kasinitz notes (1992), eating a Jamaican pattie on the Eastern Parkway assumes a symbolic significance it never had in Jamaica. The annual outpouring of tens of thousands of West Indians on Labor Day, claiming the Eastern Parkway in Brooklyn for their strut in full carnival regalia, is a further staking of political ground. Their ownership of this day has become so complete that now even New York City's mayor and national political leaders like Jesse Jackson take their place at the head of the parade.

At the same time that these immigrants seem to have become more incorporated into the work force and cultural life of the City and to have attained some material, educational, and economic success, a sizeable sector of Vincentian and Grenadian immigrants have become transmigrants. Their transnational practices cannot be attributed solely to affective ties, cultural practices, or to lingering political attachments. In concert with the immigrants' heightening ethnic identification, their continuing social and economic ties to their home countries are in large part a response to the West Indians' continuing experience of economic and racial marginalization in New York City.

Most of the immigrants we interviewed, for example, were employed in white collar service sector businesses in which whites were the supervisors and managers. Although several of the immigrants moved up the ranks relatively quickly to the tops of their occupational categories, their upward mobility soon came to a halt. Whites continued to dominate managerial positions and other jobs associated with power, which remained elusive for both West Indian immigrants and African-Americans. West Indians have found that even in situations where immigrants do move into senior slots, their positions rarely reflect the life-blood of the company. The immigrants we interviewed reported that key areas, such as production and finance, are closed to them, as they generally are to all blacks. The more usual scenario for successful Grenadian and Vincentian immigrants is to find themselves in community relations and similarly powerless positions. One Vincentian woman immigrant, who was a Vice President of Community Relations for a major bank and whose picture was frequently featured prominently in both the Caribbean and African American press, found that her salary, which was not much higher than that of a clerical worker, allowed her to live only in a basement apartment in Brooklyn. Individuals whose expectations are rising as a result of their education and success become quickly aware of the reality of the racial structure and embittered by their experiences (Basch and Toney 1988).

Within recent years, the Caribbean media have contributed to this understanding of the racial barriers that contribute to job insecurity and block upward mobility. For example, one newspaper reported that a study of 500 black managers undertaken by a black employment agency revealed that this sector was discouraged about the possibilities of further advancement (*Carib News* 1988). Other articles in the Caribbean press have emphasized the vulnerability of blacks in middle management positions, which they attribute to declining corporate responsibility and affirmative action coupled with corporate restructuring (*Black Enterprise*, August 1987; *Carib News*, April 5, 1988). Because West Indian immigrants are often at the lowest rungs of occupational hierarchies and are frequently low in seniority, they are often among the first to be laid off (see also Foner 1992).

It is in reaction to these experiences that despite their ever increasing participation in all aspects of life in the United States, a significant sector of Vincentian and Grenadian immigrants are actually transmigrants. Of those we interviewed in New York, fully 50% owned property both in New York City and St. Vincent or Grenada; 66% reported sending money home at least once annually, although the majority (56%) remitted funds more often; 54% sent goods again at least annually, although barrels of clothing and foodstuffs were usually shipped more often (Basch, Wiltshire, Wiltshire, and Toney 1990); and the majority had visited home within the past five years.

Several also had invested in economic projects at home — agricultural undertakings, transportation companies, shops, hotels, and some in state sponsored development programs, such as a spice factory and a milk company. They, like many Vincentians and Grenadians in New York, have also become increasingly involved in politics at home, as we saw in the opening vignette in this chapter. Transmigrants respond to the urgings of political leaders, many of whom they supported before their migration, to donate money, influence the political thinking of relatives and friends, and many even go home to campaign for their party.

On the level of the pragmatic, investments and economic bases stretched across a wide social field that includes the immigrants' home societies and the United States offer the immigrants greater security and more options. In many instances, the successful migrations of these poorly capitalized immigrants are dependent on transnational connections and the assistance they receive from various points in the transnational field.

Maintaining the social relationships that allow this transnational assistance requires the careful cultivation of relationships — through visits, telephone calls, gifts, cash remittances, and other forms of reciprocity. In the following sections we will explore how these increasingly transnational social fields have been built through family, economic, organizational, and political relations. While incipient transnational practices — remittances to kin at home and the ownership of property — are rooted in the Caribbean experience, the present transnationalism, as we have argued, is an effect of the global restructuring of economic and racial relations.

VII. THE WARP AND WEFT OF TRANSNATIONALISM: KINSHIP, CLASS, AND ECONOMY[12]

Mavis Carrington first came to New York in 1970 when she was 23 years old on a student visa, sponsored by her father's sister. Armed with the equivalent of a sixth grade education and some brief secretarial training, Mavis took on an assortment of jobs in New York — first doing clerical and then factory and domestic work — to support herself while attending school. She first completed the high school equivalency requirements and then received a secretarial certificate. In 1978, after eight years of living a relatively isolated existence in Brooklyn except for her relationship with her aunt and the connections she developed through the small Pentecostal church to which she belonged, Mavis realized that she was no closer to a green card than the day she had arrived in New York.

She decided to take a job as a live-in, full time domestic worker, a tested route for Caribbean immigrants with Mavis' skill level to obtaining the green card. Mavis' efforts paid off — three years later, in 1981, Mavis, approved for the green card, was on a jet bound for St. Vincent to collect her papers and legalize her status. This was her first visit to St. Vincent in eleven years, and the first time she had seen her mother and brothers in that time. Throughout her long separation, however, Mavis kept in close touch with her mother in St. Vincent through letters and phone calls. She also sent money regularly to help build the family home — by her return a concrete block house, respectably "middle class" in proportion and style, located on the perimeter of Kingstown, the capital.

Mavis came to New York because of the encouragement she received from a paternal aunt and because she knew that as a woman she could find employment as a domestic worker, if all else failed. The circumstances of her three brothers — all auto mechanics, an area of occupational overtraining in St. Vincent — who had similarly limited opportunities in St. Vincent, dictated a different strategy. They emigrated to Trinidad, where they also had relatives, because they knew that as tradesmen they would neither find jobs easily nor qualify for green cards in New York. But while they could enter and even locate jobs relatively easily in Trinidad as skilled workers, because they are not professionals they have never been able to obtain work permits. This means that similar to Mavis before she received her green card in New York, her brothers have become virtual economic prisoners in Trinidad, unable to leave for fear of not being able to reenter.

The situation in Trinidad is particularly thorny for Mavis' brother Elton, who is married to Sandra, with whom he has three children. The economic recession in Trinidad resulting from the rapid global decline in the price of oil — Trinidad's main product — left that country with sudden and unexpected high rates of unemployment. The Trinidad government's response was to discourage the very immigration of construction workers from impoverished neighboring islands that only a few years before, in the late 1970s, during the Middle East oil embargo and resulting economic boom in Trinidad, it had welcomed. To stem this immigration flow, the Trinidad government had begun to "round up" migrants without papers, even those who had been in the country for several years, putting them in prison and then deporting them. Unwilling to risk the precariousness of undocumented life in Trinidad, Sandra and the children remained behind in St. Vincent, where Sandra was employed as a beginning level secretary.

The family's resource sharing operated in other ways as well. Mavis' location in New York became a beach head for others in the family wanting to migrate to New York. Last year Sandra, because of the economic problems in both Trinidad and St. Vincent, decided to come to New York to find employment as a domestic worker. But because domestic work means "living in," which makes child-rearing in New York particularly difficult, Sandra left her children in St. Vincent with her mother and mother-in-law, Mrs. Carrington. Her game plan was first to get the green card and then bring her husband and children to New York, their long-term strategy to save money to return to St. Vincent. For the present, however, New York is the only site where Sandra can see her immediate family having adequate resources to reside together.

Mavis' plan at the moment is to help her mother obtain the green card under family reunification provisions. Although her mother does not want to reside in New York, this seems the safest strategy; since the economic recession in the United States, she has had difficulty obtaining a tourist visa to visit Mavis. In fact, she almost missed Mavis' wedding because the American Consulate (in the eastern Caribbean) refused at first to grant her a visitor's visa. Moreover, without a green card it is likely Mrs. Carrington will have problems coming to New York when Mavis has a child to assist with child care.

As this family capsule of the Carringtons suggests, historical forces, and the web of economic and political dependence and vulnerability they weave, conspire to make the family a continuing locus of Caribbean social geography. The family is the matrix from which a complexly layered transnational social life is constructed and elaborated. Almost ubiquitously at the social center of this transnational field, the family facilitates the survival of its members, serving as a buffer against the intrusiveness of individual state policies; it fosters the social reproduction of its members, their class formation and mobility; and as the repository of cultural practices and ideology shaped in the home society, it mediates identity formation in the new setting as it socializes its members into a transnational way of life.

A. West Indian Family Structures in the Context of Global Capitalism

The Carrington family, with its members stretched across three geographically distant sites, is an apt example of R.T. Smith's observation that the West Indian family has been the "major tissue ... sustaining human relations throughout a turbulent ... history" (1990:184). There are a number of historically shaped features of West Indian kinship — its plasticity and flexibility, its ideological basis — that enable the family to serve both as a primary social unit and as a key survival strategy for its members. Within the historic specificities of West Indian political economy — slavery, colonialism, chronic underdevelopment, and continuing economic and cultural penetration from the outside world — the household did not evolve as the dominant locus of economic production and the family was not necessarily residentially based. Rather, the survival of a family and its members often depended on family labor stretched across several sites, sometimes off-island. Families were linked through mating, children, and reciprocal support networks with the web of kinship extending far beyond the mating pair, consanguineal unit, or household (see Basch, Wiltshire, Wiltshire, and Toney 1990). As this family capsule of the Carringtons suggests, historical forces and the web of economic and political dependence and vulnerability they spin conspire to make the family a continuing locus of West Indian social geography.

The multi-pronged and elastic character of the West Indian family, shaped by centuries of geographic and temporal separation and border straddling, has meant that West Indian kin units lack precise contours. The West Indian family is very much an ideological unit, a symbolic construct (Schneider 1968; Yanagisako and Collier 1987), located within historical contexts of dependency, reciprocity and change. Capturing the plasticity and suppleness of West Indian kinship, Rubenstein has defined the family as a "bilateral, egocentric collection of all known or reputed consanguineal relatives of an individual regardless of genealogical distance" (Rubenstein 1987:223). The networks within the symbolic units constituted by these kin are reinforced through time and space by an intricate patchwork of transactions that can be tapped and built upon, depending on circumstances, regardless of spatial and temporal distances.

As part and parcel of transnational strategies, kin and institutions at both ends of the transnational field, in the West Indies and New York, become centrally involved in family histories at different points of the life and domestic cycle. Although he had been out of touch with Mavis for eleven years, Mavis's younger brother, who was living in Trinidad, was able, by virtue of his membership in the family, to telephone Mavis to ask her for funds to escape the deteriorating conditions of Trinidad and return to St. Vincent, where he would subsist for an indefinite period on the funds Mavis sends home. Indeed, the constant activation of such family links and networks through transnational projects strengthen the symbolic unity and identity of the family.

Mavis' experiences, in joining her aunt in New York and later being joined by her sister-in-law Sandra around the same time that she married, illustrate the multi-generational nature of households at certain moments in the migration cycle. While families often may splinter into core nuclear units within five years of the first member's migration to New York, more characteristic of the historic flexibility of West Indian kinship are households composed of layers of lateral kin, if only on a temporary basis. In fact, as part of the tendency of immigrants to utilize dense social networks to buffer themselves against the hostile environment of New York, adult Vincentian and Grenadian siblings often rent apartments for their families in the same building or jointly purchase multi-unit brownstones, where their families can live together.

B. Transnational Families, Global Economic Insecurities, and State Policies

As the vignette of the Carrington family illustrates, families, through their transnational linkages, provide a creative response to the contingencies of West Indian history and insertion into the edifice of global capitalism. At the same time, however, their shape is the product of the very transnational migration these families help foster. Family members, separated from the majority of their kin, endure vast stretches of loneliness and isolation socially, culturally, and emotionally. It is within contexts of social, economic, and political insecurity that those Vincentian and Grenadian families who are able weave their transnational strategies. In order to survive economically, the Carrington family needed to rely on three locations; no one site provided adequate resources to accommodate the family's basic economic needs.

The Trinidadian economy could provide employment opportunities and subsistence for only two family members and partial subsistence for the rest of the family in St. Vincent. The economic recession in Trinidad, with its consequent restrictive immigration policies, left family members reliant on their resources in St. Vincent — their house and plot of land for shelter and food, the small agricultural surplus yielded by their garden for vending in the local market — and the remittances of cash and goods that Mavis sent from New York. Sandra's recent migration as a domestic worker to New York attempted to take advantage of an available labor niche in New York for Caribbean women. In so doing, she will try to alleviate the precariousness of her family's economic base and the increasingly untenuous position of family members who had settled in Trinidad.

However, economic and racial conditions in New York presented similar insecurities and narrow opportunities for this family. Mavis's brothers were reluctant to trade their jobs in Trinidad, as tenuous as they were, for likely unemployment in New York. They were aware that the lagging economy that has accompanied deindustrialization and economic restructuring in the United States has meant a diminishing number of available well paying jobs — especially for black immigrants. On the other hand, immigration policies, enforced with varying stringency in the slack economic climate and at best ambivalent racial environment of New York, that have reduced the availability of visitors visas have pushed Mavis's mother toward obtaining a more permanent resident status.

The predicament of Sandra and Elton, which centers on the fact that neither person has been able to locate remunerative and secure employment in a single place that will tap both their skills, is reflective of the state economic strategy on the part of St. Vincent. The government has invested in training programs geared to external needs rather than in the development of local opportunities. The result is the overproduction of skilled workers in St. Vincent whose career opportunities elsewhere are vulnerable to the vicissitudes of global capitalism. Unlike past years, when graduates like Elton of local technical apprenticeship programs found their skills valuable in England, Canada, the United States, and Trinidad, the skilled workers overproduced in St. Vincent increasingly are encountering difficulty in being absorbed by other countries. The simultaneous recession in Trinidad and decline in manufacturing in the United States have made it difficult for Elton to locate consistent work paying enough to support his family.

However, by using transnational networks, Elton and other members of his family have been able to resist specific state policies aimed at controlling and exploiting their labor and also to challenge the terms of their subordinated insertion into structures of global capital. The Carrington's transnational family strategy of developing material bases in three locations, which has rendered them less dependent on any single national economy, in a small way is enabling them to challenge the terms of their subjugation. Through their transnational activities they have been able to accumulate property and savings, and to enhance the educational and skill levels of various family members. The price, however, has been steep: protracted separations through space and time among family members, a practice which will continue for several years. State policies which "educate for emigration" (Crane 1971) mean that for families such as the Carringtons, living together is often difficult to afford.

C. Mobilizing Resources and Support Systems

Family networks that span national borders, such as that of the Carringtons, aid in the migration projects of their members in a host of ways. Kin help migrants accumulate the capital to launch their migrations in the first instance and mind the migrants' children and property while they are away (R. Wiltshire 1992). At the migration destination, kin — and not necessarily immediate kin — provide immigrants with the much needed shelter, assistance in locating employment, and knowledge that makes negotiating their new settings possible, all the while softening the trauma of the migration experience.

Mavis Carrington's aunt, whom she had not seen since she was a baby, encouraged and assisted Mavis' migration to New York, giving her a place to live and aiding her quest for employment, and fifteen years later Mavis provided similar aid to her sister-in-law, Sandra. Mavis' older brother living in Trinidad was able to assist their younger brother. Mavis' mother "minded" Sandra's and Elton's children after Sandra emigrated to New York, as grandmothers have done for generations to assist their children who work and live away from home, frequently in situations not conducive to child rearing.

Multi-stranded involvements focused on education and family reproduction, health care, and economic and political activities span multiple locations and occur among all class strata. Obtaining educations for family members is often a transnational project. Young children may be sent home to the Caribbean to school, where the streets are safer, the racial situation less oppressive, and learning is more structured. Sending or leaving children at home for education and to be minded by close kin is an especially important interim strategy when immigrants first come to New York; their incomes are low and they cannot afford the fees necessary for either parochial schools or the growing number of private West Indian schools, or to move to suburban neighborhoods, where the schools are safer and academically stronger. This strategy is especially prevalent among women who lack proper papers and must work as live-in domestics (see Colen 1986, 1990) as well as among those who work long hours, such as nurses.

"Child-fostering" or "minding" has been a culturally sanctioned means of linking kin networks within the Caribbean, and is part of the critical interface between historically specific economic conditions and West Indian family structure. Within the Caribbean, children have often been placed in the households of family members — usually grandmothers or aunts — who could better care for them at given moments. This cultural practice has been important in facilitating the emigration of young women and men of child-bearing and -rearing age, usually the most employable members of the population. And for the elderly women, who are usually the child minders and who have few other sources of income, child-fostering has been a source of social capital, convertible into local definitions of female status as well as economic wealth.

Beyond the pragmatic, as Soto (1992) points out in her study of child fostering, by connecting transmigrants and their relatives remaining at home, children become building blocks in transnational networks. They maintain transnational cultural continuities that foster the perpetuation of transnational social fields. Thus, in addition to being both cement and rationale for transnational ties, child-fostering plays an important role in the multi-societal socialization of children.

Although primary education is prevalent, well organized, and a right of all, secondary education and training programs are severely restricted and higher education is nonexistent in St. Vincent or Grenada. Some migrants, therefore, come to New York specifically for education at a later stage. Indeed, migrants who have sent their children home when they were young often bring them to New York for secondary school and college, and kin living in St. Vincent and Grenada send their children to New York to live with migrant relatives in order to avail themselves of educational opportunities in the United States.

Health care also becomes a means of solidifying transnational family networks (Basch 1989). Migrants and their kin make regular visits home for rest and relaxation, especially after they have been in New York long enough to accumulate some capital, and retirees often spend winter months in the more congenial Caribbean climate, usually in their own homes. Family members from St. Vincent and Grenada will also come to New York to see medical specialists who do not exist on these islands. So institutionalized has the practice of looking to the United States for health care become that in some instances migrants will even include their parents living in the Caribbean in their health insurance policies.

Vacations also become important pegs in the transnational social field, contributing to its viability and continuity. Several organizations sponsor low fare flights to the Caribbean at Carnival and Christmas; indeed, some migrants go back and forth so often that when I was doing field work, it was at times difficult to recall where I had last seen them. Migrants' relatives living in St. Vincent and Grenada, and especially those with more economic resources, also vacation in New York, some fairly often, where they stay with relatives.

Reciprocal transactions — gifts of money and goods, the minding of migrants' children and the care of their property — are the symbolic and material enactments of transnational family relationships. In our study, 66% of the migrants interviewed sent money and goods to relatives annually and the majority remit something more than twice a year. These gifts are sent to relatives at all income levels and serve multiple material and symbolic purposes.

Such "gifts" are not a one way street, but rather are part of a complex web of reciprocal transactions that are at once a survival strategy for those in St. Vincent and Grenada, a symbolic statement about the depth of the transnational relationship, and a means for migrants to secure a base in the home society. Relatives at home take care of the migrants' houses and land so that migrants do not have to sell these assets and can in fact one day return to them. They enable migrants to retain a base in St. Vincent and Grenada. However, such transnational economic strategies may benefit family members differentially as migrants use the assets and education they obtain in the United States to improve their class positioning back home, as the following vignette reveals.

D. Class Reproduction and Contention

John, a 57 year old man, was born in a rural village in St. Vincent and is the only one of his six siblings who has not emigrated for long periods. Although he always thought of emigrating, except for temporary work cutting cane in Florida, he has lived his entire life in St. Vincent. He is married and is the father of two grown children.

John is employed as an agricultural worker and earns $200 every two weeks, an income only slightly above subsistence by St. Vincent standards. In addition, he spends much of his time cultivating several acres of estate land owned by his sister Joanne, who lives in New York, and from which he takes most of the produce. Because of the opportunity he has gained from his sister's migration — which he acknowledges "has helped a lot financially" — John, like many Vincentians and Grenadians who receive assistance from migrants abroad, does not need to emigrate. Additional monetary supplements to his income from other relatives abroad — in both England and New York — at holiday season make his economic situation even more secure, and during hard times John is able to sell some of the crops from his sister's land in the market.

Joanne emigrated to New York in 1970, after 13 years of living in England. In New York, she was able to build on nursing training she received in St. Vincent and honed in England to become a registered nurse. Joanne owns a three family house in Brooklyn in addition to the estate land and house she purchased in St. Vincent. Although Joanne has lived in New York since 1970, she claims she has never been comfortable there. She complains about the crime and racism she feels, and dwells on the fears she experienced raising her two children in New York. They are both now grown and live in the

United States, but outside of New York. Joanne and her husband plan
to return to St. Vincent some day to live in the estate house she owns.
Because this property once belonged to white plantation owners, in
her mind it is a major accomplishment that she was able to purchase
it. It also has elevated her class position in St. Vincent. But because
her retention of this property is contingent upon her brother John
caring for it, she is reluctant to sponsor his migration to New York,
and indeed tries, through gifts to him and his family, to encourage
him to remain in St. Vincent.

As this vignette illustrates, seemingly joint family strategies are often
part and parcel of processes of class reproduction and differentiation.
Indeed, joint strategies frequently have different implications in class
terms for the participants in family migration projects, although the
intrinsic class opposition contained in these "joint" strategies are
often submerged within the larger ideology of kinship. The different
class situations, interests, and perceptions of Joanna and John are apt
illustrations of such submerged class opposition.

In the West Indies historically, migration has provided a major
means for sustaining and advancing the class and status position of
individuals and families. Many migrants who went off to Panama or
the oilfields of the southern Caribbean remitted savings to St. Vincent
or Grenada to be invested in education, property, and housing. The
object of these migrations was the improvement of their material
circumstances and social "standing," which the migrants aspired to
translate into further local opportunities. Whole sections of
Kingstown and Georgetown, St. Vincent, and St. Georges, Grenada,
contain well-built concrete homes, testimonials to the wealth
migrants brought back from their toil in the oil refineries of Curaçao,
Aruba, and the oilfields of Trinidad. But more often than not this
wealth could not be transformed into other forms of wealth because
of the continuing underdevelopment of these islands and the absence of other resources to draw upon to multiply savings. While
individuals and families often did improve their material circumstances and status through migration, the abandoned, deteriorated, and unsold homes built with the savings of migrants during
the 1940s in Georgetown, St. Vincent, an agricultural area that
declined abysmally during the middle of this century, stand as a
public declaration of the ongoing stagnation of these small island
economies and the limited payoffs sometimes to be derived by
migrants from their individual efforts.

Transnationalism has provided migrants and their families with
new opportunities for material and social positioning, and members

of transnational families have been drawn into creating the basis for their class reproduction or mobility in the two different contexts of host and home societies. Crucial to these projects has been the differential access to economic, social, and cultural capital (Bourdieu 1977) provided by transnational kin networks. Present conditions in New York offer special opportunities to migrants. Because of limited education and training programs in St. Vincent and Grenada, many post-1965 migrants, who have come to New York armed with little more than the equivalent of a ninth grade education, have a two-fold purpose: to earn money and to gain educations.

For middle and working class Grenadians and Vincentians like Mavis and Joanna, New York is the place one can attend schools at night, earn a high school equivalency certificate and participate in training programs, and possibly even earn a college degree. Out of the 131 Vincentians and Grenadians we interviewed in New York, more than 60% had earned a high school degree plus some vocational certificate, and over 35% had gained a college degree as well. For most of these migrants, the payoff from their improved educational status is a better job with more earnings. Mavis, through obtaining a high school certificate and taking a secretarial course, moved from being a domestic worker to a secretary; and Joanne, through participating in a nursing training program, advanced from her position as a practical nurse to a registered nurse.

Mavis was able to make a statement about her education and greater earnings by building a substantial home in St. Vincent, which increased the family's symbolic and cultural capital. Building and maintaining this home was premised on her mother's assistance, and indeed her mother's standing in the community has improved because of this new modern structure with its metropolitan amenities. However, the existence of this house is dependent on Mavis's mother remaining in St. Vincent, not migrating to either New York or Trinidad to join her children or to work herself. Joanne presents a somewhat starker case. She was able to provide her children with educations in New York and a safe environment on a tree-shaded street of brownstones in Brooklyn through her earnings as a registered nurse. In fact, Joanne has gone to some lengths to induce her brother to remain in St. Vincent, a decision which has curtailed the opportunities for her brother's immediate family, especially his children.

Matters of class formation and mobility in a transnational social field, as we see, are not straightforward, but are convoluted and murky. Joanne, and to a lesser extent Mavis, have achieved some social and even class mobility in St. Vincent — with the complicity and sometimes at the expense of close relatives — which are transferable to the migrant community in New York. However, this gain is tempered by the realities of their everyday lives; they both live in a society — the United States — as members of a racial minority, for whom symbolic, social, and cultural capital are severely curtailed. Moreover, neither will be able to convert the wealth they have brought back to St. Vincent into great amounts of economic capital because of the limitations posed by St. Vincent's underdeveloped economy. Sugar from St. Vincent, after all, has limited currency in local, regional, or world markets, where stiff competition is presented by countries with more rationalized production and marketing arrangements. Houses, and often land as well, are not highly productive assets in either St. Vincent or Grenada. While away from home, transmigrants often develop notions of what they might do economically back home, only to find, if they do return, that economic conditions have deteriorated during their absences in ways they could not anticipate (see Rouse 1991 for similar experiences of Mexican transmigrants).

Yet the returns from migration, transmitted through transnational networks, do have a larger impact on class formation in both St. Vincent and Grenada. Migrant remittances and savings enable the production and reproduction of middle strata that would not be possible through internal forces alone, given the deteriorated conditions of these economies. Many families in St. Vincent and Grenada are sustained beyond subsistence levels by monetary transfers from abroad. Indeed, Wiltshire asserts (1992) that transnational families, through economic endeavors that transcend geographic and political borders, arrive at somewhat of an equilibrium in terms of the imperatives to migrate. Some 71% of the Vincentian relatives of migrants we interviewed in St. Vincent, and close to 51% of the Grenadians queried,[13] said they were satisfied with their own lives and did not wish to emigrate.

Of course, these infusions of wealth also diffuse to some extent the anger and consciousness that working and middle class members might develop and direct toward challenging the source of their islands' strongly entrenched and almost forced migration traditions — continuing metropolitan domination buttressed by the complicity of their own ruling elites.

VIII. THE FURTHER BUILDING OF TRANSNATIONAL SOCIAL FIELDS: COMMERCIAL TIES AND THE MEDIA

Over the years, a number of economic activities have emerged that build on and reinforce the transnational kin networks and add another strand to the complex tapestry of transnational social relationships being woven by immigrants and their relations at home. These activities take a number of forms, drawing variously on human resources and capital located at both ends of the migration stream, in the United States and St. Vincent or Grenada.

Some of these activities are small, commercial endeavors in which family members in New York provide capital, generated from their wages, that enables their relatives at home to import consumer goods, which they sell in St. Vincent and Grenada. These items range from clothing and other dry goods, records, tapes, and videos to raw materials to make dried floral arrangements or candied fruits for cakes, to larger items, such as electronic equipment, furniture, refrigerators, washing machines, dryers, building materials, and automotive parts. In some instances, immigrants in New York send these goods to relatives at home to sell, while in other situations immigrants serve as a base where relatives from home, who are engaged in commercial activities, can stay when they come to New York on buying trips. Some immigrants also make business contacts for kin at home who are involved in entrepreneurial activities.

The immigrant community also provides a receptive environment for the sale of goods produced in the West Indies. Restaurants, snack-ettes, bakeries, and catering establishments owned by Vincentians and Grenadians and other West Indians in New York import food items from home, news stands sell magazines and papers from the West Indies, beauty shops rely on products from home, local shops sell curative herbs grown in the West Indies, and liquor stores carry West Indian produced rum and beer.

Some economic activities have emerged in direct response to the realities posed by the transnational experience of lives spread across several geographic locations. The small shipping company created by Carl Hilaire is such an example. Capitalizing on the desire of migrants in New York to ship goods to relatives and friends at home for holidays and other special occasions as well as for subsistence, and also on the need of those migrating to bring goods to New York, Carl used the savings he accumulated as a relatively well-paid cleri-cal worker at the United Nations to create a small company that shipped barrels of goods between New York and St. Vincent.

Similar to the way Joanne is able to maintain her estate, an essential part of Carl's business is his brother, who lives in St. Vincent. Carl employs his brother to receive the barrels shipped home, to usher them through customs, and also to organize the shipment of migrants' goods to New York. Although Carl keeps his business open for limited hours only because of the demands of his primary job, the personalized service he and his brother are able to provide at both ends of the migration stream — including their willingness to accept payment in either New York or St. Vincent — make Carl's company attractive to many Vincentians in New York. Carl has enhanced the visibility and popularity of his company by being actively involved in several social service activities and voluntary organizations in the Vincentian immigrant community.

The potential growth of these transnational economic practices is not clear. The scarcity of capital available to Vincentians and Grenadians, an effect of their limited wages and savings, curtails the scale of such undertakings. Such enterprises seem confined primarily to networks of individuals, providing specific opportunities for those within these networks. Yet such economic activities also have a wider impact through the cultural symbols they transmit — whether they be botanical herbs or foods from the West Indies or clothing and household items from New York — which take on a common meaning throughout the transnational social field.

The growing entertainment industry, which also has taken on transnational dimensions, has become a major means of facilitating flows of cultural productions and ideas that unite the experiences of immigrants and those remaining in St. Vincent and Grenada. By enabling calypsonians and other musical entertainers to circulate between New York and St. Vincent or Grenada throughout the year, performing much of the same music in these locations, the entertainment industry incorporates large numbers of Vincentians and Grenadians in both New York and the West Indies into the transnational social field. Calypsonians sing at Carnival in Brooklyn as well as at Carnivals in St. Vincent or Grenada, circulating hit tunes between these locations. The growing record and tape industries, different phases of which are completed in both New York and the West Indies, further the circulation of commonly appreciated and understood cultural representations through the music they produce.

The immigrant press gives further shape to the transnational social field. *Everybody's* magazine, founded by a Grenadian, Herman Hall, has been published monthly since 1977 and has a circulation of some 75,000, with most of its subscribers located in central Brooklyn

(Kasinitz 1992:71). This magazine provides social and political coverage of events and activities in various parts of the West Indies as well as in New York and the United States that are of interest to the immigrants. During the war in the Persian Gulf, for example, *Everybody's* carried a special on Colin Powell, emphasizing his Caribbean roots, and also developed features on other West Indians who had served in U.S. military conflicts over the past half century.

The weekly tabloid, the *New York Carib News*, with a circulation similar to *Everybody's*, is published by a Jamaican, Karl Rodney. This tabloid also taps the immigrants' nationalist as well as ethnic identities. Its sweep is large, keeping immigrants involved in nation building efforts in both the West Indies and the United States. Equal attention is given to upcoming elections in West Indian countries and in the United States, in New York, and in Brooklyn. Recent issues have reported on an interview with St. Vincent's prime minister on the economic situation in his country and other regional issues, on anti-drug campaigns in Jamaica and Trinidad and Tobago, on internal conflict among political factions in Grenada, on a proposal for a political union between Barbados, Trinidad and Tobago, and Guyana, and on statements by West Indian political leaders in New York urging West Indian regional integration. The same tabloids have discussed "the Caribbean student in transition" from schools in the West Indies to schools in Brooklyn, jobs for youths in Crown Heights, the problems of investing in the uncertain U.S. economy (June 9, 1992) and have probed whether "multiculturalism work[s]" on New York college campuses (May 26, 1992).

Ideology as well as approach are debated in the columns of the *Carib News*, role models are created, and identity is shaped. Immigration policies are addressed, successful students are heralded, as are those who have achieved in the workplace, local businesses are advertised, and West Indian entertainment is reported. This tabloid has been especially vigilant in reporting common experiences confronted by almost all West Indians: the increasing racism in New York — for example, the rioting that followed the death of a seven year old Guyanese boy under the wheels of a car driven by a Hasidic Jew in Crown Heights last year, the alleged rape of a young West Indian woman at the Stony Brook campus of the State University of New York, the beating and then chase of Trinidad-born Michael Griffith across a highway in Howard Beach that led to his death, and the maligning of "Caribbean Americans" in police academy training documents.

IX. CONCLUSIONS

This chapter has traced the development and intensification of transnational practices among Vincentian and Grenadian immigrants in New York, dating back to their circum-Caribbean migrations at the turn of the twentieth century. Similar to the earlier period, these practices are both a response and a resistance to the migration that is "forced" on the transmigrants by their nation-states' marginalization in the global political economy. Migration ideologies that emphasize maintaining kin relations that straddle national borders have salience for immigrants in New York, given the present context in which immigrants continue to be economically and racially vulnerable in the United States, much as they were previously.

Until decolonization and political independence in St. Vincent and Grenada, transnational practices were confined to the private sphere of family relations, where they were protected from intrusive colonial state policies. Messages carried along transnational family networks, shaped by the *habitus* formed in the Caribbean, have reinforced the transnational practices of present immigrants and also have enabled Grenadian and Vincentian identity constructions to retain their vitality among the immigrants abroad. Transnational family networks also have been important means for the formation and reproduction of class relations and mobility on both islands.

While transnational family relations allow the immigrants to resist their subjugation in host and home societies, these relations also contain the seeds of the immigrants' complicity in their present situations and perpetuate the need for ongoing emigration. Because they allow the migrants to move between host and home societies emotionally, culturally, and materially when conditions in either become intolerable, transnational family networks diminish the likelihood that immigrants will collectively challenge either system.

In addition to the transnational social fields built by kin relations, economic activities, including the entertainment industry as well as the media, that have moved into the crevices of the transnational experience give further shape to and reinforce the transnational social field forged by immigrants. Through the symbols and representations these activities create and transmit, they enlarge the web of individuals encompassed in this field.

Decolonization and political independence in St. Vincent and Grenada set the stage for a more encompassing and public transnationalism, this time carried through immigrant organizations. The continuing global marginalization of post-colonial states such as St. Vincent and Grenada has given birth to a new hegemonic construction, that of the deterritorialized nation-state. It is through this construction, as we shall see in the next chapter, that both states attempt to capture and reinforce the transnational practices of their dispersed populations and through which transmigrants resist the terms of their incorporation into U.S. society.

NOTES

1. Portions of this chapter appeared in Basch (1992). Chapters Three and Four are based on research conducted by Linda Basch. In these two chapters, any first person narrative refers to Linda Basch.

2. Blaize and Stanislaus had attended high school together in St. Georges, the capital of Grenada, and had worked together in the 1960s to raise funds to erect a high school on Carriacou, the other small island in the Grenada triad.

3. This research was funded by grants from the United Nations Fund for Population Activities and the International Development Research Centre.

4. These chapters are also informed by Basch's earlier field research in Trinidad in 1971 and from 1972 to 1974. She studied race, class, and ethnic relations among workers in an American owned oil refinery and their families and the identity constructions spawned by their experiences (Basch 1978). There she found immigrants from Grenada, St. Vincent, and Barbados. In exploring the workers' identity constructions, the varying connections the immigrants maintained with their home countries became apparent.

5. Understandings of the ongoing transnationalism practiced by Vincentians and Grenadians living in New York were enlarged by the research assistance of Margaret Souza, Isa Soto (see Soto 1992) and Colin Robinson, the latter two of whom live transnational lives themselves.

6. The small sizes and the similar social histories and material conditions of these "small islanders," as they are known within the region, have led to common understandings that cause Vincentians and Grenadians, as many other West Indians, to identify themselves as West Indians in many instances.

7. When St. Vincent's volcano Soufrière erupted violently in 1979, it covered half the island with volcanic ash, destroyed most of the banana crop, the island's major crop, and a great deal of property and livestock, forcing 20,000 people — a full one-fifth of the population — to live in refugee camps while they slowly rebuilt their homes and

lives. The worst tropical storm of this century, which occurred in the same year, destroyed a multi-million dollar land reclamation scheme underway in St. Vincent's capital of Kingstown, along with hundreds of homes and commercial establishments, for a total loss of over $50 million. This is no small amount for an economy with an annual GDP of $59.8 million in 1975 (Nanton 1983:236).

8. Vincentian workers on U.S. farm schemes sent home compulsory savings valued at $69,226 in 1951 (cited in Toney 1986:30).

9. West Indians were a presence in the United States during this period. According to Kasinitz, the majority of the almost 200,000 foreign-born Blacks in the US in 1930 were from the West Indies (Kasinitz 1992:24).

10. Although stable marketing organizations exist on both islands for export agriculture, they are again dominated by the planter class, with little participation on the part of peasant producers (Ambursley 1983). Moreover, little funding is provided for agricultural research, insurance, or smallholder development.

11. Of the Vincentian and Grenadian immigrants we interviewed in both New York and Trinidad, we found that the intellectuals and professionals articulated a preference for remaining in the West Indies — for the most part in Trinidad or Barbados — filling positions vacated by nationals from those islands who emigrated to New York, Canada, or England. Racism in the U.S. and a more congenial lifestyle in the West Indies were cited as their primary reasons for this strategy. It is also likely that there were few professional positions available for them in the U.S. economy. Skilled and unskilled workers, who did not have the funds to travel to the U.S., also tended to emigrate to Trinidad, often for short-term construction work.

12. The relationship between transnationalism and kinship was first set forth in Basch, Wiltshire, Wiltshire, and Toney (1990).

13. The lower figure for Grenadians who expressed satisfaction with their lives may reflect the more insecure political situation in that country at the time of our interviews. They were conducted at the time the PRG of Maurice Bishop was unraveling.

Chapter
FOUR

Hegemony, Transnational Practices, and the Multiple Identities of Vincentian and Grenadian Transmigrants

I. INTRODUCTION

The St. Vincent Education and Cultural Club

The St. Vincent Education and Cultural Club, begun in 1977, had 26 active members, whose average ages ranged from their mid-twenties to their early forties, and an annual budget of close to $10,000. Most of the Club's members had their origins in the middle classes of St. Vincent and had come to New York after 1965. The goals of the Club, to enhance the educational and cultural life of Vincentians in both St. Vincent and New York, were explicitly transnational. Like many of the Vincentian and Grenadian voluntary organizations begun around the same time, the Club, through its practices in both New York and St. Vincent, was knitting together a membership in New York that was self-consciously Vincentian and that could act in both St. Vincent and New York.

The focus of this Club's activities — large cultural fairs, panel discussions, and a newsletter widely disseminated in both New York and St. Vincent (to a mailing list of over 1,000 Vincentians) — enabled the Club to influence far more than its membership. Its cultural fairs, for example, which were held annually in Brooklyn and which featured the crafts, music, and visual and dramatic arts of St. Vincent and the Grenadines, usually attracted over 1,000 people. Attesting to the Club's transnationalism, several artists traveled annually from St. Vincent to join Vincentians living in New York in exhibiting at these fairs.

Part of the concern of the Club was also the incorporation of Vincentian immigrants into the social and economic structures of New York City. To further this goal, the Club organized annual seminars that addressed such matters as education, real estate investing, black economic upliftment in New York, and the merits of U.S. citizenship. The Club's Newsletter wrote about similar issues, at the same time providing information on economic opportunities in New York.

In fashioning Vincentian identity in New York, the Club constantly brought the home society and its representations into the consciousness of Vincentian immigrants. In addition to the cultural fairs it organized, the Club joined with other organizations in sponsoring performances of calypsonians, recording stars, and dramatists from St. Vincent. Through its Newsletter the Club also kept immigrants engaged in the discourse of home. Articles highlighted upcoming Carnival celebrations in St. Vincent, giving full information on bands, costumes, and the details of who composed the music and designed the costumes. The Newsletters also featured aspects of daily life in St. Vincent and analyzed ideas and events at the forefront of political life — for example, the upcoming elections in St. Vincent and the implications for the Caribbean of the "invasion" of Grenada by U.S. troops. The images and symbols invoked through these activities played an important role in helping the immigrants to understand that they were Vincentians or Grenadians, although they were in New York.

Since the earliest settlement of Vincentians and Grenadians in New York, voluntary organizations have played an important part in the incorporation of these immigrants into the United States. Because these organizations have been able to mobilize large segments of the immigrant population across class sectors at various moments, they have also given a public face to immigrant identity. This has been a changing face over the years, with the immigrants at various moments calling attention to themselves as negroes or blacks, as Vincentians or Grenadians, as West Indians, and even as subjects of the British Empire.

While Vincentian and Grenadian immigrants have engaged in some transnational practices since the earliest years of their migration to the United States — largely through their family and personal networks — it is only since the middle 1970s that organizations such as the St. Vincent Education and Cultural Club, with explicit transnational agendas, have arisen to give public voice to these transnational practices. These organizations have made concerted efforts to encourage Vincentians in New York to straddle political and cultural borders. Beyond its cultural fairs, newsletters, and seminars, the St. Vincent Education and Cultural Club, for example, sponsors inexpensive excursion flights to St. Vincent every Christmas and Carnival for close to 300 people, which enable the immigrants to stay in close touch with people, issues, and the thinking of those at home. It also raises funds for a number of educational projects at home, arranging scholarships for young Vincentians in both St. Vincent and New York.

To understand why the transnational practices of Vincentian and Grenadian immigrants are intensifying and becoming more collective and public at this moment, we must look to the changing hegemonic contexts in both the immigrants' home societies and the United States in which these practices are being forged. As we shall see in this chapter, there are a number of interpenetrating factors in St. Vincent and Grenada — the shifts from colonialism to decolonization and political independence, the islands' continuing economic stagnation, and the institutionalized migration traditions — that account for hegemonic constructions in which political leaders have begun to define their dispersed populations as active members of a deterritorialized body politic.

At the same time, in the United States the enormous influx of immigrants of color from the former colonial world to fill jobs in the growing service sector and service industries, intertwined with the Civil Rights and Black Power movements, have produced hegemonic processes that continue, albeit in new ways, to differentiate and hierarchize the country's racially diverse populations. These economic and political forces frame the "interconnected social space" (Gupta and Ferguson 1992:15) in which the transnational practices and identity constructions of Vincentian and Grenadian immigrants emerge.

This chapter will explore the intensification of these immigrants' transnational practices and their changing formulations of identity through an ethnography of Vincentian and Grenadian immigrant organizations. Because, as we shall see, organizations have been important contexts in which the collective identities of Vincentians and Grenadians have been defined, mediated, and contested, they provide a lens for exploring the formulation of immigrant identities in response to different hegemonic processes. At the same time, an ethnography of organizations will allow us to examine the ways that constructions of race, ethnicity, and nation have influenced and been incorporated into the cultural practices of the transmigrants as the latter both resist and accommodate to these hegemonic situations.

While voluntary organizations have played a central role in the adaptation of West Indian immigrant populations to New York, they are not natural to all immigrant situations. For example, no organizations based on nationalist or ethnic affinities have emerged among the class-differentiated Vincentian and Grenadian immigrants in Trinidad, where the terms of incorporation of immigrant populations of African origin have been different (Basch 1987b). Of the same racial background as half the island's population, Vincentian and Grenadian immigrants in Trinidad have been encouraged by African Trinidadians to join militant trade unions, churches, and political organizations. An association established by primarily middle class Vincentian immigrants to raise funds for disaster relief in 1979, after the Soufrière volcano erupted in St. Vincent, dissolved almost immediately after the task was completed.

In New York, in contrast, immigrant organizations have become important loci in the invention of Vincentian and Grenadian communities. They have taken many forms through the years — benefit societies, sports clubs, social and cultural clubs, vocational and professional associations, alumni/ae and "old boys/girls" organizations linked to secondary schools back home, political clubs, performance groups, a woman's group, and churches — addressing immigrant incorporation in New York and, in recent years, connecting the immigrants to projects back home. Memberships in Vincentian and Grenadian voluntary organizations have never been large, varying anywhere from 20 to 500 members. Yet, because of the large numbers of individuals that they have been able to mobilize through their numerous social, cultural, and political activities, such organizations have constituted important sites at which collective identity has been shaped.

It is through these organizations that immigrant leaders have tried to forge political consciousness and action to respond to U.S. racial and ethnic constructions of immigrant incorporation — some of their thrusts reaching into the halls of the U.S. Congress and Manhattan's City Hall — and also to wield political influence at home. And as we shall see, immigrant organizations have been sites of hegemonic contention in which dominant forces in St. Vincent and Grenada and in the United States have made competing claims to immigrant identity and allegiance.

II. HEGEMONIC AGENDAS, VINCENTIAN AND GRENADIAN ORGANIZATIONS, AND TRANSNATIONAL PRACTICES

A. The Forging of Ethnic and Racial Identities: The Early Years in New York, 1900–65

In trying to understand the identity constructions and consciousness of Vincentian and Grenadian immigrants in the 1980s and 1990s, and the intensification of their transnational practices, it is useful to review the identities forged by migrants who came to New York during the first half of the century. Their emerging identities, and the ways they were shaped and contested in response to U.S. hegemonic processes, became the prism through which the later immigrants interpreted and then responded to the incorporative structures they encountered.

West Indians entered a hegemonic context that organized social space into a two-tier racial hierarchy, in which assimilation into U.S. cultural practices and ideology, the hegemonic agenda for absorbing the vast foreign-born population, meant incorporation into the separate, often segregated institutions and generally inferior conditions allocated to African-Americans. Race determined where the immigrants could live, the kinds of jobs they could apply for, where they and their children could attend school and seek health care, and how they would be treated by the media, civic institutions, and people of all colors.

In this hegemonic context, race was the engine that powered, gave shape to, and bounded the early organizing efforts of Vincentians and Grenadians. However, Vincentians and Grenadians responded to the barriers of race with several different types of organizing activities. Some of these activities reflected internal differentiation and hierarchies confined to a racially delimited social space.

Among the longest lasting responses were the island specific mutual benefit societies organized for the protection and support of their members. Somewhat class differentiated, the majority of the members came from the lower middle stratum and working classes at home. While built on pride in the immigrants' cultural roots, the main work of organizations such as the St. Vincent Benevolent Society and the Grenada Benevolent Fraternal Organization was providing protected space for the immigrants settled in the United States. The benefit societies provided financial assistance, housing and employment information, and moral support at a time when no state-supported social benefits or health insurance existed and few family members were in New York to provide assistance during hard times. In addition, the immigrants looked to these societies for security, support, and the status affirmation of those from their home islands. Keeping the vision of home in the minds of the immigrants, benefit societies forged a sense of "community" as they fostered immigrant adaptation.

Those who became the professionals, businessmen, and shop-keepers in the enclaves the immigrants inhabited with African-Americans also joined Vincentian and Grenadian organizations along with their clients and customers, as a means of reinforcing these relationships. However, professionals and those more firmly planted in the middle strata at home, reflecting a broader West Indian identity forged in previous decades of unrest throughout the Caribbean, built organizations that attracted members of similar strata from all the West Indian islands. Associations such as the West Indian Committee of America (Toney 1986) both fostered profes-sional and business networks and also confirmed the immigrants' status positions within social fields that had meaning in the racially segregated urban environment. It is these associations that provided the base in the 1930s upon which immigrants, again primarily from the middle classes, built nationalist or regional West Indian political organizations that both advocated and addressed the shape of inde-pendence in the West Indies.[1] Some of the immigrants even returned home to lead these movements.

Yet "home" was more often a point of reference than a location of organizational activity. During most of this period, Vincentian and Grenadian organizations developed few transnational practices. However, as we have seen, immigrants did maintain ties to home through family networks; they called upon these transnational prac-tices, embedded in the migration traditions of Vincentians and Grenadians from the previous century, when responding to the economic vulnerability and racial humiliations they suffered in the United States. Many immigrants remitted funds and invested in houses and land in St. Vincent or Grenada.

To resist the race-constituting incorporative agendas that defined them as subordinate and limited their mobility, Grenadians and Vincentians joined with African-Americans at the same time that they were building organizations that emphasized their island based and West Indian distinctiveness. In the 1920s, in their earliest collective strategy, West Indians of all class sectors joined with African-Americans to form Marcus Garvey's United Negro Improvement Association (UNIA). This mass movement looked to African representations as the unifying symbols of an ideology that opposed the U.S. social and political structuring and the place of blacks within it.[2] Opposition to racial as well as class oppression also brought West Indians into the U.S. Communist Party where they attempted to fuse the ideologies of black nationalism with working class solidarity.

It was the Democratic Party in the early 1930s, however, reflecting the U.S. hegemonic agenda of differential incorporation, that brought West Indians into the formal U.S. political process. West Indians were for the most part unencumbered by the historical experience of African-Americans that created strong antipathies toward the Democratic party. The party was therefore able to find many West Indian political activists who, disillusioned by the failures of the Garvey movement, of the Harlem Renaissance, and by their experiences with the Communist Party, yet eager to gain political and economic empowerment, were willing to accept this overture. All along, however, they were made aware that they were being brought into the Democratic Party not as ethnics with distinctive cultural roots, but as representatives of an undifferentiated black racial bloc.

West Indians who aspired to political leadership had several reasons to be interested in participating in the Democratic Party. For many educated West Indians, influenced by the U.S. ideology of democratic participation that was denied them at home as British colonial subjects, U.S. politics offered an important arena of political action. Moreover, the stark reductions in West Indian immigration after the early 1930s, owing to the Depression and World War II, shrank the size of the West Indian population and political base. Nonetheless, West Indian immigrants who rose to important leadership positions in the Democratic Party incorporated many West Indians into the political process.

Some of the noted black political figures of the 1950s and 1960s —
Justice Constance Baker Mottley, Democratic county leader J.
Raymond Jones, Manhattan borough president Hulan Jack, State
Senator Basil Patterson, New York State Assemblyman (from Brooklyn) Bertram Baker, and Brooklyn Congresswoman Shirley Chisholm
— were born either in the West Indies or in the United States of West
Indian parents. The terms of their office under a hegemonic construction that denied cultural distinctiveness to people of color meant,
however, that they participated on the U.S. political scene as blacks,
not as West Indians, with a political agenda aimed at addressing the
situations of all blacks.

By the end of this period, most Vincentian and Grenadian immigrants had come to see themselves politically, and in some senses
socially and culturally, as part of a larger black population. This was
a response both to their concrete experiences in New York, within a
context built around racial differentiation, and to the politically incorporative strategies of West Indian and U.S. political leaders. At the
same time, immigrants continued to look to their cultural roots as
Vincentians or Grenadians and West Indians to counter the low
status accorded to black people in the United States. Despite the
growing number of ethnic organizations and the immigrants' continuing transnational ties to family members and close social networks at home, the transnational practices of most immigrant
organizations up to the late 1950s remained for the most part symbolic, sporadic, and class differentiated. But the stage was set for the
eruption of more self-conscious transnational organizational practices.

B.   *Vincentian and Grenadian Nation Building and the Growth of Transnational Organizational Practices: 1965–80*

Beginning in the early and mid 1960s, organizations with explicit
transnational practices began to emerge among Vincentian and
Grenadian immigrants in New York, as did identity formulations
that in various ways began to acknowledge these practices. At the
same time, immigrants were finding new economic and political
spaces open to them in New York. They were taking part in trade
union activities, studying at universities and trade schools, and becoming homeowners.

A sector of transmigrants who began to achieve some occupational
mobility and security in the New York economy became directly
involved in projects at home that extended beyond the terrain of

family relationships to philanthropic causes. They began to participate in projects — for example, hospitals, schools, sports teams, and orphanages — in the communities they had come from. These projects were not initiated by individuals acting on their own, but rather were collective, undertaken through organizations that developed around these specific activities.

Many immigrants were already transmigrants who had created a place for themselves in the social landscape of their home island through remittances and investments in land and houses. In the 1960s, with decolonization, St. Vincent and Grenada served no longer only as bulwarks of transmigrants' self-esteem, places of refuge during hard times, locations for retirement, or imagined homelands looked to as sources of distinctive cultural roots. With plans for political independence and membership in the United Nations, St. Vincent and Grenada became sources of pride and avenues of political protection and support. Home now became a place where immigrants could be actively engaged. Even small amounts of money taken from immigrants' increased earnings in New York could leave a mark on the home countries' resource-scarce economies and bestow upon the transmigrant the status of benefactor. Moreover, the transmigrants' involvements at home through New York based organizations earned them respect and status, not only within the communities they had come from at home, but also among Vincentian or Grenadian networks in New York.

By the 1970s, the character of transnational projects had changed yet again, as had the foci of many immigrant associations in New York. While the involvement with philanthropic causes continued, new organizations emerged that were concerned with broader social and political projects at home — for example, the development of a Carnival hall in Kingstown, the capital of St. Vincent, and the election of government leaders in both St. Vincent and Grenada. What was most striking, however, was that at the very moment these organizations were addressing the reincorporation of the immigrants into their home nation-states, many — for example, the St. Vincent Education and Cultural Club — were involved with the incorporation of immigrants into the United States. Issues of housing, day care, health, education, and politics in New York, and of U.S. citizenship were increasingly on their agendas.

The explicit transnationalism evolving in these organizations was perceived as natural by both leaders and members, who increasingly seemed to see their simultaneous involvements in both their West Indian islands and in New York as parts of a single process occurring

in one interconnected transnational social field. During our research
we found that of the twenty voluntary organizations built by Vincentian migrants, thirteen had come into existence since 1970 and most
had transnational agendas. The situation was similar for the Grenadian immigrants' clubs.

With political independence, a new political consciousness was
forged in both St. Vincent and Grenada as nationalist regimes
emerged with their own nation building agendas. Yet at the same
time, the deteriorating economic conditions in both St. Vincent and
Grenada, as well as some of the political turmoil accompanying
political independence, continued to spawn emigration — increasingly to the United States.[3] Increasingly, the new nationalist leaders
saw the immigrants as part of their political strategies. The striking
demographic changes taking place in New York in the decade from
1965 to 1975, in which the entire West Indian population nearly
doubled (Kasinitz 1992:25–27), therefore introduced a more politically conscious and class differentiated population into the Vincentian
and Grenadian communities.

The heightening of transnational organizational practices made
Vincentian and Grenadian transmigrant organizations the sites of
increasing contention over immigrant identity. It is the identity formulations that emerged from these debates, within shifting
hegemonic contexts in the United States as well as in St. Vincent and
Grenada, that paved the way for the constructions of the Vincentian
and Grenadian deterritorialized nation-state. In the following sections we will review the basic outline of Vincentian and Grenadian
identity formulations and the hegemonic processes that shaped the
emerging debate as this construction gathered force.

III. VINCENTIAN AND GRENADIAN HEGEMONIC
CATEGORIES, IDENTITIES, AND CONTENTIONS

A. Race, Class, and Culture in St. Vincent and Grenada:
The Historical Perspective

In order to understand the relationship between transnational migration and argumentation over the identities of Vincentian and Grenadian transmigrants, we must first understand the historical
hegemonic processes within which transmigrants have come to understand their experiences. The layered intertwining of color, class,
and culture that mark the historical processes within West Indian
societies make the hegemonic constructs that have emerged within

even the small societies of St. Vincent and Grenada enormously complex. Shaped largely by the class contentions that have under-pinned St. Vincent's and Grenada's emergence, first from slave to colonial societies and then to decolonized and politically indepen-dent nation-states, these constructs provide the filter through which immigrants of different classes interpret and respond to the struc-tures of U.S. society. At the same time, transmigrants, although set-tled in the United States, contribute through their actions and beliefs to hegemonic processes in St. Vincent and Grenada.

In both St. Vincent and Grenada, a rigid hierarchy of class seg-ments organized along a gradation of race and color was the legacy of slave and early colonial societies. The stark divisions of white, brown, and black constituted the social pyramid in both locations and, for that matter, throughout most islands of the West Indies (see Lowenthal 1972; Hall 1977). So entrenched and fundamental to the social order were the cultural constructions that girded this system of domination that they remain part of the formulations and contest-ations that pervade class relations on both islands today.

English culture and values, imported by the white planter class and adopted by the dominant groups of these societies, represented the cultural ideal. A central stimulus for their adoption came from the fact that most of the British land owners resided in England, leaving poorer whites and mulattoes, who represented the dominant classes, to serve as the bearers of British culture. As Stuart Hall points out, they represented "the absent paradigm"; they were the "stand-ins for the invisible and ideal culture, [which served to] validate ... the whole graded structure *by its very absence*" (1979:172). This dynamic set the pattern for the West Indian cultural experience during the colonial era and thereafter, especially on St. Vincent and Grenada: the "'internalization' of external forces, ... [which] marks the [islands'] deeply structured cultural dependency" (Hall 1979:173).

The small size of the dominant class on both islands endowed the systems with a certain flexibility; this took the form of considerable growth and development within the intermediate colored group, which became the administrative class in the absence of adequate numbers of whites. Within this category, brown was the predomi-nant hue. Position in this intermediate category was carefully graded along a complicated continuum of both racial and cultural attributes. However, color, which was calculated in terms of skin shade, hair type, and facial features, could be tempered by the possession of such valued cultural attributes as education, occupation, wealth, and the proximity to behavior and values perceived to be British in origin and style.

While the expansion of this class further institutionalized the conflation of color and culture, it also provided the dynamic for color to become socially and situationally as well as physically defined. Within this framework, a person of darker skin shade with "black" features, who was educated or had some wealth, was able to move into the intermediate "colored" grouping and be ranked higher than a lighter skin person who was uneducated and poor. In contrast to the United States, with its inflexible, two-tiered racial order, the cultural formulations which framed this system allowed for some mobility and contestation across the frontiers of race and color.[4]

Rigid cultural diacritics kept the Vincentian and Grenadian peasant and working classes, whose origins were in the slave classes, socially distanced from the other classes. On the plantations and in their villages, peasants and workers elaborated their own forms of kinship, family, and religion, that drew on and reworked symbols of African culture and the plantation experience to shape a Caribbean black, folk culture that stood in opposition to European hegemony. Autonomy, community, and conviviality were prime elements of the ideology of these classes. Throughout the late nineteenth and the twentieth centuries, these cultural constructions have provided the banners under which agricultural workers on both islands have organized strikes against the plantations.

Despite the strength of peasant folk culture and the feelings it evoked among the dispossessed in this system, it is important to recognize that lower class practices and ideologies were not autonomous; they were shaped in relation to the dominant structure of legitimation. Lower classes have appropriated aspects of the beliefs and practices of the more powerful, which has served to legitimate the structure of domination and their own subordination within it. The system of legitimations on both St. Vincent and Grenada fostered an excruciating paternalism; employers were cast as "cultured" father figures and workers as "primitive," "irresponsible, indolent children" (Rottenberg 1952, quoted in M.G. Smith 1965a:15). Blackness connoted poverty, ignorance, and intemperate ways.

In a way, the discourse of class relations, which has been conducted in terms of color and culture, has tended to mask the sharp class divisions which underlie the system. Mobility between classes remained rigidly constrained by severe economic restrictions and ordered by well developed forms of cultural etiquette that defined proper conduct between people of different class statuses. Of the difficulties of crossing class boundaries, Simon Rottenberg, a labor economist studying Grenada in the early 1950s, observed that

> There are few avenues for escape from lower-class status. Persons ... who pursue upward movement ... quickly encounter checks, and several generations may be necessary for status changes to be effected. The children of agricultural laborers may, by dint of hard work and good fortune, become clerks and begin the process of escape, but in a small community they cannot conceal the status identity of their parents, and this is the major determinant of their own status. Custom is a powerful influence, and change which redefines inter-class relationships is either not accepted at all or accepted in bad grace. (Rottenberg 1952, quoted in M.G. Smith 1965a:15).

Migration provided one of the few roads to mobility. Migrants returning with or sending enough wealth from abroad to purchase "respectable" homes and property were able eventually to transcend the divides of island class culture. It is largely because of the role that migration has played in status and class mobility that migration practices and ideologies have become so deeply rooted in the firmament of Vincentian and Grenadian society and culture.

Decolonization and independence processes challenged colonial-derived constructs of race, class, and culture. The new political leaders, in their strivings to forge a sense of nation and foster national pride, rejected the close relationship between color and class and the cultural symbols of colonial stratification, emphasizing instead the historical and cultural commonalities that linked the entire population. As part of this effort, representations associated with the peasant and working classes were elevated to the repertoire of public symbols and given salience alongside those of income and property, occupation, education, and respectability. Indeed, the leaders of decolonization thrusts in both St. Vincent and Grenada, Joshua and Gairy, were themselves closely connected to the working classes and developed their confrontational styles as workers in the U.S. owned oil refinery of Aruba, "the nursery of West Indian agitational leadership" (Lewis 1968:157). Their language and presentation were those of the working classes. As Gordon Lewis said of Gairy, and it rings somewhat true for Joshua as well:

> Gairy, in his own flamboyant person, represented the Negro of working class origin and limited education who has reached eminence through union leadership and mass voting, bitterly hostile to the white plantocracy and the brown middle class, not overly concerned, even when he becomes Chief Minister, to maintain intact the conven-

tions of the established legal-political order. There is a strain of ribald
irreverence in West Indian life; Gairy brought it into the open... Not
only did he raise wage rates for his followers through stubborn trade
union pressure ... but he helped break down the rigid class barriers
of Grenadian life by teaching his followers a new class self respect
(Lewis 1968:159).

This matrix of forces has transformed the constructs that order
relations of race, class, and culture in St. Vincent and Grenada and
among migrants abroad into a contested terrain. On the one hand,
although membership in the middle classes through achievement
has accelerated, "inheritance and pedigree," [the] successful
"manipulation of symbols of 'respectability,' a compulsion to validate, if not raise, [one's] social position by trying to differentiate
[oneself] from members of the lower class, and to emulate certain
upper-class standards of behavior and belief" remain important
symbols of the bourgeoisies and middle classes (Rubenstein 1987:64).
But challenging and piercing these ideologies are those constructs
that emphasize national unity and autonomy, powered by political
independence and the lingering remnants of the Black Power movement[5] on both islands.

The rejection of the older symbols of class stratification and the
emphases on a new national 'black' solidarity and cultural and
economic independence, which are the legacies of the Black Power
movement, have been felt strongly on both St. Vincent and Grenada.
The New Jewel Movement in Grenada tried to transform these very
ideologies into a political program in Grenada from 1979 to late 1983
(see Bishop 1982), and the offshoot of this Movement in St. Vincent,
the United People's Movement (UPM), injected these principles into
political life in St. Vincent in the early and mid-1980s.

In part, the demise of the New Jewel Movement in Grenada following Bishop's death and the inability of the UPM to gain a
foothold in St. Vincent beyond young 'radicals' and some intellectuals, must be viewed within the context of the vise of economic
dependence, which continues to grip the entire region, and the forms
of class inequality that dependence fosters and indeed requires
(Levitt and Best 1975 in Austin 1984:xxiv). Yet the alternate constructions of national society and culture embodied in the New Jewel
Movement and the UPM remain part of the cultural contention on
both islands and have been incorporated into the transnational discourse about nation conducted between immigrants and dominant
forces at home.

It is the complex layering of these interpenetrating constructions, evolving from the colonial period to the present, that shapes the migrants' perceptions of and responses to their experiences in both the United States and their home islands and leads to sharp contestations as the immigrants attempt to define their identities.

B. Vincentian and Grenadian Culture and the Creation of Immigrant Identities

The hegemonic constructs, cultural practices, and consciousness the immigrants imported from their home islands have been the prism through which they interpret and respond to the shifting hegemonic sands of the United States. Drawing on these understandings and also their experiences in the United States, Vincentian and Grenadian immigrants define the nature of their relationship both to the United States and to St. Vincent or Grenada.

When they arrived in the early part of the century, the first wave of immigrants from St. Vincent and Grenada understood and confronted the dual stigma of being immigrant and black through the lens of their own colonial culture of domination. This colonial culture contained its own explanations of the relationship between race, class, and culture and included the criteria by which these immigrants, most of whom were of the middle and working classes, could attain status and respect. Many of these immigrants in fact made their journeys in order to sustain or advance their class and status positions within this cultural framework as they understood it.

Believing that the correct behavior and credentials could foster both class mobility and social respect and that they could succeed, regardless of color, even if within limited parameters, Vincentians and Grenadians worked hard, taking advantage of the limited opportunities available to them. They also created opportunities for themselves through the benefit societies and rotating credit associations they organized, which enabled them to save outside the formal banking structure with its regulations that most of them could neither meet nor grasp. And many immigrants did succeed materially, although all these successes were confined within the black community. As Lewinson has pointed out of the early West Indian migrants:

> [They] formed a percentage of the black professionals far out of proportion to their numbers, but also became labor leaders and

businessmen. Yet the role of the West Indians has largely been limited to that of leadership within the black caste. They have become doctors, lawyers, labor leaders, politicians and businessmen within the black ghetto... They have played leadership roles within the black community (Lewinson 1974:171 in Kasinitz 1992:52).

The immigrants knew that education and home ownership were critical means of enhancing their class status and social standing at home; they had seen people advance through these strategies — especially those who had gone abroad to work and brought savings back. They expected that through the correct behavior they could reach middle class status and respectability in the United States as well. These immigrants focused their energies on positioning themselves to reach these goals. As educational opportunities became available to them in New York City through night schools, trade schools, and the city colleges, many immigrants invested when they could in their own educations and those of their children. The sacrifices, during the early years in particular, were often enormous, with immigrants living in cramped quarters, sometimes working two and even three jobs at a time if they could get them, and enduring long separations from kin, waiting years before they diverted savings to expensive trips home.

Striving for mobility, immigrants purchased homes, no matter how meager, in which they rented out rooms to boarders if necessary to help meet their payments. This drive is captured by Paule Marshall in her novel *Brown Girl, Brownstones*, in which she describes the obsession of the protagonist's Barbadian mother with purchasing a house in Brooklyn in the 1940s. Vincentians and Grenadians shared this same craving and strategy.

> Every West Indian out here taking a lesson from the Jew landlord and converting these old houses into rooming houses — making the closets-self into rooms some them! — and pulling down plenty-plenty money by the week... You want to see yourself improve. Isn't that why people does come to this place? (Marshall 1981 [1959]:173–174).

But the small successes that immigrants experienced as a result of their hard work during the early years explain only a part of their continuing identification with the culture of colonial domination. The racial order of the United States that confronted the immigrants contradicted the more graded and differentiated structures of class and color that the immigrants had experienced at home and which underpinned this colonial construction. Their cultural orientation, with its genesis, paradoxically, in the colonial context, provided the immigrants with the critical perspective not only to question and confront the terms of their incorporation into the United States, but also to resist these terms and redefine who they were.

The contention occurred along the divides of both class and culture. Especially troubling to the immigrants was their allocation to the bottom of the social pyramid, a position most immigrants feared intensely. They saw themselves as far different socially and culturally from the black immigrants, often illiterate, from the U.S. South and from other blacks in Harlem who lacked their educations, skills, or manners, but with whom they were lumped.

The early Vincentian and Grenadian immigrants, like most West Indians, were eager to escape the designation of "negro" or "black," in their eyes synonymous with location at the "social bottom." For many, their migrations had been conceived as a means to avoid sliding to the bottom of the social pyramid in colonial St. Vincent or Grenada. As other colonized populations have done, the immigrants appropriated the cultural symbols of their own colonization (J. and J. Comaroff 1991; Fox 1990) — the cultural representations and symbols forged in the hegemonic context of British colonialism, into which they read new meanings — to resist their subordination by U.S. incorporative forces.

To emphasize the immigrants' cultural distinctiveness, West Indian voluntary organizations sponsored gala balls. For example, in 1937 they staged a ball in Harlem to mark the coronation of King George VI with a mock king, queen, and archbishop of Canterbury, attended by some 5,000. Church services were organized on the birthdays of the king and queen and full-dress cricket matches were sponsored by the various island sports clubs.[6] These symbols enabled the immigrants to present themselves as black British subjects, establishing distance from African-Americans through an emphasis upon their proximity to a culture still highly revered in the United States, that of the British. Taking refuge in this identity construct, when confronted with racial affronts immigrants are reported to have countered: "I am a British subject, I will report this to my consulate" (Kasinitz 1992:48).

The successes achieved by the early immigrants have become important items in the collective memories of Vincentians and Grenadians in New York and have played a role in shaping their identity constructions and cultural practices. These successes, abetted by the immigrants' identification with the colonial culture of domination in St. Vincent and Grenada, have strengthened the resolve of succeeding generations not to accept "the American Negro social status as it

[had] been fashioned by the American way of life" (Cruse 1985 [1967]:425). Many immigrants avoided public expressions of racial identity. At the same time, they stressed their ability to get along with and obtain acceptance from white Americans. As an older Vincentian man, who entered the United States in the early 1950s, said:

> We get along better with people. We're not as sensitive to black/white relations. From our upbringing, we have a pride instilled in us that Black Americans do not have.

Shirley Chisholm made a similar point when she wrote:

> I think that blacks from the islands tend to have less fear of whites, and therefore less hatred of them. They can meet whites as equals; this is harder for American blacks, who tend to overreact by jumping from feeling that whites are superior to looking down on them as inferior (Chisholm 1970:76–77).

The social validation to be found in their home societies has been especially important for those in the lower middle stratum. As we saw in the last chapter, both Joanne and Mavis endured enormous hardships in New York. These experiences were offset by the recognition each received in St. Vincent for their material achievements, such as the property they purchased at home. This continuing identification with colonial inscribed values means that investments at home, in addition to providing a place for immigrants to return to when they retire or when times get hard, are important sources of much needed status affirmation.

Decolonization and political independence introduced yet another layer to the changing self identification of Grenadians and Vincentians. With the creation of the politically independent countries of St. Vincent and Grenada, migrants were able to make a nationalist rather than a racial or ethnic presentation of themselves. As a Vincentian social scientist friend of mine said of independence: "We can now turn inward and embrace other nationals rather than outward to an inferior status and the stigma attached to blackness."

With the growing consciousness that accompanied decolonization, Vincentians and Grenadians at home and in New York appropriated new cultural representations — the steel drum, calypso, Carnival, and symbols of African Caribbean folk culture — that validated both Caribbean peasant and working class experiences and these populations' African cultural roots. These were symbols that had been used on both islands historically to express resistance to the dominant culture.

The existence of their home countries as nation-states in the world of nations introduced new feelings of cultural empowerment to the immigrants. In face of the racism and social and political exclusion they continued to confront in the United States, immigrants found their politically independent home countries increasingly important political arenas. The result was an escalation of transmigrant investments in public projects in both St. Vincent and Grenada — for example, the involvements of the St. Vincent Education and Cultural Club in St. Vincent and Stanislaus' successful collection of funds among Grenadians in New York to build a secondary school on Carriacou.

The independence ideologies that challenged the colonial system of cultural, economic, and political domination have ramifications for the nationalist identifications taking shape among Grenadian and Vincentian immigrants. The radical critiques of U.S. imperialism to which the immigrants have been exposed in New York buttress ideologies of independence, enabling the immigrants to turn a critical lens on their home societies. Earl Cato, for example, the president of a Vincentian transnational immigrant organization, feels distanced in New York from political values in St. Vincent; he claims to have little patience for the "right wing politics" of both parties at home and their lack of consideration of the "downtrodden masses." He asserts that "these are not governments of the people; they're capitalist-oriented."

The nationalist ideologies taking shape among the immigrants, with their emphasis on autonomy, are a departure from and challenge to the earlier pervading sense of partialness. The earlier hegemonic perspective, with its acceptance of dependency, continued to have an eroding influence on St. Vincent, Grenada, and other small eastern Caribbean islands in the late 1960s during the decolonization process. As Lewis noted at this time:

> So long as ... thinly disguised neo-imperialist ideas gain a welcome ... it is evident that the pathology of colonialism, the absence of a strong local pride, the failure of nerve in political leadership, are all still endemic in small island life (1968:162).

And contrapuntal to these newly forming counter-hegemonic currents with their emphases on autonomy, empowerment, and social equality, the culture of colonial domination, with its focus on hierarchy and manners, persists. It is the interpenetration of nationalist and colonial values, further influenced by the immigrants' experiences in the United States, that frame the emerging contention over what the character of Vincentian and Grenadian immigrant identity will be, over the intensity of transnational practices, and over the salience of deterritorialized nation-state constructions. It is this opposition that generates contradictions to the nation building practices of St. Vincent, Grenada, and the United States.

C. U.S. Hegemonic Agendas, Political Incorporation, and Ethnicity

The creation of a public West Indian or Vincentian and Grenadian identity in New York did not receive its sole impetus from the new role immigrants were able to play in the nation building processes of the politically independent micro-states of the Caribbean. Nor were these identity constructs solely a reflection of the pride and self-confidence the immigrants derived from the global repositioning of their home nations as independent states. Closely intertwined with the increasing transnationalism of Vincentian and Grenadian voluntary organizations, these public expressions of identity also were linked to the hegemonic contention around race and ethnicity that began to take place in the United States in the mid to late 1960s. This was a struggle, as we discussed in the introductory chapters, that resulted in a reformulated model of ethnic and racial incorporation, one of cultural pluralism. The effect of these shifting hegemonic processes in the United States and the Caribbean was to create a layered immigrant political community in which the immigrants began to see themselves as Vincentian or Grenadian and West Indian, constructs that had cultural, nationalist, and ethnic meaning (Basch 1988).

This new political narrative was given sharper focus by the differentiation process taking place within the black community itself, which was closely related to the emerging supremacy of the construct of cultural pluralism. Arising from the Civil Rights and Black Power movements in the 1960s was a new cadre of African-American political leaders. Seeing their interests as distinct from the Democratic clubhouse politics that the West Indians had dominated, these politicians were eager to carve out their own political space and form their own alliances. At the same time the new wave of West Indian immigrants, moving to New York in large numbers as a result of the 1965 immigration law and coming from decolonized and politically independent states, had a new political sense of who they were and saw the distinctiveness of their own situations.

The outcome of these converging processes — of decolonization and independence in the West Indies, of the Civil Rights and Black

Power movements and the new hegemonic model of cultural pluralism in the United States — was the emergence of West Indians as
an ethnic political constituency. The actions of government officials,
politicians, community agencies, and corporations in the United
States — reflecting the new hegemonic agenda of cultural pluralism
— which gave increasing recognition to the ethnic distinctiveness of
the immigrants, helped transform the situation from a politics of race
to a politics of ethnicity. This drive to ethnic politics was fueled from
several corners. Mayor Koch established Commissions on Black New
Yorkers and on Ethnic Affairs, both of which had separate African-
American and West Indian representatives. Howard Golden, the
Brooklyn borough president, inaugurated a Caribbean-American
Awareness Day, and white politicians campaigning in Brooklyn
strategically emphasized West Indian cultural symbols — they sponsored calypso concerts, "jumped up" in Carnival, and courted West
Indian voluntary organizations — as they tried to mobilize West
Indian votes. American corporations and government agencies
helped underwrite the fledgling Caribbean American Chamber of
Commerce, implicitly acknowledging that there was something unique about the economic situation of West Indians, and local Community and School Boards became increasingly responsive to those
who campaigned for membership in the name of West Indian interests.

Voluntary associations, the rudimentary beginnings of an ethnic
infrastructure that was put in place by the first wave of immigrants,
have become important building-blocks in this process. Previously
outside the bounds of U.S. political processes, these organizations
have been increasingly swept into the emerging ethnic politics by
West Indian immigrant leaders — ethnic entrepreneurs as Kasinitz
calls them (1992) — as well as by the formal agents of this new
hegemonic agenda. The fact that there were 158 such organizations
by 1985, according to the "Caribbean Guide" published by
Everybody's magazine (cited in Kasinitz 1992), means that these associations have been significant loci of mobilization. While these
organizations have retained their island-specific orientations, which
have become increasingly nationalist in focus since independence,
their leaders have joined forces with other West Indian ethnic political brokers in attempting to forge a wider West Indian identity and
political alliances to act on perceived West Indian interests.

Significantly, several of the new ethnic political leaders have
played leadership roles within Vincentian and Grenadian immigrant
organizations. Lamuel Stanislaus is the apt example. Recognized by

many as the informal leader of the West Indian immigrant community, Stanislaus came to the United States in 1945 from Petit Martinique, a remote island dependency of Grenada, to attend college and dental school at Howard University. He was sent for by his father, a former schoolmaster on Petit Martinique, who had emigrated to New York about a decade before. Stanislaus has lived in Brooklyn since his arrival in New York, and continues to practice dentistry there among a predominantly West Indian clientele. He has consistently been at the center of Grenadian and West Indian cultural and political activities in New York for almost half à century. Yet, attesting to the increasing transnational organizational practices developed by the immigrants, Stanislaus has played an informal leadership role in island-specific voluntary organizations such as the Grenadian Benevolent association, in pan-West Indian organizations, and in organizations linked to the political arena of Grenada, such as the support group for Blaize, described in the last chapter.

It is perhaps appropriate that a man of Stanislaus' stature within the West Indian population made one of the first forays into the New York City political arena in 1977, explicitly in the name of West Indian interests, when he organized a support group called "Caribbeans for Percy Sutton." Sutton was the African-American Manhattan borough president then running for Mayor of New York City. What was most noteworthy about this situation was that it constituted the first political thrust of a group of West Indians, acting as a self-conscious constituency and building on ties created through West Indian immigrant organizations. Although Stanislaus had supported Shirley Chisholm in the 1960s and facilitated her attempts to make contact with West Indian organizations, that political support was not conceptualized as a way to advance West Indian interests. Politics in the 1960s was still perceived and constructed along an axis of race. In supporting Sutton in the mid-1970s, however, West Indians were asserting that they were a special interest group and that they wanted access to the political system as West Indians.

The concern of the immigrants with attaining political access for West Indians demonstrates the increasing salience of West Indian ethnic identity.[7] As part of this process, Stanislaus organized a support group for the reelection of Edward Koch as mayor of New York City in 1985. He claimed:

> We need a liaison to power. The more we press for dumping Koch the greater will be the backlash. So we should support a variety of candidates, not put all the eggs in one basket ... and as an old student of

politics, I will tell you, the mayor is going to win (quoted in Kasinitz 1992:171).

What was particularly interesting about this election was the last minute candidacy of Washington Heights assemblyman Herman "Denny" Farrell, who was African-American and was put forth by a coalition of African-American political leaders. Even though Farrell's parents were born in the West Indies, Farrell only tried to gain political capital among West Indians by releasing this genealogical information late in the campaign. As Stanislaus pointed out, Farrell had never before articulated West Indian interests. In contrast, Koch had sought the West Indians out, indeed Stanislaus had been interacting with the Mayor since 1977, and Stanislaus' group had extracted promises from Koch of assistance in developing a Caribbean resource center to provide community support services,[8] a committee to address the problems of West Indian children in the schools, and continued support for the Labor Day Carnival in Brooklyn. In 1988, Koch marched in Carnival in Brooklyn as a way of showing support for the idea of a West Indian community,

Several other activists in Grenadian and Vincentian voluntary organizations joined with Stanislaus to support Koch in the 1985 mayoral election while others rallied to support groups for Carol Bellamy. The majority of these activists had come to the United States as part of the post-1965 migration swell. Roy Hastick, a Grenadian and leader of the Caribbean American Chamber of Commerce, migrated to the United States in 1976 and became an active member of Caribbeans for Koch. In defense of his not supporting Farrell, Hastick declared: "For too long West Indians have been taken for granted... We have to make sure that we have friends in high places" (quoted in Kasinitz 1992:233). While Hastick told me that he was especially concerned about "the absence of West Indian elected officials talking about West Indian interests," he did not see Farrell answering that need.

For Stanislaus, Hastick, and other West Indian political activists, what was perhaps most important about the political forays of the West Indians in the mid-1980s was that they were beginning to enter the political process under the banner of a West Indian constituency. As Stanislaus said: "A new day has come." In the service of pragmatism, these activists were even willing to overcome island-based cleavages. While some immigrant political leaders would not participate in traditional immigrant associations with immigrants of lower class standing, in the context of New York City urban politics

and the larger goal of West Indian access to this structure, old antipathies and status differences paled.

During this period, white politicians, confronted with an increasingly non-white, yet ethnically diverse population, were emphasizing ethnicity. Indeed, white politicians were the only ones actively
soliciting a specific West Indian vote and using distinctly West Indian
symbols to do so.[9]

In so doing, they were able to strike a responsive chord among
West Indians, who believed that African-Americans were insensitive
to their concerns and perspective. It was not until David Dinkins'
campaign in 1989 that West Indians began to perceive that concerted
overtures were being made to them by African-Americans as an
ethnic constituency. Indicative of this shift were changes in Jesse
Jackson's consciousness of West Indian sensitivities. In his appearance at the Labor Day Carnival Parade in 1984, in contrast, he
showed little awareness that Carnival was a West Indian cultural
representation. In 1988, he used Carnival as an opportunity to speak
on specifically Caribbean issues and remained to mingle with the
crowd.

What is particularly striking about the West Indian forays into
New York urban politics is that they have been led by individuals
who remain centrally active in organizational activities that are
clothed in nationalist goals and symbols and directed toward their
home islands. These twin involvements have led the immigrant
leaders to use these organizations as a means to participate in both
arenas. In this process, the organizations, their leaders, and their
memberships have become more self-consciously transnational. For
example, even as Stanislaus was coordinating the support group for
Mayor Koch, he was orchestrating the successful election of Herbert
Blaize as prime minister of Grenada in 1984. In both instances he was
using his network of island-specific voluntary associations to further
these efforts.

Roy Hastick became president of a block association to clean up
his street in Brooklyn as a prelude to his joining his local Community
Board in that borough; at the same time he started the Grenada
ex-policemen's association. The head of an encompassing umbrella
organization for all Vincentian immigrant voluntary organizations
became active in the support group for Carol Bellamy in 1985,
saying: "We live here; we've got to get involved in things." At the
same time that he was eliciting a block of West Indian support for
Bellamy, however, he was actively trying to influence votes at home
in favor of the opposition candidate for prime minister.

As we saw above, under the aegis of their leaders, the activities of these voluntary associations increasingly reflect transnational interests. The agendas of their meetings and the panel discussions they sponsor might as easily include the election of the next mayor of New York City as the next prime minister of Grenada or St. Vincent, and the economic climate for small investments in New York, St. Vincent, or Grenada, and contributions might be collected for all these efforts.

The hegemonic emphasis on ethnicity has provided fertile soil for the emergence of larger pan-Caribbean interests. Immigrant political leaders have acted in concert several times on an ad hoc basis to accomplish specific goals, as, for example, the election of a candidate. Yet, within this political field only one formal pan-Caribbean organization — the Caribbean Action Lobby (CAL) — has emerged. The aims of CAL are to foster explicit Caribbean alliances and to articulate formally a pan-Caribbean, transnational political identity. The cultivation of a West Indian base is central to this political effort. Headed by a black, Trinidad-born Congressman from California, the agenda of this organization is explicitly transnational: it is dedicated to the "political empowerment of the Caribbean immigrant group" and "to articulating Caribbean aspirations, whether they are in the United States or the Caribbean, to the centers of American political power." This political identity is still emergent, however. As of now, a formalized pan-Caribbean field is a hegemonic arena in which most transmigrants will not play. Its ideology cuts across two important social and ideological divides — internal class differences and nationalism.

In large part dominated by political activists who are West Indian intellectuals and professionals, the views of CAL's members frequently diverge from those of small islanders like Vincentians and Grenadians. Their different political stances reflect their varying interests. For instance, CAL was opposed to American forces landing in Grenada in 1984, viewing this as a violation of Grenada's autonomy. The majority of immigrants in Brooklyn, however, with family members at home in Grenada whom they feared were being held hostage to the squabblings among the remnants of the PRG leadership still alive, perceived this U.S. incursion as a "rescue mission." They did not want to address the larger issues of sovereignty that were troubling the leaders of CAL. CAL, for example, did not support the Simpson-Mazzoli Bill, the precursor to the revised 1985 immigrant legislation, because it would have put undocumented migrants at risk by fining employers of the undocumented. Yet the mass of West

Indian immigrants viewed this legislation positively, because it promised to grant amnesty to many undocumented immigrants then in New York, some of whom constituted part of the immigrants. They are reluctant to support CAL.

CAL's public articulation of a pan-Caribbean identity also cuts across the nationalist identities of the immigrants. The nationalist ideologies of Vincentian and Grenadian transmigrant leaders, which emphasize cultural representations of the "grassroots" and "local," delegitimize CAL as "not grassroots enough." The salience of nationalist ideologies is reflected in CAL's inability to mobilize the followings that island-based voluntary organizations can muster. CAL's events attract turnouts of less than fifty, while Vincentian and Grenadian organizations can attract up to 1,000. We will return to these issues later in the chapter when we discuss the contradictions contained in the construction of the deterritorialized nation-state.

IV. TOWARD THE DETERRITORIALIZED NATION-STATE

A. Vincentian and Grenadian Nation Building and Transnational Immigrant Organizations

1. The St. Vincent Umbrella Organization

The meeting of the St. Vincent and Grenadines Independence Anniversary Committee (the umbrella organization) took place in 1984 at the St. Vincent Consulate, which was also the St. Vincent Mission to the United Nations. Sixteen people were in attendance, all representatives of the various Vincentian voluntary associations that had agreed to constitute this resurrected umbrella organization. An umbrella organization had last functioned in 1979, when the eruption of the Soufrière volcano devastated half the island of St. Vincent and Vincentian migrants in New York, largely through the concerted effort of voluntary organizations, were able to raise tens of thousands of dollars for disaster relief. During that same year the umbrella organization had developed a round of activities in New York to mark and celebrate the Independence of St. Vincent and the Grenadines.

The agenda of this meeting was to develop a series of activities for the Vincentian community in New York to celebrate the fifth anniversary of political independence for St. Vincent the coming October. The group quickly agreed on four activities to take place in a single weekend, some of which had been discussed at a previous meeting: a panel discussion, a children's cultural show, a Saturday night dance, and a Church Service. The topics being considered for the panel discussion indicate the transnational sweep encompassed in these migrants' consciousness:

a) Advantages and Disadvantages of Independence; b) Ways and Means in Which Vincentians Can Contribute to the Development of St. Vincent; c) Government Progress and Misdemeanors; d) Problems which Vincentian Migrants Face in Adjusting to the United States.

The location and costs of these events, however, drew heated and at times acrimonious debate, reflecting some of the differences in age, class, length of stay in the United States, and gender that were causing rifts in this increasingly heterogeneous immigrant population in the mid-1980s. The greatest argument centered on the dance — whether it should include dinner and be held at a fashionable catering hall in Queens costing close to $50 per person or be merely a dance, with a band, in Brooklyn at a projected cost of $10 per person. Those in favor of the lower cost affair argued that it would be more inclusive. As one younger organizational leader said:

"My first concern is for all Vincentians to participate. We're not sure if the majority of our community would be able to support a dinner dance. A big gala occasion would exclude many who would like to attend. We want a dance where richer folks can come and where poor folks like me can go."

But there seemed to be another ideological point at issue beyond national unity, one centered on the increasing ethnic consciousness of this population. Another young immigrant said:

"I'd like to suggest Brooklyn with a local caterer. It's our Independence. Every time we want to be sophisticated, we go to Queens and give our money to Italians and Jews. We should have a Vincentian caterer with Vincentian food, not foreign food."

Another point made in favor of the lower cost function included the probability that a greater number of people would attend, making it possible to raise more money to send back to St. Vincent. The other side was tenacious, however. An older immigrant of the lower middle stratum, who had fought hard to achieve class mobility in part through organizational activities in New York and who had led many organizations in his years, argued that

"90% of Vincentians want to buy a new dress or suit just for that occasion. If we are to celebrate Vincentian independence, we can't speculate and think of making money; we want to enjoy ourselves and not think of a lower type dance. Some of us wouldn't want to associate with a $10 dance."

The group resolved the issue by deciding on a $25 per person dance, with food, to be held in Brooklyn, submerging the class differences being expressed under a nationalist label and acting in the interests of all.

The divisions expressed in this meeting had been brewing over the
past decade with the greatly expanded migration to New York from
St. Vincent. This influx created a much more class differentiated
population, as evidenced in the variations in the proposed dinner
dance that the committee members envisioned. This class segmenta-
tion also reflected different levels of political consciousness, particularly between those who had come before and after 1965. Those
arguing for a more inclusive event had for the most part come to
New York during the 1970s, like the presidents of the St. Vincent
Education and Cultural Club and of the umbrella organization, and
had been actively engaged in politics at home. They were part of the
stream of migrants who left both St. Vincent and Grenada in
response to the fragile political arrangements and post-colonial
political turmoil in those countries, which, in the 1970s, fomented
wide-scale strikes in education and health care in St. Vincent and
political repression in Grenada.

Large numbers of strikers, permanently fired from their positions
and unable to find alternative positions in St. Vincent's stagnant
economy, left for New York. Several retained their involvements with
politics at home, however, where they hoped to still make their mark,
using their base in voluntary organizations in New York to do so. In
attempting to weld together political support among migrants in
New York, these activists understood the importance of encompassing ideologies that unite rather than differentiate supporters. In contrast to these political activists were the older immigrants, more
focused on incorporation into the United States. Having left a
colonial St. Vincent, their national identity was less formulated, even
though many were deeply embedded in family networks in St. Vincent.

What was also being discussed at this meeting was the incorporation of the immigrants as loyal citizens of the deterritorialized nation-state of St. Vincent. The St. Vincent government saw the
umbrella organization as a means of fostering the immigrants' collective involvement and investment in St. Vincent's nation building
projects. This would have an effect on the continuing flow of remittances, on which the state was heavily reliant for its balance of
payments, and on contributions to development projects. It is useful
to note that in our interviews with Vincentian and Grenadian immigrants we found that 60% in our sample made such contributions
through voluntary associations.

The umbrella organization had already pledged to raise funds
through its member organizations for a Carnival hall to be located in

Kingstown, St. Vincent. Because of the potential for nation building projects in St. Vincent that such an organization could support, the St. Vincent government, through its Consulate in New York, had provided the funds to initiate the organization and space to hold the meetings. The meetings were usually attended by the St. Vincent Consul in New York.

The transnational practices of this organization, amidst the increasing incorporation of immigrants into both the United States and St. Vincent, provided a political space for immigrant leaders to participate in the political processes of both St. Vincent and the United States simultaneously and to transfer political capital from one location to the other.

2. Immigrant Leaders and Vincentian and Grenadian Nation Building

The transnational practices of immigrant organizations, like the St. Vincent umbrella organization and the St. Vincent Education and Cultural Club, are responses in large part to the nationalist agendas of political leaders at home and to the political space that nation building practices in St. Vincent and Grenada have created for immigrant leaders to wield influence at home. Earl, for example, the leader of a Vincentian transnational immigrant organization, reacting to the same economic and political forces that sent many abroad, left St. Vincent in the 1970s. A trade union leader in St. Vincent, Earl had been closely linked to the Labor Party; his departure in 1973 was related to the Labor Party's election defeat. Earl was afraid for his job and, worse, of jail. After he left St. Vincent, he found he was viewed as suspect by fellow Vincentians at home for "jumping ship" to improve his fortunes in New York. Moreover, as so many other immigrants with political aspirations, he found that he had lost his political clout at home and was able to have only limited political influence within the United States.[10] However, the situation changed once Earl became the president of a successful and well known immigrant organization in New York that donates large sums annually to various causes in St. Vincent. Regardless of which political party was in power, whenever he visited St. Vincent, Earl was interviewed on radio and television and asked his views on development and politics. For immigrants like Earl, such opportunities to be heard are indeed incentives to transnational organizing. They augment these immigrants' status among personal networks in both St. Vincent and New York and also create a field of political action within which they are treated as political advisers and representatives.

Political leaders from St. Vincent and Grenada visit regularly with their "constituents" in New York; for example, at least 14 politicians from St. Vincent visited New York in 1985, which was not atypical. They organized meetings with association leaders such as Earl to solicit their views, covering topics ranging from development plans, to party platforms, to the allocation of funds for development projects. They also reminded the immigrants of their continuing obligations to their home nation-states, solicited funds from the immigrants for political campaigns, and beseeched them to use their influence with relatives and friends at home on their behalf.

Several immigrant leaders have in fact gone home to campaign for political candidates. Reflecting the deeply ingrained cultural belief, a residue of colonial experience, that what comes from the outside is usually best, one Grenadian immigrant leader articulated the value placed on the involvement of immigrants in political activities in St. Vincent and Grenada: "If people at home see prominent people [from New York] coming home behind X, it will make a difference." These collaborations between Vincentian political leaders on the island and in the immigrant community work two ways: they augment the political capital of the immigrant leaders at the same time that they broaden the base of Vincentians and Grenadians abroad involved in the home nation-state.

As we see then, within a transnational political field immigrants need not return home to live to wield political influence. Many immigrant leaders who had become increasingly incorporated into life in New York at the same time they actively participate in political fields at home, demonstrated little interest in returning to St. Vincent or Grenada. As Earl said: "New York grew on me after a while." Reinforcing this view is the reality that few jobs are available to immigrants such as Earl. In St. Vincent's precarious economy, they cannot match the salaries or standard of living they have achieved in New York, even though both are usually less than they feel they deserve.

With transnational immigrant associations, such as the umbrella organization and the St. Vincent Education and Cultural Club, and with immigrant leaders like Earl, Stanislaus, and Hastick, the deterritorialized nation-state construction has reached maturity. Through the activities of these organizations and leaders, immigrants living in New York have been actively drawn into nation building at home — through the sponsorship of the St. Vincent state.

B. Reshaping Post-Colonial National Space and Identities

In 1982, the Caribbean Action Lobby (CAL), with the assistance of Grenadians in the United States who were supporters of Maurice Bishop, organized a meeting in Washington to advance the cause of the United States reinstituting relations with Grenada. Several intellectuals from within the West Indian community and others associated with it spoke at this gathering. The meeting had the support of the Congressional Black Caucus, which the president of CAL, a Trinidad-born Congressman and member of the Caucus, had arranged. This perhaps accounted for the presence of a representative from the State Department, who also spoke. Also in attendance were several Grenadians from Brooklyn, many associated with organizations. This group included those who had reservations about Bishop and were even somewhat sympathetic to the United States position.

The Bishop government's newly instituted relations with Cuba and the Soviet Union posed serious obstacles to its winning diplomatic recognition from the United States. Speakers on behalf of Grenada argued that these relations were not meant to be antagonistic to the United States but rather were an attempt to find new solutions for development in the region. The exhortations of the Grenadians and CAL fell on deaf ears. The United States, sensing the threat that the policies of this Grenada government posed to its hegemony in the region, never extended recognition to Grenada during the tenure of Bishop or the Peoples' Revolutionary Government (PRG).

The active engagement of dispersed populations in the political life of the home nation, reflected in the actions of the immigrants who were attending this meeting, was not perceived as aberrant by either the immigrants or the officials of the Grenada nation-state. These immigrants, even if they had been living in the United States for decades and held U.S. citizenship, were responding to the claims of their home political leaders. And although some were not in total accord with Bishop's policies, their loyalty was to their home nation; they were acting as constituents of Grenada.

The deterritorialized construction of national space reflected in the behavior of Grenadians on this occasion is in large part rooted in the colonial experiences and political traditions of both Grenada and St. Vincent. Embedded in the very definition of Crown Colony government was the geographic separation of governing institutions, located in England, from the people in the colonies. The legacy of this system, as Singham has pointed out, is that "the political community is thought of as external to the island" (Singham 1968:71). Moreover, even during the colonial period, as we have seen, the populations of both Grenada and St. Vincent were dispersed across national and territorial boundaries — with the dominant classes in England and the middle and working classes spread throughout the Caribbean. Once the colonial government's representatives and the dominant classes in both St. Vincent and Grenada recognized the value of the migrants' remittances, they began to make claims on the migrants' identities and allegiances.

The constructions of partialness engendered by the specific historic experiences of both Grenada and St. Vincent continued to pervade nation building processes during decolonization and into independence. Both nations saw themselves more comfortably as parts of larger entities, not as autonomous nation-states with loyal populations. In the mid-1960s both nations were willing candidates for inclusion in the ill-fated Federation of the West Indies, which soon collapsed. Earlier in that decade they had explored the prospect of an association with Canada on the United States-Puerto Rico model, which did not materialize. In the late 1960s Grenada voted in favor of a union with Trinidad and Tobago, which again did not come to fruition.

This history created a double stranded construction of the nation-state for both St. Vincent and Grenada. The European vision of a politically and economically autonomous nation-state, which, as Chatterjee (1986) has pointed out, became woven into post-colonial constructions, coexists with the sense of partialness embedded in both states' colonial experiences. The result of these interpenetrating ideologies has been that for both states, definitions of nation have rested on their populations, not their geographic territory. The place of the Grenadian population in Brooklyn in the body politic and social and economic fabric of Grenada was demonstrated in the frequent claims made by Maurice Bishop that "Brooklyn was Grenada's largest constituency." The political action undertaken by the migrants in Washington, in fact, followed on active lobbying among the migrants by political leaders from Grenada, including Maurice Bishop.

That Brooklyn is the geographic space where Bishop saw this segment of Grenada's population as most useful to the Grenadian nation-state is revealing of the role the governments of both Grenada and St. Vincent see transmigrants playing in these post-colonial states. No more than government officials from St. Vincent did Grenadian political leaders envision their dispersed populations returning home. At issue in both St. Vincent and Grenada were the loyalty and allegiance of the transmigrants, their political access in the United States, where they have become increasingly incorporated socially, economically, and politically, their economic support and remittances, and their political influence with relatives and friends at home — not their return.

Although Bishop did try to attract some younger migrants back to Grenada, this was selective and based on the migrants' ideological commitments and skills. No attempts were made to lure the majority of migrants home, many of whom were themselves ambivalent about some of Bishop's policies. Our interviewing in Grenada and St. Vincent revealed that people at home are frequently jealous of those who leave and are not eager for them to return unless they are close relatives. Immigrants in Brooklyn are well aware of this sentiment. As one said: "If you're on vacation, they'll love you to death; if you go back to live, it's another story." Another clarified this point further: "People at home are suspicious of you when you live abroad, they think you don't know the issues unless you go home a lot."

Gupta has argued that whether "a master narrative of the nation succeeds in establishing itself or not depends a great deal on the *practices* of the state" (1992:72). The governments of both Grenada and St. Vincent instituted a number of practices to engage their populations abroad socially, culturally, economically, and politically, as part of their inscribing the hegemonic construction of the deterritorialized state. At political independence both states offered full citizenship rights to their subjects abroad, whether or not they were United States citizens and even if they had served in the armed forces of the United States. Yet, many countries, certainly including the United States, would revoke the citizenship of nationals abroad for doing either.

Neither the Vincentian nor the Grenadian government saw a potential contradiction arising from a migrant's involvement in the political affairs of more than one nation-state. As the Vincentian Consul to New York said: "St. Vincent recognizes dual citizenship. We see nothing wrong with it so that people do not have to renounce their St. Vincent citizenship if they become American citizens." Both St. Vincent and Grenada (after the demise of the Bishop government) appointed immigrants, who were U.S. citizens, as ambassadors to the United Nations to represent them in world affairs. Interestingly, each appointment required the concurrence of the U.S. government, which was forthcoming, underscoring the subordinate and client location of these countries within the U.S. hegemonic orbit after the ideological threat from the Bishop government was removed.

As part of the rights of citizenship, both St. Vincent and Grenada allow their subjects abroad to vote in elections at home. That the governments recognize the problems attached to controlling the ideological perspectives of the immigrants abroad, however, is demonstrated in the cumbersome process attached to voter registration; in each case, the voter must spend some time in their home enumeration district. Underscoring the place of immigrants in the Grenadian and Vincentian nation, both countries promise to protect their citizens abroad and St. Vincent has acted on this several times. Its foreign minister formally objected to the government of Trinidad and Tobago about its practice of rounding up and deporting undocumented migrants or putting them in jail and appealed to the U.S. government to enlarge the immigration quota for relatives of Vincentians in the United States.

To strengthen the invention of a deterritorialized transnational community and create unifying symbols that override status and class differences, both St. Vincent and Grenada changed their Carnivals from the traditional moment just before Lent to the summer so that transmigrants can actively participate and use the summer, a moment when they and their children have more free time, to visit home.

The construction of the deterritorialized nation-state is wrapped in expectations that the migrants have continuing obligations to these states. The St. Vincent government brought migrants' organizations representing all class sectors together in encompassing umbrella organizations to collect funds for the beleaguered population at home when the Soufrière volcano erupted and again to mark the fifth anniversary of political independence. The implicit message from the agents of the state is that the migrant population, as part of a reconceived deterritorialized unit, has ongoing responsibilities to their countrymen at home and to the state.

The consulates in New York, in their attempts to foster the concept of transnational communities and deepen the transmigrants' identity with this reterritorialized space, frequently hold meetings with their citizens in New York. On these occasions, ministers of state familiarize the migrants with development issues and plans at home and actively solicit the migrants' opinions and advice, as we saw in the case of Blaize in the opening vignette of the last chapter. As the Vincentian Consul in New York said: "Vincentians, regardless of whether they ever return home, should have a say in the development of their country." To cast as wide a net as possible, both the Vincentian and Grenadian governments encourage this involvement through voluntary organizations in New York. This means that larger development projects can be developed and that all class sectors can be included. The St. Vincent government enlisted organizations in New York in selecting the project, a Carnival hall, which the immigrants wanted. The government's perception was that too many such projects had failed in the past because they had been imposed by the state. But this deference to immigrants' views also reflects the value placed on exposure to other places, a perception deeply embedded in the psyches of these small, post-colonial island states. As the Consul pointed out: "When migrants are away they learn a great deal and become less partisan. They can see things relatively objectively."

Organizations in New York play an important role in fostering transnational practices under a banner of nationalism among immigrants and also contribute to creating the symbols of this reconfigured space. Old Boys and Old Girls organizations attached to schools at home, ex-teachers and ex-policemen's organizations linked to their professions in St. Vincent and Grenada but not in New York, and independence committees and celebrations are such symbols. The organizations also sponsor activities that transcend class boundaries and engender the culturally distinct feelings and ideas of home. They bring the cultural products from home to Brooklyn — through crafts fairs, concerts featuring Vincentian and Grenadian calypsonians, steel bands, dance groups, and sports meets, which invite teams from home to compete.

At the same time, the home states treat these organizations as though they are bases for Vincentian and Grenadian national interests in New York. As part of this hegemonic vision, the Vincentian consulate organized meetings of the umbrella organization at its office at the United Nations specifically so that the prime minister could speak directly by telephone with the transmigrants.

In the aftermath of Bishop's murder in Grenada, as we saw in the last chapter, Blaize, who succeeded Bishop as prime minister, came to New York to orchestrate his political campaign. A support group was quickly organized by Stanislaus, who was well enough respected within the immigrant community to unite different class interests. Working with Blaize, the support group worked to calm the population — "to heal" in Stanislaus' words — and to unite Grenadians behind an encompassing ideology that would reclaim their loyalty to and identity with the Grenadian nation. Their aim in part was to repair the deep ruptures carved within the New York population by the wrangling among different class interests for power in Grenada over the preceding decade.

Although political leaders from home have increasingly referred to the role immigrants can play in affairs at home as part of the vision of the deterritorialized transnational nation-state, this is an issue of contention. Transmigrants are not convinced that these political leaders really want to listen to their views. As one transmigrant said: "You know they want the financing, they'll gladly take that. But sometimes they ain't hear the advice." There are instances when the transmigrants and political leaders from home read situations through different lenses. In the reinventing of a united Grenadian state following the bruises experienced during the political turmoil surrounding both the Gairy and Bishop governments and during the American imposed military activities and interim government, it was Stanislaus who cajoled and influenced Blaize into developing a slate of candidates widely incorporative of different class origins. This citizen of both Grenada and the United States, influenced by his experiences of forging cross-class, cross-island alliances to support first Sutton and then Koch as candidates for Mayor of New York City, saw the forging of such unity as imperative. Blaize, the veteran politician from Grenada, reflecting the culture of colonial domination that still shapes the identity and actions of many Grenadians, had not seen, on his own, the necessity for such an alliance.

In a sense, the reestablishment of a government in Grenada with the assistance of transmigrants in New York confirmed the reality of the deterritorialized hegemonic construction. But the seeming absence of contradiction associated with Stanislaus' political activities in this transnational political field, in fact his very appointment as Grenada's ambassador to the United Nations despite his not having visited Grenada in close to forty years, is illuminating. As we shall see, the increasing incorporation of transmigrants into the hegemonic visions of both the United States and their home nation-states poses a variety of contradictions for the nation building projects of St. Vincent, Grenada, and the United States, and also for the identity formulations, feelings, and actions of the immigrants.

C. Invasion or Rescue Mission? Contestation and the Forging of the Deterritorialized Construction

In 1983, immediately following the murder of Maurice Bishop, Grenada's prime minister, political uncertainty on that island ran high. The U.S. government sent armed troops into the political vacuum allegedly to restore order, a task that was accomplished within days and televised internationally. The justification was that U.S. students at an off-shore medical school in Grenada needed to be protected.

This military action marked the end of a government whose legitimacy had been a point of active controversy among Grenadians both at home and in the United States throughout its four years of life. Older immigrants, those arriving in the United States before 1965 who had become relatively incorporated into the United States and who were able to translate their successes into status and class mobility both in New York and at home, tended to believe that Bishop and the PRG had violated democratic principles. The violation of principles, which the immigrants identified with the British and the United States, and to which they subscribed, included the PRG's censoring of the press and resisting open elections.

But even more to the point, many of these Grenadians had been able to translate their hard earned financial gains in the United States into status mobility in Grenada through land and home ownership. The PRG's agenda to empower the masses, which openly attacked the colonially derived status hierarchy, was perceived as a threat to the migrants' class positions. These fears were heightened by the PRG's statements about confiscating idle land to redistribute to land-poor peasants and agricultural laborers.

Many immigrants fairly well incorporated into the United States were also uncomfortable with the PRG's open challenges to U.S. economic and cultural hegemony in the Caribbean. These policies had led the United States to withhold recognition of the new government throughout its four years in office. To these immigrants the American incursion was a rescue mission. Many of these immigrants also had relatives in the villages and towns of Grenada, and they feared that their lives were in jeopardy in the disorganization following Bishop's death. Citizens were reportedly advised not to leave their homes on pain of being shot, a difficult proposition for the many Grenadians who lacked refrigeration and indoor plumbing.

In contrast, intellectuals and many post-1965 younger immigrants exposed to the radicalizing ideas of the Black Power movement both in the United States and the West Indies identified with much of the ideology of the PRG. They applauded the government's attacks on the culture of domination that continued to prevail in most West Indian nations and on the continuing economic and cultural dependence of the region. They also approved of the PRG'S efforts to empower the masses and the movement's incorporation of African and Caribbean folk symbols as the cultural representations of their ideology. These migrants viewed the U.S. action as an invasion.

The furor over the PRG's legitimacy and the U.S. action underscored the depth of the transnational involvements of both the immigrants and their organizations in political processes in Grenada. Immigrants, calling on connections developed through their network of voluntary organizations, had first played a role in bringing Bishop to power in Grenada, then in expressing opposition to him, and finally in orchestrating the political alliances that enabled the government of Herbert Blaize to succeed Bishop.

Because of the wide publicity given to the political situation in Grenada by the United States, West Indian, and immigrant media during the reign of the PRG and the efforts of the PRG political leaders, including Bishop, to gain immigrants' support by visiting and meeting with them in Brooklyn, Grenadians in the United States were informed and actively drawn into the ongoing debate. Leaders of immigrant organizations and West Indian intellectuals also tried to shape the opinions of immigrants by organizing frequent meetings in Brooklyn to familiarize them with their readings of the issues and to debate their opponents. Many immigrants developed firm positions. Indeed, the rancor attached to this debate had so penetrated the immigrant community that most Grenadian immigrant associations were unable to function during the final two years of Bishop's government.

The contention over the U.S. military incursion demonstrated not only the extent to which transnational practices are at the base of the deterritorialized construction, but also the struggle that surrounds its shaping. Grenadians in the United States actively participated in formulating this construction through their political organizing. Yet, as this vignette demonstrates, the transmigrants are not a homogeneous group ideologically; their different class positions and the shifting terrain of both U.S. and Grenadian hegemonic contexts lead them to hold multiple perspectives. Different ideologies, emerging since before decolonization, clashed during the Bishop years and in the aftermath of his death.

Very much at issue in this political debate was a struggle over Grenadian culture and identity, which had implications for the political agenda in Grenada. On the one hand, there were those favoring a continuation of the values, practices, and interests that had dominated Grenada since the colonial period. Their definition of the nation-state was a more partial vision that led them to see their destinies closely linked with the United States. They found the interpretation of rescue mission more acceptable. At the other end of the spectrum were those advocating values that were at the root of nationalist claims for political independence and that were echoed in the Black Power and New Jewel movements. They represented different class perspectives. In this dichotomized political situation, cultural constructions created in the crucible of the history of class struggle in Grenada, and the entire West Indies for that matter, were politicized and used as emblems to engage different class interests. The debates that raged over the legitimacy of Bishop's government and over what had been the "true" intent and impact of the American invasion were also asking people to define further their identities.

The cultural issues raised by Maurice Bishop and the American military action in Grenada continue to gnaw at the body politic and to be redefined and contended in both Grenada and St. Vincent. The tension between these two ideological currents spurred the debate in the St. Vincent umbrella organization. Should the organization be inclusive or exclusive in the members it attracted to its events? Should it invest organization funds in public symbols such as a Carnival hall or in clothing factories, whose primary beneficiary would be the dominant economic forces in St. Vincent? These cultural struggles animated the assessment made by Earl, the leader of the St. Vincent immigrant organization, when he discussed political leaders in St. Vincent and his own political involvements. According to Earl, who migrated in 1975 and has listened carefully to radical critiques of Caribbean politics both in St. Vincent and New York: "The downtrodden masses are still collecting the crumbs off the table and the governments are doing whatever the United States and England want." Yet Earl meets with politicians from home when they come to New York and when he returns to St. Vincent, offering his views and enjoying the suggestion of influence such meetings signify.

D. Contradictions of the Vincentian and Grenadian Deterritorialized Constructions

The movements of Vincentians and Grenadians across the geographic and ideological borders of their home nation-states and the United States have generated flows of cultural products and ideologies, creating new forms of cultural interaction and new interpretations. By constructing transnational social and political fields, migrants have been able to retain and act on ties to their home nations at the same time they foster relationships in the United States. These transnational fields, which encompass both the United

States and the migrants' home societies, are also the context in which immigrants construct, contest, and reformulate their identities and strategies, interacting with the hegemonic processes generated in both locations.

The new hegemonic formulation of the deterritorialized nation-state has emerged as an attempt by dominant forces in both St. Vincent and Grenada to bound and structure the transnational flows of people, practices, and culture. Arising out of the specific histories and post-colonial situations of St. Vincent and Grenada, this construction enables the dominant strata of these small nation-states to lay claim to the allegiances and wealth of their emigrants, providing in exchange arenas of social validation, prestige, and political action for these dispersed populations. As we began to see from the dramatic political changes in Grenada, however, this new hegemonic formation is fraught with contradictions.

Some of these contradictions have been articulated by transmigrants, as we have seen in the preceding pages. Earl, the president of a Vincentian immigrant organization in New York, for example, had developed a sharp critique of the economic development practices of the Saint Vincent government; yet at the same time, he continued to acquiesce to these strategies through his continuing support of the government's political practices. Other contradictions, as we shall see, may not be so clearly verbalized or even recognized by the actors. While some of these contradictions can lead to complicity with the nation-state, as in Earl's situation at the moment, other contradictions also can undermine nation-state building projects. Bishop's regime, for example, was in part destabilized by segments of his body politic — his "constituency" — living in the United States.

These contradictions strike at the nation building projects of both the subordinate (St. Vincent and Grenada) and the dominant (United States) nation-states as well as at the reformulated and reinvented identities of the transmigrants. This section will examine some of these contradictions, exploring the ways transnationalism and transnational practices challenge, reinforce, and interact in other ways with the nation building projects of the United States and St. Vincent and Grenada. Attention also will be given to the implications of these contradictions for relations between different classes of Grenadians and Vincentians living at home and abroad and between these immigrant populations and other groups in the United States.

As we have pointed out, nation building strategies, by their very definition, are formulated by those who are or who aspire to be dominant and are designed to benefit these strata. Moreover, these strategies frequently act against the interests of other social groups, leading to their further subordination, even though this fact is masked by the ideology and unifying symbolism of the "nation," which is aimed at capturing the loyalty of its entire citizenry, both at home and abroad. Despite the fact that different classes and groups experience the rewards of the nation-state in different ways, nationalist discourse makes no reference to the social position, relationship to production, monetary worth, or access to power of the various class actors. This contradiction frames relations between the transmigrants and the dominant political and economic strata in both St. Vincent and Grenada. Indeed, there are several points of economic and political difference between transmigrants and those living on these islands that are masked by the hegemonic construction of a deterritorialized nation-state.

For both St. Vincent and Grenada, transmigrants are viewed as major sources of revenue production, not only from the remittances that are crucial to these countries' balance of payments and GNPs — but also as sources of tourist dollars, indirect tax revenues, funding for improvement projects, scholarships for higher education, paint for public buildings, and so on.

However, while transmigrant dollars generate some income, these financial infusions mask the fact that the productive bases of both island economies are eroding and that few projects to stimulate or expand development appear on the drawing boards of either state. In both St. Vincent and Grenada, off-shore banking, which favors the dominant commercial strata almost exclusively to the detriment of other classes and generates virtually no jobs or state funds for further development, has become a major focus of economic activity. Moreover, reliance on external assistance continues as a chief means for the governments of both states to address the basic needs of the lowest strata of their populations, which have among the lowest per capita incomes in the region. A matrix of government strategies wrapped around external funding sources, coupled with an absence of economic productivity, serve to further the underdevelopment of these islands, forcing the ongoing emigration of large numbers in the middle, working, and peasant classes. Somewhat ironically then, the governments that transmigrants politically support and help to keep afloat with their remittances and expenditures as tourists, become part of the dynamic that forces migrants and their family members to live and work abroad.

There is yet a further dimension to this contradiction between the interests of the political leadership and the transmigrants. While the political elites need the transmigrants' wealth, they do not welcome migrants' critiques of their nation building strategies. As both Stanislaus and Earl have acknowledged, their home governments want their money but not their advice. While Earl has begun to grasp the negative impact of St. Vincent's developmerit strategies, his allegiance at the moment to this nation-state, combined with the status validation he receives from his activities at home, paper over the fundamental contradiction in his own and the state's interests.

The deterritorialized nation-state construction fostered by both Grenada and St. Vincent can also draw the transmigrants into development schemes that further class differentiation and exacerbate these countries' dependency, again perpetuating the necessity of the transmigrants' own migration. Support for export-oriented textile firms, the production of exotic fruits, and tourist development, projects currently favored by both governments, lead to low wages, tax evasion on the part of the donors, and the repatriation of profits to the country of the funders (Nanton 1983). Such projects are known to bring little wealth into countries like St. Vincent and Grenada, but rather to further the interests of the dominant classes, again at the expense of middle and lower strata.

Moreover, the deflecting of viable land from subsistence production into crops the local population can neither afford to purchase nor consume, has the potential to erode further the fragile agricultural bases of these nation-states. This in turn forces more of the peasantry into migration in search of its subsistence. Exotic fruits, which are highly perishable and would have little currency in other Caribbean countries, which are capable of similar crop production, would also further the country's dependency on U.S. markets. That this project was supported by immigrants in New York points to another dimension of the contradiction between the interests of transmigrants and the home nation-state. For transmigrants, who also are subject to U.S. hegemonic ideologies of capitalist development and U.S. investment abroad, the negative implications of reliance on U.S. markets for their home country's development can become obscured.

The demise of the Bishop government in Grenada points to the very difficult task of breaking the yoke of post-colonial dependence and the mentality and cultural constructions that support that dependence. The PRG's construction of the nation-state, which also encompassed transmigrants, was designed to challenge Grenada's economic dependence. As part of this strategy, Bishop aimed to lessen the class differentiation and reverse the culture of domination — colonially derived, but perpetuated by the country's post-colonial political economy — that underpinned the island's dependence. Bishop's ideology of "empowering the people" — and especially those of the lower classes — by achieving economic autonomy from the United States, was perceived by the dominant classes and many of the middle strata, both in Grenada and abroad, as an attack on their interests. Many owned property there and felt particularly threatened by Bishop. Bishop's political agenda also cut across the transmigrants' aspirations for social mobility, which had been an inducement for many to migrate in the first place. The transmigrants' growing opposition to the Bishop regime contributed to the efforts of dominant forces in the United States and Grenada to destabilize the political situation in Grenada.

The ultimate fate of the Bishop government also demonstrates how the ideologies and cultural representations that transmigrants bring from abroad can be a destabilizing force to the political cultures of their home nation-states. The negative assessments developed by some Grenadian migrants of the Bishop government, for example, were in part influenced by the ideologies of democracy and a free market economy to which they had been exposed in the United States. These negative assessments helped bolster the forces of opposition to the Bishop government. Grenadians of all classes living in New York were especially fearful of, and opposed to, Grenada's ties with Cuba and the Soviet Union. Their collective reading of history also led them to mistrust Bishop's political agenda, which included curbing the press and delaying elections until the new political culture took hold.

The appointments of transmigrants as the representatives of St. Vincent and Grenada to the United Nations also pose a potential threat to the nation building strategies of these nation-states. Such appointments raise questions about whose interests such transmigrants are unwittingly serving. Their perspectives, shaped largely in the United States, can have a destabilizing effect on their home nation-states' practices. For example, the ideologies that have informed the development strategies Stanislaus has supported for Grenada — those that emphasize capitalist investment — further Grenada's deepening dependency. The United States did little to foster economic development in Grenada following its military action, and Grenada's economic conundrum has led it to allow 118

off-shore banks — almost all from the United States — to register on
its island.

Ideologies of electoral democracy developed in the United States,
when imposed on a tiny nation like Grenada, can also lead to
decisions undermining local political interests. The stand Stanislaus
took on developing a broad-based slate for the Grenada election
following the fall of Bishop's government suggests the divergence of
viewpoints that can exist between these appointees and the outlook
of various political forces in the home countries. Stanislaus had not
been back to Grenada in forty years; his experience was with the
politics of access in New York (Kasinitz 1992; Katznelson 1981),
where he put together coalition support groups for both Percy Sutton
and Ed Koch as mayoral candidates. He could not have had a clear
sense of the political climate in Grenada. Indeed, the broad-based
coalition he orchestrated, although elected, did not hold together, in
part because of its diversity of perspectives. Moreover, Stanislaus
was not in Grenada to help keep the political alliance. Political inter-
ventions by transmigrants, who become representatives of their
country of origin, confound in a way twentieth century understandings of sovereignty in independent nation-states.

There are other counts on which the sovereignty of dependent
nation-states is jeopardized by transnational social and political
fields and the ideas transmigrants transmit within these fields. The
political perspectives of younger immigrants are being influenced by
counter hegemonic ideas and radical critiques developed in U.S.
universities. The transmigrants attend classes in Black, African, and
African-American Studies departments and frequent public lectures
where the present structure of global power relations is challenged
and linkages are drawn between global capitalism, economic and
cultural dependency, and racial exploitation. To some extent, these
critiques reinforce the assertion of economic and cultural autonomy
contained within the ideologies of decolonization and political independence to which immigrants also have been exposed. Moreover,
these analyses resonate with the migrants' own experiences of
economic insecurity, racial discrimination, and long separations from
familiar places and people. Many younger immigrants have begun
to articulate an analysis of the causes of their own "forced" migrations, which they locate in the development policies of their home
nation-states. Earl's analysis of the present political situation in St.
Vincent — which, he says, is controlled by dominant classes who are
"doing whatever the United States and England want" and are un-

concerned with the plight of "the masses" — has support from other immigrants.

These developing collective representations pose the possibility of a broader alliance against the nation building strategies in St. Vincent. When Earl returned to St. Vincent just before a recent election campaign, for example, he marched with a party that articulated an ideology reflecting his analysis. He was familiar with the party through his contacts in New York. Although this party did not gather enough votes to participate in the constituted opposition at home, its message was planted in the consciousness of Vincentians by Vincentians in St. Vincent and New York acting together. There are increasing opportunities for forging larger transnational alliances with those who share this analysis and consciousness through voluntary organizations. Earl, for example, heads an organization that has large followings in both St. Vincent and New York because of the cultural and educational projects it sponsors in both places.

The role of transmigrants in destabilizing political regimes in Grenada is part of the historical narrative of that island nation-state. Gairy, who led the country into decolonization, had been a trade union leader in the U.S. owned oil refinery in Aruba and went home to challenge British hegemony. His repressive tactics in weeding out opposition, however, led to heavy emigration among all class strata. Under these conditions, the opposition movement to his regime, the New Jewel Movement developed by Bishop, had to be built in the diaspora. Indeed, some transmigrants who were early incorporated into Bishop's movement, but whose interests were later threatened by the movement's ideology, played a role in shaping the negative images attached to this regime.

The strivings for political and economic autonomy expressed by Earl and other transmigrants of his generation and class may also be reinforced by the incipient pan-West Indian identity that is being shaped in New York. A cross-island alliance, for example, was forged among intellectuals and younger middle class migrants from a variety of West Indian islands, who, becoming increasingly conscious of and opposed to the impact of U.S. hegemony in the Caribbean, were supportive of Bishop's ideologies. In fact, they played a strong part in organizing the public hearing in Washington that challenged U.S. foreign policy in Grenada and, by extension, United States domination in the region.

The rancor and contention that raged in the West Indian community over issues such as the legitimacy of the Bishop government and the conduct of U.S. foreign policy in the Caribbean brought to center stage yet another important issue related to the identity of transmigrants. This is the matter of immigrant loyalty and allegiance in a transnational political field. Which nation immigrants give their allegiance to and whose interests they are expressing are questions of central import to political leaderships in the United States, St. Vincent, and Grenada. This issue is perhaps one of the reasons that home nation-states, although they extend citizenship rights to transmigrants, leave practices in place that make voting by transmigrants in local elections difficult. As we saw in the introductory vignette of the preceding chapter, voting at home is of concern both to transmigrants and home political leaders. Loyalty is also an important issue with regard to the economic investments of transmigrants. Where will migrants invest their savings: in milk factories in St. Vincent, in agribusinesses in Grenada, or in a house in Brooklyn?

There are other threats to hegemonic constructions of a deterritorialized nation-state posed by cross-West Indian alliances. Small West Indian nation-states are currently reticent about regional integration efforts, in part because of their lack of success in mounting earlier, more inclusive initiatives, but also because of their subordinate positions within the Caribbean region. The aborted attempt to form a West Indian Federation, which the smaller states had wanted, only underscored their lack of voice within the region and their vulnerability to the more dominant West Indian states of Trinidad, Jamaica, and Barbados, all larger, with relatively more human and natural resources. The inability to form such a federation is in part a legacy of the British colonial experiment in the West Indies, which linked the island dependencies vertically to the metropole while fostering competition, sometimes intense, between them (see Basch 1992). One of the constraints on forging wider alliances has centered on the fears of states, with no prior experience in sharing resources, that such alliances would weaken their own scarce economic and political resource bases.

The position of recent governments of St. Vincent was expressed by its Consul to New York, who said: "It is better to concentrate on the Vincentian community before we think of cooperation with other West Indian communities." Yet, the incorporation of Vincentians and Grenadians into U.S. ethnic constructions that emphasize their West Indian identity, which is beginning to override the sense of "otherness" that previously pervaded relations with West Indians from other islands, nags at and could possibly unravel the deterritorialized nation-state construction. The growing West Indian identity could draw the immigrants' attention to broader, West Indian projects that foster regional integration.

As part of their allegiance to their home nation-states, many Vincentians and Grenadians, even if they opposed some of the political practices of Maurice Bishop and viewed the American intervention as a rescue mission, are concerned about the deeper implications of this incident for the autonomy and integrity of the Caribbean region. This enlarging consciousness leads the immigrants to identify with other post-colonial nation-states that are the objects of aggressive acts by the United States. West Indians, for example, have marched with Haitians to protest the removal of Aristide from power, and the West Indian press has featured this situation prominently. West Indian nation-states have also voiced strong opposition to other perceived violations of third world sovereignty, such as the recent kidnapping of a Mexican to stand trial in the United States, which the immigrant press has also headlined. This more encompassing and shared consciousness can become a potent force in challenging U.S. hegemonic agendas aimed at post-colonial countries.

On this basis, transmigrants are also beginning to challenge the predominant racial and ethnic categorizations within the United States and the terms of their own incorporation. We have seen how Vincentians and Grenadians over the past decade have been responsive to U.S. incorporative constructions that differentiate the population into ethnic groups at the same time they are more broadly united under banners of "cultural pluralism" or "multiculturalism." These constructions have enabled West Indians to feel that they occupy a middle terrain in the U.S. social structure, one to which they have aspired over the years (Sudarkasa 1983). Yet the increasing acts of public racism during the 1980s and 1990s, in which many Caribbeans have been the victims, have exposed the fiction of a three-tiered racial model within the U.S. construction. These acts of racism have led Vincentians and Grenadians, and all West Indians, to rethink these predominantly ethnic categorizations.

Their racial consciousness raised by these assaults, West Indians, simultaneously with their ethnic political assertions, have also been acting on the more encompassing identity of race in developing new alliances. West Indians have joined African-American political leaders in publicly opposing these attacks. Moreover, they have been meeting to discuss the increasing racism and have been visible together at the sites of most incidents, whether the victim is African-American or West Indian. A West Indian lawyer has taken the cases of African-American victims and African-American politicians have joined in the public outcry against the assaults on West Indian victims. The West Indian media and WLIB, a radio station jointly directed by African-American and West Indian interests, are also contributing with their ongoing accounts of racist experiences to the public articulation of this discourse.

As we saw in the last chapter, there is precedent for this shared consciousness and for the joint political action of West Indians and African-Americans. Despite the middle class West Indians' tendency to mark their own progress in the United States by emphasizing their cultural differences from African-Americans, largely to escape the social stigma of blackness, this focus on difference did not preclude active alliances with African-Americans to address their political exclusion, especially prior to 1965, when both groups were subject to intense racism. As with Garvey's UNIA and the Harlem Renaissance in the 1920s, West Indians are responsive particularly to the encompassing construction of "African" to articulate this consciousness.

A focus on symbols — those of Africa — reinterpreted as reflective and constitutive of a rich cultural tradition, does not require public acknowledgement of the racial order that continues to structure U.S. social relations, and which West Indian ethnic constructions continue to challenge. Moreover, the emphasis on the common African cultural roots of all black people captured in the imagery of Africa taps into the meaning and symbols attached to other ideologies drawing on African representations as symbols of resistance — for example, decolonization, political independence, the Black Power movement, and the New Jewel Movement.

This increasing racial consciousness not only challenges U.S. nation building constructions of ethnic incorporation, but as the immigrants remain involved in transnational social and political fields informed by other hegemonic formulations, they increasingly subject U.S. racial constructions to a new scrutiny. At the beginning of the Gulf War, the West Indian press, as did much of the U.S. media, emphasized the allegiance of the West Indian community to the U.S. war effort. West Indians serving in the Gulf were prominently featured, as was the genealogical fact of Colin Powell's Jamaican roots. But as the war progressed, and deaths and injuries mounted, the West Indian press began to raise questions that challenged the very premises of the U.S. structure of race/class relations. The press, and West Indian political leaders, wanted to know why so many foot soldiers and why so many injured in the Gulf were of West Indian background. It is possible that as racial attacks continue, as alliances between those of African-American, West Indian, and other post-colonial backgrounds are expanded, and as the transmigrants' loyalties and ties to their home nations continue to be activated, similar questions aimed at the fundamental assumptions of the U.S. social structure and the global structure of race relations will be challenged.

V. CONCLUSIONS

Voluntary organizations have become the most recent strand in the transnationalism being forged by Vincentian and Grenadian immigrants and have given a public face to transnational processes. Through an ethnography of organizations, this chapter has traced the multiple identities, very much in the process of formation, of these transmigrants and analyzed them against the shifting hegemonic contexts of both the United States and the immigrants' home societies. Embedded equally in Vincentian or Grenadian and U.S. social and political spaces, these immigrant populations have seen themselves variously as Negroes, blacks, Africans, British West Indians, ethnic and nationalist Vincentians or Grenadians, West Indians, and Caribbeans.

It is through organizations that constructions of deterritorialized nations, the attempts of the Vincentian and Grenadian post-colonial states to reclaim the immigrants' loyalties and commitments, have gained force. This construction is fraught with complexity and internal contradiction, however. Within this construction the sense of partialness and dependence, reflected in these states looking to their populations abroad for economic and political assistance, is juxtaposed to inherited colonial notions of the autonomous European nation-state. As we saw in this chapter, the gap between the lived experience of economic dependence and almost forced migration, on the one hand, and the ideal of autonomy, on the other, provides fertile terrain for ongoing contention between the immigrants and dominant strata at home. It underscores the multistranded and complex character of Vincentian and Grenadian transmigrant identity. This discrepancy leads transmigrants to challenge U.S. incorporative practices that further their subordination as blacks, as ethnics, or as black ethnics. Through reworking the meanings attached to the hegemonic categories of race and ethnicity, and creating an encompassing idiom drawing on African symbols, Vincentian and Grenadian transmigrants, along with other West Indian and Caribbean immigrants, are finding new ways to challenge global forces of power and domination.

NOTES

1. The Caribbean Union, the later incarnation of the West Indian Committee, was such an organization.

2. The goals of the United Negro Improvement Association challenged the structure of race on a global scale by seeking to "unite the Negro peoples of the world into one great body to establish a country and Government absolutely their own" (Jacques-Garvey 1969:126, cited in Sunshine 1988:36).

3. In the post World War II period, West Indians migrated to England, where they were enlisted in efforts to rebuild the British economy. This outlet ran dry by the early 1960s, when the migration stream was redirected toward the United States.

4. Recently, Hispanics and Asians have become intermediary categories in the United States racial order. However, while no longer two tiered, the system remains different from the color/class continua of the Caribbean. An individual is not able, by assimilating to the dominate culture, to change his or her positioning in the hierarchy.

5. The Black Power movement emerged on West Indian islands such as St. Vincent, Grenada, Barbados, Dominica, and Trinidad in tandem with the Black Power movement in the United States. This "bidirectional flow" of ideas (Sutton 1992a) across political borders in the early 1970s, facilitated by migrants, was early testimony to the growth of the transnational social field.

6. That these events enabled West Indians to distinguish themselves in small ways culturally and socially from other blacks is evidenced by their being noted and chronicled in such magazines as *The New Yorker* (1954:65). *The New Yorker* was particularly taken with the orderliness of cricket in contrast to the roughness of most American sports.

7. Foner 1987 discusses the increasing tendency of Jamaicans to identify culturally as West Indians.

8. It is of note that Koch never acted on this promise.

9. There were some African-Americans, especially intellectuals and cultural nationalists who, using a discourse of "black ethnicities," began to speak to the specificity of West Indian interests. However, these discussions for the most part took place at poorly attended meetings held on urban college campuses.

10. Despite their recent increasing involvement in New York ethnic politics, the West Indian immigrants' access to political power remains for the most part minimal.

Chapter FIVE

The Establishment of Haitian Transnational Social Fields[1]

I. INTRODUCTION

"We want Aristide," "No Aristide, No Peace!" On October 11, 1991 the streets of lower Manhattan, including the entire Wall Street area, were occupied by tens of thousands of Haitian immigrants. They marched from Grand Army Plaza in Brooklyn across the Brooklyn Bridge, rallied on the steps of the historic Customs House, flooded Wall Street, went on to the United Nations, and then split up into handfuls of people who marched through Grand Central Station continuing to shout their demands, "We want Aristide!" "We want Aristide!" *The New York Times*, reporting on the event the next morning, noted that not a single person was arrested in the course of the day-long demonstration (Faison 1991:32). Instead of facing opposition to what could well have been looked upon as a veritable invasion, the marchers were greeted by the Mayor of the City of New York, who warmly addressed the demonstrators.

The straightforward slogans on the placards and in the chants, which were mainly in English, made the purpose of the demonstration clear to the well dressed Wall Street regulars and the thousands of other New Yorkers who saw the demonstration. The demonstrators were delivering a message to the government of the United States and to the American people. They were demanding the restoration of Father Jean Bertrand Aristide as President of Haiti and accusing the United States of supporting the repressive military forces that had taken over the Haitian government in September 1991 and sent Aristide into exile.

What was less clear was the relationship of the demonstrators to Haiti. Who were the "we?" Certainly the different individuals who organized or who were invited to speak to the demonstrators did not perceive their assembled audience in the same way. To Mayor Dinkins, New York's first African-American mayor, the demonstrators were part of a potential constituency of "African" people in New York. About to go to Africa to validate his own African identity, Dinkins was among a number of black leaders who are working both to recognize the diverse "roots" of the black populations in the United States and to encompass these populations into a constituency active in the U.S political process. Mayor Dinkins addressed the cheering crowd as Haitian-American immigrants who might demonstrate about Haiti, the land of their ancestry, but who were firmly planted within the United States in terms of their current life and future aspirations.

The Haitian leaders who called the demonstration saw those assembled before them differently. Wilson Désir, a long-time political activist in New York who had been appointed Consul-General in New York by Aristide, spoke to the assemblage as Haitians who were inextricably part of the Haitian people. Although standing physically in New York, Désir saw this population as participants in the political life of Haiti. He accepted Aristide's construction of Haitian nationality in which Haitians abroad, no matter what the citizenship status recorded on their passports and legal papers, continued to be a part of Haiti and continued to have responsibilities to sustain Haiti.

This definition of Haitians in the United States as part of the population of the Haitian nation-state had been popularized by Aristide when he named Haitians abroad "the 10th Department" *Dizyèm Depatman-an* of a country that has 9 geographical divisions called

Depatman.[2] In their national discourse, Aristide and many persons in his government who had lived abroad for many years and maintained transnational networks were rupturing the territorial definition of the state and creating a deterritorialized nation-state. Their construction of the identity of Haitian immigrants reflected the emergence of Haitian transnationalism. At the same time these leaders were shaping the manner in which Haitians are coming to understand their migration.

In the course of over three decades of settlement in the United States, Haitian immigrants have bought homes, joined block associations, joined unions and gone on strike, run for school boards, started businesses, and reflected on their life in New York in song, poetry, and film. At the very same time, they have bought property, built houses, repaired cemeteries, started businesses, made marriages, and influenced political developments in Haiti. Familial, social, economic, religious, as well as political ties to Haiti have increased as Haitian immigrants became firmly established in the United States.

However, while lives are lived across borders, Haitian immigrants struggle to establish their identities in a world in which dominant classes define persons in terms of their relationship to nation-states. It is important to note that neither Dinkins nor Désir acknowledged the multiple ties and loyalties that are part of the daily experience of transmigrants and mark the emergence of Haitian transnationalism. Both leaders were involved in nation building processes that stressed primary loyalty to a single nation-state. They cooperated with each other in building the demonstration but competed with each other for the loyalty of the demonstrators. The transmigrant experience is not spatially localized, yet the political leadership and the representatives of institutions in nation-states — universities, philanthropies, churches — offer geographically bounded hegemonic constructions of loyalty and identity within which transmigrants struggle to understand who they are and where in the world they belong.

For their part, the demonstrators, with their diverse class backgrounds and histories of settlement, were not all equally comfortable with Aristide, the leadership of the *Dizyèm* or with Dinkins. The degree to which Haitian immigrants have engaged in Haitian politics, or identified themselves as part of the Haitian nation-state, has varied in the course of the Haitian settlement. At particular moments such as this one, Haitian immigrants might unite, identify strongly with Haiti, and become significant actors in the political arena in Haiti. The concept of *Dizyèm-nan* allowed them to express their continuing ties to Haiti without eschewing their ties within the United States. However, as a national construction, there is much that the identity of *Dizyèm-nan* does not encompass.

Haitian immigrants sometimes accept and sometimes reject self-identification as a population with a political future within the United States. While at times they see themselves as separate from other black populations in the United States, at other times they identify with these populations. Thus they might embrace or eschew the labels of "black," "African-American," Caribbean, or "African" (Fouron 1985; Charles 1990b). Moreover, these migrants, divided from each other by differences in class background, occupation, religion, color, gender, and region of origin in Haiti (Glick [Schiller] 1975), often expressed a variety of conflicting identities. In the first years of settlement, there was little sense of community and no identification with the Haitian government. The degree to which different identities have became salient and were made points of contention have varied in the course of settlement in the United States, depending on the setting and situation (Glick Schiller 1977; Glick Schiller et al. 1987; Glick Schiller et al. 1992; Glick Schiller and Fouron 1990).

Haitian transmigrants have yet to articulate fully an identity that reflects their transnationalism. They have created no language or identity that gives full voice to the complexity of their daily lives. The formulation "*Dizyèm-nan*," while reflecting their transnational connections, builds an exclusive and intense identification with the Haitian nation-state. This is only a partial reflection of the social, economic, and political location of the transmigrants. Through their social relationships and their actions, transmigrants experience the intersection and interpenetration of their countries of origin and settlement. No single identity, not *Dizyèm-nan*, African, or Haitian-American fully articulates their spatially dislocated but interpersonally connected social experience.

II. THE DIMENSIONS OF HAITIAN TRANSNATIONALISM.

This chapter will delineate the dimensions of Haitian transnationalism. First the chapter reviews the history of postcolonial economic dependency and political independence that forms the context for Haitian migration. The second half of the chapter examines the developments of family, economic, and communication networks. As they maintain these networks, Haitians have de-

veloped transnational practices in which multiple strands of relationship straddle conventional definitions of polity. The following chapter examines the emergence of transnational Haitian organizations,
addressing the implications of Haitian political practice for Haitian
categories of identity. It explores the relationship between Haitian
transnational projects and the hegemonic efforts to describe and
bound immigrant practices within the categories of nation, ethnicity,
and race.

The data in both chapters were gathered in the course of field
studies conducted that I conducted in 1969-71[3] and 1985-87[4] and
through less intense but always instructive participation and observation of the experience of Haitian immigration during a span of 25
years from 1967 to 1992. Over the course of the years my participation has included extensive visiting with families, attendance at
public activities, including cultural performances, religious cere-
monies, and demonstrations, and working as both volunteer and
paid consultant in a range of Haitian organizations. I have written
grants, newsletters, and public statements for these organizations
and assisted in various types of community organizing and case
work. I have attended public meetings and informal strategy ses-
sions. The second research project, which I developed with Josh
DeWind, was carried out collaboratively by a team of Haitian and
American researchers that included Marie Lucie Brutus, Carolle
Charles, George Fouron, Antoine Louis Thomas, Beth Rosenthal, and
Norman Yamada. From 1985 to 1987, representatives of ninety-one
Haitian and sixty-three U.S. organizations in the New York
metropolitan area were interviewed (Glick Schiller et al. 1987, 1992).
These interviews were supplemented by observations in Haiti made
by team members who visited Haiti to maintain their own transna-
tional networks, and by 35 interviews conducted in Haiti in 1990 and
1991.[5] Twenty of these interviews were of a snowball sample in
Port-au-Prince of persons who had never emigrated but who were
supported by members of their families who had settled in the
United States.

Most of the data about Haitian immigrants in the United States
refer specifically to the New York Metropolitan area. According to
the 1990 U.S. Census, there were 290,000 persons in the United States
who claimed Haitian descent (Dreyfuss 1993:21). The Census
probably undercounts those who are undocumented, overstayed
their tourist visas, or did not wish to publicly claim Haitian ancestry.
By the end of the 1980s the Haitian population in the New York
Metropolitan area had reached at least 100,000 (DeWind 1987:4) and

was estimated by some to be as high as 500,000 (Dreyfus 1993:21). Estimates for the population of Haitian descent in Southern Florida by the decade of the 1980s range from 85,000 (Stepick 1986b; Stepick and Stepick 1990:73) to 300,000 (Dreyfus 1993:21). Smaller settlements of Haitian immigrants can be found in Chicago (Woldemikael 1989),[6] Boston and Philadelphia. Haitians have also become part of the migrant stream of farm workers in the eastern United States (Cassagnol Chierici 1990; Richman 1992b).

There are significant differences between Haitian immigrant experiences in these diverse locales because of differences in the class composition of the Haitians who have settled there, variations in the manner of their insertion into local economies, and differences in the ethnic politics of different regions in the United States. However, Haitian immigrants in all areas of the United States have developed transnational practices and have been active participants in a debate about *Dizyèm-nan*.

Although this book concentrates on Haitian settlement in the United States and the relationship these migrants have developed with Haiti, Haitian transnationalism in many cases includes relationships that span more than two countries. Individuals, families, and organizations that participated in social relations in the United States often maintained ties to the Haitian migrant population of Montreal, Canada, and there are also linkages to Haitians settled in France. One of the members of the research team, for example, had a spouse living in Montreal. Their young child has spent significant amounts of time in both Montreal and Port-au-Prince, the capital of Haiti, as well as in New York and understands herself to have three homes.

Haitian transnationalism has its own particularity shaped by the interpenetration of two sets of factors: Haitian hegemonic constructions of color, class, and nation that continue to configure immigrants' understandings of their identities;[7] and the emergence in Haiti, perhaps for the first time since the Haitian revolution, of a political debate about and identification with the Haitian state that encompasses all classes and regions of the country.

In the day-to-day construction of transnational social fields, individual migrants react to insecurity and racial exclusion by building personal networks. These networks help them maintain or improve their economic circumstances, reinforce or raise their social standing, and validate their self-esteem. In this sense, the emergence of Haitian transnationalism is a product of the reactions of individual Haitian migrants of different classes to their subordination by the dominant classes of the advanced capitalist countries. At the same time, Haitian transnationalism is a product of Haiti's long and continuing post-colonial subordination to global capital. The large scale Haitian migration to the United States that began in 1957 was a product of Haiti's history of subordination first to European and then U.S. domination.

III. THE GLOBAL CONTEXT OF THE EMERGENCE OF HAITIAN TRANSNATIONALISM

A. Dependency, Class Contention, and Migration

A contradiction runs through Haitian history: although Haiti achieved early national independence from European colonialism, the Haitian economy has long been subordinated to foreign capitalist interests (Nicholls 1974). The position of Haiti in the growth and current configuration of global capitalism and the type of class domination that emerged in independent Haiti as a result of this history and positioning have set the context for the emergence of Haitian transnationalism.

Although claimed for Spain by Columbus in 1492, the western portion of the island of Hispaniola was officially ceded to France in 1697, and France was the European power that left its political and cultural imprint on the plantation society that developed there. Haiti emerged as an independent nation in 1804 after a successful revolution in which the *affranchis*, (freed blacks and mulattos) joined with the African slaves that made up the majority of the population to defeat the military might of Napoleonic France. The Haitian leadership that emerged in the decades after the revolution strove to restore Haiti's plantations but lacked sufficient labor to do so. The freed slaves resisted plantation labor by withdrawing to the mountains and beginning peasant cultivation in a mixed subsistence and cash economy.[8]

In the 19th century, the emergent capitalist centers isolated Haiti politically, ridiculed Haiti in the sphere of world public opinion, and yet penetrated Haiti economically (Bellegarde-Smith 1990). Although Haitian laws had been written to restrict the role played by foreign economic interests, these laws were increasingly circumvented or ignored (Dupuy 1989; Plummer 1984; Bellegarde-Smith 1990).[9] In the second half of the 19th century, Haitian governments borrowed from foreign banks for operating expenses and to pay interest on past loans. Haitian political leaders, although they accompanied their actions with a rhetoric of fierce defense of the Haitian nation, compromised national autonomy in order to obtain outside support for their quest to obtain and hold state power (Nicholls 1974; Dupuy 1989). Foreign firms controlled shipping and played an increasing role in Haitian internal commerce.

Haiti's subordinate position in the world capitalist system shaped the nature of the Haitian class system and the manner in which the position of the dominant class was explained, justified and challenged. The political economy that this subordination engendered in the 19th century placed the country at the margins of the developing world economy, and then, in the 20th century, led to large-scale migrations. Until the twentieth century, there was virtually no middle class. There was a small dominant class that never represented more than 2–3% of the population (Leyburn 1966 [1941]:10). Although they were landowners, they were not a landed gentry, extracting most of their wealth from the peasantry by controlling commerce and the state. Haiti produced few cash crops beyond coffee. Peasants marketed small amounts of their subsistence crops of cassava, corn, and rice.

There were actually several distinct strata within the dominant class, each with its own history and cultural roots. Most visible was a cluster of urbane families who claimed as their ancestors the mulatto descendants of French planters and African slaves. This stratum looked to Europe and especially to France for its education, culture, religion, and values and commonly married its children to Europeans. Those who studied, lived, or married in Europe were not seen as emigrants from Haiti but as continuing actors in Haitian society, since the commercial, educational, and social networks that crossed Haitian political borders were part of the on-going structuring of Haitian society. In some sense one could argue that this dominant sector of the Haitian population was always transnational, since its social and economic connections linked it to Europe as well as Haiti. In general, this stratum, perhaps because its access to positions of dominance was limited to Haiti, generally returned and settled in Haiti although its networks did span borders.

While the dominant class has often been referred by Haitians as "milat" in the color terms that mark Haitian political discourse (see Pacquin 1983), there was also a stratum of important black families based in the smaller cities and towns of Haiti (Dupuy 1989). Many were descendants of military leaders of the Haitian revolution and an array of rural military leaders who had seized the presidency at various points in Haitian history and whose families remained important and powerful. By the 20th century there was also a commercial sector of Middle Eastern and European origin who are not mentioned in Haitian political discourse but who have played an important role in the nation's economy (Charles 1990a; Dreyfuss 1993).

A number of authors have designated this dominant class "the elite" (Leyburn 1966 [1941]:4; Mintz 1989 [1974]:271; Trouillot 1990:38), a term that signals the significant cultural distinctions that have existed from the time of the revolution between the mass of agricultural producers and the dominant class. However, it would seem more helpful for our purposes to adopt the language of authors who have focused their attention on political economy and class relations (Casimir-Liautaud 1975; Bellgarde-Smith 1980; Dupuy 1989). Because this dominant class has lived off the extraction of surplus, which then becomes capital for investment in other forms of wealth production, these authors have applied the term "bourgeoisie" to the dominant class in Haiti. This usage is followed in this discussion of Haiti (as it has been in the chapters on the eastern Caribbean).

In post-colonial states, the direct control of the state may be an aspect of the manner in which the bourgeoisie extracts the surplus created by the producing classes.[10] Contention over direct control of the state between sections of the bourgeoisie, as well as the bourgeoisie's ever increasing extraction of surplus from the bottom strata, have marked all of Haitian history and set the conditions for the migrations of the 20th century (Lundahl 1979; Dupuy 1989; Trouillot 1990; Fouron 1993). Since World War II, these competing factions have included members of an emergent middle class that under the Duvalier regime became the predominant public political actors (Dupuy 1989; Trouillot 1990).

In the past, as well as in the present, most of the Haitian people have lived by working small plots of land. The Haitian peasantry speak Kreyol and have a distinctive rural culture forged from African and European colonial practices and beliefs and from the slave culture that grew up on the Caribbean plantations (Trouillot 1990). The ethnographies written in the 1930s to the 1950s project images of remote and seemingly timeless peasant villages or "habitations," isolated from the outside world by their poverty, illiteracy, distinctive language, and traditions. (Herskovits 1937; Bastien 1961; Moral 1961). In some ways the picture was and remains accurate. Measuring 10,700 square miles with only one-third of the land mass arable, Haiti is a land of many mountains and few roads, and life in the countryside moves at a different pace than life in Port-au-Prince, Haiti's capital and by far its largest settlement. But the apparent isolation of the countryside masks the reality that the term "independent peasantry" is a misnomer, since Haitian peasant production has always been a subordinated sector of Haitian society and of the larger world economy. The wealth that supported the dominant class and foreign capitalist interests has been extracted through commercial transactions and by taxes rather than by rents.

By the end of the 19th century, the ever intensifying trajectory of impoverishment among the peasantry through the extraction of wealth led increasing numbers of peasants to seek to supplement family income by periodic stints of backbreaking labor as sugar workers in the Dominican Republic and Cuba (Lundahl 1983). At first, peasants went abroad to earn income to support their families and allow them to hold and buy land. By the middle of the 20th century they went abroad to feed themselves, if not their families. By that time Haiti had the densest population in the Western hemisphere, estimated to be over 5 million people.

By the beginning of the 20th century, European and U.S. capitalists had begun a greater degree of penetration with the development of a pattern of direct investment in Haiti. In 1915, in order to keep out its European competitors and to consolidate its interests, the United States invaded Haiti and proceeded militarily to suppress any opposition to U.S. domination. This more intense penetration led not to economic development but to economic dislocation. Large-scale agriculture was instituted in some regions of Haiti, and many peasants lost their land and were forced to seek work on Haiti's growing sugar, rice, and cotton plantations or as migrant cane workers. The mechanisms of extracting wealth from the peasantry were consolidated. When the United States troops left Haiti in 1934, the United States military left behind an army it had built, a President of its liking, and a place for itself as a major force in Haitian economic, political, and military affairs.[11]

The American occupation had a profound, long-term influence on Haiti. The migrants who made up the first large scale migration to the United States in the 1950s and 1960s came with understandings of their past that had been shaped by the Haitian experience of occupation. The occupation strengthened the economic and political dominance of the mulatto stratum of the bourgeoisie and yet engendered a tradition of resistance to American domination on the part of members of all classes. Resistance took the form of an armed rebellion in the countryside from 1918 to 1920, which, although predominantly peasant in composition, came to be symbolized by leaders such as Charlemagne Peralte who was a former military officer from a landowning family (Trouillot 1990).[12] The rebellion was brutally suppressed by the U.S. military. In reaction to the suppression of the rebellion and to the U.S. racism that justified and accompanied the occupation, Haitians writers, poets, and politicians began a renewed search for the African roots of Haitian identity.

While U.S. prejudice was directed against all Haitians, darker skinned Haitians were particularly disfavored, so that darker skinned people were forced out of the army and out of political power. The lines of social exclusion based on color were so tightly drawn that the American sociologist Leyburn (1966 [1941]), observing Haiti soon after the end of the occupation, described the Haitian class system as a caste system with the different castes distinguished by skin color.

This reinforcement of the color definitions of the class system occurred at a time when a limited but real economic expansion in the capital city led to the emergence of a "klas mwayèn" (Nicholls 1979; Paquin 1986). The term klas mwayèn, though literally translated as middle class in English, refers to individuals who occupied intermediary positions in production, being neither peasants nor persons with significant landholdings or commercial interests. The klas mwayèn includes skilled artisans, mechanics, small shopkeepers, as well as teachers, doctors, and bureaucrats who have no other source of wealth (Wingfield and Parenton 1965). During and immediately after World War II there was a small-scale and short-lived period of economic expansion in Haiti that allowed the klas mwayèn to grow. Their numbers were supplemented by the offspring of rich peasants who were able to obtain some education. Under President Estime (1946–50), whose assumption of power represented a reaction to the complicity of the mulattos in U.S. rule, many members of this class became part of the state apparatus. However, defined as black in the class/color landscape of Haiti, members of the klas mwayèn found their way to further social mobility blocked by the newly reinforced lines of discrimination against those of darker skin. The klas mwayèn might send their children to private schools with the elite, but their children would not be invited home to play; men of this class might achieve professional status as doctors or lawyers and speak perfect French, but the doors of the elite social clubs remained closed to them.

It was on the base of long smoldering anger at class privileges articulated in terms of skin color, anger felt by the masses of people and voiced by the emergent klas mwayèn, that François Duvalier shaped a power base, developed a black nationalist rhetoric (Nicholls 1984; Trouillot 1990), and came to power in 1957. The Duvalierists differed from previous class alliances that had seized control of the state, not by their use of force to seize and maintain control, but by the new degree to which the force of the state penetrated into all aspects of Haitian society, both in the city and in the countryside (Dupuy 1989). A secret police force called the *tonton makout* was set up to spy on people and report any and all dissent to the presidential palace. All organizations in Haiti, from the masonic lodges and student groups to voodoo temples, were infiltrated and members were recruited into the *makout*. Lower level members of the *makout* drawn from the rural and urban poor were given guns but no salary and were free to enrich themselves by taking what they wanted at gunpoint.

The regime coupled repression with an intensified and broadened effort to engage the population in political discourse. Once in power, Duvalier attempted to legitimate the black identified faction that dominated the state by linking it to the nation. Hence François Duvalier's infamous aphorism "I am the flag." Over time, the Duvalier regime was able to develop a clientage dependent on the regime for jobs, education, and privileges (Dupuy 1989). However, the alienation of the peasantry from the state continued, as did their migration as seasonal cane workers.[13] Meanwhile, increasing sectors of the upper strata, including much of the *klas mwayèn*, which had initially been supportive of the Duvalierist black nationalist rhetoric, reacted to the worsening political and economic conditions by fleeing Haiti.

B. The Intensification of Dependency and Migration

As the Duvalier regime consolidated its political and economic stranglehold over Haiti, increasing numbers of Haitians settled in the United States. The destination of the United States reflected the immense amount of influence that the United States had developed in Haiti during and after the U.S. invasion. The anti-Duvalierist opposition, the first to flee, chose the United States as their location of temporary exile because the United States was seen as having a direct influence on Haitian affairs.[14] Their goal was to discredit the Duvalier regime in the eyes of the U.S. government and obtain support for their campaign to overthrow it. Their presence shaped the future direction of the migration.

For generations, sections of both the Haitian peasantry and bourgeoisie had resided abroad, and there had always been a trickle of

Haitian immigration to the United States (Reid 1939; LaGuerre 1980). In the two decades before the Duvalier regime came to power, approximately 3,000 Haitians arrived as legal immigrants (U.S. Immigration and Naturalization Service 1970, 1990). However, until the wave of migration precipitated by the Duvalier regime, Haiti was not perceived by Haitians or by observers as a country of significant emigration, and the Haitian presence in the United States went almost unnoted. By the 1970s the Haitian migration to the United States had become significant, with 90,834 legal immigrants arriving between 1961 and 1980 and perhaps another 90,000 arriving without permanent resident status.[15] The significance taken on by the Haitian migration to the United States and its increasing public prominence can be traced to its growing numbers, to the increased level of capitalist penetration in Haiti beginning in the 1970s, and to the emergence within the United States of the Haitians as a publicly identified black ethnic group (Glick [Schiller] 1975).

1. "We'll Be Home Next Month"

Haitian transnationalism developed slowly, as individual migrants and migrant families struggled to come to terms with the situation they had left behind in Haiti and the social and economic situation they confronted when they arrived in the United States. Among the first migrants to flee the turmoil that marked the coming to power of the Duvalier regime in 1957 were several thousand persons who were political opponents of Duvalier. Decades later, they recalled that they were so sure that they were political exiles who would be returning to Haiti in a matter of months that for years they didn't unpack their bags. By their continuing orientation towards Haiti, even as they settled into life in the United States, obtained jobs, learned English, went to school, sought to reestablish themselves in their professions, and joined organizations, these immigrants set the stage for the development of Haitian transnationalism.

However, during this initial period, Haitian immigrants actually had little contact with Haiti beyond communication with their families. Several factors combined initially to prevent the type of circulation of the population that later would facilitate and become the foundation of transnational migration. During the years from 1957 to 1972, when François Duvalier was President, a large "undocumented" sector of perhaps 50,000, perhaps as many as one half of the Haitian immigrant population, used tourist visas to enter the United States and then overstayed the terms of their visas. They were unable to go back and forth. Even those with legal status feared to return to Haiti to visit because of the continued political and economic stranglehold on Haiti maintained by the Duvalier regime. Continued political repression and fear of the secret police, whose surveillance it was believed extended into the United States, impeded Haitian immigrants' efforts to establish organized activities of any type that extended into Haiti.

Despite these limited contacts with Haiti during this first period of settlement, Haitian immigrants to the United States continued to look toward Haiti because they saw the United States as having very little to offer besides a temporary haven. The situation was sharpest for the bourgeoisie and upper strata of the *klas mwayèn*, who had left positions of social and political importance in Haiti only to face impoverishment and discrimination in the United States. Unable to transfer their landholdings and commercial position into ready cash, and without knowledge of English, diplomats became elevator operators, lawyers parked cars, doctors became orderlies, and teachers became factory workers. People who had staffs of live-in servants all their lives became maids and waiters. In seeking work in the United States, professionals faced not only the problems of their lack of documents and of facility in English, but also their loss of credentials.[16] Whether they worked three jobs to pay for the run-down house they had purchased in Queens, or lived in a single room occupancy hotel in Manhattan with the strong smell of urine in every corridor, they dreamt of returning to their lives of luxury and privilege in Haiti.[17]

Most of these immigrants linked their migration to the repressive brutal nature of the Duvalier regime and its devastating effects on the Haitian economy. However, the large scale influx of Haitian immigrants to the United States from the 1960s to the 1980s also reflected a global restructuring of capitalism in which a new wave of capital investment in post-colonial countries, in the form of export processing industries, agribusiness, and food importation, disrupted local economies and prompted large-scale migrations (Sassen 1988; DeWind and McKinney 1988). This trend became more evident in Haiti beginning in 1972, when François Duvalier's son, Jean-Claude, became "President For Life" after the death of his father.

2. Intensified Capital Penetration and the Launching of Haitian Transnationalism

Jean-Claude welcomed a greatly increased expansion of United States direct investment into the Haitian economy. Export-processing factories were established, some owned by Haitian businessmen, although the more successful projects often became directly owned by foreign capital (Dupuy 1989). The growth of the export processing industry, although the most dynamic sector of the economy in terms of the production of profits, did not provide economic development for Haiti (DeWind and McKinney 1988). The new export processing industries produced relatively few jobs and these paid wages below the level of subsistence. The statistical picture of the Haitian economy contained in reports by the United States Agency for International Development (USAID) tell the story (DeWind and McKinney 1988:107–110). Between 1971 and 1981 the population of Port-au-Prince, where the Haitian assembly industry was located, grew by approximately 35,000 persons a year. During that period new jobs in export processing plants grew at the rate of 3,000 per year. Thirty-eight percent of persons actively seeking work were unemployed; when one added those who were only able to find part-time work, those who sought but were unable to obtain full time work soared to fifty-two percent of the workforce.

In a survey of 500 assembly plant workers conducted in 1979, average wages were reported to be $55 per month, with 35% earning less than $50 (Delatour and Voltaire 1980 cited in DeWind and McKinney 1988:123). This was far under the absolute poverty level, which was $70 a month in 1980, meaning "they were unable to satisfy their essential needs for food, water, housing, clothing, health care and education" (DeWind and McKinney 1988:123). The extreme concentration of wealth at the top of the society continued. In 1981 the World Bank estimated that .8% of the Haitian population possessed 44.8% of the wealth (World Bank 1981:6 cited in Stepick 1986a:3).

The expansion of the population of Port-au-Prince reflected not a growth in employment opportunities in the urban area, but deteriorating conditions in the countryside. The problem of increased population densities on unproductive soil that confronted Haitian peasants continued to grow as the population climbed to close to seven million by the 1980s.[18] In addition, the price of agricultural goods in the internal marketplace dropped, as Haitian peasants had to compete with food imported from the United States through U.S. assistance programs. The combination of the increasingly depleted soil and the development of food imports led to the contradiction of a country of peasants relying on imported food.

The 1970s were marked by two migration trends, both of which had long-term implications for the development of Haitian transnationalism: migration from Haiti increased, while a small sector of the migrants returned to Haiti. A small but significant number of Haitian technocrats, engineers, managers, bankers, and technicians educated in the United States and Canada returned to Haiti in the wake of the growth of export-processing sector and the promise by Jean-Claude of political reforms. They returned to Haiti to work for international banks, export processing industries, and the nongovernmental agencies dispensing international aid. There is some indication that this return also included members of upper class mulatto families, who played in important role in the development and top management of export processing industries (Carolle Charles, personal communication).

But return is not quite the right word. For the mulatto families, as well as the technocrats of middle class origins, one could say that they had always stayed rooted in the Haitian social milieu. Abroad they had been extensions of their family networks, with a core of many families always maintaining a base in Haiti. On the other hand, those who "returned" to Haiti did not disrupt the commercial, professional, and familial ties they had established in the United States and Canada. The density of the connections between Haiti and Haitians in the United States grew as travel and communication between the population in Haiti and those settled abroad became less politically suspect and consequently much more frequent.[19]

Many more people left Haiti than returned in the 1970s and the class composition of the migration dramatically changed. As a result of the increasingly desperate economic situation and continued political repression, large numbers of the rural population joined their urban compatriots in leaving Haiti. The increasing numbers of Haitians who came by plane either as legal immigrants or as "tourists" who overstayed their visas were joined by an estimated 35,000–45,000 arrived in between 1971 and 1980 by small boat (Silk 1986:16). In 1981 the U.S. Coast Guard began a policy of "interdiction" of boats leaving Haiti. Boarding Haitian vessels in international waters, they took the passengers prisoner, sank the boats, and returned the refugees to Haiti.

Those who arrived by boat settled primarily in southern Florida, settling both in a Miami neighborhood that became known as "Little Haiti" and in several of the more rural counties of Florida. Suburban

Florida also became a second home for individuals affiliated with the Duvalier regime. Many wealthy families established residences in the United States in case they lost their positions in Haiti and began to commute between Florida and Haiti. The enclaves of wealthy Duvalierists lived apart from organized Haitian life and public view in the United States; Haitians of rural origin, many without schooling or experience in urban life, became the visible sector of the Haitian immigrant population.[20] Their presence affected the perceptions of Haitians held and popularized by the U.S. media. These images contributed to the formation of a Haitian identity in the United States and the configuration of Haitian immigrant organizational and political life, a sequence of events that will be described in the next chapter.

In the 1970s and 1980s, the economic dependency of Haiti on the United States grew tremendously. In addition to loans and direct investment, Haiti became tied to the United States by a large network of development, health, and social service programs sponsored in Haiti by U.S. philanthropic and religious organizations. An increasing number of these programs received funding from agencies of the U.S. government (DeWind and McKinney 1988). However, during this period the Haitian economy, according to World Bank reports, also became dependent on remittances sent by Haitians abroad. Haitian migrants sent over 100 million dollars a year, an amount that was equivalent to the foreign aid being received by the Haiti government (DeWind and McKinney 1988:164).[21]

A survey conducted in New York in 1987 of a convenience sample of 487 Haitians revealed that the vast majority of adults (91%) were sending remittances (DeWind 1987). Adult respondents reported remitting an average of $1336.70 to Haiti within the previous twelve months (DeWind 1987:4). No relationship was found between a respondent's occupation or income and the amount of money sent to Haiti. People in their fifties sent the most money, averaging $1528.30. Women sent more money to Haiti than did the men, with women who headed households in New York sending the greatest amount. The frequency of sending remittances varied from once a year to every week, with an average of 9.7 times a year. While the most frequent mode of transfer was money transfer businesses (71%), twenty-three percent usually used personal networks to hand deliver the money and the majority of the people (61%) had done this at some point during the year. In addition to providing insights into the scale of contributions that Haitian immigrants make to the Haitian economy, data on remittance give us a glimpse of the pervasiveness of ongoing transnational connections among Haitian immigrants.

3. The Duvalier Regime Collapses: Full-Fledged Transnationalism Begins

By the 1980s the Haitian population of the United States had grown enormously with estimates varying from half a million to over a million people of Haitian descent settled abroad — mainly in the United States — out of a total population of approximately 6,630,000 (Charles 1990a:152; Kaleidoscope 1991:1). The growing layers of interconnection established by Haitians in the United States and Haiti, as well as the ever deteriorating economic conditions in Haiti, contributed to the social unrest and political awakening that took place in the Haiti in the 1980s. Finally, in February 1986, Jean-Claude Duvalier boarded an American military jet and fled to France. Although ruled primarily by military juntas in the years to follow, the political conditions changed sufficiently to allow transnational political activities and organizations. Moreover, the pattern of dependency, economic deterioration, and migration continued.

With the flourishing of transnational political activities, Haitian transnationalism came of age. By 1990, when Aristide was elected President of Haiti, Haitian transnationalism had become an acknowledged part of Haitian political practices and had been incorporated into Haitian nation building projects. Under Jean-Claude, organizational ties between Haitian religious and hometown organizations had developed, but political repression imposed severe constraints on transnational political activity.

That Haitian transnationalism was to become pervasive, however, was not apparent in the first flush of excitement over the fall of the Duvalier regime in 1986. Instead, in public interviews and in private conversations between friends, one heard people of all strata declaring their intention of returning to Haiti. In the years that followed, while some people who had been active in political organizing or transnational activities of various kinds decided to "go home" to Haiti, most Haitian immigrants stayed in the United States. However, there was an upsurge in Haitian nationalism among people who had become firmly rooted in the United States. The upsurge first became highly visible in New York in February 1986 when a demonstration in support of the uprising in Haiti swelled to thousands of people who danced and sang their way down Eastern Parkway in Brooklyn and stood in the snow in Grand Army plaza, cheering wildly while waving the red and blue Haitian flag that had been outlawed by Duvalier. In the months to follow, Haitians in New York, for the first time since the beginning of the migration, flaunted their Haitian identity. Haitian taxi drivers decorated their cabs with bumper stickers declaring "Haiti Libere" ("Haiti is liberated"). Haitians could be seen in the subway wearing tee shirts or buttons with Haitian flags. Virtually all Haitian immigrant organizations were swept up in the excitement and began to discuss organizing activities towards Haiti and setting up organizational linkages or offices in Haiti.

The movement that elected Father Jean Bertrand Aristide President of Haiti in 1990 and the protest movement that called for his return to power when he was ousted from power in 1991 only eight months after his inauguration increased the interest a great many Haitians — both in Haiti and settled abroad — had in having a voice in the political processes of the Haitian state. Aristide's presidency marked the first sustained involvement of the masses of the Haitian people in the Haitian political process since the Haitian revolution of 1804. The coalition that brought Aristide to power, by awarding him 67% of the vote in the most democratic election in Haitian history, had its base in parts of the countryside, among the urban poor in Haiti's secondary towns, and in the capital city. Yet, many of the people who built the political coalition that backed Aristide's candidacy, and who then made up the personnel of his government, were transnationals who had spent long years outside of Haiti and had maintained ongoing ties that crossed borders.

In September 1991, the class coalition that had dominated the state under the Duvalier regime and continued to control the Haitian economy and military overthrew Aristide and began a brutal repression of Aristide's base. As always, the political crisis deepened the economic crisis, as political insecurity made daily commerce problematical. The small export-processing sector, already reduced by global economic slowdowns and five years of political insecurity, became further reduced. Fuel and supplies became scarce because of embargoes imposed by the Organization of American States to challenge the military dictatorship that had replaced Aristide. Again thousands of people fled Haiti by boat, putting an international spotlight on the political and economic situation in Haiti and the Haitian migration to the United States. First Bush and then Clinton upheld the interdiction begun by Reagan. The U.S. continued to capture Haitians on the high seas, refuse most requests for political asylum, and return refugees to Haiti. However, while the tide of migration was slowed by both the interdiction and the embargo, the efforts of Haitian immigrants in the United States to change U.S. foreign policy toward Haiti strengthened their commitments, both toward political participation in U.S. political processes and toward changing the political situation in Haiti.

IV. THE BUILDING OF TRANSNATIONAL SOCIAL FIELDS

A. *The Family as a Transnational Social Relationship*

Since I was a young girl, I supported my whole family, you hear? Now that I've come to N.Y., its worse. I have bills here and there to pay. My husband is dead, its been 8 years since he died, and I'm taking care of bills here and in Haiti. I'll tell you, I wake up around 4 am to go to work in New Jersey, and all the time, throughout the night, I worry that my ride will leave without me. And there is no other work, so I can't quit what I have for something else. I'll give you an example: If I quit my job now, what would I do for the bills here and in Haiti? Because once the month starts, in 15 days, they start watching the mail to see when I am sending the money. Well I can tell you, if I leave my job, my whole family would die, because I'm the one who keeps them afloat (Kerner 1991:4).

* * *

Observe a flight leaving from New York to Port-au-Prince. There are children of all ages going to stay with grandparents, aunts, or uncles, sometimes for a vacation, or for a year, or for an indefinite period of time. There are senior citizens, having come to stay for weeks or years with adult children but now returning home, attired in new clothes. There are parents, immigration papers finally in hand, returning to visit family and children left as babies who are now almost grown. There are adults on vacation, carrying every imaginable size and shape of box. Some people save all year for the several weeks that they can return to Haiti well clothed and shod with all the latest consumer items. Many of the things are for the house that they are furnishing in Haiti. Someone else may be going home for a family wedding, bringing with her not only the wedding present but the flour, sugar, and decorations to make the wedding cake. Most people returning bring food, since meat and even rice are cheaper in the United States.

Returning to Haiti costs money. Immacula Pierre Louise, who had arrived by boat in 1980, described her return in 1989 this way:

In February the children called and said my mother was sick. I decided to go to Haiti. I asked for time at work. I bought a ticket for 460 dollars. I spent three hundred dollars for clothes, sneakers, dresses for my little girl. I bought six dresses for $8, one pair of shoes for $20.00. I bought a pair of sneakers for $40, I bought material for a jacket and pants for $40. I bought 10 towels, I bought one sheet, I bought 6 night gowns for my mother, I bought six cans of Hawaiian punch, I bought a big 22 pound turkey.

I lost many things in the airport in Haiti. They took 3 towels, bras, panties, and a camera. They took it from the bags. My sister was at the airport with her husband and my nephews — 13 and 15.

I saw everyone. They all asked for money. They think that everyone who goes to New York is very rich. I said I don't have a lot of money. I had taken $600 for my pocket money. I changed American money into goudes on the street — you get more money.

I gave some to my sister, my niece, my brother. I gave my cousin money. They need it to live, to eat.

I will send things to my sister who has the funeral home. Rice, beans, ammonia, Ajax, and many things.

When I came I bought a mattress for mother and one for my children and a bed. My mother goes to a private hospital all the time. I bought shoes for my niece. I bought a lot of IV serum for my mother. I bought vitamins. They say she has a weakness. And each day I bought food. She lives in the house of my brother with my children and the wife of my brother and his children. They have two rooms.

Meeting a plane arriving from Haiti, one finds a scene similar to that at departure. Again, we see a wide variety of kin. Teenagers coming to visit or live with their parents, sometimes parents they haven't seen since early childhood. Grandparents, aunts, uncles arriving to visit and also to watch the children. Young women, poor relatives, or the children of family servants arriving to be family servants in New York. Siblings, cousins, godchildren arriving to live in the basement or attic of kin and study and work. The type and quantity of goods being carried would be much reduced, however.

While the role of family in facilitating migration is apparent, the continuing significance of kinship in the lives of migrants after they are long settled in the United States, and the growth over time in the type and quantity of transactions which take place between kin located in both countries, requires further explanation. It cannot just be assumed that an immigrating population will continue to have many relatives back home and feel obligations to them. Kin obligations, as just demonstrated in the example of Immacula returning home, can be expensive and onerous (LaGuerre 1978). Why do so many Haitians of various strata and classes send money on a regular basis to kin in Haiti? Why is money sent, less frequently, but in sizeable amounts, from Haiti to family members in the United States?

To answer these questions it is first necessary to define what is meant by family and kinship in Haiti. Most students of the Haitian family have distinguished between the peasant family, seen as African based, polygamous, and extended, and the upper class urban family, seen as European and monogamous (Herskovits 1937; Leyburn 1966 [1941]). In reality, faced with continuing uncertainty about life in Haiti, where economic life has always been circumscribed and subordinated to both global capitalist dynamics and local political uncertainties, both classes have relied on extended kin networks, nonresidentially based, that extend through consanguineal lines and affinal relationships.

In Haiti, then, the term family refers to a network of individuals in a series of households, united by an ideology of common kindred and interests, that functions as a unit of social reproduction, including the reproduction of personnel, gender divisions, and class position. As such, an aspect of family is the allocation and distribution of labor and resources. The Haitian system of personalized relations continues to have meaning in the context of the continuing capitalist underdevelopment of the Haitian economy and its subordinate position in the world system, a subordination which fuels and reinforces the conditions of political instability (Laguerre 1982).

Children have always served as a building block of the family system, since it is in the reproduction and socialization of children that the continuity of the society and its different social strata are ensured. In the upper and middle classes, the high value placed on women's chastity has allowed these families to control the relationships and alliances within which women would produce children. In peasant families, matings that produced offspring, as well as formal marriage, were ways to extend networks, and place kin on the land (Bastien 1961).

Children are a link to the future. The Haitian sayings *"petit se richès"* (children are wealth) or *"petit pi fò passe mariaj"* (children are stronger than marriage) (Smucker 1982:189) continues to represent the Haitian survival strategy of building and maintaining kinship networks. The continuity of family ties remains an important concern of Haitian immigrants. This concern is reflected in reports by Haitian social workers in the United States (Saint Cyr-Delpe 1987) that Haitian parents of all class backgrounds attempt to determine and supervise the friendships of their teenage children, especially their daughters. The protectiveness of this parental pattern as well as the struggle by parents to control a daughter's choice of mates, persists as a route to maintaining kinship networks.

In the course of the past three decades, the many Haitians who have migrated have found that maintaining their personalized kin and pseudo-kin networks has been critical to their migrations. Personnel and resources moved around within kin networks have maximized the chances for members of family networks to survive and prosper in a situation in which neither home nor host country has offered security. The impetus to maintain personal networks then comes not only from loyalty and sentiment but from a realization, which actually grows over time, of the precariousness of rooting oneself in the United States. Individuals verbalize many motivations for maintaining these connections. They talk about the growing crisis in the U.S. economy and the high rate of unemployment; the persistent racism and national chauvinism that are growing in response to the U.S. economic decline; the high cost of living and the shortage of housing; and the continued undocumented status of a portion of the Haitian immigrant population, who are never sure if they will be discovered and deported.

For those from the bourgeoisie and the *klas mwayèn*, the loss of status and social position experienced in the United States can be compensated for by continuing to invest in social position in Haiti. The widespread practice of building or buying homes in Haiti and then furnishing them with all the accoutrements of a luxurious life can be a reflection of this concern. This type of investment cannot be an individual activity; most often kin back home supervise and maintain the residency. Investment in class status takes place through the reproduction of social relationships and the continuity of family ties across borders.

Marie Rose,[22] for example, comes from the *klas mwayèn*, and from adolescence onward lived and was educated in Brooklyn, New York. She obtained a masters of nursing and became head of a unit in a Brooklyn hospital, working long hours but earning a good salary. In New York she has friends, family, and a secure position. However, throughout the year she invests in her home in Haiti. The house in New York that she shares with a sister and her sister's young child and the adolescent child of another sister is often filled with her purchases for her home in Haiti — one year a bar, another year a barbecue grill. These items will be useful in the round of parties she will host during the two weekends a year she lives in Haiti. Her husband moved back to Haiti several years ago and the Mercedes she bought was sent back with him. She has no children of her own, but on one recent trip gave an elaborate baptism party in Haiti for her sister's child, an occasion to create and reaffirm her social position and participate in the social and ritual life of her class in Haiti.

For others, money or goods sent to family members may contribute to the maintenance and education of children, siblings, cousins, or the care of elders in ways that are less of a financial drain than if they were supported in the United States. Children born in the United States, and consequently United States citizens, often are sent home to be raised by family members. Or children are left behind with family members, while first one parent and then the other make their way to the United States and begin the settling in process. This pattern of child fostering is especially prevalent in working class households, and children may move between households in the United States for weeks or months (Gutwirth 1988), as well as between households in the United States and Haiti.

Children are sent to households of various relatives located in the United States and in Haiti not only because these households provide child care but also because children can be used as a way of maintaining kin networks. Households that remain in Haiti are simultaneously a drain on resources and a staging area for ongoing migration strategies.

Because households extend transnationally, the pattern of transnational family ties is transmitted across generations. For example, Yvonne, a woman who came as a visitor to the United States in the 1950s, returned to Haiti to retire after working two jobs cleaning houses for 30 years. She had come as a visitor and had easily gotten her green card. She then sent for her sister and her husband and children. Her children grew up in the United States, but also returned to Haiti, the son after living for a period in Montreal. The education and social standing he had obtained in the United States yielded this son an excellent position as chief accountant for a big Haitian firm. The other child, a daughter, is married to an engineer who works for the government. This daughter tends a small store stocked with goods carried back from visits to the United States and Canada but there are few customers. She has begun talking about returning to the United States with the children. They have been in Haiti eleven years. She and the children are American citizens, as is her mother, the woman who began the pattern of migration over 30 years ago.

Disparities and differences of interest exist within families as well as between them. This has long been true in Haiti, where extended family networks can contain a prosperous center family linked to multiple dependent kin who provide services or loyalty in exchange for the use of land or assistance in obtaining employment (Larose 1975). To understand the development of transnational families as a collective strategy of survival is not to maintain that we are looking at a balanced and harmonious system of kin relations.

Hostility often arises between family members left behind in Haiti and those who have migrated (Richman 1987; Richman 1992b). Family members in Haiti find that too little is being sent to care for all the responsibilities that the immigrant has left behind. From the perspective of the immigrant, the burden to feed, clothe and educate those left behind may seem unbearable. "When I have work I send $200 a month for my mother and for my children," explains a woman who takes home $800 dollars a month from her office-cleaning job and pays $400 rent on her apartment.

Some of the tensions within transnational families come from the individualized goals stressed by U.S. consumer culture and the more collective familial strategies of survival that reflect the insecurities faced by the migrants both in the United States and Haiti. The base in Haiti, however precarious, is generally maintained as a necessary hedge against failure to establish or maintain employment and a household in the United States, as well as a place for retirement. The clash between different personal goals and the need to maintain the family networks may occur on a daily basis, because much of the migrant populations, from doctors to laborers, live in extended households. Household composition is shaped by the need to draw on several incomes to pay the high rents in places such as New York, by the housing of kin who provide childcare, and by kinship obligations.

A Haitian doctor welcomes into his household two of his brother's daughters. Their presence puts strains on his marriage. Used to having household work done by servants, they do not assist the doctor's wife in cooking and cleaning. She is particularly angry because she has nieces and nephews who also wish to come to New York.

* * *

A Haitian college professor and his wife, a hospital clerk, and their two teenage children provide housing for an adult male cousin who lives in the basement. The basement is the room the professor was using as a study to write the book required for him to obtain tenure. His search for space to write is compounded by the fact that his wife's cousin, a maid on Long Island, comes to stay on weekends and family members from Haiti come several times a year for extended visits.

* * *

A Haitian woman, who works as a domestic, houses in her one-room apartment both her common law husband and three small children and her brother who has arrived from Haiti for an extended stay. Her brother sends much of what he earns back home to support a business he is building in Haiti and the family he left behind. Her husband provides a part of the rent, but contributes nothing for food, the upkeep of the apartment, or for his children's clothing and care. He has children in several different households in the United States and Haiti, including two children the couple produced together in Haiti whom he doesn't support.

* * *

On the surface, the tensions within the transnational family seem to be between the separate interests of each individual and the broader family network. The underlying contradiction, in point of fact, is that neither the efforts of each individual family member nor the collective family networks provides long-term solutions to the structural inequality that confronts the entire Haitian immigrant population. Transnational family networks are the underbelly of the global penetration of capitalism. In building transnational families as strategies of survival, Haitians keep themselves from being economically and emotionally crushed by the grip of global capital. Yet by their successful use of transnational families to keep themselves alive and hopeful, Haitian transmigrants alleviate pressures on the political and economic structures that make their lives so precarious.

B. Economic Incorporation and Transnational Economic Relations

By the 1990s, the Haitian immigrant population in the United States was diverse in its class background in Haiti and had been incorporated into the United States labor force and economy in a variety of ways. However, although there are few statistics available, it would seem that the bulk of the population is incorporated into strata of the working class (Charles 1990a).

Some people arrive in the United States specifically to work for other Haitians, most commonly as babysitters and maids. From the moment of their arrival, they are embedded in transnational communications and relationships established by the family members or patrons who have sent for them. But most of the employment that the migrants find is within the larger society. In New York, Haitian workers make up an important part of service sector industries, where they are employed as home health aides, domestics, and hotel and hospital workers. They also make up sectors of small-scale garment and light industrial enterprises that have been built on cheap immigrant labor (Charles 1990a). In many of these contexts, the immigrants seem fully incorporated, and their identification seems to be as part of the work force rather than in terms of ethnicity, nationality, or race. When these industries have become unionized or when strikes have developed over working conditions, Haitian workers have been found to be among the labor militants.

However, income earned at work in the United States is deployed in ways that maintain links to Haiti. Remittances are sent to insure that kin at home have food, water, and shelter. Of the 20 persons interviewed in Haiti in 1990 who had never settled in the United States but had relatives who were transmigrants, only two of the adults had worked steadily in the past five years. They, like ever growing numbers in Haiti, were dependent on remittances for the bulk of their livelihood. Money sent home is also used, if possible, to purchase land or build houses, making building one of the only flourishing industries of Haiti. The road from Port-au-Prince to Les Cayes in the south of Haiti, for example, is lined with newly constructed cement houses or refurbished houses financed by the money of transmigrants. Earnings are also invested in small businesses in Haiti that are staffed by kin. For example, Immacula, who cleans offices, sends supplies to her sister's funeral parlor in Haiti. In exchange, her sister helps to care for those of Immacula's children who live in Haiti.

Increasing numbers of Haitian immigrants are employed in white collar jobs in both private industry and the public sector. Haitians have become bank clerks, secretaries, computer operators, and hospitals clerks. Often there is little in their workforce identity or demeanor besides a different accent that speaks of their particular cultural origins. People from this stratum also send remittances to Haiti and they are even more fully involved in purchasing and furnishing houses in Haiti. They also may set up small stores in Haiti or assist relatives who have business in Haiti by shipping goods to Haiti or by providing housing in the United States for family members who come to replenish their stock.

Haitian professionals include a large number of doctors, dentists, teachers, and increasing numbers of lawyers, engineers, social workers, psychologists, nurses, administrators, and academics. Although many have credentials valid in both Haiti and the United States, most do not carry out professional activities in both locations. However, a growing number of Haitian professionals who work in the United States seek to establish some kind of relationship to Haiti beyond family networks. For example, a group of Haitian doctors, many of whom were raised and educated in the United States, attempted to raise funds to build a research institute in Haiti devoted to the exploration of traditional medicine. In another instance, Haitian academics linked to prominent personages in Haiti, have worked to open a university that will prepare Haitian students with the skills necessary to compete in either Haiti or the United States.

When professionals return to Haiti to live, the motivation is more often political than professional. The income to be earned in Haiti is often small and uncertain, but the opportunities for political participation on the level of national politics, nearly impossible for this population in the United States, is much greater in Haiti. Many members of the Aristide government came from this sector.

In our discussions of family we have already seen that familial networks provide the capital and serve as the supply line of small commercial enterprises in Haiti. These businesses are not transnational, but they often depend on transnational ties for their existence. Haitians prefer to transfer capital back to Haiti rather than open a business in the United States, because in Haiti one does not have to worry about extensive regulation and taxes. However, New York has enough Haitian businesses that Haitian's publish their own business directory. Most of these businesses are not transnational and almost all are very small. They include car services, grocery stores, barbershops, bakeries, real estate, insurance, dry cleaners, money transfer companies, shipping companies, travel agencies, recording studios, restaurants, furniture stores, auto mechanics, photographers, electronic repairs, and house construction.

Most wealthy Haitians have not begun businesses. Although members of the Haitian upper class were among the earliest of the migrants, their capital was not liquid and they were unable to invest in the United States. People who made fortunes because of linkage to or direct participation in the Haitian government have bought expensive real estate in Florida and keep a home base there as well as in Haiti. They seem to have little interest in investing their wealth in productive enterprises in the United States — or in Haiti.

However, there is one sector of Haitian business in the United States that is proving to be a great commercial success. These are businesses that facilitate the transnational activities of Haitians by transferring money, goods, and information. Several Haitian money transfer businesses have developed with bases in many cities and towns in the United States that have Haitian settlements. Haitian travel agencies that bring people back and forth between Haiti also flourish. The money transfer business has become so big that in 1987 Citibank commissioned a study to ascertain whether the profits were large enough for them to begin to compete with the Haitian entrepreneurs who have monopolized the field. One office in Cap-Haitien in the North of Haiti was reported to be receiving $28,000 a day in 1991 (Boccio 1991:4A). DeWind (1987:4) estimated that in 1987, 99.5 million dollars was sent from New York City to Haiti. Eighty-one percent of those sending money to Haiti used money transfer houses at least some of the time. Money transfer business provide other services which facilitate communication between Haiti and the United States. Respondents in DeWind's study of remittances (1987) reported that they also sent cassettes (37%), documents (32%), letters (24%), and airline tickets (5%). It is indicative of the significance of Haitian transnationalism that the most profitable businesses are those that have developed because of the transnational activities of Haitian migrants and that contribute to the continuation and expansion of these activities.

Business enterprises that produce the transnational culture may also have begun to flourish. The growing Haitian recording business, for example, has become a fully transnational business. The production of the recording may begin in Haiti, the record may be mixed in New York, and the distribution may take place in both the United States and Haiti simultaneously (Gage Avril, personal communication). Musical styles and cultural tastes developed by and reflected in Haitian recordings take place in a transnational social field that spans and unites the experience and outlook of people living in Haiti and the United States. Although this interchange of cultural production began in the 1970s, it was really only at the end of the 1980s, in the context of the end of the Duvalier regime and the flowering of Haitian transnationalism, that cultural production in Haiti and the United States has become fused.

C. The Emergence of Transnational Communications

Kin-based communications using telephones and cassettes brought through kin networks or shipped by money transfer companies continue to provide the basic interconnections between Haiti and the

United States. However, Haitian newspapers distributed both in the United States and Haiti and radio and television programs produced in the United States, but with direct transmissions or recent footage from Haiti, intensify the immediacy of communication developed through kin networks. Cultural performance is also becoming transnational.

International phone calls are made in Haiti from phone company offices, so someone without a telephone may find it easier to talk to a family member in the United States who has a phone than to family members in other regions of Haiti. Regular phone calls from the United States allow family networks to incorporate members in both locations into the decision making of daily life. Such communications have also allowed transmigrants in the United States to obtain news rapidly about political events and changing social currents in Haiti.

Interaction between family members is maintained by many persons who have no phones, and by some who do, by sending cassettes, which can be sent and delivered through any of the money transfer services. The cassette, like the telephone, communicates personalized information in which the tone of the voice adds to the immediacy of the message. Kinship expectations are reinforced and the structure of family authority maintained among family members of rural backgrounds in an emerging formalized style of cassette communication (Richman 1987, 1992b). The post-Aristide embargo, which brought mail to a halt, did not seriously effect transnational communications because of the widespread use of both the telephone and the cassettes and letters carried back and forth by friends and relatives.

By 1985, approximately a dozen different Haitian radio programs were being broadcast and five different weekly Haitian newspapers were being printed in New York. Some of the radio programs used university stations, but Haitian entrepreneurs increasingly established themselves on commercial stations. Haitian programs on commercial stations as well as newspapers were supported by both Haitian and non-Haitian sponsors.

By the 1990s the number of newspapers and radio programs had fallen, but Haitian communications were flourishing with the addition of Haitian cable television programs and the development of two Haitian radio stations in the New York area. The radio stations, broadcasting twenty-four hours a day, were able to reach large audiences because they were accessible to the illiterate as well as to people who had little leisure time for reading or watching television.

These radio stations are a particularly interesting commercial development, because the stations sell a device or specially altered radio costing from between $75 and $100 dollars that must be used in order to receive their transmissions. Together the two stations report 60,000 subscribers (Dreyfuss 1993:81).

At first the various Haitian media, while orientated towards Haiti, were not transnational in their structure. The eruption of mass popular protest that marked the end of the Duvalier regime opened a vital but highly vulnerable space for organized transnational communications. The formal commitment of all political factions to constitutional rule, in a struggle for power played out in the realm of international public opinion, prevented the total censorship of the media that was commonplace under the Duvaliers.

Organizationally, some of the Haitian media began to span borders. In the mid-eighties a Haitian journalist, who had been expelled from Haiti several years before, returned to Haiti and began the first transnationally based radio station with money and political backing from Haitian transmigrants. Soon after, two of the Haitian newspapers based in New York began distributing their weekly publications in Haiti and continued their base in the United States. Their focus, which had always been on Haiti, continued to be Haiti, but news and advertisements from New York, Montreal, and Miami were continued.

Perhaps even more significantly, Haitian radio and television in New York began to use telephone hook ups to broadcast news directly from Haiti. Now a Haitian immigrant may be sitting in a kitchen in Brooklyn or driving a taxi up the East Side Drive in Manhattan and listening to news of a home town in Haiti. This simultaneity of communication and the ability to obtain news from Haiti became a crucial link in the ability of people in Haiti to find out what was happening in Haiti in the political repression following Aristide's ouster in 1991, when anti-government radio was suppressed in Haiti. By maintaining reporters in Haiti and utilizing the continuing telephonic connections, Haitian radio and television stations transmitting in the United States have enabled Haitians in the United States to receive immediate descriptions of events in Haiti. This news, filtered through their own perceptions, is then transmitted by Haitian immigrants back to Haiti through family networks maintained by phone and cassettes.

Cultural performance also creates a new kind of transnational moment. Prior to the fall of Duvalier, musicians, and the production of plays and music had moved between Haiti and the United States, but there were restrictions. Performers favored by the Duvalier regime tended to be boycotted in New York. Those in favor in the United States faced political repression in Haiti. For example, Ti Manno, a Haitian singer, achieved popularity before his death in 1985 in both Haiti and the United States, but not simultaneously and not for the same songs. He spent separate periods of his life in Haiti and in the United States. His critique of Haitian society and his visions of a transformed Haiti became known in the United States before they were known in Haiti (Gage Avril, personal communication).

Since Duvalier, the audience for cultural performance has became more fully transnational, with musicians and actors performing the same works to both audiences. Musical groups as well as records and other forms of artistic production go back and forth, allowing audiences in both locations to participate in the creation of trends and stars.

V. CONCLUSION

Haiti has been called the world's first post-colonial society (Trouillot 1990). Haitians were the first European colonial subjects to win their political independence. The dramatic revolutionary upheaval through which Haitian slaves faced and defeated the military might of France became a trope both for Haitian autonomy and the resistance of people of color to European subjugation. Yet, as a product of colonialism, the new world constructed by independent Haiti continued the class divisions of the old, divisions that were reinforced by Haiti's continued subordination to foreign capital.

This subordination has long led sectors of the Haitian population to migrate. However, unlike migrants from the eastern Caribbean, Haitians developed neither a migration ideology nor constructed themselves as a "partial society." Rather than seeing themselves as an outer orbit of a world centered elsewhere, Haitians saw themselves as standing alone and autonomous, even in the 1960s through the 1980s, as an ever increasing proportion of the Haitian population began to settle permanently abroad.

As in the case of the eastern Caribbean, however, once settled in the United States, Haitians began to build a multi-stranded social field that connected them intimately to home. Those immigrants who became most settled were those who became engaged in forging familial, economic, and cultural connections with people living in

Haiti. Haitian immigrants of all class backgrounds have lived their lives across borders, creating a new kind of space defined not by geography or by the legalities of political borders, but by social relations. For more than two decades, however, the political repression in Haiti has made it difficult for Haitian immigrants to develop organized transnational activities, and political activities have been particularly restricted.

The next chapter will describe the development of Haitian organizations in the United States. As we shall see, the sphere of organizational activities proved to be an arena of hegemonic contention over the public identities of Haitian immigrants. U.S. institutions from private philanthropies to governmental offices sought to shape the manner in which Haitian immigrants understood their relationship to the United States and to Haiti. At the same time, Haitian political activities called for a nationalist commitment to ending the Duvalier dictatorship and rebuilding Haiti. Haitian immigrant organizations found themselves presented with what seemed to be an antinomy: identification as an ethnic group committed to the U.S. political process or identification with the Haitian nation. As we shall see, it was not until the Lavalas movement that transnational linkages came to be both publicly acknowledged by Haitian immigrants and celebrated. And when transnationalism did come to be publicly acknowledged, it was done within a Haitian nationalist idiom. How and why, in opposition to the U.S. hegemonic agenda, a politicized Haitian transnational identity developed and came to wear a nationalist guise will be the subject of the next chapter.

NOTES

1. Portions of this chapter appeared in Glick Schiller (1992). All first person references in Chapters Five and Six are to Nina Glick Schiller.
2. George Anglade (1990), the well-known Haitian economist was among those who first used the term Le Dixième Département. In Kreyol this term becomes Dizyèm Depatman-an. Note that in Kreyol the article *an* appears after the noun and varies in pronunciation depending on the sound that proceeds it so that the 10th becomes Dizyèm-nam.
3. The research begun in 1969 with funding from the National Institute for Mental Health investigated the manner in which Haitian immigrants in New York responded to and participated in hegemonic constructions of Haitian ethnic identity as developed by major U.S.

institutions (Glick [Schiller] 1975; Glick Schiller 1977). Data from this project and the 1985–87 research will be presented in Chapter Six.

4. From 1985 to 1987 Josh DeWind and Nina Glick Schiller received funding from the National Institute for Child Health and Human Development (Grant #281-40-1145). The research explored whether Haitian organizations that received support in the form of resources, social recognition, and technical assistance from American institutions would be more oriented to the U.S. political process and would be more likely to define the Haitian population in the United States as an ethnic group than those organizations that did not receive such support (Glick Schiller et al. 1987, 1992).

5. In 1990 Raymond Deronvil provided assistance by conducting 20 open-ended interviews with persons in several different locations around Port-au-Prince. These interviews explored the transnational ties and the concept of Haitian identity from the perspective of persons who remained in Haiti. In the summer of 1991 George Fouron and I went to Haiti and explored the knowledge of and support for the concept of *Dizyèm-nan* on the part of people of various strata, including some who had never left Haiti and others who had returned after living many years abroad.

6. See Wodemikael (1989) for a description of instances in which Haitian immigrants begin to identify as African-Americans.

7. Haitian immigrants, defined globally as "black" people from a "black republic" are subject to both national and global racial constructions as they live their lives across national borders and relate to two or more states. The construction of blackness in Haiti differs from the way in which race has been defined in either the United States or globally. See Chapter Six.

8. Trouillot argues convincingly that the trend toward coffee cultivation in the mountains began under colonial rule with small coffee estates established by French planters. The Haitian mixed economy of production for use and market also can be traced to the colonial practice of allowing slaves to plant gardens and to market the surplus (Mintz 1989 [1974]; Trouillot 1990).

9. The drain of capital from the new nation of Haiti can be dated from 1825, when Boyer, Haiti's fourth chief of state, agreed to pay a vast indemnity to France to obtain recognition for the new nation and to reestablish commercial and political relationships.

10. While many colonies and post-colonial states continue to display aspects of a domestic production, we define the mode of production as capitalist if the dominant system of production in a specific colony or state is part of the world capitalist system. In such cases, the surplus produced, is extracted and controlled by a capitalist class, wherever it is territorially situated. A state may be defined as a centralized hierar-

chy or hierarchies of offices that maintain social order within a territory. Such maintenance includes assisting the reproduction of the mode of production by maintaining either differential access to the means of production and/or differential appropriation of surplus. This function is backed ultimately by the use of force, which the state effectively monopolizes or regulates.

11. The Haitian constitution was rewritten so that foreigners and whites could own property in Haiti.

12. Bellegarde-Smith (1990) describes three phases of armed resistance: (1) resistance to the invasion in 1915; (2) a more politicized phase from 1918 to 1920 that opposed U.S. agribusiness and the corvée; and (3) a final phase in the South in 1929.

13. Neither the migrants themselves nor most analysts who have described this migration (Grasmuck 1982) thought of the cane workers as emigrants, as people permanently leaving their country. In point of fact, the effort to distinguish Haitians as temporary outsiders distinct from the Dominican population is a political construction. See Lundhal (1983) about the origins of the Dominican population.

14. The coming to power of previous Haitian rulers was usually followed by the exile of the political opposition, and at first the exiles from the Duvalier regime seemed no different. Not all fled to the United States. Some went to France and Canada, and many went to francophone areas of Africa where employment was readily available for French speaking professionals.

15. The number of Haitians living in the United States are guesstimates usually made by taking the total number of immigrants from 1951 to the present as reported by the Immigration and Naturalization Service and doubling it to account for those who stayed on as "visitors" or whose arrival was otherwise undocumented. Often the number is again doubled to account for the birth of the next generation (see, for example, Laguerre 1984:24–25). It should be noted that while the number of granted immigrant visas in 1989 was only 13,341, those arrived who arrived as "temporary visitors for pleasure totaled 72,191 in 1989 (U.S. Immigration and Naturalization Service 190:75). Charles (1990a:151) reports that it is estimated that for every legal immigrant in the United States, there are three undocumented people.

16. Professional training in Haiti, whether medical or legal, was not directly transferable into professional credentials in the United States, although physicians arriving at the time of a doctor shortage found it possible to obtain retraining and apply for an American license; lawyers could not use their law degrees at all.

17. During the first decade of settlement a sharp dichotomy existed between Haitians living in Queens, who were seen as mulatto and high

status, and those living in Brooklyn, depicted as black and of lower status.

18. There is no accurate census of the Haitian population. In the 1980s various sources reported the Haitian population as ranging from around five million (Francisque 1986) to 6,630,00 (Kaleidoscope 1991).

19. Those from the mulatto sector who did not return dissociated themselves from the broadened class composition of the Haitian immigrant population by fleeing to the New York suburbs of Rockland County and Long Island and establishing themselves in exclusive neighborhoods. There they were generally seen as French-speaking foreigners, without a clear identification as Haitian. These mulattos seem to have kept their family and property in Haiti and intensified their transnational kinship and economic relationships throughout 1970s and 1980s, although these field observations cannot be substantiated with other forms of documentation about this stratum.

20. The Haitian "boat people" were portrayed in the United States press as extremely impoverished, ragged peasants. In point of fact, it often took a considerable amount of money to come, and the majority of the people who arrived owned some property or had access to resources in Haiti as well as a skill or trade (Buchanan 1981; Stepick 1984). Yet there were small coastal settlements in Haiti from where passage was cheap, so that a section of the rural poor was able to come (Richman 1992b).

21. Based on an estimate of 100,000 Haitian immigrants in the New York metropolitan area, DeWind projected from his survey that 99.5 million dollars was being to Haiti each year. DeWind also reported that if the Haitian population in the New York area was actually 400,000 in 1987, as estimated by Haitian community leaders, the amount of yearly Haitian remittances from New York would be $398 million. Boccio (1991:4A) reports that since 1986 more than 93 million dollars a year was being sent to Haiti.

22. With the exception of Immacula Pierre-Louis, who requested that her name be included in this book, and most public figures, the names used in Chapter Five and Six are pseudonyms.

Chapter
SIX

Not What We Had In Mind: Hegemonic Agendas, Haitian Transnational Practices, and Emergent Identities

"We were very happy to be rescued, but this is not what we had in mind." Vilson Destin, a Haitian refugee embarking from a U.S. Coast Guard ship in Port-au-Prince after trying to flee to the United States in 1992 (Newsweek 1992:15).

I. THE SEARCH FOR HAITIAN IDENTITY: THE ORGANIZATIONAL RESPONSE

Carolle's description of the interview she had just completed merged with the background street noise, even though she was shouting into the phone. "I finally interviewed the leader of that group and they are Taoists," she said. "Taoists?" I responded, fairly sure I had misheard. "Taoists, like from ancient China?" "Yes," came the reply, and through the car horns and roar of buses I could sense her amusement. "Haitian Taoists, right here on Flatbush Avenue!"[1]

The Haitian Taoists that Carolle Charles encountered in our search for Haitian organizations in New York in 1985 were in many ways similar to the Haitian Muslims from an African-American Muslim mosque in Harlem, whom I met that same year, or a Haitian Bahai, whom I had interviewed in 1969. The Taoists, Muslims, and Bahai were searching for some activity and collective identity that would give their life meaning and purpose. The search for collective representations of self has been an ongoing theme among Haitian immigrants, a theme reflexive of and shaped by historical and ongoing debates within Haiti about the content and nature of Haitian culture. However, in their search for identity, Haitian immigrants have not always looked to Haiti and have not always sought out organizational activities that linked them to Haiti. As in the case of the Haitian Taoists, Haitian immigrants may not have denied that they were Haitian, but the organizations they formed or joined often were not organized around being Haitian and did not locate their cultural roots in Haiti.

Transnational Haitian organizations were the last component of Haitian transnationalism to develop. Even during the 1970s, when Haitian transmigrants began to develop organizations whose orientation and practices were transnational, Haitian immigrants did not linguistically mark or publicly discuss their practice. They were slow to articulate public and collective identities that gave voice to their transnationalism. When Haitians finally did begin to develop a collective representation that acknowledged their transnationalism, the identity that emerged became highly politicized and the politics were nationalist. Haitians living abroad, although territorially dispersed, were seen as an integral component of the Haitian nation-state.

To understand why Haitian immigrants, although living lives that extended across borders, were slow to conceptualize transnationalism is to embark on a study of hegemonic processes. This chapter will explore the hegemonic processes within which definitions of Haitian immigrant identity have emerged and have been contested. Of particular concern will be the manner in which constructions of race, nation, and ethnicity, as they are constituted within Haitian cultural practice, have reflected ongoing processes of domination and resistance.

The ethnography in this chapter will be an ethnography of organizational activity. It is in organized activity that transmigrants construct a public face, and therefore it is immigrant organizations that are often the locus of hegemonic contention. Immigrants from professional and intellectual backgrounds will be shown to be key players in this arena. However, at critical junctures, these organizations have influenced a much larger population than those who directly participated in organizational activity, and they have been able to mobilize members of all class sectors of the migrant population. At such moments, we will see that a debate about Haitian identity has spilled out of organizational offices, forums, and public meetings into living rooms and onto street corners. At such times, Haitian immigrants have asked themselves and each other, "which country claims our loyalty and in which country does our future lie?"

A. The Haitian Historical Process.

> Since we arrived on American soil, we have been mistreated... We are asking why you treat us this way? Is it because we are Negroes? Why are you letting us suffer this way, America? ... Why among all the nations that emigrate to the United States have only the Haitians known such suffering? (Haitians kept in a U.S. detention camp for five months in the 1970s cited in Stepick 1982:4).

Concepts of color, culture, and nation produced during two centuries of class contention in Haiti have been incorporated into the lives of migrants of all class backgrounds. They filter Haitian immigrants' perceptions of their relationship to the United States and Haiti and contribute both to individual decisions on the part of Haitian immigrants to become transmigrants and collective understandings of Haitian immigrant identity. Consequently, it is useful for us to examine in some further depth the hegemonic constructs that have emerged from within the Haitian historical process.

Historically, "[t]he class discourse ... [has been] couched in color ... referents" (Dupuy 1989:156). The Haitian bourgeoisie used the markers of light skin color, as well as French culture, the French language, and Catholicism to differentiate themselves from the lower class, which was conceptualized as black, Kreyol-speaking, and African in its religion and cultural roots. While the Haitian bourgeoisie have defined themselves as "French" in their culture, it can be argued that Haitian bourgeois culture

"is a set of norms, values, and traditions haunted by cultural definitions formulated by the African-born peasantry but it is also a formulation of a denial of a peasant way of life... [This] French culture
of Haiti is a culture of domination" [because] "(i)nsofar as the
dominant groups were concerned, the utility of this culture lay in its
reinforcing and imposing a dominant position" (Casimir-Liautaud
1975:43).

At the same time, in attributing value to their light skin, the French
language, and a French identified culture, the Haitian bourgeoisie
were looking outward to their positioning in a world system. Although formally independent, Haiti remained a subordinated state
within a world in which European culture and its standards of
beauty were used as the measure of whether an individual or a
people could be considered civilized and fully human (Gates 1986;
Comaroff and Comaroff 1991; Gilman 1986).

For their part, Haitian peasants, even as they developed their own
pattern of settlement on the land, family system, and cosmology
(LaRose 1975; Mintz 1989), reinterpreted, reworked, and reappropriated the dominant culture in ways that served to legitimate the
position of the Haitian bourgeoisie. Peasants saw blackness not as a
fixed, subordinated social category but as a situational identity based
on poverty and illiteracy. Hence one could move out of blackness
with the acquisition of wealth and a European education (Charles
1990a, 1990b; Labelle 1988). The awareness of class divisions, the
correlation of class and race, and the possibility of mobility within
the system are succinctly expressed in the saying "*Nèg rich se milat,
milat pòv se nèg*" (a rich Black man is a mulatto, and a poor mulatto is
a Black man).

The possibility of mobility included in the discourse about color
obscured the enduring divisions of class. However, the use of a
terminology of color as a gloss for class served not to divide the
population into mutually exclusive color categories, as in the United
States, but to promote a vision of a single people situated along a
continuum. The continuum was conceptualized as a gradation along
the lines of color, but actually it was a complex system of physical
features including hair type, facial features, and skin tone. These
features were combined with an evaluation of wealth and social
position to determine a person's "color."

A further sense of national unity, despite the sharp distinctions
drawn between two cultural worlds of peasant and bourgeoisie,
came from the contrast made in Haiti since the Haitian revolution
between color and race. Haitians have understood that the lightest

mulatto was still a black to the rest of the world. Forged in the successful defiance of the Haitian revolution, the Haitian response to the pejorative of blackness has been a racial pride that has served to unify the population when the Haitian nation was confronted with external threats and challenges (Nicholls 1979; Lewis 1983; Trouillot 1990; Charles 1990a). In their conflation of race and nation all Haitians accept that they are Black and assert that to be Black is to be truly human; the word for a human being in Kreyol is in fact *"nèg"* which is also translated as "black." Looking out to the world with this redefined concept of Blackness, Haitians define their nation as the symbol of the dignity and pride of the black race, and themselves as the rightful leaders and spokespeople of all black people.

National unity has been reinforced continually by the use of the Haitian revolution as a common point of reference that underlies both political and social discourse within and between classes in Haiti. Most Haitians of all classes have a knowledge of and pride in the Haitian revolution, which is widely seen as the moment in time when black people stood up and forever disproved racist theories about the inferiority of Black people. Although color differentiation historically has been the preoccupation of Haitian internal political and economic discourse, the concept of Haiti as a "Black Republic," without reference to the language of color, has provided an essential core of Haitian concepts of nation.

The congruence of race and nation can be found in the articulation of Haitian identity throughout Haitian history and among Haitians of all class backgrounds (see Woodson 1990). It was articulated by political leaders in the 19th century such as Edmond Paul, who, although from a black family, was a leader of a mulatto-identified political party. Paul argued that the independent Haitian nation symbolized the dignity of black people (Paul 1863, cited in Nicholls 1974:15). In the 1970s a group of Haitians (quoted above) intercepted by the United States Immigration and Naturalization Service and held in a detention camp for five months made this same equation of race and nation.

Identification with the Haitian nation must be sharply distinguished from identification with the Haitian state (Charles 1990a; Trouillot 1990). Haitian peasants historically have not identified with the Haitian state and have tried to minimize any contact with representatives of the government (Prince 1985; Dupuy 1989; Trouillot 1990). Until the Presidency of François Duvalier in 1957, the state reinforced the culture of dominance, using French for all legal transactions, communications, and public education, but it did not develop further nation building projects and did not extend nation building projects into the countryside.

The U.S. occupation reinforced the class divisions in Haiti and the representation of class in the language of color. At the same time the occupation sparked a cultural resistance in the form of a Negritude movement that elaborated the Haitian conflation of race and nation. Tracing Haiti's cultural and racial roots to Africa as well as Europe, the Negritude movement defended Haitians as black people confronting the racism and dominance of the United States (Hoetink 1985).

However, one section of intellectuals from the *klas mwayen*, which included François Duvalier, incorporated a concept of Negritude into the internal Haitian political struggle by constructing black to mean the dark skinned majority in opposition to the mulattos (Duvalier and Denis 1958). Duvalier used his construction of Negritude in his successful bid for political power. It became his justification for obtaining control over the state apparatus by eliminating prominent mulatto members of the bourgeoisie from the posts in the army and state bureaucracy. Although Duvalier excluded mulattos from the definition of the nation, he did not contest the culture associated with them. French was maintained as the official language of both government and education and was used in all radio broadcasts and on public occasions.

Consequently, when tens of thousands of Haitians began to flee from the Duvalier regime, they arrived in the United States with constructions of Haitian identity in which the cultural domination of the Haitian bourgeoisie remained salient. For the first two decades of settlement, the racial pride embedded in Haitian concepts of nation persisted only as a muted crosscurrent of identification. The Duvalierist monopoly of the discourse on race and the need of Haitian immigrants to resist their placement in the U.S. racial order led Haitian immigrants to present themselves publicly as bearers of French culture rather than as citizens of a black nation.

C. Haitian Hegemonic Categories, Migration, and Identities

The definition of Haitian culture as "French" gained some public credibility in the United States, because in the first years of settlement the Haitian immigrant population was composed of a disproportionate number of mulattos. It was this mulatto stratum, with its fluency in French, light skin color, sophisticated manners, and urbane style that both personified and promoted the public construction of Haitians as a people with a French culture. However, Haitian immigrants from all class backgrounds shared an interest in representing themselves as French in culture, language, and manners. Members of the *klas mwayen*, who had achieved their class position in Haiti through their acquisition of the French language and French-based education and who sought to maintain their class standing in Haiti, readily adopted this "French" identity. Even many of those who had little or no formal education and had a poor command of French or did not speak it at all welcomed this public definition of Haitian culture and presented themselves as French-speaking.

In the early years of settlement, the identity of Haitian immigrants as "French" was publicly legitimated in a variety of ways. France-Amérique, the newspaper of French residents and immigrants in the United States, carried tidbits of news about Haiti or Haitian immigrants. The New York City Board of Education listed Haitian children as speaking French. Within this context, the pejorative designation, "French fried," given these children by African-American neighbors or school mates was accepted with pride.

In part, the construction of a French identity by Haitians in the United States was a reaction to the loss in status that almost all Haitians experienced when they migrated. This loss of status contributed to the urgency with which Haitian immigrants, from early on, sought to build and maintain the social and family networks that connected them to Haiti. The loss of status was precipitated not only by moving to another nation-state with a different set of markers of class standing, but also because Haitians, by migrating to the United States experienced the full force of the U.S. racial hierarchy.

However, building on their own class/ color system, Haitians reacted to their positioning at the bottom of the racial strategy as if, as in Haiti, one could opt out of the socially imposed stigma of blackness though acquiring an education and speaking French. Many members of the *klas mwayen* became consumed by the goal of regaining a position of social value by achieving middle class status in the United States, as well as by maintaining, reinforcing, or even raising their position in Haiti. To do this it was necessary to retrain to obtain credentials for their Haitian education or to begin anew and obtain an American education.

In point of fact, the growing Haitian migration of the 1960s and 1970s coincided with the movement toward black empowerment. Although the racial hierarchy continued in the United States, the movement yielded some white collar positions for educated black people and made some social mobility possible for Haitian immigrants. Haitians tended to attribute such gains to their successful presentation of a French identity that differentiated them from African-Americans.

D. *The Culture of Domination and the Initial Lack of Immigrant Organization*

When Haitians began to arrive in significant numbers in the late 1950s, they found that life in the United States was difficult and that New York City was not welcoming. However, Haitian immigrants did not group together to organize a collective defense. In fact, during the first decade of settlement, they rarely organized as Haitians, and the few organization that Haitian immigrants did form could hardly be said to represent any shared Haitian identity. The first Haitian organizations were either elite social clubs or political cliques.

There were many reasons why the early Haitian arrivals avoided any collective activity, did not wish to organize as an ethnic group, and formed no transnational organizations. The undocumented legal status of many Haitians contributed to the desire for anonymity. Even if you had permanent resident status, a member of your household or a family member or friend in your personal network probably did not. Fear was a big factor. Fear of immigration authorities, fear of the *makout*, and fear of a loss of class standing kept Haitian immigrants from relating to people who were unknown to them, whether or not they were Haitian.

Haitian immigrants also were divided by political differences. These differences reflected not divisions of political ideology but of political loyalty. Politicians who had competed with François Duvalier for the presidency and were exiled by him arrived with a contingents of supporters. From the first days of their settlement, these forces attempted to build a politics of return. They publicly identified themselves as political exiles rather than as immigrants (Glick Schiller et al. 1987) and used a nationalist rhetoric linking the unsuccessful presidential "candidates" with the heroes and symbols of the Haitian revolution. Though totally oriented toward life in Haiti, these groups were unable to establish any more than surreptitious links to Haiti and were isolated in the United States.

In addition, class differences divided Haitian immigrants, and these differences were more salient to Haitians than any idea of common cause based on common origins in Haiti. While the actual class composition of the migration population in the first decade of settlement was quite diverse, the presence of the Haitian bourgeoisie among the migrants had a great influence on the identity and organization of the entire migrating population. Haitians of bourgeois backgrounds avoided any form of public organization because they did not wish to be associated publicly with Haitians of lower social strata. Lines of class, delineated by categories of color, shaped the initial Haitian settlement. Determined to return to Haiti, members of the upper strata — who were referred to and called themselves "les mulâtres" — looked to preserve their class status in Haiti through their comportment in the United States and their maintenance, while away from home, of markers of social differentiation.

Meeting for the first time, members of the bourgeoisie exchanged not greetings but last names, and conversations were continued and relationships struck only if both speakers could claim bourgeois class status. Efforts to maintain status also marked consumption patterns, with members of the bourgeoisie willing to pay higher rents, buy houses at higher prices, and live in crowded quarters in order to obtain housing in white neighborhoods away from African-Americans, Caribbeans, and other Haitians.

Members of this class joined with white Americans in occupation-based organizations, such as associations of insurance agents, and were accepted into Masonic lodges organized by French immigrants. When the mulattos did form organizations, these organizations, which proved to be the first Haitian organizations in the United States, were not open to all Haitians. They were elite social clubs with membership and entrance to club dances by invitation only. There was no sense of the Haitian community. In fact, Haitian immigrants, whether they were making a speech or speaking privately to a friend, did not refer to the Haitian settlement as a "community." Instead the world "*colonie*" was employed.

E. The Faltering Attempts to Create a Haitian Ethnic Identity in New York: 1965–71

Often newly developed hegemonic models are disseminated through publicized academic and political debate and through general social processes in which the media play an important role. However, when Haitians began to form ethnic organizations in the 1960s they were responding to more than the general dissemination of a model of cultural pluralism. The model was "hand carried" by representatives of an array of U.S. institutions who worked to organize the disparate Haitian population in New York into a Haitian ethnic constituency.

Along with advice, funding, and assistance came an agenda for the construction of a Haitian ethnic community that would be incorporated politically into the United States. However, even within the organizations that did grow up to represent Haitians as an ethnic group within the United States, some Haitians began activities that eventually formed the basis for a transnational agenda.

By 1970, organizations contributing technical assistance and funding to foster Haitian ethnic organizing included several Catholic Archdioceses, the Episcopalian Diocese of Brooklyn, the Southern Baptist Convention, the National Democratic Party, the New York City Community Development Corporation, the Ford Foundation, and the Community Service Society. In 1986 we identified sixty-nine U.S. organizations providing support to Haitian organizations in the New York Metropolitan area.

These organizations, whether they were a fundamentalist church, a private foundation or a government agency, explained their mission in similar terms. Haitian immigrants were seen as a "community" that needed a "voice" so that they could adequately compete with other ethnic communities that made up a culturally plural United States. They were said to be similar to the Italians, Irish, and Jews, who had succeed through ethnic organizing. In the 1960s and 1970s, no mention was made of race. Haitians were assumed to identify, not with others of African ancestry or with coworkers of all nationalities, but with other Haitians with whom they shared a desire for united action.

In these organizing efforts by U.S. institutions, the Haitian nation-state and Haitian politics were also absent categories. To the extent that Haitian immigrants were encouraged to have a political voice, they were directed toward participation in the U.S. electoral process. U.S. politicians, priests, and social workers were observed delivering the same message to the Haitian immigrants that they were trying to organize. They told Haitians that in order for them to obtain a larger "piece of the pie" in the form of jobs, community services, and housing, they needed to become politically active as Haitians. This advice was given to Haitians from the *klas mwayen* and bourgeoisie, who aspired to regain status and achieve leadership positions.

At the same time, representatives of these U.S. organizations built up a constituency for Haitian community organizing. Workers from Haiti found that they were able to obtain valuable free services, including English language training, job placement, and assistance with immigration regulations, by identifying themselves as members of the Haitian community. In this way hegemonic forces encouraged the incorporation of Haitian laborers as ethnics.

For example, in 1967 white American social workers representing New York City anti-poverty agencies approached prominent individuals of Haitian origin working in a multiethnic community and suggested establishing a separate Haitian agency to serve the growing Haitian immigrant population of the Upper West Side of Manhattan (Glick 1975). The Haitian Neighborhood Service Center (HNSC) in Manhattan became the first organization to speak for the "Haitian community" in New York. A major activity of the HNSC was finding entry level blue collar employment for Haitian migrants of all class backgrounds.

However, even at this early stage, when the political repression in Haiti made transnational activities of any type perilous, Haitians engaged in ethnic organizing began to develop their own distinctive agenda, and it was transnational. They sought incorporation in the United States, but also tried to maintain ties to Haiti. The history of the Haitian-Americans Citizens Society (HACSO) provides a particularly interesting example of Haitian immigrants following an alternative agenda because HACSO was officially affiliated with the Democratic Party. Despite this affiliation, there are indications that the Haitian members of HACSO entered American politics with some thought of obtaining political influence in Haiti as well as in the United States.

Before its founding in the late 1960s, the future leaders of HACSO were flown to Washington to a meeting in the White House with President Johnson, national party officials, and an array of experienced local ethnic politicos. Since at the time Haitians had absolutely no political clout in terms of voting power, with only several hundred individuals of Haitian origin in the whole country who were citizens, the wooing was quite remarkable.

The inclusion of Haitians at this White House meeting seems to have been part of a larger effort directed at the incorporation of migrants of color in ways that would keep them separate from subordinated populations within the United States. Within the Democratic Party, Haitians were placed in the All Nationalities Divisions together with Irish-Americans and Slovakian-Americans.[2] The placement of Haitians with white ethnics represented a construction of Haitians as ethnic Americans who were part of the larger American nation, a nation made up of multiple ethnic groups. This integrative effort came at the precise historical moment that advocates of black and Latino empowerment were advocating separatism and revolution.

The career of Louis Brun, one of the founders of HACSO, who had been wined and dined in the White House as a result of his interest in participating in U.S. politics, provides evidence of the transnational orientation of members of HACSO. Brun accepted ethnic incorporation, but he also wished to maintain ties to and a social position within Haiti. Brun, together with another founder of HACSO, were the first Haitians to run for political office in the United States, making unsuccessful bids for positions as New York State Representatives. For him there was no contradiction between his U.S. political activity, which was contingent on his acquisition of American citizenship, and his desire to maintain his social and economic ties to Haiti. When Jean-Claude Duvalier came to power, Brun returned to Haiti, parlaying the prestige he had obtained through his political participation in the United States into social capital in Haiti.

However, if members of the Haitian bourgeoisie, such as Brun saw no problem in wanting to obtain influence within the U.S. political system while using their membership in HACSO to preserve and reinforce their class position in Haiti, their dual goals posed an unresolvable dilemma for efforts to build the organization. HACSO could only succeed in U.S. politics if its members were united, but its bourgeois members sought to preserve their class position in Haiti by refusing to associate with persons of lower status. At times, the class divisions in HACSO were so acrimonious that the organization was paralyzed, tickets were not sold for fund-raising dances, and important decisions about who would represent or lead the organization could not be made.[3]

The history of the first Haitian religious "community" organization in the United States provides us with a further example of Haitians working at cross purposes with a U.S. hegemonic agenda. When the Haitian Christian Community was formed in 1968, the purpose of the organization, according to its charter, was to "encourage and incite persons of Haitian birth to provide leadership in guiding Haitians to work within the American political system" (Haitian Christian Community 1968). The charter language reflected the advice and support provided to the organization by both Paul O'Dwyer, a prominent Irish-American politician, and an Irish-American parish priest. Père Auguste, the Haitian priest in charge of the new organization, saw things differently.

As early as 1969, Père Auguste began developing organizational practices that transcended geographic location and reconfigured political space. His first step was to initiate a discussion group focused, not on American politics, but on child rearing in the United States. This organizing effort was a great success. Several dozen people attended and the discussion was heated. Haitian families, just beginning to settle in the United States, were greatly concerned that their children not become *mal lève* (raised without manners). Unmannerly children would threaten the norms of reciprocity and obligation which were fundamental to the transnational family networks upon which so many in Haiti were coming to depend for survival. Moreover, embedded in the discourse about properly raised children were also concerns about class position and social mobility. Parents feared that in inner city neighborhoods their children would take on the language and stance of the Black American poor and thus forfeit their family's opportunity to maintain or improve its class position in the United States and in Haiti.

Once the Haitian Christian Community became solidly established, Père Auguste went a step further, directly building transnational organizational ties. Much to the dismay of his U.S. mentors, and in opposition to their wishes, Auguste used the organization's treasury to maintain at school in Switzerland young Haitian priests who were then to return to work with youth in Haiti. Auguste and his Haitian immigrant parishioners saw Haitians in New York and in Haiti as part of the same population.

The contention between the U.S. mentors and the leadership of Haitian immigrant organizations that emerged in this early example of the Haitian Christian Community was to repeat itself in different ways in the decades to follow. The Haitian agenda was transnational in its orientation, although the concept of Haitian transnationalism was not articulated fully until the 1990s.

F. The Development of Explicit Transnational Activities and Multiple Identities: 1972–85

Ten Haitian men gather in a Long Island living room for a meeting of their home town association. The members come from different classes in Haiti, although all are fairly successful in New York. Each member has pledged $10.00 a month to support the indigent elderly of their home town.

Dr. Paule addresses the meeting. Doing well in New York as a doctor, Dr. Paule lives for his yearly return to his home town, where his mulatto family is part of the local elite. Voicing the general sense of malaise that has contributed to the formation of the association, he states, "I'm making money and I am not happy. My life here has no meaning." Dr. Paule's solution to his existential dilemma is to propose that the association build a sports complex for the youth of their home town. He indicates that he already has bought the land, which he will donate, and he will also donate $4,000–5,000 dollars for the building.

Dr. Paule is not alone in his aspirations to make a mark back home in a way that maintains or asserts status both in Haiti and among his personal networks in New York. In 1985 there were more than twenty Haitian home town associations in New York, composed primarily of people who had lived in New York for many years. The core of most of these associations were migrants who had established a fairly secure base in the United States and then supplemented their personal and family ties to Haiti by forming or joining a home town association. Their background in Haiti ranged from peasant to professional. The public identification of this sector was not with the country or the government of Haiti, but with people from the same "peyi" (country or region), or in this case, home town in Haiti.[4]

These organizations were not organized for the mutual benefit of members in New York but to sponsor community development projects in Haiti. However, the assistance sometimes took on a dramatic rather than a practical nature. Members have seemed more interested in strengthening or developing their social standing in Haiti and in the United States than in performing good works for the town.

While this kind of organizing can be explained in terms of individual status aspirations, more needs to be said. That immigrants began to identify publicly with their home town in Haiti can be read as an indicator of several larger trends that contributed to the growth of Haitian transnationalism. Such public identification was a new phenomenon. Before the 1980s, people from small towns often claimed they were from Port-au-Prince, eschewing identification with rural black culture and claiming the sophisticated and implicitly European-linked culture of the capital.

Haitians began to identify with their home towns at a time when Haitians were the subject of vicious public attack in the United States. As the recession of the 1970s grew, Haitians became scapegoats. Visibly black and immigrant, Haitians found themselves constructed by the U.S. media as the undesirable other, differentiated as illiterate, impoverished, and ragged boat people. This stigmatization continued into the 1980s, when Haitians were the only nationality designated by the U.S. Center for Disease Control (CDC) as a "high risk group" for AIDS. The linkage continued long after the HIV virus and the means of transmission were identified and although no behavior peculiar to Haitians that raised their risk of transmission of HIV was found.[5] The message was clear. The risk lay in the identity itself: to be Haitian was to be diseased, dangerous, and undesirable.

On an individual level, this stigmatization had catastrophic effects on the sense of well-being and security of the Haitian immigrant population. Although no systematic accounting was kept, there were widespread reports among Haitians of people losing their jobs, housing, or friends because they were Haitian. There were numerous incidents of Haitian children being beaten or harassed at school.

Initially, most Haitian immigrants did not respond to this attack through organization and public protest. Throughout the 1970s, only a few Haitian organizations publicly spoke out against the attacks on Haitian immigrants. Organizing efforts that tried to speak in the name of Haitians as an ethnic group in the United States abated after the retreat of federal and municipal governments from sponsorship of anti-poverty programs and the waning of the civil rights and black power struggles. Instead, as the attack on Haitians escalated, Haitian immigrants formed an increasing number of organizations that provided a safe haven by making salient a variety of identities other than Haitian. In addition to the hometown associations, Haitians organized around religious, professional, fraternal, athletic, hometown, Caribbean, and African identities (Glick Schiller et al. 1987, 1992). The majority (58%) of the 91 Haitian immigrant organizations we studied in 1985 had not chosen a Haitian public identity (Glick Schiller, Brutus, and DeWind 1985).

Yet a persistent, although in most cases not publicly prominent, aspect of organizational life of that period was the effort of organizations to forge links to Haiti. Eighty-five percent of the leaders interviewed said that Haitians "should maintain their own culture" in the United States and their emphasis on cultural persistence was linked to their identification with the future of Haiti. Haiti was seen not as a source of past cultural roots but as a part of the transnational arena of activities that they were then quietly constructing.

Forty percent of the organizations we studied had some relationship to Haiti. As organizations, they were sending money, personnel, and equipment to an array of small development projects and philanthropic activities in Haiti. A much greater number (60%) said that their organizational activities contributed to Haiti. If they trained youth, in soccer for example, this contributed to the development of the Haitian youth, who were important for the future of Haiti. If they taught people to read in New York, this would aid in the development of Haiti. The majority of the leaders of these organizations saw Haiti and the United States as two different locales within a single social field.

At the time of the interviews, many political leaders in the Haitian diaspora publicly criticized organizations that had ties to Haiti as implicitly contributing to the maintenance of tyranny in Haiti and the oppression of the Haitian people. At the same time, the Duvalier regime made organizational activity, especially independent transnational activities, difficult. Therefore, it is highly significant that leaders of forty percent of these organizations admitted to Haitian interviewers during the year before the fall of the Duvalier regime that they were involved in organizing activities in Haiti. It was a measure of the degree to which activities in Haiti were integral to the goals of Haitian immigrant organizations in the United States.

Many Haitian immigrants found that Protestant churches were receptive to their desire to develop both alternative identities in the face of the stigmatization of Haitian immigrants and transnational linkages with Haiti. Protestant churches, unlike many other U.S. based organizations, did not see programs that assisted with immigrant incorporation in the United States and programs that encouraged immigrants to maintain home ties as contradictory. The religious mission of the church was thought to transcend national loyalties and politics.

During the period of attack, Protestant congregations grew rapidly among Haitian immigrants in New York. By 1986 there were, for example, 23 Haitian churches linked to the Southern Baptist Convention out of a total of about 160 congregations that belonged to the Convention in the New York Metropolitan area. The five congregations we randomly chose to study all engaged in transnational activities (Glick Schiller and Charles 1992). Protestant congregations, many of which were evangelical, ranged in size from tiny store fronts to substantial church structures supported by a membership of over one thousand that included many second and third generation members. Many of these congregations were intensely transnational in their activities.

Although Haiti is predominantly a Catholic country, Protestantism has been growing rapidly, and many denominations conduct missionary work in Haiti, so that Haitian pastors and congregants arrive with some type of transnational connection to the United States. At the same time that Haitian pastors established congregations in the United States, they sought to maintain their congregational ties in Haiti and expand them.

II. THE CHALLENGE TO HAITIAN HEGEMONIC CATEGORIES AND EMERGENT TRANSNATIONAL HAITIAN IDENTITIES

A. Contestations Over Culture

> The one room inside the little shack is crowded with young people, and a few who are not so young. It's hot. A young woman standing at the back is directing the discussion. What are those words we hear the people saying? *Libète* Liberty. *Dwa Moun.* Human rights. *Teyoloji liberasyon.* Liberation Theology. A pot of hot rice and beans is being distributed, paid for by contributions of everyone present. What is this place, what is this group, why are they gathered here under the light of one bare bulb to talk about liberty? You know what this is, brothers and sisters, as well as I do. This is an ecclesial [sic] base community; In Haiti, we call them *ti kominote legliz* (Aristide 1990:13).

While most Haitians in the United States in the 1970s tried to keep a low public profile, the countryside in Haiti became the location of a cultural revolution that was ultimately to transform the representation of Haitian culture and identity in both Haiti and the United States. Although continuing to repress any open political activity, the Duvalier regime, as part of its overture to foreign capital, replaced its black nationalist rhetoric with one of democratic reform. The government also allowed a myriad of international organizations from USAID to the Quakers to begin hundreds of projects in Haiti. These projects promoted the participation of peasants in grassroots development, which was defined as an economic rather than political activity. Haitian Catholic priests committed to liberation theology used the new language of reform and the possibility of grassroots organizing to build a *ti legliz* (little church) movement that addressed both the needs and aspirations of the poor.

While some priests were eventually exiled, others were able to continue their work, using the weapons of culture in their challenge to the dominant forces in Haiti. The Kreyol language, which had long been dismissed by the Haitian bourgeoisie as a menial patois, became the language of the mass. People prayed to the beat of drums that had been equated in Haiti with voodoo and the Afro-Haitian culture of the peasantry. As the movement grew, it found a voice in the Church radio station, Radio Soleil, that could unify scattered remote congregations and link localized concerns to national political developments.

The priests exiled by the Duvalier regime continued their organizing activities in New York and Miami. The presence of these priests in the United States linked the Haitian immigrants ideologically and organizationally to the political and cultural movement in Haiti.[6] The priests launched a campaign among Haitian immigrants in the United States to displace the culture of domination by redefining the Kreyol language and the customs and practices of the peasantry as the core of Haitian culture and reappropriating them into the practice of Catholicism.

In the 1970s a debate raged in living rooms, barbershops, on the radio, and in churches in New York City. The key point of contention seemed to be whether Kreyol, the only language spoken by the majority of the Haitian population, was a real language suitable for communication with God (Buchanan 1980). Haitians of all classes insisted that the Catholic mass, with which they marked their baptisms, marriages, and funerals, could not be celebrated with the proper respect unless the priests spoke in French. The priests maintained that Haitian masses should be in Kreyol because Kreyol was the language of the Haitian people.

The debate over language was a challenge to the dominance of Haitian bourgeois culture as well as an effort to redefine the nature of Haitian identity, both in the United States and in Haiti. A political agenda for Haitian immigrants was linked to these issues of culture and identity because, at its core, the struggle over culture raised questions of political as well as cultural representation. At issue was who had the right to speak for the Haitian nation. The debate challenged the legitimacy of the dominant forces in Haiti and their control of the state. The ferocity with which the debate was waged, and its extension into every aspect of Haitian immigrant life, brought broad numbers of Haitian immigrants into what was essentially a political debate.

However, for more than a decade in the United States, and even longer in Haiti, this was an embedded politics. The priests made no political speeches. It was through their stance on issues of culture that they repudiated both the French identified bourgeoisie and their cultural hegemony and the Duvalier regime, which claimed to speak for the black masses in Haiti yet continued the use of French as the official language.

Reappropriating representations of the Haitian nation into a challenge to the prevailing political forces in Haiti and their U.S. backers, the radical priests named the community center they founded in Brooklyn, "Charlemagne Péralte." Péralte was the Haitian leader whose troops took up arms to resist the American occupation.

It was only at the end of the 1970s that the movement that celebrated Haitian Kreyol and Haiti's African-based culture began to gain ascendancy among Haitians in the United States. One measure of the transformation was the acceptance of Kreyol in public discussions. By 1985, most meetings of Haitians in New York were conducted in Kreyol rather than French. To some degree, the adoption of Kreyol reflected the changing composition of the Haitian immigrant population. In the course of the 1970s an increasing number of new arrivals were unable to speak French. However, politics as well as demographics had brought about this change. The use of French in public gatherings was increasingly taken as evidence of arrogance rather than erudition.

However, Kreyol and peasant culture are still not fully legitimated among Haitian immigrants and continue to be contested from many different sources. Haitian parents, for example, registering their children for school in New York City in 1992, continued to claim that their children were French speaking and needed French bilingual instruction, even when neither they nor their children could speak French. Nonetheless, a profound cultural transformation has occurred in New York, although the political significance of this change and its linkages to an awakening taking place in the Haitian countryside did not become apparent for some time. It was only in 1990, when Aristide's Lavalas movement organizationally linked the two domains of cultural struggle into a single transnational political arena, that the importance of these developments became evident.

B. Nationalist Responses to Attack:
The Politics of Return, 1972–85

The struggle to reject the culture of the Haitian bourgeoisie that had long been dominant in Haiti took place during the same decade that increasing numbers of Haitians fled to the United States by small boat and Haitians were derided and attacked in the U.S. media. While most Haitians initially responded to the attacks by a reluctance to identify themselves publicly as Haitians, a handful of Haitian organizations openly challenged the detention of the boat people and the attacks on Haitian immigrants. By the end the 1970s the few voices lifted in protest had swelled to become the thunderous roar of a political movement. The demands of this movement were transnational, directed toward both political change in Haiti and justice for Haitian immigrants in the United States. However, Haitian transnationalism was not openly acknowledged by this movement. The nationalist organizations advocated a politics of return.

Reflecting the development of the left in Haiti, the United States, and Europe, a small but vocal cluster of Haitian revolutionary nationalists based in New york contributed to these politics. Analyzing Haitian politics in terms of class rather than color, they used theater, radio, newspapers, and leaflets to celebrate the culture and language of the Haitian peasantry.

There was a direct connection between the development in New York of Haitian nationalist organizing and the growth of Haitian newspapers and radio programs. Beginning in 1970, every Sunday morning in New York thousands of Haitian immigrants listened to impassioned discussions in Kreyol of the political situation in Haiti and the need for revolution. The fact that the student radicals were broadcasting from the location of WKCR, the radio station at Columbia University, lent prestige and weight to the arguments.

Soon after, other Haitian nationalists that were both anti-Duvalierist and anti-communist began *Haiti Observateur*, the first Haitian newspaper in the United States. By the 1980s, there were several newspapers and a handful of radio programs proclaiming that the future for Haitian immigrants lay in changing the political situation in Haiti. At first the political and media organizations began with a transnational orientation rather than actually having a base in both Haiti and the United States. Whether on the left or right, Haitian political activists insisted that Haitian immigrants in the United States had a responsibility to overthrow Duvalier and return to reconstruct Haiti.

Throughout this period, Haitians fleeing Duvalierist repression were being systematically refused political asylum, while Cubans fleeing a communist government were designated political refugees. In 1980 the dramatic arrival and detention of thousands of Haitian boat people, at the same time that tens of thousands of Cubans arriving by boat were being welcomed by the U.S. government, highlighted the inequalities in U.S. refugee policy. The situation became a focus of national attention when Haitians, imprisoned in the Krone Detention Center of the Immigration and Naturalization Service in Florida, rebelled, and photographs of dark skinned Haitians in concentration camp-like settings appeared in U.S. newspapers.

At the same time, the decade of nationalist organizing began to bear fruit. Large numbers of Haitian immigrants became intensely involved in the future of the Haitian state for the first time (Glick Schiller et al. 1987, 1992 [1987]). The movement attacked both the

Duvalier regime and the United States, which supported Duvalier and jailed and abused black immigrants. In 1981, while supporters in the Black Congressional Caucus lobbied for change and the national press looked on, ten thousand Haitians demonstrated in Washington DC.

The awareness and increasing advocacy of the Haitian case on the part of the U.S. media were fueled by the glaring contradiction between the treatment accorded Haitian and Cuban refugees. However, the publicity that the media finally gave to the Haitian situation also reflected the growing success of the Haitian nationalist movement within the United States and the political alliances it was making with human rights groups and African-American political leaders. Paradoxically, while the majority of Haitian immigrants continued to believe that to obtain economic success and social acceptance in the United States they must distinguish themselves from African-Americans, leaders of Haitian nationalist organizations, while advocating a politics of return, began to build a broader, race-based identity for Haitian immigrants in the United States.

In the end, some rights and benefits were won for Haitian boat people. Although they did not concede the justice of the Haitian claims, the U.S. government responded to the protests and public spotlight put on the inequities of its refugee policy. Both newly arrived Haitians and Cubans were accorded a new temporary status of "Entrant." Entrants became entitled to some federal benefits, although they were not offered a secure legal status until the round of compromises that accompanied the immigration legislation of 1987. Along with the federal benefits, which included millions of dollars for resettlement and training, came a new effort to incorporate Haitian immigrants politically into the United States. At the same time, the upsurge in Haitian nationalist organizing led to another round of contention between Haitian immigrants and U.S. hegemonic forces over the political allegiances and identities of Haitian immigrants.

C. The New Hegemonic Efforts to Incorporate Haitian Immigrants as Black Ethnics: 1980–85

At first glance, the agenda set by the U.S. organizations in the 1980s seemed to be a replay of the hegemonic fostering of Haitian ethnic organizations of the 1960s. Interviews conducted in 1986 with representatives of most of the organizations that worked with Haitian entrants in New York revealed a set of common goals. Most of these

organizations sought to incorporate Haitian immigrants into the social and political fabric of the United States and build a Haitian
leadership that could serve as ethnic spokespersons for the broader
Haitian immigrant population. Their project was to strengthen the
unity of the U.S. as a nation. They opposed organizational activities
devoted to addressing the political and economic situation in Haiti.
Efforts by Haitian immigrants to participate in the political process of
Haiti were seen by these representatives of U.S. organizations as
subverting their agenda of incorporation.

However, there were some important differences between the cultural pluralist message carried to Haitians in the 1960s and the model
of U.S. society presented to the Haitians in the 1980s. For the first
time, there was explicit mention made of race. For example, citing
Supreme Court Justice Blackmun, Franklin Thomas, the African-
American President of the Ford Foundation, said "In order to get
beyond racism we must take account of race," (Ford Annual Report
1984). The introduction of race into the pluralist paradigm was, in
part, a response to the influx of immigrants of color into the United
States in the 1970s.

In this hegemonic response, African-American professionals and
politicians emerged as key players in shaping a pluralist paradigm
that explicitly acknowledged histories of racial discrimination. In the
years since the first ethnic organizing of the Haitians, a visible core of
African-American politicians, social workers, and bureaucrats had
developed. They were in a position to serve as mentors in the next
wave of incorporative initiatives that framed the settlement of the
Haitian boat people. These African-American mentors approached
Haitians as an ethnic group, but saw ethnicity and race as overlapping identities for Haitians. An African-American social worker who
helped set up one of the first programs to resettle Haitian entrants
told us that "Haitians should be part of a [black] network, should be
part of NAACP and all that good stuff, should pay some attention to
organizing of blacks, but the main focus should be to build up the
political conditions for Haitians here."

By the 1980s, however, it was evident that Haitian transmigrants
had directly and intensively entered into the Haitian political
process. Representatives of U.S. organizations responded to the
Haitian nationalist movement by being much more explicit than had
past U.S. advisors about the necessity for Haitian immigrants to
become U.S. citizens and give up their allegiance to Haiti. Abandon-
ing Haiti and developing a commitment to the United States was a
prominent theme among both African-American and white Ameri-

can policy makers, planners, social workers, and program consultants who worked with Haitian entrant programs.

An African-American representative of the Community Service Society, an influential philanthropic organization in New York City, made explicit the question of the political allegiance of Haitian immigrants: "I have problems with dual citizenship, I believe in allegiance to one country. Haitians should not assimilate but should 'Americanize,' just to the extent that they can make it" in America. They should become "part of American life, vote, gain political allies, convey their needs to elected officials in Washington, and educate their community about issues, citizenship, voting."

An Irish-American grant writer summarized this position for us: "Community organizing for political and strategic purposes in the United States is most important, while continuing interest in Haiti threatens this priority. Haitians should become citizens. Our organization has encouraged them to adopt U.S. ways — including capitalist values." Even the Ford Foundation, which became directly involved in Haiti in the 1980s and began to fund a "Human Rights" organization there, was not supportive of Haitian efforts to organize in the United States to attend to the problems of Haiti.

A small, although significant, group of Haitian leaders responded to this renewed effort to build community organizations among Haitians after a decade of cutbacks in public monies. However, while they embraced the goal of incorporation into the United States, they also continued to look to Haiti. Most of the leadership of the Haitian organizations that received entrant funding were transmigrants. They lived in a transnational rather than national terrain, embedded in transactions and networks that connected the United States and Haiti. Neither the leadership of these organizations nor the Haitian immigrant population as a whole were deterred from continuing and increasing their transnational practices by the renewed effort at constructing a Haitian immigrant identity. However, these hegemonic efforts did affect the ability of Haitian immigrants to articulate an identity that could publicly acknowledge and legitimate their transnational practices.

In New York, three different U.S. organizations initiated programs for Haitian entrants, working with a core of well-established Haitian organizations. President Carter personally called the Director of the Community Service Society (CSS) and asked him to take responsibility for the resettlement money allocated for Haitian entrants in New York. CSS proceeded to identify a cluster of Haitian community centers in New York and began to work closely with them.

Meanwhile, the Center for Human Services, a private Baltimore grant-writing firm, knowing nothing about Haitians but attracted by an announcement in the Federal Register of a multi-million dollar program for Haitian resettlement, located and brought together many of these same community centers into a coalition and won a contract to do language training for Haitian entrants. Shortly afterwards, the Ford Foundation, as part of an initiative to "stabilize the Haitian community" (interview with a Ford representative), decided to fund this New York coalition of Haitian organizations.

The Haitian Centers Council that emerged in 1982 from this collaborative effort looked publicly like a black ethnic organization with the sole purpose of incorporating Haitian immigrants into life in the United States.[7] The Council represented six community centers that provided job and language training, employment counseling, and community advocacy for Haitian immigrants. The Council described itself as "the voice of the Haitian community," and its Director, Joe Etienne, was invited to represent "the Haitian community" at an array of ritual and political events from picnics at the Mayor's mansion to private meetings with foundation heads and special Gubernatorial committees. Depending on the situation, Etienne was presented publicly as a Haitian, Caribbean, or black leader.

At the time of the founding of the Council, Etienne was one of a handful of Haitian leaders who explicitly repudiated the politics of return. In 1985, Etienne recalled ruefully to me his past hopes of returning to Haiti to build a political career and talked about the wasted energies that so many of his friends continued to expend towards trying to change Haiti. He saw more political possibilities in the United States, and had himself taken some small effort in that direction, having tried to run, albeit unsuccessfully, for a local school board. The decision of Etienne and several other Haitian leaders to focus their energies solely on incorporation in the United States was a response both to the renewed interest of hegemonic institutions in encouraging Haitian ethnicity and to the growing incorporation of Haitian immigrants within the United States. Although even these leaders tended to be transmigrants, their focus on U.S. incorporation reflected the broader U.S. hegemonic context.

No ideological terrain had been cleared to explore the implications of Haitian transnational practices for Haitian constructions of identity. Those who preached the politics of incorporation assumed, as did the advocates of the politics of return, that building organizations and identities that linked them to the Haitian political process was antithetical to focusing their political energies on participation in U.S. politics.

The politics of incorporation in the United States received a Haitian public voice in 1979 in the form of *Moment Créole*, a highly influential commercial Haitian radio program. *Moment Créole* was developed and produced by Inner City Broadcasting, a "black" corporation owned by African-American and Caribbean-American capitalists including Percy Sutton, who had run unsuccessfully for Mayor of New York City in 1977, and David Dinkins, who was to become the first African-American Mayor of New York City in 1989.

Broadcast throughout the entire afternoon on Sundays, *Moment Créole* filled the airwaves with advice to Haitian immigrants about how to improve their situation in the United States. It provided information about legal rights, education, housing, and employment. The programs encouraged Haitians to become involved in and committed to the political process in the United States. In its broadcasts between 1983 and 1986, *Moment Créole* portrayed Haiti as the source of the cultural roots of Haitian-Americans rather than as a continuing part of the daily life of Haitian transmigrants. However, at times, despite the efforts of its broadcasters, alternative voices intruded and the air space of *Moment Créole* was encompassed within the Haitian transnational terrain in which both broadcasters and listeners lived their lives. Such moments came when insistent listeners responded to call-in shows by directing attention back to Haiti.

Only in 1986, after the overthrow of Duvalier, did *Moment Créole* become transnational in its programming. The program began to feature live hourly reports on the unfolding political events transmitted by phone calls directly from Haiti. Soon impassioned discussions between broadcasters and callers about the political future of Haiti and their role within it became a regular feature of the broadcast. At the same time, *Moment Créole* continued its efforts to build a constituency of Haitian voters in the United States.

Moment Créole was joined in its pre-1986 effort to focus the political energies of Haitian immigrants solely on U.S. political processes by a new organization that emerged in the mid-1980s, the Haitian Americans Citizens for Action (HACFA). Unlike the Haitian American Citizens Society, its predecessor of the 1960s, this new organization was not formally affiliated with a U.S. political party. However, it was envisioned almost as a political club by its founder, Père Darbouze, a Haitian priest, and its sponsor, Congressman Major Owens. Congressman Owens provided technical assistance to

HACFA. At a time when some African-American politicians in New York were still reluctant to recognize black ethnicities, Owens, who had cut his political teeth in the cultural pluralist politics of the anti-poverty programs of the 1960s, encouraged the participation of Haitian immigrants in U.S. politics as Haitians.

However, neither Owens nor Père Darbouze was able to build a core of activists fully committed to entering U.S. politics. Shortly after they organized HACFA, the Duvalier regime came crashing down and members of HACFA, along with large numbers of Haitian immigrants throughout the United States, started talking, dreaming, singing, and planning to transform Haiti. A core member of HACFA, the founder and director of a private school in Brooklyn that taught Haitian children about their culture, packed up and moved her school to Haiti. In Haiti, the goal of her school became to prepare Haitian children to feel at home in both a Haitian and American milieu.

With the Duvalier regime gone, Haitian organizations begun in the United States began to operate openly in Haiti. Haitians became fully transnational. Social fields of family, economy, communications, religion, politics, and culture could now publicly be constructed and organized across borders. Yet it remained difficult for Haitians to formulate a transnational identity. The concept of immigrants as transmigrants belonging fully to more than one nation-state continued to cut against the hegemonic nation building constructions in both the United States and Haiti.

After two decades of organizing, both by U.S. organizations and Haitian nationalist forces, Haitians in New York had come to believe that there was indeed a "Haitian community" in New York, perhaps even in the United States. Yet there was no consensus as to which nation-state this community belonged. Although the politics of return was never widely accepted and was always openly contested, Haitian immigrants found their lives too enmeshed in Haiti not to see themselves continuing to be part of Haiti. At the same time, the efforts on the part of U.S. hegemonic institutions to incorporate Haitians within the ethnic constructions of the United States resonated among those Haitians who had in fact become incorporated into the social and economic structures of the United States.

In 1986 our research team of Haitian and U.S. researchers could not see transnationalism, even though we found that four of the six member centers who made up the Haitian Centers Council, "the voice of the Haitian community" in the United States, were committed to organizational activities in Haiti. One of the centers was a

Protestant evangelical congregation in Brooklyn whose religious mission extended to Haiti. The leaders of three other centers were intensely involved in anti-Duvalierist politics. One of these centers was Charlemagne Péralte, the organization formed by Haitian priests committed to liberation theology and the transformation of Haiti.

However, it was only with the election of Aristide that Haitians developed a vocabulary with which to describe and legitimate their incorporation in the United States and their continuing ties to Haiti. With more than a sixth of the Haitian population living outside of the country, Aristide moved to reclaim the Haitian "community" for the Haitian nation-state and publicized the concept of *Dizyèm-nan* as a way of both acknowledging and encapsulating Haitian transnationalism. Although receptive to participation in the U.S. political processes, those who shaped the construct of *Dizyem-nan* insisted that at the same time, Haitian immigrants, wherever they settled, remain a part of the Haitian nation-state. Emblematic of this transnationalism was the appointment of Joe Etienne, the Director of the Haitian Centers Council, as Ambassador to the Bahamas.

D. Explicit Haitian Transnational Political Organizing and the Articulation of a Nationalist Haitian Identity: 1986–91

The efforts to popularize a concept of *Dizyèm-nan* came only after five years of explicit transnational political organizing that followed the fall of the Duvalier regime. In their efforts to challenge the Duvalierist forces that still controlled Haiti, Haitian leaders in both the United States and Haiti sought to link Haitian immigrants with the political struggles in Haiti. They sought to represent and legitimate the interconnections between immigrants and Haiti. As part of this quest they reshaped the way in which the term diaspora was used and understood by Haitians both in Haiti and abroad.

Previously, nationalist leaders had sought to popularize the term *"dyaspora"* as part of the narrative of exile told by immigrants committed to the politics of return. In this context, the word diaspora invoked an image of a population in exile whose mission was to return and rebuild their promised homeland. On radio shows and in newspapers, nationalist leaders spoke of "the diaspora" when referring to the Haitian immigrant population settled in the United States, Canada, France, and the Bahamas. In the contestation between the politics of return and incorporation, references to Haitian immigrants as "the diaspora" signaled continued allegiance to Haiti. In contrast, references to Haitian immigrants as the "community", the term popularized by U.S. politicians, social workers, often reflected a commitment to U.S. ethnic politics.

In 1985 Haitian leaders of working class backgrounds and those who avoided any form of political activity had never heard of the word "diaspora" and heard it as a foreign English word. By 1990 the word diaspora was well known and had entered Haitian Kreyol both in Haiti and among Haitian immigrants among all classes and degrees of political activism. However, in the course of those few years, the definition of diaspora had changed. While some sense of exile remained, among Haitians abroad the term had come to refer to Haitians who settled permanently outside Haiti but who continued to be responsible for Haiti. In Haiti it could mean "Haitians abroad" or carry a more pejorative connotation such as "upstart."

In reconstructing their concept of diaspora, Haitian leaders used as a model and made public reference to "Zionists," whom they envisioned as Jews who were permanently part of the political, social and economic life of the United States but who understood that they had a "homeland" in Israel. Jews became a potent example of the manner in which a people maintained obligations to their homeland and contributed to its reconstruction while remaining within the United States. Similarly, the Haitian diaspora was not obligated to return to Haiti but was obliged to provide Haiti with support and assistance. While connecting Haitians abroad and Haitians living in Haiti, the concept of the diaspora still drew a distinction between those in Haiti and those deyò (outside). Haitian immigrants had not yet been clearly located as an organic part of the Haitian nation-state.

Among those who appealed to the Haitian diaspora to take an active part in the rebuilding of Haiti were Père Antoine Adrien and Père William Smarth, two of the Haitian priests who had been part of the Haitian Centers Council and who had returned to Haiti after the fall of Duvalier. Beginning their organizing in Haiti with a massive literacy campaign in Haitian Kreyol, they sought financial assistance from Haitians abroad. They called their campaign Tèt Ansanm (Heads Together) and the persons joined together by their project were not confined within the geographic borders of Haiti.

The diaspora was expected to provide political as well as financial assistance, although the entry of the diaspora into the internal politics of Haiti was not welcomed by some of the political forces in Haiti. In the years between 1986 and 1991, when Haiti was ruled by a series of military juntas, those who defined themselves as leaders of the diaspora called on Haitian immigrants to participate in the campaign in Haiti for a new constitution and new elections.

Haitian politicians began campaigning in the United States for the Presidency of Haiti, even though Haitian citizens abroad were unable to vote without returning to Haiti. Many of the major Presidential candidates were persons who had lived abroad for a long time and who had a political base in the United States. Their political supporters included both Haitian immigrants and hegemonic institutions outside of Haiti, including the Catholic church, sectors of the Protestant evangelical movement, and the World Bank.[8] A number of candidates for the Chamber of Deputies, the Haitian Parliament, including several who went on to win seats in the 1990 election, also had lived and had ongoing connections in the United States.

There was constant talk in New York of Haitian elections, even after the abortive election of 1987, during which military forces massacred people at polling places. A sector of the *klas mwayen* settled in the United States began negotiating for a political voice for the "diaspora" in the Haitian political process. They wanted full dual citizenship with the right to vote in Haiti as well as in the United States, and they wanted "the diaspora" to have official representatives within the government of Haiti.[9]

By 1991, the diaspora had actively entered into the political affairs of Haiti. That this political interconnectedness reached up to the level of the top leadership in Haiti was first apparent in the manner in which Pascale Trouillot, the interim President who preceded Aristide, was selected. She came to power because of the backing of a coalition of forces that included the Haitian Centers Council priests and a human rights organization in Haiti that received funding and support from the Ford Foundation.

As transnational networks began to enter into active political life in Haiti, they also began to enter into the U.S. political process. In 1989 Trouillot appointed as representatives of the Haitian government in Washington and New York two long-time members of the diaspora. One, Raymond Joseph, was an editor of *Haiti Observateur*, the oldest Haitian newspaper in New York. The other, Henry Frank, was the Director of the Haitian Neighborhood Service Center, a community center that had begun in the 1960s with the explicit goal of organizing Haitians as an ethnic group. This organization had been continuously funded by the Community Development Agency of NYC and had joined with other Haitian community centers to form the Haitian Centers Council. Therefore the Haitian immigrants who officially represented the Haitian government were people who, at the same time, were participating within the U.S. political arena. Moreover, their political participation in the United States was framed by multiple identities that included black, Caribbean, and Haitian ethnicity. In the election that brought Aristide to power, several of the candidates, including Aristide, had transnational bases and had campaigned in the United States.

II. NEW HEGEMONIC CONSTRUCTIONS: THE DETERRITORIALIZED NATION-STATE

A. Redefining the Haitian Nation-State

Alone we are weak.
Together, we are strong.
Together, we are the flood.

Let the flood descend, the flood of
Poor peasants and poor soldiers,
The flood of the poor jobless multitudes (and poor soldiers),
Of poor workers (and poor soldiers).
The flood of all our poor friends (and poor soldiers) and
The church of the poor, which we call the children of God!
Let that flood descend!
And then God will descend and put down the mighty
     and send them away,
And he will raise up the lowly and place them on high (cf Luke 1:52).
                                        (Aristide 1990:104)

Despite its commitments to the electoral process and its lack of a radical platform of societal transformation, the Aristide presidency threatened the Haitian bourgeoisie and their hold on the state. For the first time since the Haitian revolution, the poor of the Haitian countryside, who make up the vast majority of the population, entered directly into the formal political processes of the nation-state. Aristide's candidacy built on the broad anti-Duvalierist movement that had ousted Jean-Claude and had been marked by the entry of the peasantry into the national political arena. In its mobilization of and efforts to empower the Haitian peasantry and urban poor, the anti-Duvalierist movement moved Haitian politics beyond the domain of the traditional competition between political factions based in Port-au-Prince.

The anti-Duvalierist movement put aside the traditional political language of black against mulatto, and built instead on the language of the *ti legliz* who spoke of the "poor, jobless multitude." However, it was not accompanied by a critique of the political economy of Haiti; there was no analysis of the role of the Haitian bourgeoisie in the impoverishment of the Haitian people, and of their links to global capital.[10] Although radically new in its mass base and transnational constituency, in its political direction the movement did not advance beyond previous Haitian political contention. Its most militant demand was for *dechoukaj* (uprooting), a campaign of direct action to uproot the Duvalierists completely from their grip on Haiti's political and economic system. As direct action *dechoukaj* was liberating but certainly not transformative. Once again the problems facing Haiti were attributed to the misdeeds of a particular clique.

Nonetheless, the entrance of the *ti legliz* into Haitian political life represented a challenge to the dominant strata in Haiti that went beyond a bid for formal political leadership. What was at stake was the legitimacy of the old regime and the definition of the state. When Aristide claimed leadership of the mass movement through his campaign for the Presidency, he named the movement *Lavalas*, the "avalanche, flood," and promised that the countryside would descend and overwhelm "the mighty." As the first President of Haiti to address the United Nations, Aristide entered the world stage speaking Kreyol. *Lavalas* contested the cultural values that had long been used in Haiti to reinforce and legitimate formal political domination. Lavalasians projected a national culture that originated in the Haitian countryside, but that was said to represent all Haitians who were on the side of rebuilding Haiti.

In their effort to validate rural Haitian culture, the Haitian revolution remained a potent national symbol, but its non-European and rural origins were made salient in public gestures such as the official celebration of the 200th anniversary of *Bwa Kaymen*. *Bwa Kaymen* is a commemoration of the voodoo ceremony in the north of Haiti said to be the beginning of the slave uprising in 1792. After Aristide won the Presidency, the 200th anniversary of the ceremony became a national holiday acknowledged by the Ministry of Culture and with commemorative activities broadcast on public television.

In place of a clearly articulated political program or an analysis of the roots of Haiti's underdevelopment, Aristide's movement offered a revitalized sense of nationalism in which the state belongs to and is responsive to the nation. Both the ancestral spirits and biblical scripture were invoked to produce a national vision in which God would "raise up the lowly and place them on high [cf. Luke 1:52]" (Aristide 1990:14).

Aristide's conceptualization of *Dizyèm-nan* must be understood in this context. Aristide moved to reinvent the Haitian state by adopting a nation building process that ruptured the territorial definition of the state. In doing so he gave to the Haitian population, both in Haiti and abroad, a new way to conceptualize their transnational experiences. He was creating bonds that had not previously existed between the Haitian population, wherever they were living, and the Haitian state. In Aristide's construction, no matter where Haitians had emigrated and settled, or how many generations in the past their ancestors left Haiti, they continued to be belong to the Haitian nation-state.

In envisioning Haitian immigrants as *Dizyèm-nan*, Aristide was telling Haitians abroad (*moun dèyo-yo*) to stay settled as immigrants but devote themselves to the reconstruction of Haiti. The concept of *Dizyèm-nan* spelled political opportunity to aspiring Haitian political leaders in the United States and they proceeded to hold a series of meetings to choose official representatives of the 10th Department (Haiti Progres 1992:8).

Despite Aristide's use of the term *Dizyèm-nan* to signify the full incorporation of the diaspora, on the level of political representation, the reclamation of those abroad remained symbolic. The majority of the Haitian Chamber of Deputies, representing factions opposed to Aristide, refused to give *Dizyèm-nan* official status. Dual citizenship was debated by the Haitian legislature but not granted. The Chamber also challenged some of the appointments that Aristide made to governmental and ambassadorial posts on the grounds that those nominated to represent the Haitian nation-state had become citizens of other countries and consequently were no longer citizens of Haiti. Indeed, a number of the people that Aristide recruited to work in his government and represent it were transmigrants who may well have become citizens of other countries.

Aristide's conception of a deterritorialized nation-state, as well as the specter of the rhetoric of popular empowerment becoming a revolutionary movement in Haiti, were threatening to dominant political forces in the United States. Aristide was very specific in insisting that his government had a right to intervene on behalf of Haitians living in other countries. In his address to the United Nations he committed his government to address the wrongs that Haitians suffered in the United States. That week a coup by the Haitian military forced him to flee Haiti.

Aristide was overthrown in September 1991, after only eight months in office. Aristide had talked about the "marriage" of the people and the army, and included the "poor soldiers" as members of Lavalas. Nonetheless, he was overthrown by the army, supported both by the bourgeoisie and by elements of the *klas mwayen*, whose grip on the state had been threatened by the Lavalas movement.

Marc Bazin, the 1990 Presidential candidate who had been away from Haiti for long periods while working for the World Bank, was appointed by the Chamber of Deputies as Prime Minister of Haiti. Bazin was widely rumored to be the candidate of the U.S. government. Despite Aristide's democratic election, which was validated by international monitoring, U.S. officials strove to delegitimate him by charging that he had violated the Haitian constitution. The campaign to delegitimate Aristide became transnational, waged simultaneously in Haiti and in the United States. Aristide had contributed to setting the terms of the debate by confining the mass movement in Haiti to winning his election as President. When he declared his candidacy for Presidency in 1990, he lent the weight of the prestige he had earned from years of fearlessly ministering to the poor to the electoral process. By participating in the election campaign, he endorsed U.S. and Haitian hegemonic concepts of the manner in which political power must be won and exercised. He reinforced the notion that change could be brought about by the democratic election of a new Chief of State.

The participation of transmigrants in election campaigns in Haiti reinforced the ideology of constitutional democracy that had long been part of Haitian political culture, despite the equally long history of coups d'état and military rule. For generations, political factions, displaced from power by the use of force, have cited the violation of constitutionality by their opponents as a justification of their own efforts to seize the state. Transmigrants who returned to Haiti to visit or settle brought with them the conviction that governments must be legitimated through formal democratic processes. When Haitian immigrants were being urged to form an ethnic constituency, become U.S. citizens, and vote, they also were being told that empowerment of people is actualized by their participation in formal democratic processes.

Haitian conceptions of formal elections as a measure of a government's legitimacy also have been influenced, within the past few decades, by the foreign policy of the U.S. government. For example, although U.S. foreign aid and military equipment continued to flow to the military juntas that proceeded Aristide's election, the assistance was often accompanied by statements that these governments were moving toward democracy.

In a contradictory way, the coup against Aristide served yet again to restrict debate about bringing fundamental change to Haiti to a question of constitutionality; the level of discourse remained focused on whether the army or Aristide were champions of constitutional government and democracy. While U.S. officials did not formally recognize the military-based government that overthrew Aristide, they said nothing about the constitutionality of a military coup. The United States also did not acknowledge or condemn the political violence the armed forces unleashed against the poor and the political opposition in Haiti.

The military and its new government suppressed all opposition, but they made special targets of the rural and urban organizations of the *ti legliz*, beating, raping, arresting, drowning, and shooting both leaders and supporters (see, for example "Human Rights Report" in *Haiti Info* 1992a,b, 1993b–d). It is widely believed in Haiti that several thousand people, almost all of them poor, have been murdered (Cable News Network 1993). However, the cultural hegemony that the Haitian bourgeoisie has long maintained in Haiti was considerably shaken. They were confronted with the impoverished majority of the population who, for the first time, believed that the Haitian nation-state belonged to them. They were forced to attempt to reestablish legitimacy in a situation transformed by the utilization of Kreyol as the language of political discourse.

At the same time, the political significance of a nation building strategy that envisioned a deterritorialized nation-state became apparent. The dominant strata in Haiti were unable to suppress the 10th Department, which turned into a powerful political opposition. Key to their potency has been the ability of Haitian transnational political leaders to speak as representatives of the deposed Haitian government at the same time they are also able to mobilize constituencies within the United States. The vast throng of tens of thousands of Haitians in the streets of New York City in October 1991, demonstrating in support of Aristide and holding the United States responsible for his ouster by the Haitian military, indicated the strength of the construction of a deterritorialized nation. So did the demonstrations of thousands of Haitians in other major U.S. cities. Their positioning within the United States has enabled transmigrants to gain access to U.S. media, to lobby in the halls of Congress, and demonstrate in the streets. A campaign to build public opinion has followed. An expensive full page advertisement signed by 3,500 organizations and individuals exposing the hypocrisy of the U.S. government's position on Aristide and Haitian refugees was placed in the *New York Times* (1992).

When Candidates in the 1991 Presidential primary in New Hampshire were greeted by a Haitian demonstration demanding that the United States government support Aristide's return to Haiti and grant refugee status to those fleeing Haiti, Haitian transmigrants entered directly into the campaign for the U.S. presidency. A year after the coup, the Haitian campaign to win over public opinion within the United States for support of Aristide was brought to the viewers of public television through the film "Haiti: Killing the Dream" that was shown across the country and reviewed by many newspapers. In Boston, where there is a politically vocal Haitian population a Boston Globe Editorial provided a quotation from Ossie Davis, the film's narrator. "Washington's promise to defend democracy in a new world order rings hollow in its own back yard" (Boston Globe 1992:12).

B. Uses and Contradictions of Deterritorialized Nation Building

From the beginning, Aristide's bid for political power, a bid that was supported and welcomed by many transmigrants living in the United States, was laden with an oppositional stance to the U.S. domination of Haiti. This stance was symbolized by pictures of Aristide that linked his image to that of Charlemagne Péralte, the martyred leader of the resistance to the U.S. occupation. After Aristide was overthrown, his concept of *Dizyèm-nan* gave a voice and political identity to Haitian immigrants that set them in opposition to American foreign policy. When they continued to support Aristide and oppose all moves on the part of the military and the United States to create an alternative leadership in Haiti or force Aristide to accept the military leaders, Haitian immigrants were opposing both the dominant class in Haiti and the continuing efforts on the part of the United States to dominate Haiti. In this spirit, when Marc Bazin was appointed Prime Minister by the de facto government that replaced Aristide, he was nicknamed "Mr. America" by the supporters of Aristide in both the United States and in Haiti (Haiti Info 1993:3). This labeling and Aristide's denouncement of both Bazin and of "American" policy in Haiti separated Haitian transmigrants from the United States and put them even more clearly in opposition to the United States.

At the same time, by building national unity between the classes and between those at home and the diaspora, a borderless nationalism has become part of the Haitian struggle against the subordination of the Haitian economy to both United States and global capital. The waging of this struggle within the borders of the United States strengthens the political potential of this movement. Aristide's use of funds raised from Haitian immigrants to create a funding base independent of foreign loans was just such a strategy, although the amount of money raised made it more significant symbolically than financially.

Even before formal deterritorialized nationalism was articulated, transmigrants living in the United States began to critique the effect of U.S. AID and World Bank policies on Haitian efforts to become economically strong. In 1986, for example, the Haitian Americans United For Progress (HAUP), a community organization based in Queens, New York, met to discuss what Haitians both in the United States and Haiti dubbed the "American Plan for Haiti," a development strategy of export processing industries, agribusiness, and food imports. HAUP, over the years, had built ties to a number of U.S. politicians, both in New York State and in the U.S. Congress. As it became engaged in critiques of U.S. foreign policy and global capital investment, HAUP was able to oppose U.S. policy both by radical public discourse and by lobbying within the U.S. political system. When, beginning in 1990, members of HAUP became intensely committed to the Lavalas movement, this critique of U.S. foreign policy that directly challenged capital penetration in Haiti, was joined to a potent transnational political movement.

In one sense Haitian transnationalism has come of age. The concept of *Dizyèm-nan* allowed Haitian immigrants to express their continuing ties to Haiti without eschewing their ties within the United States. Haitians publicly acknowledge and even celebrate their transnational practices, transforming themselves from a dispersed people to a people with many locations but with an enduring national bond. By constructing a political field that exists across borders, Haitian transmigrants reclaim for themselves the symbolic capital denied them within the U.S. racial order. However, as a construction which focuses Haitian transmigrant energies on the Haitian nation-state, there is much in the Haitian transnational experience that the idea of *Dizyèm-nan*, or any other formulation of Haitian borderless nationalism, does not encompass. The lived experiences of class, gender, and race are not fully encompassed in the refurbished nationalism of the postcolonial diaspora. The degree to which the population of Haitian immigrants is embedded within U.S. lifeways is not articulated. The differences in outlook and interests between transmigrants and those who remained in Haiti is not credited.

Contradictions of class underlie any construction of national identity, including that of the deterritorialized nation-state. As a nation building process, Aristide's concept of *Dizyèm-nan* privileged concepts of national unity over recognition of the class divisions within the Haitian population. Haitian immigrants and the population living in Haiti were offered a common set of symbols and a construction of history that opposed the hegemonic culture of the dominant class. Incorporation of the culture of the majority into the identity of the nation-state may have legitimated the state to the people, but it did not put the subordinated sections of the population in control of the state apparatus. Aristide's reconstruction of Haitian nationhood did not do away with the class divisions which have run through all of Haitian history. His upholding of the formal constitutional process as the means of empowering the disempowered, impoverished minority disregarded the differing interests and the differential power of the various classes within Haiti and amongst Haitians abroad.

Little was done programmatically to countermand the dominant class's control of the economy and the army. The program of Aristide and the Lavalas movement in some ways became reduced to the nation building project itself. The reform measures that were taken served only to threaten the interests of the dominant forces in Haiti without effectively reducing their power. For example, some of the corrupt personnel entrenched in the state apparatus were removed and the technocrats who came to staff the Aristide government were probably less corrupt. This step was necessary if any further economic and social change was to be implemented. However, most of the multiple means by which wealth is extracted from the rural majority were not challenged.[11] While some attempt was made to begin to collect taxes from the wealthier strata, the fundamental issue of the vast inequalities in the distribution of wealth and power were not addressed. The dynamic of impoverishment that impels and maintains migration was therefore not addressed within the new representation of the nation-state. The construction of national unity, a unity so inclusive that it encompassed Haitians wherever they might be living, had the vitality of inclusiveness, but the very breadth of its construction left no room to speak to the very real divisions of class in Haiti.

Also not addressed by the construction of the deterritorialized nation-state were class differences within the immigrant population.

Those who emerged as leaders of *Dizyèm-nan*, tended to come from the technocratic, professional, and business strata and, in general, had a base only within those strata. Among the exceptions was Wilson Désir, who was appointed to head the New York Section of *Dizyèm-nan*. A former military officer in Haiti, Désir had functioned for years as an old time political boss in New York. He built a base among the Haitian working class by means of personal favors and assistance to immigrants struggling to obtain legal immigrant status for themselves and their families, jobs, and housing. However, even in cases such as Désir's when official spokesmen have a broader following, they display different priorities than those of their compatriots living quietly desperate lives, trying to keep body and soul together in the United States and maintain kinfolk in Haiti. While members of diverse strata have become transmigrants and share an interest in developing and maintaining their home ties, their programmatic needs may be starkly different. Publicly validating immigrant ties to Haiti might speak to the needs of transmigrants who have investments in Haiti, those who hope to build transnational political bases, and professionals who desire to substantiate their status in both locations. But a transmigrant such as Immacula, whose one child is brain damaged from eating lead paint in her Brooklyn apartment, while another child back in Haiti suffers from malnutrition and neglect in the care of an ill grandmother, finds herself with the same spokesmen.

The word spokesmen is directly to the point. If divisions of class lie unarticulated within a deterritorialized nationalism, also silenced, although not dormant, are divisions of gender. Shortly after the ouster of Jean-Claude, thousands of Haitian women took to the streets of Port-au-Prince. From class backgrounds that included women factory workers, rural market women, professionals, and mulatto women of the bourgeoisie, these women had been brought together for the first time in Haitian history as a separate political force (Charles 1992b). The differential impact of political and economic crisis, including the strains of social reproduction with family members separated by large geographic distances, had brought them into motion. Their experience of the gender constructions of the United States and Canada and their ongoing transnationalism contributed to the creation by Haitian women of a self-conscious women's movement and the entry of this movement into the political arena. However, much of this political energy became absorbed into the Lavalas movement. This movement did not propose changes that could lighten the burden of social reproduction carried by Haitian women who wake each morning in both the United States and Haiti knowing, "if I leave my job, my whole family would die, because I'm the one who keeps them afloat" (Kerner 1991:4). The hyperspace of the deterritorialized nation-state leaves no room for the recognition that a disproportionate burden of the responsibility of insuring the physical survival and education of family members falls to Haitian women.

The concept of deterritorialized nation-states does more than obscure the class and gender structures within the Haitian population. Such nation building constructions conceal the ties of dependency that link national economies and their dominant classes to the global capitalist system. Yet it was this global system of domination and inequality that made it necessary for people to migrate to obtain employment and that perpetuates their inability to find economic or political security either at home or abroad (Glick Schiller and Fouron 1990). Global capitalism makes it increasingly likely that the concept of independent nation-state will exist, for postcolonial countries, only in rhetoric.

It is not only transmigrants like Mark Bazin, the former World Bank employee named Prime Minister in June 1992, who advocate development schemes that tie Haiti to global capital. Aristide, although wary of international capital, was forced during his eight months in office to negotiate a large loan for Haiti from the World Bank in order to try to keep the country afloat. At the very time that transmigrants are learning to identify with the Haitian nation-state and make sacrifices for its development, the policies of the entire Haitian leadership may be contributing to the increased subordination of Haitians at home and abroad to global capital.

Yet *Dizyèm-nan*, as a concept of a deterritorialized nation-state, is proving to be a double-edged sword. If it can be wielded in ways that maintain the class divisions within the Haitian population and further the interests of global capital, at the very same time, the very success of the construct can be directly threatening to the U.S. nation building project. By nationalizing the identity of Haitian transmigrants so that they begin to identify with the Haitian nation-state, Aristide and other Haitian political leaders have pulled Haitian immigrants away from a cultural politics that incorporated them within the U.S. body politic. Until the past few years of Haitian immigration, as we have seen, Haitian immigrants in the United States did not link their pride in nation to the Haitian state, although their strategy of adaptation to the U.S. racial order led them to identify themselves as culturally distinct. Haitian cultural distinctiveness based on pride in the Haitian national past could be encompassed within more recent U.S. nation building projects that make ethnicity salient within a pluralist model or, more recently, black ethnicities within a multicultural paradigm.

For over twenty years the dominant class forces within the United States and the various forces that have contended for leadership in Haiti have sought to shape the outlook and win the political allegiance of Haitian immigrants. But the growth of the Lavalas movement, the construction of *Dizyèm-nan*, and the subsequent ouster of Aristide have raised the stakes. They have demonstrated the potency of Haitian transmigrants as an awakened Haitian nationalist political force implanted right within the U.S. body politic.

The transformation of the manner in which Haitian immigrants have come to identify themselves was made apparent when, after Aristide's ouster, Haitian refugees again began to take to small boats and flee the political and economic situation in Haiti. The very different reception that the Haitian diaspora gave Haitian boat people in the 1970s compared to the 1990s encapsulates the extent of the changes. In both instances, the U.S. government, as well as sectors of the press and U.S. politicians, defined the Haitian boat people as undesirable, impoverished, and diseased people seeking economic opportunity rather than political asylum. In both instances the U.S. economy was in a recession and black impoverished immigrants made good scapegoats. As we have seen, when Haitian boat people began arriving in the 1970s, they were not at first championed by Haitian organizations. Haitian doctors in New York showed no interest in assisting them. Many strata among Haitian immigrants tried to distinguish themselves from the Haitian refugees and, if fact, shrank from identifying publicly as Haitian. The Haitian boat people of the 1990s, who fled the political repression and economic deterioration that accompanied the ousting of Aristide, received a dramatically different reception from the Haitian diaspora. The 10th Department embraced these refugees. Their detention became the symbol of the Haitian people — a single people living in both Haiti and the United States whose desire for liberty was being blocked by the U.S. government. However, in the face of a dramatically weakened economy, this show of Haitian unity was not warmly welcomed by dominant forces in the United States and the Haitian refugees were denied political asylum and returned to Haiti (Masland, Katel, and Mabry 1992).

Haitian transmigrants have accepted the advice of U.S. hegemonic agents from foundations and government agencies to churches and philanthropies who, as we were able to document in the history of

Haitian ethnic organizing, persistently advised immigrants to gain empowerment in the United States by becoming citizens and participating in the U.S. political process. However, Haitian transmigrants did not follow the hegemonic agenda of eschewing commitment to and political participation in the nation-state from which they or their parents originated. By accepting the construction of the deterritorialized nation-state that defines them as perpetual citizens of their countries of origin, they used their participation in U.S. politics in ways that went contrary to the U.S. hegemonic agenda.

C. Moving Beyond the Nation-State

As Haitian immigrants have become more thoroughly incorporated into the United States and Haiti, Haitians' sense of race pride has begun to form broader senses of identity that pose additional challenges to United States nationalism. Small but increasing numbers of Haitians have begun to construct their identities in the United States, not only as part of Haiti, but also as part of an African diaspora. They have begun to respond publicly to political movements that identified them as African people.

Alliances between Haitian immigrant leaders and African-American leaders began in the 1970s during the first wave of Haitian boat people, but they took on a new tone when the dimensions of Haitian transnationalism became publicly visible after 1986. Haitians have found that African-Americans have simultaneously sought to bind Haitian political identification to the U.S. polity and worked to mold forms of identification that go beyond loyalties to either the United States or Haiti. The efforts to engage Haitians to identify with U.S. national interests have taken many forms. We have seen that African-American political leaders, such as Major Owens, and African-American representatives of U.S. hegemonic institutions, such as the Community Service Society, worked to build organizations of Haitian immigrants committed to participation in the U.S. political process. Members of the Black Congressional Caucus have worked to obtain influence and connections with Haitian transmigrants who were recognized as potential leaders in Haiti and to embed them within a sphere of U.S. influence. In the days that directly preceded the fall of Jean-Claude, for example, Major Owens approached Haitian organizations with a proposal to build a Haitian government in exile based in the United States.

However, these African-American leaders have been part of a broader movement to forge a broader black identity that serves to critique the U.S. racial order and generate a post-nationalist identity for black people. Increasingly open racist attacks and a more public racism by the end of the 1980s led to more active political alliances between Haitian politicians and African-American leaders and organizations. Broad sectors of the African-American leadership, from Dinkins, African-American radio personalities on WLIB, and the black nationalists who organized to oppose attacks on black people in various neighborhoods in New York City made appeals that went beyond African-Americans and constructed and popularized the term "African" for black people in the United States. For example, when a Haitian woman became involved in an altercation in a Korean vegetable store in Flatbush in 1988, a neighborhood of dense Haitian settlement, the attack was defined as an attack on African people, and a mobilization of forces that was based on African-Americans but reached out to the leadership of Haitian organizations took place.

As compared with the term African-American, in which the bottom line identification is with the United States, the category "African" has some resonance for many Haitian transmigrants. Our 1985 interviews with Haitian leaders revealed that fifty-nine percent of the leaders identified themselves as black/African. The transnational reconstruction of Haitian culture as an African originated culture, and the legitimation of this culture in the course of Aristide's presidency, strengthened the readiness of Haitian immigrants to identify as African.

This African identification became a political force in the massive demonstration of support for Aristide by Haitians in New York in October of 1991. The demonstrators were not only greeted by Mayor Dinkins, New York's African-American mayor, who saw Haitians as potential constituents within the U.S. political process, they were also greeted as African people by African-Americans committed to this more global racial identification. This newly emergent African idiom contained an acknowledgment of a global racial order and of the necessity of resistance, but did not link the perpetuation of this racial order to the structure of global capital.

NOTES

1. The data about Haitian organizations were gathered through field work in the New York metropolitan area in 1969–71 and 1985–91. It included attending organizational meetings and activities and in

gathering and in some cases participating in the writing of organization documents. In addition, in 1985 the leaders of 91 Haitian organizations were interviewed and in 1986 representatives of 63 American organizations that had funded and provided technical assistance to Haitian organizations were interviewed. The Haitian organizations were selected out of a universe of 189 organizations that we had identified and an estimated total of 250 organizations in the New York Metropolitan area in 1985. The American organizations were identified as having contributed to the development of the Haitian organization in the sample of 91. The goal was to interview 100 organizations, but interviewing was stopped after the fall of Duvalier because the change in the political situation in Haiti had a profound impact on the goals, public statements, and activities of Haitian organizations in New York.

2. Haitians were separated from African-Americans, who were organized into another sector of the Democratic Party. However, although organized as a "nationality" rather than as a race, Haitian-Americans were to be a nationality who were not expected to look to their homeland. In their meetings with Haitian immigrants the Democratic party officials said nothing about the political situation in Haiti and nothing about race. The other "nationalities," particularly those from Communist countries such as Soviet Union and Eastern Europe, were encouraged to talk about their "imprisoned" homelands. This discussion about the "old country" fed into cold war politics. But Duvalier was anti-communist and Haitians received no encouragement to talk of Haiti; discussions with the Democratic party always focused on participation within the United States political process.

3. As a result of one such stalemate, I became the HACSO representative to the Goldberg-Patterson campaign for Governor of New York State in 1970. The two factions of the organization, which represented persons of different class backgrounds in Haiti, could agree on no other representative.

4. The English translation for this phenomenon became "regional associations."

5. In 1990 the U.S. Food and Drug Administration prohibited Haitians from giving blood without making a clear cut case that justified the targeting of a nationality. The highest risk in the United States was actually to be found among New Yorkers. See Glick Schiller (1992).

6. It is interesting to note that Catholic priests made a significant contribution to the formation of an overarching Italian ethnic identity among Italian immigrants in the 19th century who came to the US with loyalties that did not extend beyond their village or region in Italy.

7. The social workers who actually worked to build a coalition of Haitian centers, who wrote the Ford grant, and who linked HCC to the New York City Department of Social Services were African-Americans.

8. Leslie Manigat received sponsorship from the Catholic Church in New York. Marc Bazin has worked for and is closely associated with the World Bank. He was widely believed in Haiti to be the candidate of the United States. Slyvio Claude was linked to U.S. Protestant evangelism.

9. Some Haitians had de facto access to dual citizenship, but it was by sham. It became a fairly widespread practice for one to apply for U.S. citizenship, in the interim period report that one's "green card" (permanent residency card) had been lost or stolen, and obtain a second green card. One could then turn in this replacement card when the citizenship papers were complete. Upon returning to Haiti an individual could then display a U.S. green card rather than a U.S. passport, therefore having the right to vote and hold political office in Haiti. The fact that the individual was in point of fact a U.S. citizen would not be known.

10. It should be noted that Aristide, before he was elected President, did make reference to American imperialism, but did not offer a consistent radical critique of capitalism. In 1988, for example, in the same radio message in which he denounced a coup that merely replaced one Haitian general for another and called for the flood to descend, he said "To prevent the flood of the children of God from descending, [t]he imperialists in soutane have conspired with the imperialists of America" (Aristide 1990:104).

11. A significant expectation was the elimination of the *chefs de section*, local rural authorities that had both police and civil authority and who often lived by intimidation of and theft from the rural population that they were appointed to administer. However, these individuals were not brought to justice and jailed, and after the military coup that replaced Aristide, they were returned to their posts, where they proceeded to persecute supporters of Aristide.

Chapter
SEVEN

Different Settings, Same Outcome: Transnationalism as a Global Process[1]

Shots rang out ... people and guards ran on the airport tarmac... Horror was reflected on the faces of Benigno Aquino's relatives and friends, who were forced by guards to stay inside the plane that had just landed at Manila International Airport but who had heard some of the commotion... The crowd assembled outside the airport to welcome him, wearing yellow ribbons of hope, heard the news... Emotions ran high.

Five years before, Benigno Aquino had joined his wife, Cory, and their children in suburban Boston, Massachusetts. Their children were studying in the United States as their parents had before them. From their simple home Cory and Ninoy supervised from a distance their considerable land and business holdings in the Philippines. Then Benigno decided to return to the Philippines.

For months after the televised and shocking assassination of Benigno Aquino upon his return to the Philippines in late August, 1983, news programs throughout the United States and around the world conducted a complex investigation into the crime and its political consequences for an already compromised and extremely bankrupt Philippine government. The battle for public opinion that was being waged daily in the media came to a head again in November 1985. During prime time President Marcos addressed U.S. television viewers from his presidential palace, giving them his reassurances that justice would be carried out and explaining to them his plans for an upcoming "free" national election that would be held two months later.

Between 1983 and 1985 many new Filipino organizations such as the Ninoy Aquino Movement (NAM) and Justice for Aquino, Justice for All (JAJA) formed in New York and Washington. Other more radical organizations — such as the Committee to Advance the Movement of Democracy and Independence (CAMDI) and the Organization of Filipinos in America Aiming for Democracy (KAPATID) — continued, but with new appellations that publicized their commitment to democracy. Using their contacts in the Philippines, all of the organizations started providing information to Filipinos in the United States about the political situation at home. They jointly sponsored prominent Filipinos to speak to audiences of Filipino transmigrants. They also showed underground videos, exhibited photographs, and presented theater plays on the issues. At the same time they provided information to anti-Marcos groups in the Philippines about the international and U.S. perspectives on the crisis. This news was then fed into rapidly developing underground newspapers that were becoming readily available on the streets of Manila and elsewhere in the Philippines.[2]

This intensified level of political activity began to mobilize other Filipino-American organizations of professionals that had previously concerned themselves primarily with incorporating their members into the U.S. work force with full professional rights and appropriate credentialing. Coordinating with groups like NAM, which had opened branches on the West Coast, these Filipino-American organizations started co-sponsoring speeches by Filipino politicians, bankers, civic leaders and intellectuals. They mobilized Filipino voters to pressure the United States Congress to support Cory Aquino, since Marcos was still strongly supported by the Reagan administration. These transmigrant organizations, already transnational in their other activities, were entering the U.S. political process in order to obtain change in the Philippines.

Over and over again NAM's president Heherson Alvarez, a former Philippine Senator and Delegate of the Pre-Martial Law Constitutional Convention, pointed to the lack of democracy in the Philippines under Marcos and called for its restoration. Another transnational Filipino organization, the National Movement for Free Elections (NAMFREL), collected considerable funds among transmigrants and U.S. sympathizers, which allowed them to monitor, together with the official commission on elections (COMELEC), the presidential elections of February 1986 in almost every precinct in the country.

Following the elections and their heavily publicized monitoring by United States congressional leaders, the United States made a quick turn-about to support Cory Aquino and sustain the image of the United States as a friend of democracy. Globally televised images showed Filipinos willing to sacrifice their lives for democracy in their nation. Filipinos at home and abroad were united in their pride of their newly won democracy, legitimated by global news coverage and world wide praise.

The newly elected President Aquino recognized the contribution of transmigrants by inviting many of them to become cabinet ministers or to enter different levels of government. Others were elected under her sponsorship to important provincial posts, which, when these people were later identified as American citizens, created quite a stir in the Philippines. A good number of these returnees, disappointed by what they saw happening in the new government and no longer feeling at home either in the Philippines or the United States, soon returned to their careers and families in New York.

Having contributed to the development of a new transnational political field based on a new reading of Filipino nationalism, and having been instrumental in electing a new Filipino President, the United States-based transmigrants began to make some demands of Philippine presidential candidates. They asked for expanded citizenship rights that included the right to vote in Philippine elections, the right to own land in the Philippines without restrictions as foreigners, and dual citizenship. At the same time they continued to struggle in the United States for rights as immigrants or citizens.

* * *

The drama of the decline and fall of Marcos and the rise of Cory Aquino at first seems a uniquely Philippine event. Colonized for more than half a century by the United States, the Philippines certainly has a different historical relationship to the United States than Haiti, Grenada or St. Vincent. These past colonial relationships have contributed to the tenor of political discourse about the relationship between the Philippines and the United States. The current ability of Filipino immigrants in the United States to make known their views of U.S. foreign policy and to influence the course of events in both places is a reflection, in part, of the wealth and status of these immigrants. A significant sector of the Filipino immigrant populations in the United States comes from dominant strata within the Philippines and has achieved success in the United States as professionals and business people. Nonetheless, in many ways Filipino immigrants strongly resemble those Caribbean immigrants whose transnational practices we have described.

Different in cultural and political history and racial designation from those of the Caribbean, but suffering from the same progressive erosion of their standard of living, Filipino newcomers to the United States have also become transmigrants, constructing for themselves multifaceted layers of connection between the United States and their "home" country. They, too, have entered the contentions over immigrant identity that characterize nation building processes in the United States. At the same time, responding to their national leaders, these Filipino immigrants have also expanded their visions of the nation-state into one of a deterritorialized nation that can encompass the Philippine diaspora. In this chapter we will compare the Philippine and Caribbean contexts, exploring the areas of difference in order to highlight the similarities and argue that the transnational processes we have identified are global in scope.

I.   COMPARATIVE HISTORICAL OVERVIEW: CONDITIONS LEADING TO TRANSNATIONALISM

A.   The Position of Postcolonial National Economies in the World System

At first glance, the colonial and postcolonial trajectories of economic development in St. Vincent, Grenada, Haiti, and the Philippines seem to have strikingly different contours. However, despite the relative wealth of the Philippines, as compared to the ecological devastation of Haiti and the minimal resource bases of St. Vincent and Grenada, by the 1970s all these countries were sending significant sectors of their populations abroad. By the 1990s several common trends among the four countries had become clear: (1) the development of postcolonial states that have become direct agents of extraction of wealth from the majority of their populations; (2) the intensive penetration of global capital in the form of both loans and investment by multinational corporations; (3) the domination of all four countries by the United States; (4) a resultant deterioration of the standard of living for all but the dominant classes; and (5) a vast emigration, from all classes, including broad sections of the middle strata, who could only maintain their class positions by migrating.

There never was much industrial development in St. Vincent, Grenada, or Haiti, although their societies and economies were the very creations of early capitalist expansion. Their colonial plantation economies were central to the growth of European economies throughout the sixteenth, seventeenth, and eighteenth centuries. However, by the 19th century, although St. Vincent, Grenada, and Haiti were never totally without plantations, these islands had became backwaters. For the most part, their economies were dependent on subsistence and small scale cash cropping. Precluded from 19th century industrial development by their colonial or neocolonial positioning, these islands moved into the 20th century with a large base of agricultural or peasant laborers, a very small middle stratum, and a dominant class linked to and dependent on European capital. Their current economic situations are dismal, the increased presence since the 1970s of foreign capital only intensifying the fragility of their economies.

An economic trajectory that would include extreme dependency and massive migration did not seem to be what was awaiting the Philippines in the first few heady decades after the Philippines finally won independence from U.S. colonial rule in 1945. In comparison with the relatively smaller Caribbean islands we have examined, the Philippines, although also an island economy, has a much larger population (80 million in 1990) and land base, consisting of 114,830 square miles spread across some 7,000 diverse islands, many agriculturally and minerally rich, with plentiful rivers, streams, and high mountain ranges of volcanic origin.

Although comprised of several ethnically and racially differentiated groupings, including aboriginal Negritos, Chinese immigrants, and small, scattered, culturally diverse upland populations, the bulk of the Philippine population consists of Malay lowlanders who come from three major island groups[3] and speak eight main languages.[4] After three hundred years of Spanish indirect colonial rule, initiated in the sixteenth century and extending to the takeover by the United States in 1898, Spaniards and Spanish mestizos still amounted to no more than one percent of the population (Abella 1971:9–10; Phelan 1959:24–25).[5] The marked linguistic, cultural, and racial heterogeneity of this population is reflected in the composition of Filipino migrants in the Unites States. However, this study focuses primarily on people of Cebuano and Ilongo origins (Visayas) which migrate in large numbers and belong to the Philippines' second largest linguistic group. These cultural origins shape the migrants' kinship and gender relations and many of their organizational practices.

The Filipino colonial experience and more recent nation building projects have tempered the cultural differences that characterized much of the nation's population. Spanish rule resulted in the conversion of large lowland sectors to Roman Catholicism, the religion which predominates today among approximately 70% of Filipinos (Pido 1986.) Colonial and postcolonial economic policies and practices also led to processes of class formation that today override many regional differences.

During the early years of colonial rule and well into the nineteenth century, the Philippines remained primarily a subsistence economy. There was some commercial development based on accumulation by local elites and the growth of a stratum of Chinese merchants. They were kept in place however under Spanish indirect rule. Subject to taxes, labor corvee and tributes, the Philippines experienced only limited economic growth. By the 19th century, foreign capital, which was primarily British, began to transform the productive base in ways that allowed local elites to increase their wealth and power by developing large sugar plantations and extracting rents from tenant rice farmers. Capital penetration further accelerated when the Philippines became a direct colony of the United States in 1898. The United States developed plantations of pineapple, coconut and hemp and expanded the mining of the mineral resources of the islands which include copper, gold and chromite.

Unlike Haiti, St. Vincent, or Grenada, the postcolonial experience for the Philippines was marked by an initial period of relative economic development. For two decades after the Philippines won their independence from the United States, the country began to develop an industrial base. The Philippine state followed a focused policy of import substitution that expanded industries developed under U.S. rule. Thus, in the 1960s the Philippines seemed to be a showcase of economic development, poised for a successful economic future. Analysts based their assessment of the promise of Philippine development on the fact that in addition to an industrial base and extensive natural resources, the Philippines had the technical know-how and sufficient local capital to develop a strong national economy (Cheetham and Hawkins 1976; Golay 1968; Wurfel 1988; Baldwin 1975).

However, the condition of the rural economy which supported the bulk of the population contained important warning signs. During the 1960s and 1970s the World Bank and USAID and other substantial foreign investors had developed a sector of export agriculture. At the same time, "green revolution" and "land reform" programs actually displaced rice tenant farmers and lease holders, increased the cost of rice, which is the basic staple of the Filipino diet,[6] and led to a tremendous deterioration of the living standards of rural workers. By 1971 half of the rural families had less than adequate nutrition and life essentials (Russell and Hawkins 1976:94–95).

The intensive penetration of global capital into Philippine industry began in the 1970s. By the mid-1970s, the IMF and the World Bank had thrown the Philippines into a path of economic "liberalization" and export-led industrial and agricultural growth. These agencies dismantled the Philippines' former import-substitution protected industries, using as an incentive large structural adjustment loans and requesting further peso devaluations in 1981 and 1982 (Hawes 1987; Broad 1988).[7] By 1981 the "liberalization" of the Philippine economy was virtually completed, thus bringing about its fuller integration into the world economy.

During that period, Marcos, who became President in 1965, initiated export processing zones for multinational companies in order to increase the foreign exchange that would help repay these loans. In sterile laboratory type factories, young uniformed women workers produced, at low cost, microelectronic chips, micro conductors, and garments for export. Marcos also opened the doors wide to tourism and facilitated the transfer of lumber and rice land to agribusinesses, often foreign-owned.

Although a positive growth of the GNP continued throughout the 1970s, underlying this apparent success story were serious problems of redistribution and development.[8] Rather than producing a flourishing national economy, these development strategies proved suicidal for the Philippines (Wurfel 1988; Broad 1988; Shalom 1981). The country was bankrupt, with vast and increasing balance of payments deficits (Sussman, O'Connor, and Lindsey 1984). The world prices of key Philippine agricultural exports dropped, oil prices rose and Western countries, who were themselves facing recession and structural crisis, erected tariff barriers against manufactured goods from the third world. By the mid-1980s, the Philippines was the post colonial country most indebted to the International Monetary Fund, with no relief in sight. At much the same time that economic crises became severe in St. Vincent, Grenada, and Haiti, the Philippines, despite its earlier promise, was facing economic disaster.

The import substitution policies of the 1950s had not improved the existing disparities between rich and poor. Despite the overall growth between 1956 and 1965, the share of income going to the lowest fifth and the lowest three-fifths of families declined, while the share going to upper-income groups increased. The top 5 percent of families throughout this decade reported more income than the bottom 60% (Shalom 1981:146–147). The development strategies of the 1970s and 1980s resulted in ever declining incomes among many strata and a serious erosion of the ability of Filipinos in a wide range of occupations to meet their basic needs. The standard of living of the middle strata eroded dramatically. By 1973, the earnings of a Philippine secretary were 15% lower than the next lowest paying Asian country, accountants received 13% less, and mechanical engineers 50% less (Russell and Hawkins 1976:94–95). By the 1980s, even a schoolteacher could not afford to buy more than two chickens a month and could only purchase low quality rice. The export of foodstuffs continued to grow and the middle strata could not feed themselves.[9] As the economy deteriorated, increasing numbers of people of all classes began to leave the Philippines.

During the early 1970s, while the Filipinos faced the beginnings of an economic crisis of major proportions, they also confronted major political transformations. Many of these political transformations were taking place under a declaration of martial law by Marcos in September 1972.[10] Promising a "New Society" that would transform the Philippines into a more egalitarian, prosperous nation, Marcos consolidated his state power under a nationalistic slogan of "Isang Banwa, Isang Diwa" (One Nation, One Mind) (Magno 1983). In the name of ridding government of graft and corruption, he sapped the strength of regional and municipal elites. In the name of a "democratic revolution from the center," he attacked the left and student opposition. Political restructuring, and particularly the centralization of power under the Marcos regime, as well as repression contributed to the vast migration that had begun to take shape.

The defeat of the Marcos regime and the assumption of the presidency by Aquino in 1989 did nothing to remedy the downward decline of the Philippine economy. On the contrary, tenant farmers experienced another U.S. financed Land Reform that actually assisted agribusinesses in their efforts to consolidate their landholdings. Meanwhile all development efforts were sacrificed to the constraints of debt repayment. The "liberalization" of the economy continued and with it the destruction of the independent Philippine industrial sector. Under Aquino, therefore, significant sectors of the population continued to look to migration as a means of survival.

B. Migration

Economic conditions, combined in some places with political repression, were already difficult enough by the 1960s in all four countries to lead increasing numbers of people from all strata to migrate. As conditions deteriorated during the next two decades, with intensified penetration of capital and concomitant dislocation and unemployment that eroded salaries and reduced living standards, the dimensions of the migrations grew and the United States became an important area of settlement.[11] Eastern Caribbean immigrants built on settlements in the United States established earlier in the 20th century.[12] Filipino migration to the United States jumped from 19,307 during the decade of the 1950s to 98,376 in the 1960s, and then to 354,987 in the 1970s and 477,485 in the 1980s (U.S. Immigration and Naturalization Service 1990). By the late 1980s, Filipinos had become the largest and fastest growing Asian population in the country (Gardner, Robey, and Smith 1985).

As we saw in the Caribbean case studies, Caribbean populations in New York in the 1960s contained a sector of persons who had relatively high levels of education and skills compared to their countrymen and whose migrations reflected family strategies to protect hard fought gains and also obtain additional resources. Maintaining social position was also a major concern of the Filipinos who began to migrate in the decades of the late 1960s and 1970s. The first to migrate were a highly educated middle stratum of professionals,[13] mainly the children of the entrepreneurial provincial elites. Between 1965 and 1969, the Philippines had replaced all of the European countries as the leading source of foreign physicians in the United States and, along with India, was providing the bulk of foreign scientists and engineers settling in the United States (Morales 1974). Subsequently, the bulk of the legal migration to the United States consisted of family reunifications (16,760 out of 20,810 in 1989, for example), which, by drawing on different strands of family networks, as well as new provincial populations, led to a more diversified mix of managers, accountants, teachers, service workers, and domestics.

Important political personages and sectors of the bourgeoisie also began to establish transnational bases for their families, as competition between Philippine local and national elites intensified over control of the state apparatus. Sectors of the dominant class who were displaced by Marcos as well as sectors of the Marcos clique established political and economic bases within the United States. In addition to Cory Aquino, a sector of the Aquino-Cojuanco family, which represents a sector of the Philippine bourgeoisie with extensive agricultural holdings and financial interests, settled in the United States and built a political base. As a representative of this sector, Cory Aquino was able to capture the Presidency of the Philippines and stay on through her term of office in great part because of her use of a politicized constituency of Filipino transmigrants in the United States. But the Aquinos were not the only capitalists who migrated. The Vice President under Marcos, Fernando Lopez, also developed a base overseas, as did many after the defeat of Marcos.

C. Racial Barriers as Incentive to Transnational Connections

Whatever the class background or nation-state of origin of migrants of color who enter the United States, they come as subordinated people. This political and economic subordination is a process that continues to structure all aspects of their experience in the United States. Sitting on his front porch in Port-au-Prince, a 40 year old carpenter who had lived on remittances sent by family members living abroad for 20 years and who had never even visited the United States was able to verbalize a widespread Haitian conclusion about the racial structuring of the United States. "You can become a citizen of the United States, but you will always be Haitian because they will continue to see you as Haitian." In one way or another the members of each of the populations — Vincentian, Grenadian, Filipino, and Haitian — have found, although they don't always openly acknowledge it, that no matter what their citizenship or place of birth, U.S. racial constructions continue to see them as outside of the "real America." Consequently, and despite the impoverishment of their home countries, Caribbean and Filipino migrants, although they have physically moved away, have felt constrained to produce and maintain multiple layers of transnational social connections. The more they come to know America, the more they take up as their own agenda the building of deterritorialized national identities.

In each case, however, the manner in which immigrants from these populations have come to articulate their sense of estrangement from the United States is shaped by their own national constructions about race and nationality formed in their home countries. All Caribbean immigrants face overt racism: whether they are seeking employment, promotion, housing, walking down a street, or entering a shop, they do so as blacks. Haitians have found themselves specially targeted, their national identity turned by U.S. health authorities from a symbol of black defiance to a trope for lethal transmissible disease in the form of HIV infection.

The Filipino experience of discrimination often has been more subtle but just as pervasive. Filipinos arrived with images of the United States that were the legacy of U.S. colonial educators. Expecting the United States to be a land of "equal opportunity for all" — unlike the personalized patron-client relationships underlying the rigid stratification of the Philippines — they often have found their ability to advance blocked by racial discrimination. A Filipino doctor explained,

> After years of work overseas and after passing our U.S. professional exams, our white colleagues in the hospital treat us condescendingly, as not equally experienced or knowledgeable, a bit as second-class citizens.

A secretary found she was easily able to find a job, but

> I realized after a while that I was paid less than some of the American secretaries, while often being given more responsibility, and that when career possibilities opened up they were not offered to me despite my achievements on the job.

Anger about these experiences of daily racial discrimination at the workplace has been exacerbated by the projection of media images of Asian migrants as the "model immigrants" who are all well educated and successful (Bell 1985; Kasindorf et al 1982; Newsweek 1984; Time 1985; U.S. News and World Report 1984). In the early 1980s, Filipinos were among those Asian immigrants singled out as exemplars of prosperous, well incorporated immigrants and held up as a model to other ethnic groups (Takaki 1990). Filipinos have found increasingly, however, that this very publicity has exacerbated the racism and hostility they face, both at work and in the neighborhoods where they settle. The hostility often comes from Hispanics and from African Americans. In general, verbal and physical attacks on anyone perceived as "Asian" increased in the late 1980s, together with the across the board resurgence of xenophobia and an increase in racial incidents registered country-wide (Filipino Reporter 1989b).

In fact, the success of this celebrated "model minority" is in part mythical. Images of having "made it in America" mask the professional credentialing Filipino immigrants brought with them and discount the racial barriers prominent in the career experiences of the Filipinos quoted earlier. In terms of personal income, Filipinos have in no way achieved parity with whites. Household incomes, as with the Caribbeans, include several more family members, working many hours. Households with professionals may also include family members located in a secondary sector of the economy where both wages and promotional prospects are low. And similar to the Caribbean immigrants, promotions at all levels are limited, so that even managers may only be able to see, but not reach, the top (Takaki 1990). This explains both the anger expressed by Filipinos about reports of their success and their joining with other Asians in recurrent public denunciations of racial discrimination in the United States.

Filipinos, together with other immigrants from Asia, have challenged racial discrimination through a variety of means, including law suits and community organizing. Even as they have continued to insist on full and equal incorporation into the United States, many Filipinos have become increasingly committed to a pan-Asian identity or have begun to develop broad racial constructions. A U.S. based Filipino publication editorialized that

> America is largely owned and operated by white anglo-saxon protestants (wasps) ... [And though] as a large country, America makes a good effort at providing equal protection under the law for people of different races, it also does not hold non-white people in high esteem (Philippine News, 1990).

II. TRANSNATIONAL SOCIAL FIELDS AND DETERRITORIALIZED STATE PRACTICES: FAMILY, BUSINESS, AND ORGANIZATIONAL ACTIVITIES

A. Family Connections: Transmigrant Families Compared

Adela B. first came to New York with her husband Raoul in early 1986. Their situation in Manila, with their eight children (seven boys and a girl) had been deteriorating steadily, because rampant inflation linked to the repeated devaluations of the peso, mandated by the IMF, had seriously eroded their purchasing power. Adela and Raoul had known much better times. In 1965 they had owned a sprawling and beautiful Filipino-Spanish style house in the old city of Iloilo where Raoul was the successful manager of the business interests of his half brother. Adela at the time took care of her many children with the help of housemaids.

But Raoul lost his job because of a family misunderstanding and was unable to find adequate employment, and so Adela, a high school graduate, was forced to look for work. Although she finally landed a good secretarial position in the National Bureau of Investments, the family's changed circumstances meant they faced increasing difficulty supporting their children in school. Part of the family strategy had been to obtain educational advantages for the children but they could no longer afford the tuition of the private schools the children had been attending. As the situation in the Philippines worsened both economically and in terms of personal security, Adela and Raoul could see that the entire family faced a lowering of their class position and reduced social status. They were particularly concerned that in the situation of widespread unemployment in the Philippines, their children would face serious difficulties.

Adela and Raoul took a calculated risk and migrated to the United States, although it meant they had to leave two of the children behind to finish school. With the assistance of relatives who had preceded them, the family settled in Queens, where they tried to economize on housing so as to be able to send money back to the Philippines for their children to continue their educations. In 1992 they were still in the same apartment, living with two of their children and two recently arrived nieces, who are part of their extended transnational family network.

Adela has found work as an administrative secretary in the pulmonary wing of a hospital. Raoul, who found work as a watchman, continues to search for the right business opportunity. From their salaries they have been able to give most of their children college educations, but only by keeping the family divided. While three children live in different locations in the United States, assisted by relatives who have settled in California and Chicago, several children have maintained a family base in the Philippines.

Child rearing decisions have been made by phone with Adela and Raoul constantly monitoring their children in the Philippines. When their only daughter, troubled by having been left behind in constrained economic circumstances to watch over her brothers, had an unfortunate romance, a friend visiting the Philippines was dispatched to investigate the situation. In the past six years Adela has been back three times. Each time she has brought *pasalubong* (gifts) for everyone. In order to recover some of the costs of the trip she has bought inexpensive watches, for example, in Manhattan and sold them for a profit in Manila.

The two sons, now married and living in Manila, have started a small business with the help of their parents and plan to buy a piece

of land on which to build a family house. The daughter who
remained behind, once she was educated, was able to secure a position with the Bank of New York in Manila. She is marrying a
prosperous dentist there.

The marriage and return visit to Manila for the wedding represent
the triumph of Adela and Raoul's transnational family strategy. The
family returned laden with *balikbayan* boxes filled with high status
items purchased in the United States such as electronic equipment,
kitchen gadgets, and expensive cosmetics. The celebration of the
family victory cost many thousands of dollars — the tickets were over
$1,000 each for the parents and four siblings, even when bought
within the Filipino network.

Raoul became a citizen last year and this year Adela took her turn
at swearing her citizenship oath of allegiance to the United States, but
she is hoping that the Philippines will soon pass a bill that will allow
dual citizenship. She has made American friends at work and is involved in local Filipino affairs in Queens.

Adela and Raoul, as we saw in the vignette above, became transmigrants as they began to make family decisions across national
borders. In the Philippines, as well as in the Caribbean, transnational
family processes and relations between people defined as kin constitute the initial foundation for all other types of transnational social
relations. Immigrants from each country of origin we studied come
with family structures and kinship expectations shaped by distinctive cultural histories and separate experiences of colonial domination. Yet kinship, however defined, has been stretched and
reconfigured as households and families have been extended transnationally.

Historically, Caribbeans of all classes have used family networks
of kin to provide access to resources. Flexibility, for centuries a
hallmark of Caribbean family patterns, continues to be important in
the continuity of Caribbean transnational families. Among the Caribbean rural and urban poor, women bear much of the burden of
responsibility for supporting children. This expectation has facilitated situations in which women have often been able to migrate first
because of the availability, until recently, of employment and permanent residency papers for those who worked as domestics. Although family structures in the Philippines are very different from
those of the Caribbean, in the process of becoming transnational
some striking similarities have emerged.

Middle class family households in the areas from which Filipino
immigrants to the United States originate are increasingly nuclear.

However, in the United States Filipino households resemble Caribbean households in their inclusion of extended kin. These Filipino families, like Caribbean families, have a strong bilateral base and by extending this bilaterality they develop transnational kin networks. Filipino immigrants also have found ways within their structures of kinship to respond to the greater ease with which women have sometimes been able to obtain immigration visas as nurses, teachers, and domestics by calling on their cultural construction of "elder daughter." Transmigrant kin networks frequently center around women who are said to have special responsibilities as "elder daughters" for their kin. When additional staffing for family networks has been needed, Filipinos have been able to extend their networks to encompass fictive kin constructions of "compadre" or "comare," in much the same way that Caribbean peoples have created fictive kin under the rubric of "cousins," "aunts," and "uncles."

The patterning of the transnational family connections of the migrants from the Caribbean and the Philippines are so similar that we can draw some general conclusions. Because, in all of these societies, the family domain is considered a zone of private affiliation rather than commerical relations, it can operate more flexibly beyond state policies and impediments. This allows for the flexible mobilization of extended family labor and resources somewhat outside the orbit of immediate state intervention and direct regulation. This location facilitates "family" strategizing and income generating activities that make the family a transnational base. Family networks, stretched across political and economic borders, provide the possibility for individual survival within a situation of subordination to world capitalism both at home and abroad.

At the same time, as we saw in both the Caribbean and Filipino family vignettes, transnational family strategies are used to maintain and, if possible, enhance social position. These strategies contribute to class reproduction and differentiation. In both the Philippines and the Caribbean, class processes are embedded within transnational family dynamics.

1. Family Production and Reproduction: Issues of Class Formation

Adela and Raoul, living in their crowded apartment in Queens and working at dead-end jobs, plan their home in the Philippines. The uncertain and insecure circumstances immigrants encounter in the United States intensify the role played by the home societies as a symbolic and at times actual security net. Within this context of global insecurity, constructing a base back home becomes a shared Filipino family project. This means building a proper family home that can become a haven during hard times — if only in the family's imaginings — and a place to shelter children and family members unable to migrate. The symbolic and concrete import of this structure is realized on occasions when children are sent home to be minded by grandparents, or when members of the family use it as a haven to which to return or from which to plan the next migration voyage.

Base building is something that immigrants from all four countries frequently do. We saw the Carrington family members from St. Vincent living in three locations — New York, Trinidad, and St. Vincent. They collectively invest their savings and energies in the project of fashioning a well equipped and comfortable family home in St. Vincent, even though Mavis Carrington married a man from the even smaller island of St. Kitts and rarely visits St. Vincent. The modern structures they build with all their appointments serve as the symbol, as much to the family as to the outside world, of its social progress. The rural areas and small towns of the home countries are strewn with cement houses with metal sheet roofing, signaling status, commonly called "dollar houses" in the Philippines because they are built on such remittances.

On the other hand, members of the family networks left at home may serve as an important social and political base for transmigrant kin, providing a place for the migrants to stay on their visits home, making the arrangements necessary for their visit, and systematically sustaining the migrant's connection to the local community. Kin at home provide the necessary support for migrant kin with political aspirations in their hometowns by orchestrating and managing the migrants' visits and soliciting support within the home community. While the survival and well-being of kinsmen left at home is enhanced by remittances, many transmigrants also build prestige and influence in the home community. Adela and Raoul transfer consumer items from the United States back to the Philippines, where they have utilized a whole variety of activities to establish reputation and status.

The migratory efforts of individuals are often made possible only through the collective efforts of family networks. These collective efforts take many forms. The pulling together of capital and labor resources across transnational social space may allow a poor family member to migrate. A woman may be freed for additional income earning activities by bringing a niece, cousin, or low cost hometown domestic helper to the United States. A young relative may become a Filipino shopkeeper's helper or a business trainee. The ideology of kinship helps to ensure workers who are reliable and trustworthy and willing to exchange their labor for only a small stipend. The rubric of family solidarity, shared mutual interest, trust, and responsibility is used to justify both at home and abroad the exploitation of individuals as cheap labor. As we have seen, transnational survival strategies are not of equal benefit to all players. Consequently, the tensions of family life may at the same time reflect the tensions of class struggles. Those who find themselves entrapped and severely limited by family circumstances and ideology may develop festering resentments.

Immigrants who are brought to the United States to provide cheap labor that sustains family enterprises and strategies often begin to feel exploited. Caribbean or Filipino migrants brought to work as domestics within households so that members of the family can attend to professional careers often rebel when they compare the subsistence they receive to other employment possibilities in the United States. Family members left at home in both the Philippines and the Caribbean to look over the migrants' interests at home often live on remittances that provide them with only bare subsistence, while the mobility they might achieve through migration is severely curtailed.

John, the man in Saint Vincent who manages and farms his sister's land holdings, certainly gains a livelihood this way, but the affective bonds of family may at times keep him from actively searching for other paths to social mobility for himself and his family. His opportunities as well as those of his children differ from his sister's, but his incentives to migrate have indeed diminished. Adela's daughter, who stayed behind to look after her brothers, was helped by remittances, but until her marriage she felt that her chances of building a future for herself were reduced because she was assuming this family responsibility. Even when there are tensions produced by the dynamics of class reproduction and differentiation, there are tremendous human costs involved in transnational migration. These costs often play themselves out in family separations, such as that experienced by Adela and Raoul, who had to leave some of their children behind in the Philippines to be educated. The separation of the Carringtons, trapped by the undocumented status of their various members in Trinidad and the United States and stretched across three different countries, echoes this pain. Immacula's efforts to sustain her children by leaving some of them in Haiti, only to

return to find her daughter, once bright and eager but now listless
and malnourished, also speaks to the price being paid.

These costs have a number of dimensions: the personal, emotional
cost for the individuals involved, who must live daily with the pain
and strain of separation; a shift in the quality of family relationships
away from ties built in the process of daily interactions and conversations to relationships built on brief interactions, occasional phone
conversations, and voice or video tapes; and the stress that accom-
panies surviving in a transnational double world that forces migrants to adapt to considerable shifts in habits, expectations, and
locale much too rapidly and frequently.

Each of these examples spotlights the sacrifices that constitute
transnational family strategies. In a world configured into nation-
states, each claiming that its population maintains a unique history,
culture, and identity, those who must live their lives across borders
may come to see themselves as perpetually unauthentic, feeling at
home in neither their "home country" nor the United States. "My
life," we heard Dr. Paul confide to his home town association, "has
no meaning." Imaginings of the deterritorialized nation build on
these yearnings for belonging and acceptance.

2. Is Transnationalism Reproduced?

At first glance, it might seem that transnationalism is more
epiphenomenon than process, since most transmigrants we have
described as constructing transnational life spaces are first generation immigrants. There may continue to be multiple processes by
which cultures flow into each other, but will successive generations
continue social relations in which distant locations and discrete
countries become fused within a single arena of human interaction?
In the understanding of transnational processes developed in this
book, continuity will depend not on memories or ideas but on the
practices of the second and third generations. Is it likely that
transnationalism will emerge as a transgenerational process?

Because family networks underlie the dense intertwining of
transnational connections, we think that transnationalism will continue as an arena of social relations. Families of immigrants are
continually being reconstituted across generations as well as borders.
The fact that family strategizing is often intergenerational is an important indication that transnational processes reflect more than the
experience of first generation immigrants. It is likely that transnational relations will continue as long as conditions in both locations

remain insecure and the flow of migration to the United States is unimpeded.

Actually there is not just one "second generation." The tendency for children to move between linked households in both the United States and the home country means that one sector of the next generation experiences multisocietal socialization by kin residing in multiple locations, and is somewhat prepared to assume roles within transnational family networks. Children sometimes return to the Caribbean in the summer or for a period of their educations. Some children are only brought as young adults to the United States from the Caribbean or the Philippines where they live with siblings who have grown up primarily in the United States.

On the other hand, many children raised in the United States avoid identification with the home country as adolescents and then become drawn into transnational family networks and enterprises as adults. In all instances, the political upsurges among the transmigrant population have transformed youth living in the United States who may previously have avoided identification with their "home country" into active players on the transnational stage. For example, young Filipino high school and college students were galvanized by the death of Benito Aquino and the rise of Cory Aquino and participated actively in transnational political activities, even though they were born here. The Lavalas movement, including the election and the ouster of Aristide, motivated large numbers of Haitian youth to begin to identify with Haiti. The Haitian students at Cornell, some born in the United States, who organized a conference on transnationalism are an apt example. Similarly, the ascendancy of the Bishop government in Grenada transformed many young immigrants living in the United States into politically conscious transmigrants, some of whom returned to Grenada to participate in nation building activities.

B. Business Connections

Transnational family networks may be used to develop large and small businesses across national borders. These can include (1) businesses of facilitation that nurture and assist transmigrant connections; (2) businesses physically located in only one part of the transnational social field, but which are dependent on influxes of goods or capital from transmigrant connections; and (3) transnational capital investments built up as the capitalist class in postcolonial countries become transmigrants.

Businesses that facilitate transnationalism owe their existence to, and in fact arise from, the interstices created by ongoing transnational social relations. Whether they are shipping and air cargo businesses, courier businesses, shippers of *balikbayan* boxes, travel agencies, remittance or money transfer houses, import-export establishments, or contractors of transnational manpower, these undertakings all thrive on the interconnections established between people in the United States and the home society. Some of these businesses facilitate migration by recruiting workers in the home country to work in the United States. They also assist people in their efforts to travel back and forth and to send consumer goods, products for businesses, and cash from one location to the other. In addition, these businesses expedite the rapid communication that makes it possible for transmigrants to share the same life space and make their daily life decisions together with people from whom they are separated by great physical distances.

The full potential of facilitating businesses has rarely been realized among Caribbean migrants, both because of the racial barriers that confront black people in the United States and the difficulties of capital accumulation in their resource-scarce home economies. While some Haitian money transfer companies have accumulated sizeable amounts of capital, which they have invested in expanding their businesses in Haiti, the continuing political insecurity in Haiti limits the growth potential of these companies. The ability of eastern Caribbean businessmen to generate large blocks of capital in the United States through transnational facilitating businesses has been particularly restricted by the limited resources of the eastern Caribbean.

For example, Carl's shipping company, which transports goods for transmigrant families and businesses between New York and St. Vincent, has remained confined to localized Vincentian immigrants in Brooklyn. Carl's efforts to expand into other economic arenas have confronted racially discriminatory bank policies. Moreover, the narrowness of Carl's own resources, compounded by the relatively meager amount of goods most Vincentians are able to send home, make it difficult for Carl's business to grow if it remains confined to transmigrant shipping. His company's existence is premised on the inexpensive labor provided by his brother in St. Vincent; Carl lacks such connections on other Caribbean islands.

It is by turning to the Philippines that we are able to see the full extent to which transnational migration provides for the growth of business interconnections on the one hand, and on the other, how these businesses then strengthen the transmigrants' multistranded social fields. The larger population size and resource base of the Filipinos, the approximately two million Filipinos settled in the United States with increasingly dense transnational ties, and the greater industrial development of the Philippines have all contributed to the development of large scale transmigrant businesses. Johnny Air Cargo and Man Asia provide examples of such businesses.

Well incorporated in New York as an accountant in a U.S. firm, the founder of Johnny Air Cargo, Mr. Valdez, began to build a business to provide him with a second income while still in his 30s. He began by selling rice and vegetables to Filipino nurses scattered around the New York metropolitan area, but moved into transnational facilitating when he began to deliver boxes filled with goods sent by nurses to the Philippines. At first, Johnny Valdez took these boxes to the Philippines himself, as if they were his personal *balikbayan* boxes. When the Philippine customs agents objected to the large number of boxes Mr. Valdez was importing and began taxing them, he decided to specialize in the bulk air shipment of transmigrants' packages. He also started a courier system to pick packages up in the New York area and deliver them personally to relatives in the Philippines. He now has offices in New York, Manila, and six other Philippine cities, a fleet of some 100 couriers, and a special agreement with certain airlines. Recently voted one of the top businessmen in New York City, Mr. Valdez has become a millionaire through his multiple facilitating enterprises.

Man Asia is another Filipino enterprise that demonstrates the manner in which transnationalism can create business niches for migrants. The founders, who were lawyers and U.S. permanent residents, initiated the firm in Manila in 1972 and began to act as labor contractors. At first they specialized in short-term contracts for nurses with a large hospital in New York City. They then discovered that they could generate other niches for migrant workers by having offices in New York as well. Using their transnational connections, they began to place female teachers in private Catholic parochial schools and health professionals in hospitals in the New York metropolitan area.

A second type of commercial activity, while located in one national setting or another, utilizes transnational social and family relations and resources to further its undertakings. Such activities include the transfers of goods, food, and labor across national borders. This may take the form of dry goods, book or record stores, religious activities such as healing or voodoo, or the staging of musical and cultural events. Businesses often develop in the home societies and depend on transnational connections to facilitate their growth. Such activities include entrepreneurs who come to New York to buy goods to sell back home — clothing, flowers, beauty products, video tapes, records — or to become familiar with current styles and ideas at the "cultural center" that they will take home. Begun with tiny bits of transmigrant capital, often by individuals who have returned home after years as migrants, they remain transnational, since they build and depend upon continuing family networks for infusions of cash, products, or ideas.

A third form of economic activity is linked to transnational capitalists, who because of the social and economic bases they have established in two or more societies, are able to move their capital to the areas of greatest opportunity. While this practice is an economically significant trend among Hong Kong Chinese (Ong 1992) or Indian transmigrants (Lessinger 1992) settled in the United States, only the Filipino migrants in our study had control of sufficiently large amounts of liquid capital that could be transferred between bases of operation in different societies. These capitalists may rely on family members located in several countries to protect political relationships that are basic to their efforts at capital accumulation.

Transnational businesses generate more than money. Economic enterprises, while generating entrepreneurial capital for their owners, also facilitate the transfer of social status, consumer goods, and information on social relations that is critical to social mobility and the restructuring of class positions at both ends of the transnational migration continuum. Such transnational economic activities also have a political dimension. When transmigrant organizations support the economic policies of national governments, as we saw in the cases of St. Vincent and the Philippines, or when national governments try to create an economic base among migrants, as in the case of the Aristide government in Haiti, the political interests of the national governments and the economic activities of transmigrants become directly intertwined and politicized.

III. TRANSMIGRANT ORGANIZATIONAL LIFE

1985. In Lower Manhattan, May 1985, an inauguration party launched a new organization, the Philippine Center for Immigrant Rights. The organization's main objective is to help less fortunate Filipino workers in the United States — nurses, teachers, etc. — by providing legal advice about discrimination and illegalities on the job and by helping them locate jobs. Initiated by a mixed group of expatriates and long-term transmigrant residents, they also exchange information and help radical, anti-Marcos groups back home. Their popular newsletter informs Filipinos (and Americans) in New York about the problems the migrants face both here and there. The organization's inauguration, set up as a Philippine style festival, began with a panel of Filipino immigrants and keynote speakers that included an old-time immigrant living in the United States since the 1930s, a political refugee, an undocumented worker, the President elect of the Association of Philippines Practising Physicians in America (APPPA), and others who shared their experiences as immigrants to the United States (Filipino Reporter 1985). Also included were Filipino food, music by the Anauan artists group, art/photo exhibits by Filipino expatriate artists and American women photographers, and cultural presentations such as theatrical skits by Filipino authors. The aim was to unify the Filipino overseas experience, give it a common agenda, and clarify some of the political linkages with the situation at home.

1987. When more than 1,000 delegates from over 300 Filipino-American professional and umbrella organizations, including some Hawaiian and Canadian counterparts, met in Los Angeles, August 4–9 1987, to celebrate a newly found "unity" among Filipinos overseas and to promote a renewed effort to work for the Filipino-American "place in the American sun," as they had done in the 1970s, their speeches contained new dimensions. In addition to Representative Solarz, Los Angeles Mayor Tom Bradley, and the speaker of the Hawaii House of Representatives, David Kihano, talking about Filipino participation in American political life, prominent Filipino government guests, sponsored by the meeting organizers, insistently asked the participants to invest back home in development projects and reminded them of problems at home.

1991. Filipino-American organizations are also developing new Pan-Asian lobbies to respond to what has been increasingly perceived as a renewed racist threat. "We are submitted to increased discrimination in hiring practices, in job careers, in the streets and feel that we deserve as naturalized Americans a better deal" (Philippine News 1991).

In developing organizations that are transnational in their practices, as these vignettes illustrate, Filipino immigrants resemble Vincentians, Grenadians, and Haitians who have settled in the United States. When we analyze the histories of immigrant organizations among all these populations we confront the same paradox: the entry of immigrant organizations into the political arena back home has worked to strengthen their incorporation into the United States. For the Filipinos, this trend emerged after 1983, when hometown associations, organizations of Filipino-American professionals, and radical groups developed or enlarged their transnational activities. By the 1990s, organizing for incorporation in the United States and the Philippines had become closely connected and mutually reinforcing processes that stretched across national borders. For all four populations the paradox of increased political practice back home, coupled with heightened incorporation into the United States, has generated new contradictions. Organizations of transmigrants embrace the nation building projects of the political leaders of their "home countries" at the same time that they struggle against the limitations of constructions of deterritorialized nation-states.

A. Organizational Practices and Individual Social Positioning

From a transnational perspective, past debates about whether immigrant organizations retard assimilation or promote incorporation are rendered meaningless. At the current moment all four populations consist of transmigrants who look increasingly to organizations to provide ways and means for building relationships across national borders and for developing projects in home countries at the same time that organizational activities also embed them within the United States. As we have seen in previous chapters and in the vignettes, organizations that engage in transnational activities come in many forms. Transmigrants have formed benefit societies, hometown associations, churches, fraternal lodges, sports clubs, social clubs, cultural clubs, professional and vocational organizations, advocacy groups, alumni or "old boy/girl" school networks, and philanthropic groups. The projects these organizations have built "back home" have been many and diverse. They have provided money for small development projects in hometowns, disaster relief, education of the youth, or local activities that celebrate, continue, and in some situations help invent local culture, such as Carnival in St. Vincent and Grenada.

In some cases, transnational organizations have branches of the same organization in the United States and in the country of origin. Caribbean evangelical churches and masonic lodges and Filipino Civic Associations (Lions, Rotary, Jaycees) have such interconnections.[14] In other instances, organizations in the United States count on trusted individuals back home, such as a priest, a member who has returned, or kin of leading members to supervise activities in the home country. During the 1960s and early 1970s, the Philippine organizations in the United States that were later swept into the political processes that brought Cory Aquino to power had such double agendas.

Filipino organizations have differed from those formed by Caribbean immigrants in two respects, although the outlines of their organizational histories and their agendas are similar. The wealth of a stratum of Filipino transmigrants has rendered the transnational projects of their organizations larger in scope. Moreover, organizations of doctors, lawyers, and nurses play a prominent role among Filipino transmigrants because cf the comparatively larger stratum of professionals among Filipino immigrants in the United States. Because of their clout, large Filipino professional organizations have been more successful than their Caribbean counterparts in easing the movement of professionals from the Philippines, where they were trained, and assuring their insertion into the U.S. work force. Filipino professional organizations have both facilitated the credentialing of professionals in the United States and helped recruit professionals in the Philippines for employment in the United States.

At this moment, activities to further the collective good among each of the four populations often take a form that works to promote or maintain the social position of the organizations' most influential members. We saw that Earl Cato, after becoming president of a Vincentian voluntary association, found himself defined as a political authority on his return trips to St. Vincent. Doctor Paul, from a prominent family in a small town in Haiti, wanted his hometown organization to build a sports center there as a way for him to maintain and validate his family position in Haiti as well as his success as a professional in the United States.

Transnational organizational practices provide another vehicle for individual transmigrants to obtain and reinforce their social position. Joining, and even more significantly leading, such transnational organizations provide migrants with a chance for public validation and recognition both within the United States and in their country of origin. Such status validation becomes a high priority for the many immigrants who, through migration to the United States, have achieved a higher standard of living, but only by accepting lower status positions within the United States and withstanding the daily assaults of racism. Framed around philanthropic and cultural projects — for example, reclaiming a cemetery, sending food, medicine, hospital beds, and school books back home, and building a migrant Carnival hall — activities of these organizations serve to make both the organizations and their members known among the population back home.

In the Philippine case, such activities are on a large scale because the membership of transmigrant organizations consists, in large part, of the educated children of provincial elites, who have developed a multitude of transnational practices to maintain and enhance the status of their families in both the United States and in their hometowns. Organizations that are part of larger transnational systems — for example, the Filipino Rotary, Lions, Jaycees, and Charismatics — have been particularly successful through their activities in small towns in reinforcing the positions of local elites. Aspiring political candidates in these towns have recently campaigned for elective position in the Philippines using Lions clubs organized in the United States as their base. Philanthropic projects and care for the poor, as well as broader projects — for example, rebuilding the church, fixing the school grounds, beautifying the municipal hall plaza, helping to improve the health center, and sponsoring local fiestas — carried out by these transnational organizations contribute to the image of wealthy families as benefactors of the people. The long standing practice of local small town and regional elites of enhancing their political and social positions by sponsoring fiestas has been sustained by the contributions of transmigrant family members able to donate large sums to fiestas in the Philippines.

As we saw in the Philippine vignettes that opened this chapter, as well as in the Caribbean case studies, transmigrants' organizations of all types may become drawn into ever more explicit political activities. The very nature of transnational organizational activity enables migrant associations to wield political influence in both the host and home societies. In the act of spanning and connecting host and home societies, these organizations become important channels for the transmission of ideologies, political and social capital, and personnel. They are important terrains for the contestation of political ideologies and constituencies.

In all our case studies, political events in the countries of origin, connected through multiple layers of transnational networks, reach into the United States and penetrate deeply into immigrant life. Associations organized to obtain more rights and benefits for immigrants in the United States, organizations of self-defined exiles, staunchly apolitical Christians, health professionals, voodoo priests, ex-police, ex-teachers, and hometowns were brought together around common national symbols and politicized at moments of crisis "back home." The bottom line of such mobilization was not sentiment but concrete ongoing transnational social fields that gave broad numbers of immigrants an immediate stake in what was happening in the country of origin. In all our cases, the results were dramatic. Transnational political organizations and politically mobilized transmigrants actually played a role in toppling regimes and putting new governments in place. The Philippine case is the most striking. The Aquino government came to power with the assistance of transnational oppositional organizations in the United States that were able both to sustain organizing at home and rally public opinion in the United States.

B. Organizational Responses to Hegemonic Constructions of the United States and Home States

As we have seen, transnational organizational activities build on family networks that have proven to be the foundation of transnational social fields yet that intersect with personal transnational agendas. They strengthen and are strengthened by the interconnections of transnational businesses. Organizational activities, however, differ from other domains of transnational practices, because it is organizational activities that give transnationalism its most public face. The presence, as well as the practices of these organizations, have contributed much to the subjectivities of transmigrants. Because they are engaged in constructing meanings and identity, as we have seen, immigrant organizations have always been an arena of active hegemonic contestation for the political loyalty of migrants. As they have become increasingly transnational, these organizations often directly confront and respond to the hegemonic agendas of both the United States and the leadership of their home countries. By so doing, they help to shape the terrain of contestation between hegemonic nation building projects and the ongoing transnational practices of transmigrants that engender multiple identities.

As we have seen in our introduction and in subsequent chapters, the hegemonic contexts, in both the United States and the postcolonial countries of origin, have changed over time. At different moments immigrant populations have been exposed to — and at times have reappropriated and created — public constructions that have emphasized race, ethnicity, and nation. The first wave of eastern Caribbean immigrants entering the United States in the early decades of the twentieth century confronted a rigid two-tier racial structure. Their identities and cultural practices were forcibly shaped by the institutionalized racism that permeated all aspects of U.S.

social life. Realizing that African-Americans were defined at the social bottom, and eager to escape this social designation, some Vincentians and Grenadians formed their own organizations. These functioned as benefit societies to assist in their members' adaptation to the United States, but they also allowed them to maintain their separate systems of status validation. Vincentians and Grenadians brought into these organization some of the hegemonic constructs that had shaped their subjectivities in their home countries. But since their own home locations were colonies of Britain, there was no strong national sense in those constructions, so that their identities were articulated in other terms. Eastern Caribbean immigrants called on cultural symbols of King, Queen and the British empire to describe who they were and to establish their social and cultural distance from African-Americans and racial stigma.

The Filipino experience of the first few decades of the 20th century was also formed by both colonialism at home and the racial structure of the United States. Filipino subjectivities had been shaped by their experience as colonial subjects of a new U.S. imperialist project. They grew up reciting the American "Pledge of Allegiance" every day in their schools, saluting the American flag, and hearing about Lincoln and the United States from their idealistic U.S. teachers. Mostly young men of rural backgrounds, once settled in the United States these early Filipino migrants — about 45,000 by 1930[15] — were confronted with segregation, miscegenation laws, and exclusion from the possibility of naturalization and access to opportunities in the larger society. This was traumatic for them since they had come with very different expectations and had enthusiastically accepted the idea of the United States as their land of opportunity. Instead, they found that their representation as "little brown brothers" gave them no claims to belonging in the United States (Ilar 1930:13).

Within the context of the racial constructions of the time, Filipinos tried, unsuccessfully, to counter the legal discrimination they encountered by arguing that as members of the Malay race, as opposed to the Chinese and Japanese Mongoloid race, they should not be subject to racial barriers. By so doing, however, they accepted the racial terms of the debate, rather than attacking its racist base.[16] They also became active in California labor conflicts during the 1930s. Even though they dreamt of returning home, they did not have a strong sense of nation; their identities had been largely defined by their colonial relationship to the United States. Not very different from the eastern Caribbean immigrants in their attitude toward Great Britain, the Filipinos laid claim to the same United States that had made them colonials while adamantly challenging their subordination. Most of them never returned to the Philippines (Pido 1986; Takaki 1989).[17]

By the middle 1960s, the context that framed immigrant organizing changed dramatically. Former colonies were on the road to becoming or had already become politically independent nation-states, and people of color in the United States had begun to talk of liberation and empowerment. U.S. hegemonic constructions of nation were widened to include those who were "culturally plural," that is, those who were different from the WASP mainstream because they were immigrant, people of color, or both. A reading of American political and economic history that portrayed immigrant populations as able to obtain economic opportunity by joining in the U.S. political process as members of organized ethnic groups was popularized. Some U.S. institutions even funded and accorded public recognition to immigrant organizations and leaderships that represented themselves as the public voices of particular U.S. ethnic groups.

The initial response of the eastern Caribbeans, Haitians, and Filipinos to the pluralist model varied, but over time each population developed organizations that claimed empowerment under the rubric of cultural pluralism. Filipino immigrants chose public invisibility rather than public ethnicity during the 1960s and early 1970s. For them, to accept an ethnic identity was to accept a status perceived as outside and subordinate to the mainstream. Because they were for the most part well-educated professionals emerging from a recent U.S. colonial past, they wanted to be treated as individuals and to become part of the mainstream society of their former colonizers. Choosing not to settle close to other Filipinos, as part of their striving to remain unobtrusive, they tried to merge with the mainstream population. Collectively they were ambivalent about racial conflicts, even though a number of the children of the 1930s immigrants became active in the civil rights struggle. The numerous small organizations they created, however, provided them with professional networks and support, an incipient sense of Philippine identity in their quasi-isolation, and the fertile soil from which to create small philanthropic projects back home. Filipino immigrants were so inconspicuous that a Filipino social scientist interested in ethnic empowerment labeled them the "invisible minority" (Pido 1986).[18]

Similar to those of the Filipinos, the earliest Haitian organizations were elite social clubs; efforts in the 1960s to organize around a

Haitian common ethnic identity were weakened by the interests of the upper and middle strata in preserving the lines of color and class distinction that ordered political and economic life in Haiti. During the initial period of settlement, and for some time after, many of the newcomers shunned the construction of themselves as ethnic subjects. They also kept their distance from African-Americans, believing that by "not being black twice" they could avoid positioning on the social bottom of U.S. society. Intense stigmatization drove Haitian immigrants to organize around a myriad of public identities from Taoists to teachers.

The eastern Caribbean migrants, in contrast, already had structures that were compatible with representations of pluralism. Ethnic organizations forged by the immigrants during the early part of the century remained in place and reinforced the immigrants' island-based and West Indian identities. For West Indians, invisibility meant a social and cultural merger with African-Americans (see Bryce-Laporte 1972). For this population, eager to escape the stigma and social position associated with race, pluralist ideologies insinuated that West Indians constituted an intermediate social category, culturally distinct from African-Americans. Eastern Caribbeans, as other West Indians, began to differentiate themselves publicly from African-Americans with whom they had previously organized to obtain greater rights and access to employment, housing and education. The leaders of eastern Caribbean organizations, as part of a larger West Indian constituency, increasingly recognized their need to become actors in the political processes of the United States as West Indians, carrying out political lobbying, mobilizing local constituencies, and becoming identified by U.S. Institutions as "ethnic leaders" who spoke to the situation of West Indians within the United States. Their ethnic thrusts were expressed in Caribbean support groups for New York City mayoral candidates who held out the promise of access in exchange for votes.

Eventually the hegemonic pressures for immigrants to define themselves in terms of culturally distinctive ethnic groups bore fruit among all four populations. Some organizations among Haitian and Filipino as well as Eastern Caribbean immigrants began to identify themselves as hyphenated Americans, with organizations such as the Haitian-American Citizens Society, the Caribbean-American Chamber of Commerce, and the Filipino-American Political Organization making their appearance. The term "American" verified that they were now part of the U.S. body politic as a voting constituency, albeit one that kept the symbols of their "culture" and addressed the situations of their homelands.

But the initial reluctance of Philippine immigrants to be publicly differentiated, and their subsequent enthusiastic adoption of pluralist rhetoric, can be traced to a strong commitment among many sectors of Filipino immigrants to become part of the U.S. mainstream. The first national newspaper for Filipino migrants, the *Philippine News*, appeared in California in 1972, and another, the *Filipino Reporter*, on the East Coast, followed later that same year. Over the course of the next two decades, the assertion by Filipinos that they were an American ethnic group became more public. A number of the main professional associations (e.g., nurses, doctors, lawyers) became regional or national in their focus. However, as with the Haitian and even to some extent the eastern Caribbean transmigrant populations, although a more public ethnic presence began to emerge, Filipinos as a whole remained divided by regional, occupational, linguistic, and class differences grounded in their home societies.

Accompanying the unfolding narrative of ethnic politics were subtexts that increasingly connected transmigrant organizations to the nation-states that transmigrants continued to call home. Transmigrants were thus responding to several different contexts as they crafted identities — and accommodative resistances — in response to their situations as immigrants in the United States. Some of the Filipinos, Vincentians, Grenadians, and Haitians who arrived during the 1970s were radicalized youth, intellectuals, and political elites who brought with them experiences with or knowledge of anti-imperialists struggles. Each brought a "pride in nation" that grew in response to periods of political upheaval in their home societies and the racial barriers the immigrants confronted in the United States. The Filipinos built their sense of nationhood in counterposition to their colonial history, both absorbing and rejecting colonial images of Filipinos. The Haitians came with an historic sense of the Haitian nation as a symbol of both political independence and opposition to white domination. This identity became a base for simultaneously opposing their racial subordination in the United States and for organizing around nationalist projects directed at Haiti. The eastern Caribbeans built on an emerging nationalism derived from their more recently achieved political independence as they redefined themselves as part of a West Indian ethnic group. Nationalist organizing had a resonance among Caribbean immigrants, who were already constructing multiple transnational fields. In many ways

Bishop in 1983 and Aristide in 1991 articulated constructions of the citizenry of transmigrants that many of these immigrants had long struggled to have officially stated and thus legitimated.

In the case of the Philippine State, these articulations had occurred as early as 1973, when Marcos started defining former Filipino citizens overseas as *"balikbayan"* (homecomers) to entice them back home. This continued as the Philippine State began to act as a labor contractor for workers and professionals migrating to the United States and to the Middle East. Such articulations reached a climax when the Philippine government began taxing overseas earnings. As these state policies developed, those who settled outside the Philippines began being identified as still citizens, and addressed by Philippine Presidents as if they were still part of, the Philippines.

It was not until the Aquino crisis of 1983–86, however, that they responded to Filipino state policies by directly addressing the issues of the Philippine state. The specifically Aquino-oriented organizations, estimated to number four thousand in 1987 (Filipino Reporter 1987:8, 1989a:1), convinced many of the numerous U.S. oriented Filipino-American organizations, composed of mostly professionals, to go beyond their relatively small transnational projects and address instead the overall problems of the country, including the development process in the Philippines. At the same time the nationalist impulse propelled some of those Filipino organizations squarely into the heart of U.S. electoral politics and motivated them to link their participation in the United States to their engagement, politically and economically, with the Philippines. Paradoxically, acting in the interests of home strengthened their incorporation into the United States. Meanwhile some new organizations were formed with an explicitly transnational focus.

Living their lives beyond the confines of national borders in ways that gave new meanings to concepts of space and geography, immigrants from St. Vincent, Grenada, Haiti, and the Philippines still find themselves constructed as the citizens of discrete nation-states. They organize transnational fields, yet they continue to tread in the domain claimed by hegemonic nation building processes. The name plates on the fence posts have national identities.

IV. DETERRITORIALIZED PRACTICES: POSTCOLONIAL STATES' ATTEMPTS TO INCORPORATE EXISTING DIASPORAS

In the crowded terminals of the Manila airport in 1990, the large bulky crates marked *"balikbayan"* sit piled up waiting for their owners, who are lined up at a special desk. At the desk sits an official whose job it is to ascertain the *balikbayan* status of Filipinos who are returning to visit the Philippines while living abroad. This status, indicated by a special stamp on their passport or an ID, entitles them to up to fifteen hundred dollars worth of duty free purchases upon arrival. In addition they pay no taxes on whatever goods they have been able to fit into two large *"balikbayan"* crates. Once duly certified, the returnees crowd into special duty free shops to buy cosmetics, liquor, cigarettes and electronic items. These returnees are often enticed to return by special discounts on airfares and tours around the country.

The *balikbayan* procedures that are now a routine part of the life of Filipino transmigrants began as a limited one-year program to encourage Filipinos to return for a maximum of four months around the Christmas holidays. The immigrants were given a special name, *"balikbayan"* (homecomers), and reduced airfares. They were also able to bypass the red tape that surrounds visa applications and were allowed safe passage after curfew. The program, "Operation Homecoming," announced by President Marcos with great fanfare in 1973, was a great success (Filipino Reporter 1973a; 1973b) and the program contributed, as Marcos had hoped, to improving public opinion in the United States about the loss of democracy and the beginnings of Martial Law in the Philippines.

In the course of the following two decades, the program was extended from year to year and then expanded. During that period the definition of who was considered *balikbayan* varied. Addressing at first all overseas Filipinos, for a period it included only those who had given up their Filipino citizenship. By 1989 *balikbayan* again included both citizens and non-citizens who wished to return for a visit that could last up to a year.[19]

Although fostered by both Marcos and Aquino, the Filipino transmigrants soon discovered that the status of *balikbayan* could be used for their own projects, because it was difficult for the government to keep track of the number of annual trips, the precise immigrant status of the users, and the number of *balikbayan* boxes sent.

By 1989 the *balikbayan* box business was contributing 4.2 billion pesos (or $ 190 million) annually to the country's economy and of that, 3.3 billion pesos went directly to Filipino families in the form of basic commodities, 155 million pesos went to the state in custom duties and taxes on boxes that were shipped, and the remainder went to the businesses involved in the shipments (*Philippine News* 1990).

The use of the word "home" by the Philippine government turned into state policy the transmigrants' term of reference for their country of origin. As we have seen, as the migration process began, Marcos intervened directly, defining migrants as legally and ideologically an important part of the nation-state. While the Philippine state has not impeded the flow of migration, it has tried to control migration and obtain funds from the migrants. During the 1970s and 1980s, the Philippine government systematically regulated and sponsored the export of Filipino manpower services overseas. Since the late 1980s, the Philippine State has collected income taxes on all Filipino citizens residing abroad on a special overseas visa. Meanwhile, Filipino migrants were actively encouraged to visit their homeland and Filipino migrants encountered little opposition to their transnational organizations, despite their growing anti-Marcos feelings and the strong political repression Marcos implemented in the Philippines.

Without as much official regulation, St. Vincent also has persistently created a welcoming environment for individual tourism by transmigrants as well as for transnational organizational activities. Various political forces in St. Vincent have perceived transnational organizations as an essential component of the islands' development. It was through the direct intervention of the state that Carnivals in both St. Vincent and Grenada were moved to the summer, enabling transmigrants to return as tourists with their children and deepen their relationship with their country of origin, at the same time investing their savings in various ways in St. Vincent.

Not all "home" governments have been as welcoming. The Haitian government under François Duvalier viewed any connection between immigrants and those who remained in Haiti as suspicious and threatening to its hold on the populace. Suspicion of transnational organizations and political repression continued under Jean Claude, but transmigrant connections were easier and transmigrant family activities grew.

Remittances have been welcomed by all governments and have been the basis of policies that encourage investment by transmigrants. The Philippine, Grenadian, and Vincentian governments have tried to convince transmigrants to invest in national economic plans that include developing specific agricultural export crops, industries, and tourism. As part of this effort, despite the limited capital generated by most Vincentian transmigrants, the St. Vincent government has created opportunities for migrants to buy bonds in development projects — a milk factory for example — that officials actively advertise among the immigrants, largely through immigrant organizations. Aristide specifically identified the Haitian transnational population as the "bank of the diaspora." While his initial contention that he could build an independent economic base capitalized by this "bank" proved grandiose, and may have been primarily meant as symbolic, he was able to obtain a million dollars that he controlled through the fundraising of the Lavalas movement.

With its relatively wealthy constituency, the government of the Philippines has paid a great deal of attention to obtaining investment capital from transmigrants. The Filipino consulate in New York and visiting senators and provincial governors have presented transmigrants with investment possibilities for development-type projects at "home." In one such instance, the governor of Western Negros assembled transmigrant Filipino sugar growers and landowners in Philippine House on Fifth Avenue in New York City to describe the great financial opportunities currently offered by shrimp farming for international export from their home island of Negros.

Passioned exhortations to invest in these types of projects for the greater good of the home country, whether the project is a milk factory in St. Vincent, exotic fruits in Grenada, a health facility in Haiti, or shrimp farms in the Philippines, sometimes are greeted with skepticism by transmigrants. In weighing personal ambitions, family commitments, and collective goals, transmigrants look at relative opportunities within their entire transnational space. Projects at home have often proven to be financially unsound. The shrimp farms, for example, have been reported as destroying the fresh water supplies of Negros, depleting its water table, and possibly bringing disease into the area (personal communication: senior official of the Bureau of Forestry and Fishing).

Transmigrants from both the Caribbean and the Philippines have tried to use state policies to their advantage, subverting regulations, such as those governing the *balikbayan*, and making new claims on their home governments. Filipino transmigrants, for example, are now requesting specific rights from the Philippine government, such as the right to vote, to own land on a foreign passport without being submitted to special regulations, to dual citizenship, and to run for elective office in the Philippines.

Filipino and Caribbean transmigrants have all at various times made demands on their home governments for greater incorporation into the political processes of their countries of origin. In this they have responded to, but also have helped generate, state policies and practices that have implicitly or explicitly defined transmigrants as part of the body politic of their home nation-states. While transnational connections are actualized through the flows of money, material goods, ideas, and ways of thinking across national borders, such connections are reinforced by a language of allegiance and loyalty to nation created by the home states.

In this new type of nation building, the idiom of the autonomous nation-state remains intact even though the geographic boundaries of the state no longer can be understood to contain the citizens of the nation-state. And so we get Marcos and Aquino's definitions of *balik-bayan* as "heroes and heroines of the nation" (Marcos 1980:1–5; Aquino 1986), and Bishop referring to Brooklyn as his largest constituency. Postcolonial states are attempting to transform existing multifaceted transnational practices into new loyalties that encompass those living beyond their borders and they are sanctioning these complex relationships with special regulations. The new construct of the 'deterritorialized' nation-state is a hegemonic construct representing the interests of the dominant sectors within each nation. But we also must recognize that it is in response to this construct that hundreds of Filipinos demonstrated for months on Fifth Avenue and at the United Nations to sway U.S. public opinion in favor of their candidate in the Philippines, that hundreds of Grenadians in the United States, joined by as many other West Indians, made public entreaties to the U.S. Congress and held public meetings to influence the U.S. government to extend formal recognition to Grenada, and that an estimated 100,000 Haitians, calling themselves the 10th Department of Haiti, took over downtown New York City in October 1991 when Aristide was overthrown.

V. CONCLUSION: TRANSNATIONAL PRACTICES AND UNDERLYING CLASS-BASED STRUCTURES

A close examination of the familial, economic, and organizational practices of immigrants in the United States from the Caribbean and from the Philippines points to the same conclusion: immigrants from St. Vincent, Grenada, Haiti, and the Philippines are developing and elaborating transnational practices that allow them to remain incorporated in their country of origin while simultaneously becoming incorporated into the United States. These practices are multi-stranded, in other words they permit the utilization of a variety of overlapping and intertwined relationships.

Underlying the multiple transnational linkages developed by both the Caribbean and the Philippine transmigrants is the position of these countries in a changing global economy based on unequal relations of power. This has meant that these countries increasingly depend on transmigrants to ensure the survival of sectors of their populations, the maintenance of their class structures, their hopes for social mobility, and their viability as nation-states. In addition, the continuing racial ordering of the United States, which places people of color on the lower rungs of the social hierarchy, consistently contributes to the development of transnationalism. In response to U.S. racial constructions, transmigrants perceive themselves as full-fledged citizens of their "home" nation-states.

At the same time, the present conjuncture of capitalism sets the context not only for transnationalism but for changing constructions of the nation-state. Although often deficient in national capital, or unable to sustain their populations, these home locations provide vital sources of symbolic capital for their migrants. It is striking that, in both the Philippines and the Caribbean, many transnational practices have been motivated by a concern for maintaining or improving the migrants' class and social position. We encountered this concern with status in all the domains of practice we reviewed: familial, economic, and organizational. The case studies in this book are replete with examples of individual migrants accumulating status. Adela desperately struggled to insure that her children obtained educations in good schools in the Philippines and made the right marital unions at the cost of long, painful separations. Marie Rose worked double shifts to insure that her house "back home" in Haiti would be furnished with all the accoutrements including a barbecue grill and a Mercedes, although she was only able to be "at home" two weeks a year. Sylvia purchased a sugar estate in St. Vincent that she rarely sees and that provides a low return on her investment. Items are exchanged, decisions made, and organizational leadership sought in a multitude of instances as part of overall efforts at obtaining social position. These efforts at status enhancement are linked to issues of class formation and reproduction in a dynamic in which enhanced status facilitates access to the political process.

Increasingly, in postcolonial countries such as the ones described in this book, control of the state apparatus is essential to maintaining or improving class position, because the political process controls access to the means of production. The use of transnational migration to maintain or enhance class positions at home has important implications for the maintenance of power by the dominant sectors of the home societies. Key middle strata are reproduced in ways not possible internally, given the deterioration of these subordinated economies.

At the same time, anger and discontent at the deteriorating life circumstances experienced by the lower and middle classes are diverted from challenging the penetration of their nation-state by foreign capital. Rather than question the role of the dominant classes in perpetuating the massive impoverishment of their countries' populations, migrants channel their energies into transnational strategies for achieving individual social mobility and economic security. Class opposition is masked and class-based action submerged. The transnational moves and family deployment strategies, which seem to have yielded transmigrants so much economically, giving them a sense of improvement and empowerment, at the same time contribute to the maintenance of the larger structures of exploitation in which they are enmeshed.

If issues of class pervade and underlie the transnational social fields migrants build, they also underlie the manner in which transmigrants identity themselves and understand their transnational experiences. In the next chapter we will examine the class contradictions, hegemonic contentions, and interpenetrating resistances and accommodations that shape the ways in which transmigrants think and speak about their transnational practices.

NOTES

1. The use in Chapter Seven of the first person refers to Cristina Szanton Blanc. Data on Filipino-American transnationalism and Philippine migration will be developed in forthcoming papers.

2. For example, an article by an historian in an Australian newspaper revealed that, rather than being engaged in resistance, Mr. Marcos had been profiteering during World War II and never received the US war medal so often mentioned in his speeches. The story was picked up by the New York Times the next day and appeared in the Philippine underground press one week before the hurriedly called presidential elections. The article did much to undermine Marcos' legitimacy as a heroic defender of the nation.

3. Of the three major island groups that constitute the Philippines, Luzon, the largest is in the North; Mindanao, the second largest is to

the south; and the Visayas, the smallest grouping, is located between the other two (Pido 1986:16).

4. The Philippine population belongs to eight major ethnolinguistic groups, comprised of some 200 dialects (cited in Pido 1986:17).

5. The Spanish colonists were mostly concentrated in the capital Manila, which functioned as an entrepôt for the Spanish China-Mexico trade.

6. From the 1960s to the early 1970s, Filipino rice farmers found themselves facing increasingly difficult conditions and rural inequalities. Many of the problems were fostered by US foreign assistance programs. Changes in land tenure led to increased production costs for farmers, land reform increased mechanization and illegal evictions, and the introduction of high-yielding varieties or "miracle rice" under a Green Revolution led to an increased reliance on credit, pesticides, fertilizers and irrigation, and also to catastrophic plant diseases (International Labour Office 1974:9).

7. There were peso devaluations in 1962, 1969, 1970, 1973, and 1975, which led to a constant erosion of the standard of living of the population and contributed to the emigration of the middle strata.

8. A 1974 study for the International Labour Office (ILO) provided some insight into the problems that eventually triggered an extensive migration from the Philippines. It noted that in the twenty-five years after World War II, "satisfactory growth rates [were] accompanied by more and more unacceptable outcomes in terms of employment and income distribution" (International Labour Office 1974:3).

9. The Philippines continued to export an increasing array of agricultural goods, including 350 million tons of sugar, 95 million tons of canned pineapple, 22 million gallons of fruit juice, $80 million worth of fish and $100 million worth of bananas. In 1984 there was a call for the additional export of nontraditional food products such as mangos, papayas, citrus fruits, cacao, feed grain and shellfish (McAffee 1985).

10. Rampant dissatisfaction about the economic situation was expressed among many sectors of the population including radicalized students and elite provincial families (Tutay 1970). A few days after Marcos' imposition of martial law he arrested hundreds of his "enemies" including more than a dozen constitutional delegates. Other officials went underground or fled the country and became influential transmigrants.

11. During the 1960s and increasingly between 1975 and 1984, over 500,000 Filipinos migrated to Canada, Australia, Europe, Japan, Hong Kong, Singapore, and Malaysia, while an additional 500,000 had become overseas contract workers, primarily in the Middle East (Fawett and Carino 1987; Commission on Overseas Filipinos 1988).

12. There was also Haitian migration to the United States in the first decades of the twentieth century but it was relatively small, left no

institutional trace, and did not provide any continuity for the Haitian migration that began in the late 1950s. The early Filipino labor migration similarly was very different from the migration that started slowly after World War II and escalated in the 1970s and 1980s.

13. Education for both men and women had been a key policy of the US colonial administration in the Philippines. It made the Philippines one of the most highly educated third world countries after 1946 (Rojas-Aleta et al. 1977:96–112; Blanc-Szanton 1982).

14. Within the Philippines there has been a succession of new organizations, such as the "Colorums" in the 1960s and the "Charismatics" in the 1980s that formed transnational connections. Such organizations are often exclusively male, swear their members to secrecy and usually develop in close connection with the local church. They are used to validate local social status, but they are also pan-Philippine. Some Charismatics groups that originated in New York and California in the 1980s have also developed connections back to the Philippines.

15. These young Filipinos were recruited, as most other Asians at the time, to do manual work. By 1930 there were up to 30,470 Filipinos in the expanding agricultural fields and fisheries of California and 45,208 in the whole country (Takaki 1989:317). Their status as US colonial subjects gave them special exemption from the immigration laws of the 1920s that excluded Asians. From 1898, when the United States annexed the Philippines as a colony, until 1934, when the Philippines were organized as a Commonwealth, Filipinos, as members of a US colony, obtained American passports when leaving their country. They entered the United States without any impediments. They were, however, excluded, along with Chinese, Japanese, Hindus and American Indians, from citizenship, a policy confirmed by the Supreme Court decision of 1934 that clarified the meaning of the Naturalization Law of 1790.

16. On the basis of the 1880 anti-miscegenation law, California prohibited marriage between whites and "negroes, mulattos, or mongolians." Filipinos challenged the law, and Salvator Roldan successfully secured a California Court of Appeals decision allowing him to marry his white fiancée. The state legislature almost immediately amended the anti-miscegenation law and added the "Malay Race" to the restricted category (Pido 1986:58–61,69; Takaki 1989:329–333).

17. In the 1930s, these Filipino workers, facing very difficult working conditions, created Filipino unions, struck, and ultimately allied themselves with unions of Mexican workers. They ended up intermarrying extensively with white women in the 1930s and kept very limited ties to their home country.

18. In an attempt to create distance between themselves and other non-whites, Filipinos became dispersed throughout the New York-New Jersey Greater Metropolitan Area. Some concentrations of Filipino

immigrants, however, have developed in areas settled by other Asians, such as Flushing, Queens, or Jersey City.

19. As of March 1, 1980, only citizens or permanent residents of other lands and their families were classified as *balikbayans* (Filipino Reporter 1980). A revised set of rules and regulations issued in December 1989 defined the *balikbayan* as "a. a Filipino citizen who has been continuously out of the Philippines for a period of at least a year from date of last departure; b. a Filipino overseas worker; c. a former Filipino citizen and his family as this term is defined hereunder (spouse and children) who had been naturalized in a foreign country and comes or returns to the Philippines" (Philippine Consulate 1989).

Chapter
EIGHT

There's No Place Like Home

Bishop's standing in a meeting hall in Brooklyn and addressing Grenadian migrants in Brooklyn as part of his "constituency," Aquino's speaking in Manila and making stirring references to Filipino migrants as "heroes and heroines of the nation," and Aristide's meeting in the Haitian presidential palace with representatives of the "diaspora" and naming them the "10th Department" are all constitutive acts. In all these cases national leaders were actively engaged in nation building projects that bound transmigrants into the body politic of their states of origin in ways that resonated with the practices and aspirations of the transmigrants themselves.

After all, it is transmigrants who have been establishing and constantly renewing ties of kinship that set the foundation for multiple transactions across national borders. They are constantly making room for the requirements and sensibilities of worlds geographically removed but not left behind. Yet these same transmigrants are at the same time incorporating themselves into the United States, as they learn to deal with expressways and subways, shopping malls and cable television, plastic slipcovers and school board elections.

We began the book with a series of propositions that contained within them a paradox. First, we argued that to perceive and analyze transnationalism we need a global perspective on migration that moves beyond the bounded categories of ethnic group, nation, and race and forces us to reconceptualize our concepts of society and culture. Once we reconfigure our field of vision, we argued, we can begin to acknowledge and to theorize the development by trans-migrants of social fields that cross national boundaries and challenge hegemonic categories of identity. Yet we have also argued that trans-migrants reinscribe their newly unbounded hyperspace into recon-ceptualized categories of deterritorialized nation-states and of race. Transmigrants are constrained in their understanding of the global forces that form the context of their lives by nation building proces-ses that continue to be generated by the dominant strata of the states within which they are being incorporated. Both the transnational processes that challenge bounded thinking and the pressures on transmigrants to reconstitute their identities in terms of nation-states and race reflect ongoing hegemonic contention within which constructions of identity are constantly being reformulated, trans-formed, and modified. Underlying this contention stand contradic-tions between the transnational practices of the migrants and the manner in which all hegemonic constructions simultaneously reflect, distort, and delimit aspects of lived realities. Consequently the newly reconceptualized categories represent simultaneously both resis-tance to domination and new hegemonic categories that perpetuate domination.

In this final chapter we will turn our attention to the ongoing contestations that underlie hegemonic efforts to shape and construct transmigrant identities. We will focus on two hegemonic constructs that have emerged in all four cases as potent means of resistance and domination: (1) the reinscription of transmigrants as citizens of deterritorialized nation-states, and (2) the construction of global, race-based identifications by people of color that breach national and ethnic boundaries. We will assess the ways and means by which these two emergent constructions articulate and empower, yet simul-taneously delimit and constrict, the lives, struggles, and imaginings of current day immigrants. In other words, we will examine the processes through which constructions of race and nation are being reconfigured and newly embedded within the national constructions of both the United States and the transmigrants' countries of origin.

I. TWO TERRAINS OF CONTESTATION

A. Contestations, National Loyalties, and Citizenship: The Deterritorialized Nation-State as a Form of Postcolonial Nationalism

The contradiction between the construction of the nation-state, with its equation of territory, state, and people, and the existence of transmigrant populations is the terrain upon which diverse labor exporting countries have begun to forge constructions of deterritorialized nation-states. In Grenada, St. Vincent, Haiti, and the Philippines, the idiom of the autonomous nation remains intact, but in the new world of transnational practices, geographic boundaries are no longer understood to contain all the state's citizens or political processes essential to its perpetuation.

Deterritorialized nation-state building is something new and significant, a form of post-colonial nationalism that reflects and reinforces the division of the entire globe into nation-states. To conceive of a nation-state that stretches beyond its geographic boundaries involves a social fabrication different from diasporic imaginings. To see oneself in a diaspora is to imagine oneself as being outside a territory, part of a population exiled from a homeland. Diasporas are populations that, while dispersed across boundaries and borders, salvage from their common loss and distance from home their identity and unity as "a people." Peoples living in the diaspora — Jews and Armenians, for example — are thought to have preserved their spiritual or cultural essence even when they had no state. The concept of diaspora is closely related to that of "nation" which envisions a people with a common past and a biological bond of solidarity who may or may not at any one time have its own state. In counterdistinction is the deterritorialized nation-state, in which the nation's people may live anywhere in the world and still not live outside the state. By this logic, there is no longer a diaspora because wherever its people go, their state goes too.

This state controls a territorial homeland and operates within the "community" of states. However, a large sector of its "citizens," perhaps even the majority, live their lives within other states to which they may come to belong in the sense of having legalized residency, naturalization, or birth. The national leaderships of these deterritorialized nation-states claim their dispersed populations as "citizens," because the members of their diasporas conduct economic, political, social, and cultural transactions that are essential for the maintenance of the home state's survival. Grenada provides perhaps an extreme yet apt example: its political leaders claim a total adult population of 90,000, only 30,000 of whom live within the homeland; the other 60,000 adults live outside the state's geographic borders.[1]

Throughout U.S. immigration history, certain sectors of immigrant populations have defined themselves as political refugees. They have lived physically in the United States, but their intense emotional attachments and political activities have been directed elsewhere. They were refugees because they had been expelled by or fled from those who controlled their home state and they existed in opposition to it. In contrast, the citizens of a deterritorialized nation-state do not insist that their return is contingent on a change in the government of their home country. The new construct of the deterritorialized nation-state reconfirms and even encourages the permanent settlement abroad of a large sector of the nation. Both the national leadership of the postcolonial nation-states and their populations abroad have actively participated in this new projection of polity.

As part of their nation building process, those who claim to lead deterritorialized states have taken steps both practically and symbolically to serve as representatives, protectors, and spokespeople for their dispersed populations. The Vincentian and Grenadian consulates have worked to address the situations that face their nationals in Trinidad and New York and have striven to create more opportunities for migration to the United States. Aristide promised his 10th Department that they had a government to defend them against attacks and defamation, and he spoke as their advocate at the United Nations. During the 1992 elections, at least two of the five top Filipino presidential candidates formally and emphatically expressed their concern for improving the situations and increasing the legal rights of Filipino transmigrants. The new President, Fidel V. Ramos, officially praised the migrants' contributions during his first days in office.

In addition, leaders who are involved in the nation building projects of deterritorialized nation-states have worked to enlist the enthusiastic participation of transmigrants of different classes. Some transmigrants have responded by assuming ongoing responsibility for promoting the national interests of their home countries. Vincentians in New York raised thousands of dollars for national rebuilding when a volcanic eruption ravaged the island in 1979. The leader of this effort was soon appointed St. Vincent's Ambassador to the United Nations. Both Vincentians and Grenadians contribute actively to political campaigns back home in response to the urgings of political leaders who meet with them in New York several times a year to discuss issues of the home country. Substantial typhoon damage as well as a recent very large volcanic eruption on Mount Pinatubo have been occasions of active U.S.-based Filipino transmigrant assistance to the Philippine nation. From 1986 to 1991 three major fund-raising campaigns among Haitians in the United States raised large sums of money for national reconstruction in Haiti, including the million dollars that the Lavalas movement placed at Aristide's disposal. These national leaderships also have worked to foster many types of transmigrant interconnections, paying special attention to those that harness the migrants' savings and return them to the home countries. Vincentian, Grenadian, and Filipino transmigrants are actively encouraged to invest at home, while Grenadians and Filipinos in the United States have been organized by their home governments to lobby for foreign aid from the U.S. government.

The national leaderships have waged campaigns to insure that when transmigrants come home to visit and spend their money, they will feel welcome. In the past, immigrants who returned found that they were the objects of ridicule and criticism from those who had stayed at home, including the national leadership and intellectuals. Persons in the diaspora were devalued as inauthentic opportunists. In Haitian Kreyol, for example, the word *dyaspora* became a somewhat pejorative term. In contrast, the national leaderships, who are building a concept of the deterritorialized nation, accord recognition and high status to transmigrants.

U.S. permanent residents and even U.S. citizens have gone "home" to St. Vincent, Grenada, Haiti and the Philippines, to stand for elections to legislative bodies, and some have been elected. Some transmigrants have been appointed consuls to the United States or ambassadors to the United Nations. National leaderships, who are building deterritorialized nation-states, move their personnel within their borderless polities in accordance with particular circumstances. Bishop tried to strengthen his Peoples' Revolutionary Government by bringing selected transmigrants back to Grenada. Aquino moved from the position of long-time permanent resident of the United States to that of President of the Philippines. She then recruited transmigrants with similar backgrounds who had helped her dislodge Marcos to become members of her cabinet. She also appointed them to represent her government to the United States at the same time that they lobbied for it as citizens of the United States. Bishop and Blaize did the same. A few Representatives of the interim Trouillot government, many members of the Aristide government, and Bazin, the Prime Minister appointed by the military, have been transmigrants. Many of these political actors have remained "transmigrants" even if they have officially "returned home" to live. They have retained homes, families, multiple social ties, and sometimes even jobs in the United States while participating in the political processes of their home countries, just as they had previously participated in the political processes of the United States while maintaining multiple connections to their home nations.

Yet underneath the efforts to fashion a deterritorialized nation-state lie a myriad of ever-present contradictions. We will focus on three different types of contradictions that arise from the construct of the deterritorialized nation-state: (1) ideological contradictions between transmigrants and the national leaderships of their countries of origin; (2) contradictions between global capital and the autonomy of subordinated nation-states; and (3) class contradictions within the deterritorialized nation. Aspects of these contradictions are openly discussed by transmigrants, while others are rarely made explicit. In the following section we will examine the reasons some contradictions have led to active contention while others are not voiced.

B. Contradictions between Transmigrants and the National Leaderships of their Countries of Origin

The concept of the deterritorialized nation-state projects a unity of economic and political interests between those who have settled abroad and those who control the state apparatus in the home country. However, both the economic and political relationships of the transmigrants to their home countries have been points of contention and struggle. As we saw in all the case studies, the nature of financial transactions between transmigrants and the home state is one that often becomes a point of public controversy. For example, while for Aristide the Tenth Department was a part of Haiti, it was a separate part. This became clear when Aristide distinguished between those who remained in Haiti, whom he called "Lavalas at home," and those living abroad, who were "Lavalas for home." In these "inflections of nationalism" (Richman 1992a), Aristide was asserting that it was by settling away from home that transmigrants were able to claim Haiti as their home. They were to be the "good Kreyol tourists" who were welcome to visit with their suitcases full of gifts and their pockets full of money, but not to stay. As the "bank of the diaspora" they produced foreign exchange by living in foreign lands, yet they belonged to Haiti because what they earned belonged to Haiti, This view of the Haitian immigrants as a "bank" caused some political critics of Aristide to charge that transmigrants were seen by Lavalas leaders less as citizens and more as cows to be milked (Haiti Observateur 1992).

Filipino leaders have followed a similar approach in their relationship to Filipino transmigrants. These transmigrants have been systematically exploited as a source of state revenue by state policies. Beginning with the Marcos regime, Filipino citizens have been encouraged and assisted in their migrations by state agencies that act as labor contractors. Migrants, however, are not allowed to return to the Philippines or to visit without paying taxes on the incomes they earn abroad. Marcos also carefully fostered return tourism through his *balikbayan* policy, attracting migrants to maintain their links to home and then taxing them on their foreign earnings. For all her rhetoric about emigrants as heroes and heroines of the state, and despite the major role they played in bringing her to power, Aquino's relationship to transmigrants was also exploitative. For this reason, apart from the period of political upsurge and optimism that surrounded Aquino's election to office, some of the practices related to *balikbayan* have been repeatedly contested by Filipino transmigrants.

Both St. Vincent and Grenada changed the dates of their carnivals to the summer to maximize the influx of transmigrant tourist dollars. Moreover, the St. Vincent consulate in New York encouraged a loose "federation" of Vincentian voluntary organizations as part of the umbrella group discussed in Chapter 4 to invest in a joint project in St. Vincent. The project selected by the transmigrants, a Carnival hall in St. Vincent's capital from which the celebration could be comfortably observed, was low on the list of development priorities for this resource poor country. St. Vincent's political leaders, however, correctly recognized that a Carnival hall would serve both as a public symbol of the transmigrants' continuing commitment to St. Vincent and as a means of encouraging the transmigrants' repeated return visits — as Carnival tourists — and the continuing flow of U.S. dollars from them. In addition, approximately fourteen state officials from both St. Vincent and Grenada visit with transmigrants in New York annually to sustain their participation as investors in development projects at home.

The role of dispersed populations in the political processes of their countries of origin remains another point of contention. When transmigrants act as agents of the deterritorialized nation-state in support of government policies, their political participation is welcomed and encouraged by their "home" country. Consuls and ambassadors often organize transmigrants to pressure the U.S. Congress. Grenadian transmigrants were encouraged to lobby on Bishop's behalf and Aquino deployed transmigrants to lobby for her government.

However, national leaderships are somewhat fearful of their transmigrant populations because they can have a direct impact on the internal politics of the home countries by stabilizing political regimes. Filipino transmigrants played a crucial role in ousting Marcos and in placing a transmigrant, Cory Aquino, in power. The military dictatorship that replaced Aristide has been hindered in its attempts to establish legitimacy by the continuing agitation of Haitian transmigrants in the United States.

Transmigrants are well positioned to challenge leaders in their countries of origin or establish themselves as national leaders because of their ability to wage battles for public opinion that can have international reverberations. In addition to having their own media, transmigrants have access to reporters for U.S. radio, television and newspapers and U.S. media are increasingly global with stations like Cable News Network broadcasting throughout the world. From this vantage point, they can challenge dictatorial regimes by calling on them to institute formal democratic processes. Finding that calls for democracy are resonant with U.S. political discourse and play well in the press, Filipino, Haitian, and Grenadian transmigrants have all popularized and supported the idea that national leaderships need to be legitimated through democratic elections. These campaigns for democracy then directly enter into the political process of the home country, challenging the legitimacy of governments. While ideologies of formal democracy and/or constitutionality were embedded within each of the postcolonial nation-states, they have gained new currency there when they have been were forcefully articulated by transmigrants.

The conceptualization of formal democracy that Grenadian transmigrants brought back to Grenada from the United States added to questions about the legitimacy of the Bishop government being raised inside Grenada. In the course of a half century, U.S. colonialism had instilled in Filipinos a belief that democratic procedures are a measure of the degree to which a nation is capable of determining its own future. In the United States Filipino immigrants were further influenced by the rhetoric of democracy. In challenging the Marcos regime and its rule by martial law, and the U.S. support for this regime, Filipino transmigrants voiced their opposition in terms of a call for democracy. When Marcos manipulated the election, Filipino transmigrants educated the U.S. public about this violation of democratic process, forcing a reversal of the policies that supported Marcos.

Haitians organized vocal opposition to the Duvalier government and vigorously lobbied against it, asserting that U.S. support for a dictatorship was contrary to U.S. principles of democracy and freedom. They also bolstered internal opposition to the military juntas that replaced Jean Claude Duvalier by building public opinion for constitutional government and democratic elections. When the democratically elected government of Aristide was overthrown, Haitian transmigrants organized public support for Aristide in the United States and against the military backed governments that replaced him, insisting that he was the democratically elected, and hence legitimate, leader of Haiti.

However, with their subjectivities at least in part forged within the crucible of U.S. political processes into which they have become incorporated, transmigrants may become a political force that supports unwittingly the national interests of the United States rather than those of their countries of origin. Such a dynamic seems to underlie the manner in which many Grenadian transmigrants greeted the U.S. invasion of Grenada. Although some Grenadian transmigrants initially lobbied for the recognition of the Bishop government, many, including some of those who participated in the lobbying efforts, did not challenge the U.S. military intervention. Concerned that their property at home might be confiscated by the Bishop government and their kin harmed, they saw their interests as aligned to some extent with U.S. foreign policy goals in Grenada.

At the same time, transmigrants may bring back home radical critiques that not only challenge the composition of the leadership of the "home country," but that also raise fundamental questions about the structures of class, gender, and power within those countries. Transmigrants from all four countries have contributed to anti-imperialist movements that have directly challenged United States dominance in the global economy and targeted the complicity of their home country national leaderships. On occasion, Vincentian transmigrants have critiqued the development plans of the Vincentian government, charging that they increase Vincentian dependency on the United States. Sectors of the transmigrant populations also organized against Marcos, emphasizing an anti-capitalist position, as exemplified by their strong anti-IMF, anti-Filipino ruling families stance (Philippine News 1989a:3; Katipunan 1988:5,8).

Feminist movements in which transmigrants have played a role have also critiqued the distribution of power in the home countries. Many of the leading figures in a woman's movement that raised fundamental questions about gender and power and brought tens of thousands of Haitian women to the streets of Port-au-Prince in the weeks that followed Jean Claude's departure were transmigrants. The particular plight of female workers in the Philippines has been a central issue in a budding Filipino feminist movement, exemplified by organizations like Gabriella and built with the active participation of transmigrants (see among others Philippine News 1987:11).

In addition, transmigrants play significant roles in challenging the nationalism of their home countries by building regional identifications and movements. In the eastern Caribbean, transmigrants have been open to and brought home pan-Caribbean ideologies that counterpose a regional identity and regional development strategies to hegemonic conceptions of national autonomy presented to them by their national leaderships. This more encompassing Caribbean identity, forged first by a regional migration experience that created a circum-Caribbean migrant population, and added to by the construction of Caribbean ethnicity in New York City, are echoed in calypsos popular regionally and among the transmigrants, such as "The Caribbean Man." Through joint participation in Carnival in Brooklyn and political activism as part of a wider Caribbean constituency in New York, transmigrants become subject to messages underscoring a common Caribbean experience and set of interests which they import to their home societies. Filipinos, in their participation as part of Asian political coalitions in the United States, also come to understand and bring home constructions of identity that are contradictory to exclusionist nation building processes.

It is not surprising, therefore, that governments in Grenada under Bishop, in the Philippines under both Marcos and Aquino, and in Haiti, before, during, and after Aristide's presidency, have tried to encourage transmigrants to play a financial role at home while sending out mixed messages about the degree to which they are in fact welcome in the country they are encouraged to call "home." Aristide, Aquino, Bishop, and the present leaderships of Grenada and St. Vincent invite their populations living "abroad," "to return home," but only as tourists. That the welcome mat remains extended for the short-term only indicates the ambivalence which marks the relationships between these labor-exporting governments and their deterritorialized subjects.

The political participation of transmigrants in the political processes of their "home countries" has been a point of ongoing contention. The Grenadian government may have granted its emigrants dual citizenship, but although the majority of the its citizens are overseas, the government has not initiated a simple system of absentee ballots. Aristide might on his own transform the *dyaspora* into the 10th Department of Haiti, but the dominant political forces in Haiti have been uninterested in granting them dual nationality, and even those citizens living abroad cannot vote unless they return home for the election. Filipino migrants may be encouraged to return to visit, but they have not been given dual citizenship nor any way to participate in the electoral process while living outside of the Philippines. Transmigrants get the message. As one Grenadian transmigrant said, "They want our money but not our advice."

C. Contradictions Between Global Capital and the Autonomy of Subordinated Nation-States

The conception of labor-exporting states as autonomous nations, whose citizenries may be incorporated elsewhere but who are still separate and equal partners in a world of individual nation-states, obscures the domination of global capital and core capitalist states in the economies and political affairs of the these countries. We have seen this occur in many ways. As they participate in development schemes for the home "country," transmigrants contribute to the belief that each of these states has a discrete and viable national economy. Older understandings of eastern Caribbean states, which cast these islands as partial societies, inextricably linked to core capitalist interests and states have been overridden by projections of national development. Development schemes, such as the construction of a milk factory in St. Vincent or a traditional medicine institute in Haiti, contribute far more to the ideology of national autonomy than do the realities of these economies. Sitting in formal meetings of organizations of transmigrants to discuss such development plans as export processing factories and tourism, officials from the "home countries" contribute more to the construction of images of viable national economies than to the building of such economies.

In the name of building up the home country, transmigrants are in fact pulled into development schemes that actually make the home country even more subordinate to global capital. Bishop, despite his discourse about development strategies that steer a course independent of western capital penetration, nevertheless tried to convince his constituencies in Grenada and in Brooklyn to embrace the development of an exotic fruit industry and a jet port for tourists. Blaize, with the active support of significant sectors of the transmigrant population, continued the plan to build tourism as a mainstay of the Grenadian economy. While such projects may raise some foreign currency and enhance the quality of life for the upper middle class in the capitalist core, they cannot place a resource poor island such as Grenada on an independent trajectory to development.

Similarly, the remittances sent "back home," which provide vital foreign exchange as well as a quantity of consumer goods, make the economies of the labor-exporting countries seem more viable and independent than is actually the case. By bolstering the standard of living of the middle strata and allowing sectors of the poor to survive, they make it possible for these states to continue to project images of economic viability. The transmigrants' remittances also offset, to some degree, internal discontent and unrest borne of the severe economic fragility of these nation-states.

The subordination of these states to the political interests of the United States and the economic interests of transnational capital is both obscured and muted when transmigrants, who are incorporated into the United States, serve as representatives of the governments of their "home" nation-states. They fill such posts as ambassadors, consuls, legislators, and even presidents, as Aquino in the Philippines, and prime ministers, as Bazin in Haiti. Stanislaus, representing an independent Grenadian nation-state he had never lived in, helped put together a coalition government that accepted U.S. involvement in Grenada. Bazin, chosen by the Haitian military in 1992 to be Prime Minister and an opponent of the return of Aristide, was a long-time employee of the World Bank. As Prime Minister he immediately set out to insure World Bank investment in Haiti. Although Aquino opposed U.S. military bases in the Philippines, as some of the Filipino press repeatedly pointed out, her ties to the United States were deep and long standing and she strongly depended on U.S. aid as soon as she took office (Katipunan 1988:5,8; Philippine News 1989b:1,8).

D. Class Contradictions within the Deterritorialized Nation-States

As we have seen in the case studies from the Caribbean and in the contrastive case of the Philippines, transnationalism can lead to further class differentiation within the home societies, and even within families, as wealth produced through migration is used to establish or buttress class positions back home. Wealth gained in the United States has been used to improve the class positions of transmigrants in both the United States and back home. On the other hand, many transmigrants come to the United States impoverished and remain at the bottom levels of the working class. Indeed, segments of this class are able to survive in the United States only by keeping aging relatives and children back home, which requires that they send all surplus funds home rather than use savings to further their situations in the United States.

As a hegemonic construction, the concept of the deterritorialized nation-state gathers power from its lack of reference to class position or difference. All nationalist formulations derivative of European nation building, including constructions of the deterritorialized nation-state, homogenize differences of class, gender, region, and history. According to such formulations, common nationality, often glossed as citizenship, unites all who are considered part of "the people." Within this construction, all are equally actors empowered to pledge loyalty, hate the nation's enemies, and display the flag. No flagpole is even needed; national loyalties can be made public on a lapel or a t-shirt. Nationalist discourse contains no reference to life circumstance, social position, monetary worth, or access to power.

Yet differences of class, gender, region, and history continue to exist and are central to the hierarchy of power, privilege, and wealth upon which nation-states are based. Constructions of the deterritorialized nation-state not only fail to acknowledge inequalities within the nation, they contribute to identity formulations and status assertions among transmigrants that implicate them in furthering the structures of domination and inequality within their home states.

Organizations that bring together transmigrants on the basis of their shared citizenship in a deterritorialized nation provide a sphere for those who have greater amounts of economic advantage and education to obtain status and better their social positions. The Vincentian and Grenadian organizations of ex-teachers or ex-police and the Haitian and Filipino hometown and community organizations all provide such possibilities. The opportunities that these organizations afford may contribute to these transmigrants' business interests and investments at home, including the purchase of land lived on or worked by relatives, thus providing a basis for furthering or consolidating their class positions. As we have seen in the case studies, this mobility may be built with the assistance and often at the expense of kin and other close relations at home.

For those from the more dominant classes within the transmigrant populations, as well as individuals who are upwardly mobile in their aspirations and opportunities, the political sphere of the deterritorialized nation becomes an arena in which they can sustain or improve their class positions. The geographically borderless, deterritorialized nation-state allows these transmigrants to move back and forth between the United States and their home societies to take advantage of positions of influence in either part of the field. The organizing efforts of transmigrants have done little in general, however, to address the daily struggles of the impoverished sectors of the populations of their deterritorialized nation-states. Although envisioned to include all Haitians who are *moun deyò-o* (people outside), the interests of all classes have not been represented or even mentioned in passing in the construction of the Tenth Department. It is significant that those who scrambled to establish and fill a series of official positions and committees to represent *Dizyèm-nan* did not include in their organizing efforts impoverished Haitian immigrants in the United States and made no mention of Haitian cane cutters living in virtual slavery in the Dominican Republic.

II. THE DETERRITORIALIZED NATION-STATE AS TRANSMIGRANT RESISTANCE: STRENGTHS AND WEAKNESSES OF A COUNTERHEGEMONIC CONSTRUCTION

Despite the multiple levels of contradiction that underlie constructions of deterritorialized nation-states, this construct serves both as a resistance to the incorporation of immigrants into subordinate positions within core capitalist countries and as a challenge to the unequal power between nations within a global system of capitalist relations. There are moments in time when deterritorialized nation building efforts stand opposed to the nation building agendas of the United States.

We saw in the case studies of Grenada, St. Vincent, Haiti, and the Philippines how, in certain political circumstances, migrants acting as nationals of their home states opposed the foreign policy of the United States vis-à-vis their home countries. Not all of this is new. To some extent "ethnics" from past migrants have participated in organizing activities in relation to their home countries, although this fact has largely been ignored by cultural pluralist models focused on the struggle of immigrants for a stake in the United States (Vassady 1982; Higham 1984).[2] However, current transmigrants' actions differ from the political movements of past immigrations in terms of the pervasive, ongoing ways in which transmigrants are dually incorporated into both states and participate in the political events of the United States and their home societies. Filipino transmigrants first actively opposed U.S. support of Marcos and helped create the public opinion in the United States that discredited the actions of the U.S. government in the Philippines. Then they pressed for greater assistance and more public support for Aquino than the U.S. government was ready to give. Haitians increasingly built public opinion in the United States against the Duvaliers and for the Haitian boat people, forcing the Carter government to honor its public posture about human rights by freeing Haitian refugees from detention and providing them with money for resettlement. The tens of thousands of Haitian immigrants who virtually took over lower Manhattan to demonstrate in support of Aristide shortly after his ouster in 1991 were an indicator of the strength of transmigrants. In the face of the refusal by the U.S. government to recognize the Bishop regime, Grenadian transmigrants worked to obtain legitimacy for Bishop by popularizing his political views, which were contrary to U.S. national interests, through the U.S. media, courses and programs at universities, and at conferences and meetings.

Using their access to U.S. media, to the halls of Congress, and to the streets, transmigrants have challenged the U.S. construction of the immigrant as one whose incorporation in the United States is accomplished through the severing of political ties to the country of origin. Transmigrants have accepted the advice of representatives from foundations, government agencies, churches, philanthropies, and from politicians who, as we were able to document in the history of Haitian ethnic organizing in the United States, have persistently encouraged immigrants to gain empowerment in the United States by participating in the U.S. political process, including becoming citizens. However, the transmigrants have not followed the hegemonic agenda of eschewing commitment to and political participation in the nation-states from which they or their parents originated. By accepting the constructions fostered by the national leaderships of their home countries that make them perpetual citizens of these deterritorialized nation-states, they have used their participation in U.S. politics in ways that were contrary to the U.S. hegemonic agenda.

This is not to say that the concept of the deterritorialized nation-state provides actual and ongoing empowerment for transmigrants. Whether or not the particular demands of these movements are realized in either the home or host society at any one time is linked to the character and intensity of struggles in the home country and the degree of economic, political, and cultural penetration of the home country by the United States.

However, the dilemma of postcoloniality is that "the local is being reinvented as idiom and spectacle, masking the complexity of transnational financial, political and cultural economies" (Hansen 1993:184). Because of the increasingly subordinated position of labor-exporting countries vis-à-vis global capital, it becomes increasingly difficult for political movements in those states to find a political, economic, and conceptual terrain from which to resist the compromising of the interests of most sectors of their countries' populations. Constructions of the nation-state, whether or not they are conceived as borderless, provide a problematic location for resistance (Chatterjee 1986; Rafael 1988). As we have seen above, even as Bishop strove to move Grenada out of the sphere of U.S. dominance, he created a development plan for tourism and export agriculture that tied Grenada to a dependent position in the world market. Even in their finest moments of resistance, post-colonial constructions of identity remain just that — post-colonial; their understandings of context and situation are framed by the language and positioning of the colonial experience.

Confined to constructing their resistance in terms of the oppression of a unitary people who share a common culture and history, post-colonial resistance has a hard time locating the voices, outlooks, and aspirations of those not visible through the hegemonic lens — the voices of those who produce, who live without work, whose voices are feminine. When connections are made beyond the geography of the state, they stay bounded by constructions of shared nationhood. And although room is made for dispersed national populations in the construction of the deterritorialized nation-state, those at home who give body and soul to produce in agribusinesses and export processing zones what they can never afford to consume have no place.

III. RACE AND HEGEMONY

The current hegemonic contention around the identities of populations that are subordinated, both in the United States and globally, has led to the emergence of new or reclaimed forms of racial construction. Constructions of race in the United States have been given a geocultural frame of reference — African, Asian, and Hispanic. Such race thinking is arising simultaneously and out of the same context as formulations of the deterritorialized nation-state. They both are ways in which those who are subaltern speak (Spivak 1988). Race thinking, however, although historically linked to nation building processes, creates different sites of resistance, since racial constructions cross-cut the boundaries of nationality.

The use by subordinated populations of racial identities as forms of resistance is not new in the United States. Its current resurgence, however, is strengthened by the presence of transmigrants of color such as Caribbeans and Filipinos. In continuing to be shaped by and to shape the nationalist ideologies of their home countries, transmigrants are affected by conceptions of racial identity formulated within their home countries as well as within the United States. In the case of each of the home societies with which we have dealt, national identities have been forged in processes of signification in which assertions of racial difference, cultural autonomy, and national equality have been merged.[3]

Haitians, who broke the bonds of colonial domination as early as the late 18th century, elaborated a concept of nation built on a racial construction, claiming that black people have a right to an equal place in the family of nations. They further believe that their uniquely successful revolt against a European power conferred on them an historic mission to lead all black peoples. The Filipino sense of national identity has been built upon refractions of their designation by their U.S. colonizers as "little brown brothers" (Pido 1986). In being paternalistically encouraged by their U.S. colonizers, Filipinos both accepted and struggled against the constructions of "childish immaturity" communicated in many ways by their colonizers as well as against the color hierarchy implied by the racial self-identifier of "brownness." The national leaderships of Grenada and St. Vincent have sought to define national identities that speak to an African-Caribbean past. Their oppositional, racialized nationalisms have challenged colonially derived constructions in which "white" and "British" were the primary standards for national culture.

Race is explicitly part of these national constructions, in contrast to and in dialogue with, the U.S. national construction that is implicitly white. For Caribbean and Filipino transmigrants, the racial pride contained in the nationalism of the deterritorialized nation-states can serve as a means to resist assimilation into the United States as a subordinated population of African-Americans or Asian-Americans. It also can serve as a basis to unite with subordinated U.S. populations in ways that defy U.S. racial constructions and political and economic domination.

During the period of open, legal segregation, immigrants of color confronted a discourse among African-Americans centered on pride in "the Race." Throughout this period, appeals to unity from African-American leaders as well as those from the Caribbean who filled leadership roles, emphasized the structural situation of all peoples of color, a population that was portrayed without distinct ethnicities and as classless.

The formulation of "African-American," articulated by leaders such as Jesse Jackson in the late 1980s, was meant to encompass the entire black population of the United States. Blacks, who had previously designated their history within the United States by identifying as "Black Americans," took up this new representation, which gained acceptance in hegemonic discourse during the next few years. It fit neatly into the idiom of cultural pluralism, making those of African descent parallel to those of European descent by providing an acknowledgment of their roots; it also placed their loyalties within the U.S. polity. However, as in previous formulations of "the Race" and of "Black Americans," this hyphenated identity denied the separate nationalist agendas generated among Caribbean immigrants, who fear being socially located on the bottom of U.S. society. While appeals calling on African-American identity formulations recognized the racism that all peoples of color experienced in the United States, they did not take into account the cultural specificities of the immigrant populations. In denying the distinct cultural backgrounds of the immigrant populations, this idiom of racial unity and pride cut against the nationalist components of the agendas of immigrant leaders that had become salient by the mid 1960s and 1970s. It denied the distinctive Caribbean experiences of gaining political independence from colonial powers and of managing their own countries politically.

However, the emergence and growth of an ideology of cultural pluralism in the 1960s enabled Caribbean and Filipino immigrants to begin to present themselves as discrete and competing ethnic populations, which in their eyes removed them from social placement on the bottom. In some ways, rather than uniting with U.S. blacks, they became intermediate groups between U.S. blacks and whites. Diverging from, although simultaneously with, this strategy of differentiation, Caribbean immigrants recently have drawn on their experiences in the explicitly ethnic, but implicitly racial, politics of the United States and on their home-based constructions of nation that incorporate elements of racial pride to find ways to unite once again with other peoples of color.

With the resurgence and reclaiming of the racial identifier of African, Caribbean transmigrants have found ways that speak to their particular histories to confront the U.S. racial order in a way that unites them with African-Americans as well as the growing influx of immigrants from African countries. Within representations such as "Afrocentricity" (Asante 1991), various black populations are able to maintain their separate identities yet acknowledge they are all African people. Caribbean performers, whether Bob Marley, Ti Manno, Sparrow, or other calypsonians from St. Vincent and Grenada, have long used Africa to establish such a common frame of reference. This is a positive identity that accentuates common cultural roots; notions of racial unity, although latent within the signifying framework, are not necessarily part of the public discourse.

In New York in the late 1980s, WLIB, the radio station controlled by African-American and Caribbean businessmen and whose constituency is comprised of members of both these populations, began using the term widely in broadcasts. Callers to this radio station both from the Caribbean and the United States have begun to refer to themselves as African people. The visit of Nelson Mandela to the United States in 1990 further popularized the concept among broad strata of black people by giving a positive personification to this term of reference. In Trenton Sate Prison a number of prisoners were reported wearing hand shaped medallions of Africa after Mandela's visit (personal communication, Joyanne Jeuvelis). In 1990 Haitians, carrying banners demanding an end to discrimination against all African peoples, demonstrated in New York against the United States Food and Drug Administration statements that linked immigrants from Haiti and Africa to AIDS.

In comparison to the term "African," the identifier "Asian" has remained fairly confined within a U.S. political discourse. In the past Asian has been used as a racial label imposed from the outside which denied through conflation particular histories (Takaki 1989). It continues to encompass an extraordinarily diverse immigrant population, ranging from fishing people from Cambodia to wealthy capitalists from Hong Kong. As we have seen, Filipino immigrant leaders, although they have at various times resisted such labeling, have increasingly been drawn to organizing political constituencies of "Asian" immigrants. In contrast to the label African, the identifier Asian, as well as the that of Hispanic, when taken up by immigrants as tools of organization are used as means of differentiating populations from the bottom of the racial order within a strictly U.S. political dialogue about the political and economic positioning of populations (Ong 1992). However, like the term African, Asian has the potential to pull immigrants in the United States from the U.S. nation building project and into a more global discourse about power. Especially with the growth of the Pacific rim economy and the flourishing economies of Japan and Korea, immigrants from Asia may be brought into political life in complex ways that extend beyond nationalist politics.

To date, contestation over the identity designation of people of color continues to be a discourse about the manner in which those of non-European descent should be linguistically signaled. Whether the racial order itself will be more directly challenged by this debate and ensuing political actions remains to be seen. The shaping of the identities of immigrant populations in the United States has the potential of exposing the racial dynamics that underlie the U.S. relationship to its client states and its location within a larger global racial order. The global ordering of race is part of a process of differentiation fundamental to the dynamics of capitalism (Wolf 1982; Worsely 1984). In this sense, "race-thinking" has a counterhegemonic potential, one that has been developing within Latin America as pan-Indian movements increasingly speak with voices that move them beyond the reach of nationalist claims (Field 1991; Kearney 1991b).

IV. THE U.S. HEGEMONIC RESPONSES TO TRANSMIGRANT RESISTANCES: MULTICULTURALISM OR REACTION

We have seen that for nation-states, creating citizens is not just a matter of legal documents but is something that requires fashioning "subjects" (Foucault 1972). Nation building consists of multiple and often antagonistic projects. There is no single message, but rather a struggle to define the limits of the debate that provide the various antagonists with conceptualizations of their conflicting positions.

The manner in which both anti-immigrant messages and the incorporative welcome to immigrants are framed can be seen as elements of hegemonic nation building projects.

Previously, the construction of U.S. nationhood was shaped by an assimilationist ideology that defined cultural difference as opposed to the interests of the nation. Later, largely in response to changes in the configuration of world economic and political relations and processes, an ideology of cultural pluralism emerged as predominant. The people of the United States were seen as having diverse cultural roots but sharing an overarching American identity and loyalty to the U.S. At the same time, however, an openly racist message of white supremacy and anti-immigrant sentiment coexisted with constructions of the U.S. nation, and were at various moments legitimized through restrictive legislation and official pronouncements. The U.S. continues to be defined as the "land where our fathers died, land of the pilgrim's pride," as immigrant children are taught to sing of common symbols that remain exclusionary.

As we have seen, the current U.S. response to transnationalism and the identity constructions with which transmigrants challenge their incorporation contain renewed and invigorated efforts at both incorporation and exclusion. The incorporative drive now takes the form of a discourse on multiculturalism; at the same historical moment, a publicly articulated racism forms a substrate of legitimate U.S. political discourse.

Unlike cultural pluralism, multiculturalism grants some recognition to the barriers of race by positing a diversity of populations whose experiences of discrimination have given particular histories to people of color in the United States. Under a banner of multiculturalism, educational institutions and public officials signal their acknowledgement that previous definitions of the nation and of the cultural canon have excluded populations constructed as racially and cultural different. Clearly, the legitimization of polivocality through specific reference to the cultural heritages of people of color does not contain the virulence of white supremacy. However, in the forms in which it has been popularized, exactly because it is part of the U.S. nation building project, multiculturalism does not encompass the domains of practice that are within the daily province of transmigrants. The paradigm validates and celebrates cultural roots but leaves no conceptual space for interconnections beyond the borders of the United States.

Whether articulated in racist attacks on immigration or in the nuanced nationalism of multiculturalism, the U.S. nation building project conceptually excludes political identification and participation in other national locations for populations who are racially differentiated. In practice, as we have seen, the U.S. State Department, in particular situations, has been willing to grant certain transmigrant leaders permission as U.S. citizens to become official representatives of their "home country." Stanislaus, who has lived in the United States for 40 years, was granted permission by the United States to be Grenada's ambassador to the United Nations. Perhaps this is because of a growing identification of a section of the leadership of transmigrant populations with the national interests of the United States. This type of active involvement is not the political path generally advocated, however. Multiculturalism encourages a discussion of empowerment within the United States.

As we have seen, messages concerning the multicultural agenda for populations of color in the United States are sometimes made quite explicit. This was the case with the U.S. foundations, Catholic Diocesan officials, and governmental agencies in the 1980s that provided funding for Haitian organizations. Their mission was to encourage ethnic politics, but to discourage transnational activities and continuing political loyalties to Haiti. Jesse Jackson, finding himself addressing an essentially Caribbean audience in 1985, told his listeners that they must become citizens and register to vote. Sometimes the message is encapsulated in the terms by which immigrants from post-colonial states are addressed and the types of coalitions that U.S. politicians try to build. Dinkins sees Haitians and West Indians as Haitian-Americans or Caribbean-Americans. The array of African-American, Hispanic, and white speakers who addressed the 1992 Democratic Presidential Convention sounded the call. The Horatio Alger myth was clothed in a rainbow of skin colors and ethnicities, each of which had been able through hard work and participation in the political system to achieve the American dream. The words "national unity," "the American nation," and "revival of pride in America" resounded through the hall as they were beamed via TV into the living rooms of the country.

However, the older image of the U.S. nation-state as white has been perpetuated during the 1980s and 1990s as transmigrant populations have grown and the U.S. has faced an intensified economic crisis. Accompanying this national construction and assisted by it, have been attacks on affirmative action policies and public thrusts against civil rights, culminating in racially inspired attacks on people of color, both on school campuses and in neighborhoods.

The legitimization of this strand of the debate is reflected in a 1992 Op-ed article to the *New York Times* entitled "Bar the Doors." Reviving images of immigrants who take jobs and resources from Americans, the article encourages sealing the borders by building "insurmountable barriers" along the Mexican border. The reader is informed that

> Our immigration policy is conducive to the proliferation of a foreign underclass that may be permanently unassimilable, thus fostering inner-city ghettoes and ethnic tensions. What's more, the economic effects of the growth of such an underclass will weaken our power to compete in the global marketplace (Daniel James 1992:21).

Immigrants, permanently foreign, are the enemy within and constitute a threat to national well-being — even survival. However, it must be noted that hegemony is a process of defining the parameters of the thinkable, the common place, the taken-for-granted. Within the contentious spiral of hegemonic discourse, racist, anti-immigrant sentiment can be maintained in a dialectical relationship to multiculturalism. Immigrant voices may be celebrated as the future strength of the nation or castigated as manifestations of a festering sore on the body politic. Yet both readings may draw from a wellspring of thought that maintains and sanctions identification with nation-states.

V. WHAT POSITION FOR THE OBSERVER? CLASS, GENDER, AND THE GLOBE

The current historical moment, a time of both disjuncture and reinscription leads us to ask what lies ahead? Will we see the processes of transnational migration continue over time, with new generations maintaining their multiple ties to nation-states that are ancestral homes? What are the implications of transnationalism for the hierarchy of power between states? Will transmigrants contribute to embedding the intensive penetration of capital and the displacement of populations into the taken-for-granted cultural politics of postcolonial states? Or will labor-exporting states prove to be locales from which transmigrants can formulate an anti-imperialist politics. Will the many contradictions that arise from the practices and multiple identities of transmigrants fracture imaginings of a world divided into discrete nation-states, leaving conceptual space for a politics of liberation.

And finally, what are the implications of our acknowledgement that we are positioned observers of transnationalism? Both in the past and at present U.S. social scientists have been intimately involved in formulating and popularizing the concepts of ethnicity, race, and nationalism that shape the experience of immigrants. The question, therefore, is not whether we should play a role in the political struggles over the identity of immigrants. We are already playing a role as we describe the manner in which immigrants live lives stretched across national borders and create a vocabulary of transnationalism that acknowledges and makes salient such practices. The question is rather what part should we play.

Although we have stressed that since transnationalism is an ongoing process of linkage rather than a unitary phenomenon, by applying a label we risk recreating a bounded, classless reification similar to the very construct of "ethnic group" and "nation." On the other hand, by conceptualizing transnationalism, not as flows of items and ideas, but as social relations constructed by subordinated populations, we may be contributing to social movements that think beyond what is deemed thinkable. By giving primacy to the agency of transmigrants, we seek to participate in the formulation of what Gilroy has called "an explicitly transnational perspective" (Gilroy 1992). We join with those transmigrants who are striving to locate areas of resistance not yet fully encapsulated within hegemonic domains as well as to reappropriate what has been limited and bound by the constraints of nationalism. There are indications that multinational conglomerates not only operate beyond national boundaries but also reflect globally articulated class interests rather than national concerns. By focusing attention on transnationalism and insisting that it must be understood in relationship to global capital we hope to contribute to a response that also moves beyond the boundaries and blinders of nation-states.

We have documented the manner in which processes of class formation within postcolonial nation-states have been relocated into transnational spaces. Transmigrant struggles to obtain resources and improve their social positioning are part of processes by which transmigrants try to maintain their relationship to global capital. This relocation of the processes of class formation has not produced a globalized politicized proletariat. As have immigrant populations in the past, current transmigrants react to their positions of subordination by identifying bases of resistance within multiclass populations that are seen as culturally and/or racially differentiated from the dominant class in the United States. In this sense, constructions of the deterritorialized nation-state do not challenge the growing global capitalist class. And yet.

Questions of loyalty are being decentered as the constriction of identities within the geography of national borders is being openly challenged by deterritorialized nation-state constructions and global racial categories. Transnational spaces, overflowing with daily life experiences that are not congruent with hegemonic boundaries of identification, provide a terrain for new and different subjectivities and public descriptors. The transnational practices of transmigrants, though thoroughly embedded in historically specific cultural understandings, contain the basis for developing broader critiques of the manner in which the domination of an emerging global capitalist class penetrates both postcolonial states and supersedes the national interests of all nation-states. Identifications that are not being articulated elsewhere, identifications as workers subordinated by global capital (Nash 1983), as women who face domination in all nations (Sutton 1992b), and as inhabitants of the earth threatened by global capitalist interests, all become possibilities once loyalties to nation-states are dislocated.

What is certain is that race is reemerging at the core of many of the arguments about identity and as a deeply embedded and effective way to group populations globally on biological/"natural" grounds. The potential of racial signification as a form of struggle will always hold within it a contradictory current. To uphold an African or Asian identity which emphasizes a biological unity beyond the domains of particular cultures and histories means entering into a discourse about human difference in a terrain already claimed by those who maintain whiteness as a realm of superiority. Global identities, whether constructed as "African" or "Asian," have the tendency to "biologize" the discourse around the present structure of global social relations at the same time that they challenge this structure.

Social scientists as observers of transnational processes can play a role in breaking through the bounded thinking that has defined and delimited the dialogue that challenges nation building agendas. Defining culture and society in ways that are not coterminous with national borders and are not confined within national borders is one way of opening this discourse.

Transmigrants accommodate to global capitalist restructuring and even reinforce hegemonic constructions of nation-states and race that legitimate their subordination in the world system, while at the same time they engage in practices that undermine loyalties basic to preserving this global structure of dominance. Underlying our emerging awareness of transnationalism is a conundrum that faces us all, the interpenetration of structures and practices of domination and resistance.

NOTES

1. This figure has not been corroborated by official records because of the wide dispersal of Grenadian migrants to Trinidad, Barbados, England, and Canada, as well as to the United States, and the large number of migrants who live without official documents in these countries. The enormous size of adult diasporic populations relative to those remaining "at home" seems to hold for all small eastern Caribbean countries, however.

2. Jewish Americans, in their relationship to Israel, present a special case that needs further exploration. Until the influx of immigrants to Israel during this century, Israel was for most an imagined homeland that they supported but in which they were not embedded by multiple fields of social relations. As individuals and families from the United States went to Israel to settle in the forty-five years since the founding of the state, transnational family networks have been built. Until recently, however, most Jewish American organizations served as lobbyists for Israel rather than as participants in transnational political organizing for political positions within Israel. There are indicators that this political situation is changing and that many Jewish Americans are becoming fully transnational. For example, Meyer Kahane of the Jewish Defense League, based in the United States, built a political constituency and won election to the Israeli Parliament in the 1980s.

3. The links between race signification and class domination in the Caribbean are explored in Austin's discussion of Jamaican postcolonial nation building processes (Austin 1984).

References

Abella, Domingo
　1971　From Indio to Filipino. Philippine Historical Review
　　　　4:1–34.

Ambursley, Fitzroy
　1983　Grenada: The New Jewel Revolution. *In* Crisis in the
　　　　Caribbean. F. Ambursley and R. Cohen, eds., pp. 191–
　　　　222. New York: Monthly Review Press.

Anderson, Benedict
　1991　Imagined Communities: Reflections on the Origins
　　　　and Spread of Nationalism. Revised ed. London:
　　　　Verso.

Anglade, George
　1990　La chance qui passe. November 15. Unpublished
　　　　document of Operation Lavalas. *In* files of Georges
　　　　Fouron.

Anzaldua, Gloria
　1987　Borderlands, La Frontera: The New Mestiza. San
　　　　Francisco: Spinsters/Aunt Lute.

Appadurai, Arju
　1986　Theory in Anthropology: Center and Periphery. Com-
　　　　parative Studies in Society and History 28(1):356–361.
　1990　Disjuncture and Difference in the Global Cultural
　　　　Economy. Public Culture 2(2):1–24.
　1991　Global Ethnospaces: Notes and Queries for a Transna-
　　　　tional Anthropology. *In* Recapturing Anthropology.
　　　　R. Fox, ed., pp. 191–210. Santa Fe, NM: School of
　　　　American Research Press.

Appadurai, Arjun, and Carol Breckenridge
　1988　Why Public Culture? Public Culture 1(1):5–9.

Apter, David E.
　1965　The Politics of Modernization. Chicago: University of
　　　　Chicago Press.

Aquino, Corazon
	1986	Public Speech, July.

Aristide, Jean-Betrand
	1990	In the Parish of the Poor: Writings from Haiti. Maryknoll, NY: Orbis Press.

Asante, Molefi Kete
	1992a	Afrocentric Systematics. Black Issues in Higher Education 9(12):16–17,21–22.
	1992b	Multiculturalism: An Exchange. *In* Debating: The Controversy Over Political Correctness on College Campuses. P. C. Paul Berman, ed., pp. 299–311. New York: Dell.

Asad, Talal
	1986	The Concept of Cultural Translation in British Social Anthropology. *In* Writing Culture: The Poetics and Politics of Ethnography. James Clifford and George Marcus, eds., pp. 141–164. Berkeley: University of California Press.

Austin, Diane J.
	1984	Urban Life in Kingston, Jamaica: The Cultural and Class Ideology of Two Neighborhoods. New York: Gordon and Breach.

Bach, Robert
	1980	On the Holism of a World System Perspective in Hopkins' and Wallerstein's Processes of the World-System. Beverly Hills: Sage Publications.

Baldwin, James
	1971	Nobody Knows My Name. New York: Dial Press.

Baldwin, Robert
	1975	Foreign Trade Regiemes and Economic Development: The Philippines. New York: Columbia University Press.

Ballard, Roger
	1987	The Political Economy of Migration: Pakistan, Britain, and the Middle East. *In* Migrants, Workers, and the Social Order. J. Eades, ed., pp. 17–43. New York: Tavistock Publications.

Barnes, J.
1954 Class and Committees in a Norwegian Island Parish. Human Relations 7:39–58.

Barth, Fredrik (Ed.)
1969 Ethnic Groups and Boundaries: The Social Organization of Cultural Difference. Boston: Little Brown.

Basch, Linda
1978 Workin' for the Yankee Dollar: The Impact of a Transnational Petroleum Company on Caribbean Class and Ethnic Relations. PhD dissertation. Department of Anthropology, New York University.

1982 Population Movements Within the English-Speaking Caribbean: An Overview. New York: United Nations Institute for Training and Research.

1987a The Vincentians and Grenadians: The Role of Voluntary Associations in Immigrant Adaptation to New York City. *In* New Immigrants in New York. Nancy Foner, ed., pp. 159–193. New York: Columbia University Press.

1987b Ethnicity, Race and Migration: Changing Dimensions of West Indian Identity in New York and Trinidad. Paper presented at 86th Annual Meeting of the American Anthropological Association. Chicago.

1988 Multiple Meanings of Ethnicity: Eastern Caribbean Immigrant Consciousness in Transnational Perspective. Paper presented at 87th Annual Meeting of American Anthropological Association. Phoenix.

1989 Barriers to Health Care for Immigrants: Institutional, Ideological, and Cultural. Paper presented at New York City Conference on The Barriers to Health Care for Immigrants. New York Academy of Medicine.

1992 The Politics of Caribbeanization: Vincentians and Grenadians in New York. *In* Caribbean Life in New York City: Sociocultural Dimensions, rev. ed. C. R. Sutton and E. M. Chaney, eds., pp. 147–166. New York: Center for Migration Studies.

Basch, Linda, and Joyce Toney
1988 Eastern Caribbean Labor Force Participation in New York: Implications for Race and Ethnicity. Paper

presented in Migration and Population Studies
Series. College of Staten Island Center for Immigrant
and Population Studies and Massachusetts Institute
of Technology Department of Urban Studies.

Basch, Linda, Rosina Wiltshire, Winston Wiltshire, and Joyce Toney
1990   Caribbbean Regional and International Migration:
Transnational Dimensions. Ottawa, Canada: International Development Research Centre.

Bastien, Remy
1961   Haitian Rural Family Organization. Social and
Economic Studies 10(4):478–510.

Bell, David
1985   The Triumph of Asian Americans: America's Greatest
Success Story. New Republic, July 15:24–31.

Bellegarde-Smith, Patrick
1980   Haitian Social Thought in the 19th Century Caribbean Studies 20(1):5–33.

1990   Haiti: The Breached Citadel. Boulder, CO: Westview.

Bentley, G. C.
1987   Ethnicity and Practice. Comparative Studies of
Society and History 24:24–55.

Berreman, Gerald D.
1972   Race, Caste and Other Invidious Distinctions in Social Stratification. In Majority and Minority. Norman
Yetman, ed., pp. 21–39. Boston: Allyn and Bacon.

Bishop, Maurice
1982   Forward Ever! Three Years of Revolution: Speeches of
Maurice Bishop. Introduction by Jim Percy. Sydney:
Pathfinder Press.

Black Enterprise
1987   When the Going Gets Tough ... The Tough Get
Going. August.

Blake, Judith
1961   Family Structure in Jamaica. New York: Glencoe.

Blanc-Szanton, Cristina
1982a   People in Movement: Mobility and Leadership in a
Central Thai Town. PhD dissertation. Department of
Anthropology, Columbia University.

1982b   Women and Men in Iloilo Province, Central Philip-
         pines (1906–1970). *In* Women in Southeast Asia. P.
         Van Esterick, ed. Northern Illinois University
         Monograph Series.

1985a   Thai and Sino-Thai in Small Town Thailand: Chang-
         ing Patterns of Inter-Ethnic Relations. *In* The Chinese
         in Southeast Asia Volume II: Identity, Culture and
         Politics. P. Gosling and L. Lim, eds., pp. 99–125.
         Singapore: Maruzen Press.

1985b   Ethnic Identities and Aspects of Class in Contem-
         porary Central Thailand. Paper presented at Sym-
         posium on Changing Identities of the Southeast
         Asian Chinese since World War II. Australia National
         University, Canberra.

1988   Field Interviews.

1990   Collision of Cultures: Historical Reformulations of
         Gender in the Lowland Visayas, Philippines. *In*
         Power and Difference. J. M. Atkinson and S. Er-
         rington, eds., pp. 345–384. Stanford, CA: Stanford
         University Press.

1990   Review of Contrasting Colonialism: Translation and
         Christian Conversion in Tagalog Society under Early
         Spanish Rule, by Vicente L. Rafael. Pacific Affairs 21.

1992   Change and Politics in a Western Visayan
         Municipality. *In* From Marcos to Aquino. B. J.
         Kerkvliet and R. B. Mojares, eds., pp. 82–104.
         Honolulu: University of Hawaii Press.

Blaustein, Arthur, and Geoffery Faux
1972   The Star-Spangled Hustle. Garden City, NJ: Anchor
         Press.

Block, Fred
1987   Revising State Theory: Essays in Politics and Postin-
         dustrialization. Philadelphia: Temple University Press.

Boccio, Rose
1991   They Dream of America. Sun Sentinel 26:1,4A.

Bossen, Laurel
1984   The Redivision of Labor: Women and Economic
         Choice in Four Guatemalan Communities. Albany:
         State University of New York Press.

Boston Globe
1992 Editorial: Partners in Haiti's Crimes. October 1:12.

Bourdieu, Pierre
1977 Outline of a Theory of Practice. Cambridge, MA: Cambridge University Press.

Broad, Robin
1988 Unequal Alliance 1979–86. The World Bank, the International Monetary Fund and the Philippines. Quezon City: Ateneo de Manila Press.

Brow, James
1988 In Pursuit of Hegemony. American Ethnologist 15:311–327.

Bryce-Laporte, Roy
1972 Black Immigrants: The Experience of Invisibility and Inequality. Journal of Black Studies 3:29–56.

Bryce-Laporte, Roy (Ed.)
1980 Sourcebook on the New Immigrants. New Jersey: Transaction Books.

Buchanan, Susan
1980 Scattered Seeds: The Meaning of the Migration of Haitians in New York City. PhD dissertation. New York University.
1981 Haitian Emigration: The Perspective from South Florida and Haiti. Port-au-Prince, Haiti: U.S. Agency for International Development.

Cable News Network
1993 Haiti, Death of a Nation. January 14.

Carib News
1988 Black Execs on Firing Line. April 5.

Carmichael, A. C.
1833 Domestic Manners and Social Conditions of the White, Coloured, and Negro Population of the West Indies. Two Volumes. London: Whittaker, Treacher.

Casimir-Liautaud, Jean
1975 Haitian Social Structure in the Nineteenth Century. *In* Working Papers in Haitian Society and Culture. S. Mintz, ed., pp. 35–49. New Haven: Antilles Research Program Yale University.

Cassagnol Chierici, Rose Marie
  1990   Making It: Migration and Adaptation Among Haitian
          Boat People in the United States. New York: AMS
          Press.

Centre for Contemporary Cultural Studies
  1982   The Empire Strikes Back: Race and Racism in 70s
          Britain. London: Hutchinson.

Chaney, Elsa
  1979   The World Economy and Contemporary Migration.
          International Migration Review 13:204–212.

Charles, Carolle
  1990a   A Transnational Dialectic of Race, Class, and Eth-
          nicity: Patterns of Identities and Forms of Conscious-
          ness among Haitian Migrants in New York City,
          PhD dissertation. Department of Sociology, Suny–Bin-
          ghamton.
  1990b   Distinct Meanings of Blackness: Patterns of Identity
          among Haitian Migrants in New York City. Cimarron
          (2)3:129–138.
  1992a   Transnationalism in the Construct of Haitian
          Migrants' Racial Categories of Identity in New York
          City. In Towards a Transnational Perspective. N.
          Glick Schiller, L. Basch, and C. Blanc-Szanton, eds.,
          pp. 104–123. New York: New York Academy of
          Science.
  1992b   Feminism and Power: Haitian Women and Political
          Struggle in Haiti and the Diaspora, 1930–1990. Paper
          delivered at the Haitian Studies Association
          Conference, Boston.

Chatterjee, Partha
  1986   Nationalist Thought and the Colonial World:
          A Derivative Discourse. London: Zed Books.

Cheetham, Russell, and Edward Hawkins
  1976   The Philippines: Priorities and Prospects for Develop-
          ment. Washington DC: The World Bank.

Chisholm, Shirley
  1970   Unbought and Unbossed. New York: Houghton
          Mifflin.

City Planning Commission
  1985   Private communication.

Clifford, James
  1988   The Predicament of Culture: Twentieth-Century
          Ethnography, Literature, and Art. Cambridge, MA:
          Harvard University Press.

Colen, Shelle
  1986   'With Respect and Feelings:' Voices of West Indian
          Child Care and Domestic Workers in New York City.
          In All American Women: Lines That Divide, Ties that
          Bind. J.B. Cole, ed., pp. 46–70. New York: Free Press.
  1990   'Housekeeping' for the Green Card: West Indian
          Household Workers, The State and Stratified
          Reproduction in New York. *In* At Work in Homes:
          Domestic Workers in World Perspective. R. Sanjek
          and S. Colen, eds., pp. 89–118. Washington, DC:
          American Anthropological Society.

Colthurst, John B.
  1977   The Colthurst Journal: Journal of a Special Magistrate
          in the Islands of Barbados and St. Vincent, July 1835–
          September 1838. Millwood, NY: KTO Press.

Comaroff, Jean
  1985   Body of Power, Spirit of Resistance: The Culture and
          History of a South Africa People. Chicago: University
          of Chicago Press.

Comaroff, Jean, and John L. Comaroff
  1991   Of Revelation and Revolution: Christianity,
          Colonialism, and Consciousness in South Africa.
          Chicago: University Of Chicago Press.

Comaroff, John L.
  1982   Dialectical Systems, History and Anthropology: Units
          of Study and Questions of History. Journal of South
          African Studies 8(2):144–172.

Commission on Overseas Filipinos
  1988   Annual Report, Quezon City, Philippines.

Cone, James H.
  1991   Martin & Malcolm & America: A Dream or a
          Nightmare. Maryknoll, NY: Orbis Books.

Cooper, Frederick, and Ann Stoler (Eds.)
  1989   Special Section: Tensions of Empire. American Eth-
          nologist 16(4).

Crane, Julia G.
 1971   Educated to Emigrate: The Social Organization of
        Saba. Assen, the Netherlands: Van Gorcum.

Cruse, Harold
 1985   [1967] The Crises of the Negro Intellectual. Boston:
        Little Brown.

Dahl, Robert Alan
 1961   Who Governs?: Democracy and Power in an
        American City. New Haven: Yale University Press.

Dandler, Jorge, and Carmen Medeiros
 1988   Temporary Migration from Cochabamba, Bolivia to
        Argentina: Patterns and Impact in Sending Areas. *In*
        When Borders Don't Divide: Labor Migration and
        Refugee Movements in the Americas. P. Pessar, ed.,
        pp. 8–41. Staten Island, NY: Center for Migration
        Studies.

Davy, John
 1971   [1854] The West Indies Before and Since Slave
        Emancipation. London: Frank Cass.

Delatour, Frantz, and Karl Voltaire
 1980   International Subcontracting Activities in Haiti.
        Washington DC: Brookings Institution.

DeWind, Josh
 1987   The Remittances of Haitian Immigrants in New York
        City. Unpublished Final Report prepared for
        Citibank. In files of author.

DeWind, Josh, and McKinney, David
 1986   Aiding Migration: The Impact of International
        Development Assistance on Haiti. Boulder, CO:
        Westview.

Diaspora
 1991   Spring Issue 1(1).

di Leonardo, Michaela
 1984   The Varieties of Ethnic Experience: Kinship, Class,
        and Gender among California Italian-Americans.
        Ithaca, NY: Cornell University Press.

Dreyfuss, Joel
 1993   The Invisible Immigrants. New York Times May 23,
        pp. 20, 21, 80–81.

Dupuy, Alex
    1989   Haiti in the World Economy: Class Race, and Under-
            development Since 1700. Boulder, CO: Westview.

Duvalier, François, and Lorimer Denis
    1958   Le problème des classes à travers l'histoire d'Haiti.
            2ème Edition. Port-au-Prince: Collection "Les Griots."

Eades, Jeremy
    1987   Anthropologists and Migrants: Changing Models and
            Realities. In Migrants, Workers, and the Social Order.
            J. Eades, ed. ASA Monographs 26, pp. 1–16. London:
            Tavistock Publications.

Ehrenreich, Barbara
    1992   The Challenge for the Left. In Debating. P. C. Paul
            Berman, ed., pp. 299–311. New York: Dell.

Enloe, Cynthia
    1990   Bananas, Beaches, and Bases: Making Feminist Sense
            of International Politics. Berkeley: University of
            California Press.

Epstein, A. L.
    1958   Politics in an Urban African Community. Manchester:
            Manchester University Press.

Faison, Seth
    1991   Manhattan Rally Supports Arisitide. New York Times
            October 12:31–32.

Field, Les
    1991   Ecuador's Pan-Indian Uprising. Report on the
            Americas XXV(3):39–44.

Filipino Reporter
    1973a   The Return of the Natives. September 16.
    1973b   24 Flights to Bring in 4,000 Tourists. December 21:9–
            10.
    1985   Philcir is Inaugurated. May 3–9:8.
    1987   Agenda of the Unity Conference. August 9–11:8.
    1989a   Florida Fil-Ams Active in the Unity Movement.
            Feb 8–14:1,10–11.
    1989b   Editorial. September 8–14:12.

Fitzpatrick, Joseph P.
1971   Puerto Rican Americans: The Meaning of Migration
        to the Mainland. 2nd ed. Englewood Cliffs, NJ: Pren-
        tice-Hall.

Foner, Nancy
1992   West Indians in New York City and London: A Com-
        parative Analysis. *In* Caribbean Immigrants in New
        York, Revised ed. Constance Sutton and Elsa Chaney,
        eds., pp. 108–120. New York: Center for Migration
        Studies.
1987   The Jamaicans: Race and Ethnicity Among Migrants
        in New York City. *In* New Immigrants in New York
        City: Race and Ethnicity Among Migrants in New
        York City. Nancy Foner, ed., pp. 195–217. New York:
        Columbia University Press.

Ford Foundation
1984   Annual Report. New York: Ford Foundation.

Foster, Robert
1991   Making National Cultures in the Global Ecumene.
        Annual Review of Anthropology 20:235–260.

Foucault, Michel
1972   The Archaeology of Knowledge and the Discourse on
        Language. New York: Pantheon Books.

Fouron, Georges
1984   Patterns of Adaptation of Haitian Immigrants of the
        1970's in New York City. PhD dissertation. Teachers
        College, Columbia University.
1985   The Black Immigrant Dilemma in the United States:
        The Haitian Experience. Journal of Caribbean Studies
        3(3):242–265.
1993   Dependency and Labor Migration: Haiti in the Fold
        of Global Capitalism. Durham, NC: Duke University
        Press.

Fox, Richard
1987   Gandhian Socialism, Hindu Identity and the JP Move-
        ment: Cultural Domination in the World System. The
        Journal of Commonwealth and Comparative Politics
        xxv(3):233–247.

1990a   Hindu Nationalism in the Making, or the Rise of the Hindian. *In* Nationalist Ideologies and the Production of National Cultures. Richard G. Fox, ed., pp. 63–80. Washington, DC: American Anthropological Association.

1990b   (Ed.) Nationalist Ideologies and the Production of National Cultures. American Ethnological Society Monograph Series, Vol. 2. Washington DC: American Anthropological Association.

Francisque, Edouard
1986   La Structure Economique et Sociale D'Haiti. Port-au-Prince: Henri Deschamps.

Fried, Morton
1975   The Notion of Tribe. Menlo Park, CA: Cummings Publications.

Friedman, Jonathan
1992   Myth, History, and Political Identity. Cultural Anthropology 7(2):194–210.

Gardner, Robert W., Bryant Robey, and Peter C. Smith
1985   Asian Americans: Growth, Change and Diversity, Population Bulletin 40(4). Washington DC: Population Reference Bureau Inc.

Gates Jr., Henry Lewis
1986   Editor's Introduction: Writing "Race" and the Difference it Makes. *In* Race Writing, and Difference. 'Race,' Writing, and Difference. ed. H. L. Gates Jr., pp. 1–20. Chicago: University of Chicago Press.

Geertz, Clifford
1983   Local Knowledge: Further Essays in Interpretive Anthropology. New York: Basic Books.

Gellner, Ernest
1983   Nations and Nationalism. Ithaca, NY: Cornell University Press.

Georges, Eugenia
1990   The Making of a Transnational Community: Migration, Development, and Cultural Change in the Dominican Republic. New York: Columbia University Press.

Ghosh, Amitav
   1988   The Shadow Lines. New York: Viking Press.

Gilman, Sander
   1986   Black Bodies, White Bodies: Toward an Iconography
            of Female Sexuality in Late Nineteenth-Century Art,
            Medicine, and Literature. In 'Race,' Writing, and
            Difference. H. L. Gates Jr., ed., pp. 223–261. Chicago:
            University of Chicago Press.

Gilroy, Paul
   1991   'There Ain't No Black in the Union Jack': The Cul-
            tural Politics of Race and Nation. Chicago: University
            of Chicago Press.
   1992   Cultural Studies and Ethnic Absolutism. In Cultural
            Studies. L. Grossberg, C. Nelson, and P. Treichler,
            eds., pp. 187–198. London: Routledge, Chapmin and
            Hall Inc.

Glazer, Nathan
   1954   Ethnic Groups in America. In Freedom and Control
            in Modern Society. Morroe Berger, Theodore Abel,
            and Charles H. Page, eds., pp. 158–173. New York:
            Van Nostrand.
   1983   Ethnic Dilemmas 1964–1982. Cambridge, MA: Har-
            vard University Press.

Glazer, Nathan, and Patrick Moynihan
   1970   [1963] Beyond the Melting Pot: the Negroes, Puerto
            Ricans, Jews, Italians, and Irish of New York City.
            Cambridge, MA: MIT Press.

Glick (Schiller), Nina Barnett
   1975   The Formation of a Haitian Ethnic Group. PhD disser-
            tation. Department of Anthropology, Columbia
            University.

Glick Schiller, Nina
   1977   Ethnic Groups Are Made Not Born. In Ethnic
            Encounters: Identities and Contexts. George Hicks
            and Philip Leis, eds., pp. 23–35. North Scituate, MA:
            Duxbury Press.
   1992a   Haitian Transnational Practice and National Dis-
            course. In Caribbean Immigrants in New York,
            Revised ed. C. Sutton and E. Chaney, eds., pp. 184–
            189. New York: Center for Migration Studies.

1992b   The Implications of Haitian Transnationalism for U.S. Haitian Relations: Contradictions of the Deterritorialized Nation State. Paper delivered at the Meetings of the Haitian Studies Association, Boston.

1992c   What's Wrong with this Picture? The Hegemonic Construction of Culture in AIDS Research in the United States. Medical Anthropology Quarterly 6(3):237–254.

Glick Schiller, Nina, and Georges Fouron
1990   'Everywhere We Go We Are in Danger': Ti Manno and the Emergence of a Haitian Transnational Identity. American Ethnologist 17(2):329–347.

Glick Schiller, Nina, and Carolle Charles
1992   'Layers of the Onion' in a Transnational Stew: Haitian Immigrant Identity in the United States. Paper delivered at the Annual Meetings of the Eastern Sociological Society, Boston.

Glick Schiller, Nina, Linda Basch, and Cristina Szanton Blanc
1992a   Towards a Definition of Transnationalism: Introductory Remarks and Research Questions. *In* Towards a Transnational Perspective on Migration: Race, Class, Ethnicity and Nationalism Reconsidered. N. Glick Schiller, L. Basch, and C. Szanton-Blanc, eds., pp. ix–xiv. New York: New York Academy of Sciences.

1992b   Transnationalism: A New Analytic Framework for Understanding Migration. *In* Towards a Transnational Perspective on Migration: Race, Class, Ethnicity and Nationalism Reconsidered. N. Glick Schiller, L. Basch, and C. Szanton-Blanc, eds., pp. 1–24. New York: New York Academy of Sciences.

Glick Schiller, Nina, Marie-Lucie Brutus, and Josh DeWind
1985   Right Here on Flatbush Avenue. The Development of Multiple Organizational Identities Among Haitian Immigrants. Occasional Papers of the Immigration Research Program. New York: Center for the Social Sciences, Columbia University.

Glick Schiller, Nina, Josh De Wind, Marie Lucie Brutus, Carrolle
Charles, Georges Fouron, and Louis Thomas
  1987   Exile, Ethnic, Refugee: Changing Organizational
          Identities Among Haitian Immigrants. Migration
          Today. xv(1):7–11.
  1992   [1987] All in the Same Boat? Unity and Diversity
          Among Haitian Immigrants. *In* Caribbean Immi-
          grants in New York, Revised ed. C. Sutton and E.
          Chaney, eds., pp. 167–184. New York: Center for
          Migration Studies.

Gmelch, George
  1992   Double Passage: The Lives of Caribbean Immigrants
          Abroad and Back Home. Ann Arbor: University of
          Michigan Press.

Golay, Frank
  1968   The Philippines: Public Policy and National
          Economic Development. Ithaca: Cornell Univer-
          sity Press.

Gonzalez, Nancie L.
  1988   Sojourners of the Caribbean: Ethnogenesis and
          Ethnohistory of the Garifuna. Urbana: University of
          Illinois Press.

Gordon, David
  1988   The Global Economy: New Edifice or Crumbling
          Foundation? New Left Review 168:24–64.

Gordon, David, Richard Edwards, and Michael Reich
  1982   Segmented Work, Divided Workers: The Historical
          Transformation of Labor in the United States. New
          York: Cambridge University Press.

Gordon, Ted, and Wahneema Lubiano
  1992   Statement of the Black Faculty Caucus. *In* Debating:
          The Controversy over Political Correctness on Col-
          lege Campuses. P. C. Paul Berman, ed., pp. 249–257.
          New York: Dell.

Gramsci, Antonio
  1971   Prison Notebooks: Selections. Quinton Hoare and
          Geoffrey Smith, trans. New York: International
          Publishers.

Grasmuck, Sherri
  1982   Migration Within the Periphery: Haitian Labor in the
          Dominican Sugar and Coffee Industries. International
          Migration Review 16:365–377.

Greeley, Andrew
  1971   The Rediscovery of Cultural Pluralism. The Antioch
          Review 31:343–367.

Greenberg, Stanley
  1980   Race and State in Capitalist Development: Compara-
          tive Perspectives. New Haven: Yale University Press.

Guha, Ranajit, and Gayatri Spivak (Eds.)
  1988   Selected Subaltern Studies. New York: Oxford
          University Press.

Gupta, Akhil
  1992   The Song of the Nonaligned World: Transnational
          Identities and the Reinscription of Space in Late
          Capitalism. Current Anthropology 7(1):63–77.

Gupta, Akhil, and James Ferguson
  1992   Beyond "Culture": Space, Identity, and the Politics
          of Difference. Cultural Anthropology 7(1):6–23.

Gutwirth-Winston, Linda
  1988   Domestic and Kinship Networks of Some American-
          Born Haitian Children. *In* Social Networks of
          Children, Adolescents and College Students.
          S. Salzinger, J. Antrobus, and M. Hammer, eds.,
          pp. 263–283. Hillsdale, NJ: Lawrence Erlbaum
          Associates.

Haitian Christian Community
  1968   Charter. Document in files of Nina Glick Schiller.

Haiti Information
  1992a   Human Rights Report 1(2):2.
  1992b   Human Rights Report 1(3):2.
  1993a   Bazin: Or the Mystification of a People 1(10)3.
  1993b   Human Rights Report 1(12):2.
  1993c   Human Rights Report 1(13):2.
  1993d   Human Rights Report 1(14):2.

Haiti Observateur
  1992   July 16.

Haiti Progres
  1992   Organisation du Dixième: resolutions du deuxième
          Congrès. August 5–11:17.

Hall, Stuart
  1977   Pluralism, Race and Class in Caribbean Society. *In*
          Race and Class in Post-Colonial Society: A Study of
          Ethnic Group Relations in the English-Speaking
          Caribbean, Bolivia, Chile and Mexico, pp. 150–180.
          Paris: UNESCO.
  1988   The Toad in the Garden: Thatcherism among the
          Theorists. *In* Marxism and the Interpretation of
          Culture. C. Nelson and L. Grossberg, eds., pp. 35–57.
          Urbana: University of Illinois Press.

Handlin, Oscar
  1973   [1951] The Uprooted. 2nd ed. Boston: Little, Brown.

Hannerz, Ulf
  1989   Scenarios for Peripheral Cultures. Paper presented at
          the symposium on Culture, Globalization and the
          World System: University of Stockholm.

Hansen, Miriam
  1993   Unstable Mixtures, Dilated Spheres: Negt and
          Kluge's *The Public Sphere and Experience*, Twenty Years
          Later. Public Culture 5(2):179–212.

Harris, Marvin
  1964   Patterns of Race in the Americas. New York: Walker.

Harvey, David
  1989   The Condition of Postmodernity: An Enquiry into the
          Origins of Cultural Change. Cambridge, MA: Basil
          Blackwell.

Hawes, Gary
  1987   The Philippine State and the Marcos Regime. Ithaca:
          Cornell University Press.

Hegeman, Susan
  1991   Shopping for Identities: 'A Nation for Nations' and
          the Weak Ethnicity of Objects. Public Culture
          3(2):71–92.

Helm, June
  1975   [1968] Essays on the Problem of the Tribe. St. Louis:
          University of Washington Press.

Herman, Judith (Ed.)
1974 The Schools and Group Identity: Educating for a New Pluralism. New York: Institute on Pluralism and Group Identity.

Herskovits, Melville
1937 Life in a Haitian Valley. New York: Knopf.

Herskovits, Melville J., and S. Frances
1947 Trinidad Village. New York: Knopf.

Herzfeld, Michael
1985 The Poetics of Manhood: Contest and Identity in a Cretan Mountain Village. Princeton: Princeton University Press.

Higham, John
1984 Send These to Me: Immigrants in Urban America. Baltimore: The Johns Hopkins University Press.

Higham, John, and Charles Brooks
1978 Ethnic Leadership in America. Baltimore: Johns Hopkins University Press.

Hobsbawm, Eric J.
1990 Nations and Nationalism since 1780: Programme, Myth and Reality. New York: Cambridge University Press.

Hobsbawm, Eric J., and Terence O. Ranger
1983 The Invention of Tradition. Cambridge, MA: Cambridge University Press.

Hoetink, Harmannus
1985 "Race" and Color in the Caribbean. *In* Caribbean Contours. S. Mintz and S. Price, eds., pp. 55–84. Baltimore: Johns Hopkins Press.

Hourihan, John J.
1975 Rule in Hairoun: A Study of the Politics of Power. PhD dissertation. Department of Anthropology, University of Massachusetts.

Hurston, Zora N.
1979 (1948) Crazy for Democracy. *In* I Love Myself: A Zora Neal Hurston Reader. A. Walker, ed. New York: Feminist Press.

Ilar, Julian
1930 Who is the Filipino? Filipino Nation, November:13.

International Labour Office
1974   Sharing in Development: A Programme of Employment, Equity and Growth for the Philippines.
Geneva: International Labour Office.

Jacques-Garvey, Amy
1969   Philosophy and Opinions of Marcus Garvey. New
York: Antheum.

James, Daniel
1992   Bar the Door. New York Times, July 25:21.

Kaleidoscope
1991   Current World Data. Santa Barbara: ABC-CLIO
Publishers.

Kallen, Horace M.
1956   (1924) Cultural Pluralism and the American Idea:
An essay. *In* Social Philosophy. Philadelphia:
University of Philadelphia Press.

Kamenka, Eugene
1973   Political Nationalism: The Evolution of the Idea.
In Nationalism: The Nature and Evolution of an Idea.
E. Kamenka, ed. pp. 2–20. Canberra: Australia National University Press.

Kapferer, Bruce
1988   Legends of People, Mythos of State: Violence,
Intolerance, and Political Culture in Sri Lanka and
Australia. Washington, DC: Smithsonian Institution
Press.

Kasindorf, Martin
1982   Asian Americans: A 'Model' Minority. Newsweek,
December 6:40–51.

Kasinitz, Philip
1992   Caribbean New York: Black Immigrants and the
Politics of Race. Ithaca: Cornell University Press.

Katipunan
1988   The Mini Marshall Plan: What's In It For For the Big
Guys? June 1(8).

Katznelson, Ira
1981   City Trenches: Urban Politics and Patterning of Class
in the United States. New York: Pantheon Books.

Kearney, Michael
  1991a   Borders and Boundaries of the State and Self at the
           End of Empire. Journal of Historical Sociology
           4(1):52–74.
  1991b   Rights of Passage and Human Rights. Ethnicity and
           Politics in the Mixteca. Paper delivered at the 90th
           Annual meetings of the American Anthropological
           Association, Chicago, November.

Kedourie, Eli
  1960   Nationalism. New York: Praeger.

Keesing, Roger
  1989   Creating the Past: Custom and Identity in the
           Contemporary Pacific. Contemporary Pacific
           1(1–2):19–42.

Kerner, Jon
  1991   Focus Group Notes: Women's General Health Issues.
           Sloan-Kettering. Unpublished document.

Knight, R.
  1989   The Emergent Global Economy. In Cities in a Global
           Society. Urban Affairs Annual Reviews. R. Knight
           and G. Gappert, eds., pp. 24–33. Newbury Park, CA:
           Sage.

Kritz, Mary M., Charles B. Keely, and Silvano M. Tomasi
  1983   Global Trends in Migration: Theory and Research on
           International Population Movement. New York: The
           Center for Migration Studies.

Labelle, Micheline
  1988   Idéologies de couleur et classes sociales en Haïti.
           Montréal: Les Presses d'Université Montreal.

Laclau, Ernesto
  1977   Politics and Ideology in Marxist Theory. London:
           Verso.

Laguerre, Michel
  1978   Ticouloute and His Kinfold: The Study of a Haitian
           Extended Family. In The Extended Family in Black
           Societies. D. B. Shimkin et al., eds., pp. 407–45. The
           Hague: Mouton.
  1982   Urban Life in the Caribbean: A Study of a Haitian
           Urban Community. Cambridge, MA: Schenkman.

1984   American Odyssey: Haitians in New York. Ithaca: Cornell.

1980   Haitians in Harvard Encyclopedia of Ethnic Groups. S. Thernstrom, ed., pp. 446–449. Cambridge, MA: Harvard University Press.

Larkin, John
1972   The Pampangans: Colonial Society in a Philippine Province. Berkeley: University California Press.

Larose, Serge
1975   The Haitian Lakou, Land, Family, and Ritual. *In* From Family and Kinship in Middle America and the Caribbean. A. Marks and R. Romer, eds., pp. 35–49. Leiden, Netherlands: Institute of Higher Studies in Cucacao and the Department of Caribbean Studies of Royal Institute of Linguistics and Anthropology.

Lessinger, Johanna
1992   Investing or Going Home? A Transnational Strategy amongIndian Immigrants in the United States. *In* Towards a Transnational Perspective on Migration: Race, Class, Ethnicity, and Nationalism Reconsidered. N. Glick Schiller, L. Basch, and C. Blanc-Szanton, eds., pp. 53–80. New York: The New York Academy of Sciences.

Levitt, K., and L. Best
1975   Character of Caribbean Economy. *In* Caribbean Economy. G. L. Beckford, ed. Mona, Jamaica: Institute of Social and Economic Research.

Lewinson, Edwin
1974   Black Politics in New York City. New York: Twayne.

Lewis, Gordon K.
1968   The Growth of the Modern West Indies. New York: Monthly Review Press.

1983   Main Currents in Caribbean Thought: The Historical Evolution of Caribbean Society in Its Ideological Aspects, 1492–1900. Baltimore: The Johns Hopkins University Press.

Leyburn, James
1966   [1941] The Haitian People. New Haven: Yale University Press.

Lieberson, Stanley
    1980   A Piece of the Pie: Blacks and White Immigrants
            Since 1880. Berkeley: University of California Press.

Lowenthal, David
    1972   West Indian Societies. New York: Oxford University
            Press.

Lundahl, Mats
    1983   The Haitian Economy: Man, Land and Markets. New
            York: St. Martins.

Magno, Alexander
    1983   Developmentalism and the New Society: The Repres-
            sive Ideology of Underdevelopmentalism. Quezon
            City: Third World Studies Center.

Malkki, Liisa
    1992   National Geographic: The Rooting of Peoples and the
            Territorialization of National Identity Among
            Scholars and Refugees. Cultural Anthropology
            7(1):24–44.

Marcos, President Ferdinand
    1980   Philippines National Commission on the Role of
            Filipino Women. Annual Reports 1977–1980.

Marcus, George
    1986   Contemporary Problems of Ethnography in the
            Modern World System. In Writing Culture. J. Clifford
            and G. Marcus, eds., pp. 165–193. University of
            California Press.

Marshall, Paule
    1981   [1959] Brown Girl, Brownstones. New York: The
            Feminist Press.
    1991   Daughters. New York: Atheneum.

Marx, Karl, and Frederick Engels
    1964   [1846] The German Ideology. S. Ryazanskaya, ed.
            Moscow: Progress Press.

Masland, Tom, Peter Katel, and Marcus Mabry
    1992   Haiti: 'We Could Turn Our Back.' Newsweek
            February 24:30–31.

Mayer, Philip
    1971   Townsmen or Tribemen: Conservatism and the
            Process of Urbanization in a South African City.
            Capetown: Oxford University Press.

McAffee, Kathy
    1985   The Philippines: A Harvest of Anger, Facts for
            Action. Oxfam Educational Publication, No. 15,
            Boston.

McCoy, Alfred W., and E. C. de Jesus
    1982   Philippine Social History, Global Trade and Local
            Transformations. Quezon City: Ateneo de Manila
            University Press.

Mintz, Sidney
    1989   [1974] Caribbean Transformations. New York:
            Columbia University Press.

Mitchell, J. Clyde
    1956   The Kalela Dance. Rhodes-Livingston Papers No. 27.
            Manchester: Manchester University Press.
    1969   Social Networks in Urban Situations. Manchester:
            Manchester University Press.

Model, Suzanne
    1991   Caribbean Immigrants: A Black Success Story?
            International Migration Review 25(2):248–276.

Mohun, Simon
    1983   Capital. In A Dictionary of Marxist Thought. Tom Bot-
            tomore, ed., pp. 60–67. Cambridge, MA: Basil Black-
            well.

Montagu, Ashley
    1974   Man's Most Dangerous Myth: The Fallacy of Race.
            Fifth edition. New York: Oxford University Press.

Moore, Colin
    1984   The Caribbean Community and the Quest for
            Political Power. Carib News, August 28:13.

Moral, Paul
    1961   Le paysan haitien: étude sur las vie rurale en Haiti.
            Paris: Maisonneuve et Larose.

Morales, Royal F.
    1974   Makibaka: The Filipino-American Struggle. Los An-
            geles: Mountainview Publishers.

Nanton, Philip
    1983   The Changing Pattern of State Control in St. Vincent
            and the Grenadines. *In* Crisis in the Caribbean. F. Am-
            bursley and R. Cohen, eds., pp. 223–246. New York:
            Monthly Review Press.

Nash, June
    1983   The Impact of the Changing International Division of
            Labor on Different Sectors of the Labor Force. *In*
            Women, Men, and the International Division of
            Labor. June Nash and Maria Patricia Fernandez-
            Kelly, eds., pp. 3–69. Albany: The State University of
            New York Press.

Nash, June, and Maria Patricia Fernandez-Kelly
    1983   Women, Men and the International Division of Labor.
            Albany: State University of New York Press.

Navarro, Vincente
    1991   The Limitations of Legitimation and Fordism and the
            Possibility for Socialist Reforms. Rethinking Marxism
            4(2):27–60.

New York Times
    1992   Restore Democracy in Haiti. March 16:A11.

Newsweek
    1982   Asian-Americans: A 'Model' Minority. December
            6:40–51.

    1984   Asian-Americans: The Drive to Excel. April:4–15.

    1992   Overheard. June 8:15.

Nicholls, David
    1974   Economic Dependence and Political Autonomy: The
            Haitian Experience. Montreal, Canada: Centre for
            Developing Area Studies McGill University .

    1979   From Dessalines to Duvalier: Race, Color, and
            National Independence in Haiti. Cambridge, MA:
            Cambridge University Press.

    1984   Past and Present in Haitian Politics. *In* Haiti — Today
            and Tomorrow. Charles Foster and Albert Valdman,
            eds., pp. 253–264. Lanham, MD: University Press of
            America.

Noble, David
    1977   America by Design: Science, Technology and the Rise
            of Corporate Capitalism. New York: Alfred A. Knopf.

Novak, Michael
   1973   The Rise of Unmeltable Ethnics: Politics and Culture
           in the Seventies. New York: Macmillan.

Ong, Aihwa
   1992   Limits to Cultural Accumulation: Chinese Capitalists
           on the American Pacific Rim. *In* Towards a Trans-
           national Perspective on Migration: Race, Class, Eth-
           nicity, and Nationalism Reconsidered. N. Glick
           Schiller, L. Basch, and C. Blanc-Szanton, eds., pp. 125–
           143. New York: The New York Academy of Sciences.

Owen, Norman G.
   1971   Compadre Colonialism: Studies on the Philippines
           Under American Rule. Michigan Papers on South
           and Southeast Asia, No. 3. Ann Arbor: University of
           Michigan, Center for South and Southeast Asian
           Studies.

Paquin, Lyonel
   1983   The Haitians: Class and Color Politics. Brooklyn:
           New York: Paquin.

   1986   Classes sociales en Haïti: classe moyenne et super
           classe. New York: Paquin.

Park, Robert E., and Ernest W. Burgess
   1969   [1924] Introduction to the Science of Society. 3rd ed.
           Chicago, IL: University of Chicago Press.

Parsons, Talcott
   1951   The Social System. Glencoe, IL: Free Press of Glencoe.

Patterson, Orlando
   1987   The Emerging West Atlantic System: Migration,
           Culture and Underdevelopment in the United States
           and the Circum-Caribbean. *In* Population in an
           Interacting World. William Alonso, ed., pp. 227–262.
           Cambridge, MA: Harvard University Press.

Pessar, Patricia (Ed.)
   1988   When Borders Don't Divide: Labor Migration and
           Refugee Movements in the Americas. Staten Island,
           NY: Center for Migration Studies.

Phelan, John Leddy
   1959   The Hispanization of the Philippines: Spanish Aims
           and Filippino Responses, 1565–1700. Madison:
           University of Wisconson Press.

Philippine Consulate
    1989   Form For Balikbayan. Manila: Philippines.
Philippine News
    1987   Filipinos for Hire: The Other Women. October
              21–27:11.
    1989a   What Is the Real Anti-Aquino Campaign In the
              United States. April 5–11:3
    1989b   Canada, U.S. Pledge Economic Support. November
              ⁻ 15–21:1,8.
    1990   Editorial. February 7–13.
    1991   The National Unity Conference. February 13–19:1,6.
Philpott, Stuart B.
    1973   West Indian Migration: The Montserrat Case.
              London: Athlone Press.
Pido, Antonio J.A.
    1986   The Filipinos in America: Macro/Micro Dimensions
              of Immigration and Integration. Staten Island, NY:
              Center for Migration Studies.
Plummer, Brenda
    1984   The Metropolitan Connection: Foreign and Semi-
              Foreign Elites in Haiti, 1900–1915. Latin American
              Research Review 19(2):114–142.
Portes, Alejandro
    1978   Migration and Underdevelopment. Politics and
              Society 8(1):1–48.
Portes, Alejandro, and Robert Bach
    1985   Latin Journey: Cuban and Mexican Immigrants in the
              United States. Berkeley: University of California Press.
Portes, Alejandro, and Ruben Rumbaut
    1990   Immigrant America, A Portrait. Berkeley: University
              of California Press.
Portes, Alejandro, and John Walton
    1981   Labor, Class, and the International System. New
              York: Academic Press.
Prince, Rod
    1985   Haiti: Family Business. London: Latin American
              Bureau.

Proudfoot, Malcolm
    1950   Population Movements in the Caribbean. Port-of-Spain, Trinidad: Central Secretariat.

Pye, Lucien
    1966   Aspects of Political development: An Analytic Study. Boston: Little, Brown.

Rafael, Vicente
    1988   Contracting Colonialism: Translation and Christian Conversion in Tagalog Society Under Early Spanish Rule. Ithaca, NY: Cornell University Press.

Rebel, Hermann
    1989   Cultural Hegemony and Class Experience: A Critical Reading of Recent Ethnological-Historical Approaches (part one). American Ethnologist 16(1):117–136.

Reid, Ira De A.
    1939   The Negro Immigrant: His Background, Characteristics and Social Adjustment, 1899–1937. New York: AMS Press.

Richardson, Bonham
    1983   Caribbean Migrants: Environment and Survival on St. Kitts and Nevis. Knoxville: University of Tennessee Press.

Richman, Karen
    1987   They Will Remember Me in the House: The Song-Pwen of Haitian Cassette-Discourse. Paper delivered at the 87th Annual Meetings of the American Anthropological Association, Chicago.
    1992a   A *Lavalas* at Home/A *Lavalas* for Home: Inflections of Transnationalism in the Discourse of Haitian President Aristide. *In* Toward a Transnational Perspective on Migration. N. Glick Schiller, L. Basch, C. Blanc-Szanton, eds., pp. 189–215. New York: New York Academy of Sciences.
    1992b   They Will Remember Me In The House: The Power of Haitian Transnational Migration. PhD dissertation. Department of Anthropology, University of Virginia.

Roberts, Bryan
    1976   The Provincial Urban System and the Process of Dependency. *In* Current Perspectives in Latin

American Research. A. Portes and H. Browning, eds.,
pp. 99–131. Austin, Texas: Institute of Latin American
Studies.

1978   Cities of Peasants. The Political Economy of Urbanization in the Third World. London: Edward Arnold.

Roberts, Michael D.
1991   Grenada's Second Invasion. Carib News, November
12:3.

Rodman, Hyman
1971   Lower-Class Families: The Culture of Poverty in
Negro Trinidad. New York: Oxford University Press.

Rojas-Aleta I., Teresita L. Silva, and Christine P. Eleazar
1977   A Profile of Filipino Women: Their Status and Role.
Manila: Philippine Business for Social Progress.

Roosens, Eugeen
1989   Creating Ethnicity: The Process of Ethnogenesis.
Newbury Park, CA: Sage Publications.

Rosaldo, Renato
1989   Culture and Truth, the Remaking of Social Analysis.
Boston: Beacon Press.

1993   Borderlands of Race and Inequality. Paper delivered
at the Spring Meetings of Society for Cultural
Anthropology. Washington DC.

Roseberry, William
1989   Anthropologies and Histories: Essays in Culture,
History. New Bruswick, NJ: Rutgers University Press.

Rothstein, Frances Abrahamer, and Michael L. Blim, (Eds.)
1992   Anthropology and the Global Factory: Studies of the
New Industrialization in the Late Twentieth Century.
New York: Bergin & Garvey.

Rottenberg, Simon
1955   [1952] Labor Relations in an Underdeveloped
Economy. Caribbean Quarterly 4(1):50–61.

Rouse, Roger
1991   Mexican Migration and the Social Space of
Postmodernism. Diaspora 1:8–23.

1992   Making Sense of Settlement: Class Transformation,
Cultural Struggle, and Transnationalism among
Mexican Migrants in the United States. *In* Towards A

Transnational Perspective on Migration: Race, Class, Ethnicity, and Nationalism Reconsidered. N. Glick Schiller, L. Basch, and C. Blanc-Szanton, eds., pp. 25–52. New York: New York Academy of Sciences.

Rubenstein, Hymie
    1983   Remittances and Rural Underdevelopment in the English Speaking Caribbean. Human Organization 42(4):306.

    1987   Coping with Poverty: Adaptation Strategies in a Caribbean Village. Boulder, CO: Westview Press.

Rushdie, Salman
    1988   The Satanic Verses. New York: Viking.

Russell, Cheetham, and Hawkins Edward
    1976   The Philippines: Priorities and Prospects for Development, pp. 94–95. Washington DC: The World Bank.

Sahlins, Peter
    1989   Boundaries: The Making of France and Spain in the Pyrenees. Berkeley: University of California.

Saint Cyr-Delpe, Marie Marthe
    1987   The Impact of Haitian Migration on the Family Structure. Unpublished manuscript in files of Nina Glick Schiller.

Sassen, Saskia
    1988   The Mobility of Labor and Capital: A Study in International Investment and Labor Flow. New York: Cambridge University Press.

Sassen-Koob, Saskia
    1981   Towards a Conceptualization of Immigrant Labor. Social Problems 29(1):65–86.

    1985   Changing Composition and Labor Market Location of Hispanic Immigrants in New York City, 1960–1980. *In* Hispanics in the U.S. Economy. M. Tienda and G. Borjas, eds., pp. 299–322. New York: Academic Press.

Schneider, David
    1968   American Kinship: A Cultural Account. Englewood Cliffs, NJ: Prentice-Hall.

Shalom, Stephen R.
    1981   The United States and the Philippines. Philadelphia: Institute for the Study of Human Issues.

Sider, Gerald
    1985   When Parrots Learn To Talk And Why They Can't:
            Domination, Deception, and Self-Deception in Indian-
            White Relations. Comparative Studies in Society and
            History 24(3):3–23.

Silk, James
    1986   Despite a Generous Spirit: Denying Asylum in the
            United States. Washington, DC: U.S. Committee for
            Refugees, American Council for Nationalities Service.

Singham, A. W.
    1968   The Hero and the Crowd in a Colonial Polity. New
            Haven: Yale University Press.

Siskind, Janet
    1992   The Invention of Thanksgiving: A Ritual of American
            Nationality. Critique of Anthropology 12(2):167–191.

Smith, Anthony
    1981   The Ethnic Revival in the Modern World. Cambridge,
            MA: Cambridge University Press.

Smith, Carol
    1984   Local History in Global Context: Social and
            Economic Transitions in Western Guatemala.
            Comparative Study of Society and History
            26(2):193–227.

Smith, M.G.
    1965a   Stratification in Grenada. Berkeley and Los Angeles:
            University of California Press.
    1965b   The Plural Society in the British West Indies.
            Berkeley: University of California Press.

Smith, Raymond T.
    1990   Kinship and Class in the West Indies: A Genealogical
            Study of Jamaica and Guyana. New York: Cambridge
            University Press.

Smucker, Glenn
    1982   Peasants and Development: A Study of Haitian Class
            and Culture. PhD dissertation. Department of
            Anthropology, New School for Social Research,
            New York.

Society for Cultural Anthropology
1993   Cultural Borders. Program for Spring Meetings.
        Washington DC.

Soto, Isa Maria
1992   West Indian Child Fostering: Its Role in Migrant
        Exchanges. *In* Caribbean Life in New York City:
        Sociocultural Dimensions, Revised ed. C. R. Sutton
        and E. M. Chaney, eds., pp. 120–137. New York: Cen-
        ter for Migration Studies.

Sowell, Thomas
1981   Ethnic America: A History. New York: Basic Books.

Spivak, Gayatri Chakrovorty
1988   Can the Subaltern Speak? *In* Marxism and the Inter-
        pretation of Culture. L. Nelson and L. Grossberg,
        eds., pp. 271–313. Urbana: University of Illinois Press.

St. Vincent Development Corporation
1977   Incentives for Investors. St. Vincent: Government
        Printing Office.

Stavrianos, L. S.
1981   Global Rift: The Third World Comes of Age. New
        York: William Morrow.

Steinberg, Stephen
1981   The Ethnic Myth: Race, Ethnicity and Class in
        America. Boston: Beacon Press.

Stepick, Alex, and Carole Dutton Stepick
1990   People in the Shadows: Survey Research among
        Haitians in Miami. Human Organization 49(1):64–76.

Stepick, Alex, with Dale Swartz
1982   Haitian Refugees in the U.S. Minority Rights Group
        Report No. 52: London: Minority Rights Group.

1986a   Unintended Consequences: Rejecting Haitian Boat
        People and the Demise of Duvalier. Paper presented
        at the Seminar on International Migration, May,
        Havana, Cuba.

1986b   Flight into Despair: A Profile of Recent Haitian
        Refugees in South Florida. International Migration
        Review 20(74):329–50.

Stoler, Ann
1989   Making Empire Respectable: The Politics of Race and
        Sexual Morality in the 20th Century Colonial Cul-
        tures. American Ethnologist 16(4):634–660.

Sudarkasa, Niara
1983   Race, Ethnicity and Identity: Some Conceptual Issues
        in Defining the Black Population in the United States.
        Conference on Immigration and the Changing Black
        Population in the United States, May, Ann Arbor.

Sunshine, Catherine
1988   The Caribbean: Survival, Struggle, and Sovereignty.
        2nd ed. Washington: EPICA.

Sussman, Gerald, David O'Connor, and Charles W. Lindsey.
1984   The Philippines 1984: The Political Economy of a
        Dying Dictatorship. Philippine Research Bulletin,
        Summer 1984.

Sutton, Constance
1992a   Introduction. In Caribbean Immigrants in New York,
        Revised ed. C. Sutton and E. Chaney, eds., pp. 15–29.
        New York: Center for Migration Studies.

1992b   Some Thoughts on Gendering and Internationalizing
        Our Thinking about Transnational Migrations. In
        Towards a Transnational Perspective on Migration:
        Race, Class, Ethnicity, and Nationalism Reconsidered.
        N. Glick Schiller, L. Basch, and C. Blanc-Szanton,
        eds., pp. 241–258. New York: New York Academy of
        Sciences.

Sutton, Constance, and Susan Makiesky–Barrow
1992   [1975] Migration and West Indian Racial and Ethnic
        Consciousness. In Caribbean Life in New York City:
        Sociocultural Dimensions New York, Revised ed. C.
        Sutton and E. Chaney, eds., pp. 86–107. New York:
        Center for Migration.

Takaki, Ronald
1989   Strangers from a Different Shore: A History of Asian
        Americans. New York: Penguin Books.

1990   Iron Cages. Race and Culture in 19th Century
        America. New York: Oxford University Press.

The New Yorker
1954   Well Caught Mr. Holder. September 25:65.

Thomas-Hope, Elizabeth M.
  1978   The Establishment of a Migration Tradition: British
          West Indian Movements to the Hispanic Caribbean in
          the Century after Emancipation. *In* Caribbean Social
          Relations. Colin G. Clark, ed., pp. 66–81. Centre for
          Latin American Studies, Monograph Series No. 8.
          Liverpool, England: University of Liverpool.
  1985   Return Migration and Its Implications for Caribbean
          Development: The Unexplored Connection. *In* Migra-
          tion and Development in the Caribbean: The Unex-
          plored Connection. Robert Pastor, ed. Boulder, CO:
          Westview.

Time
  1985   The Changing Face of America, Special Immigrants
          Issue. July 8:24–101.

Tomasi, S.M., and M.H. Engel
  1970   The Italian Experience in the United States. Staten
          Island, NY: Center for Migration Studies.

Toney, Joyce Roberta
  1986   The Development of a Culture of Migration Among a
          Caribbean People: St. Vincent and New York. PhD
          dissertation. Teachers College, Columbia University.
  1988   Emigration from St. Vincent and the Grenadines: Con-
          textual Background. Unpublished manuscript in files
          of author.

Trouillot, Michel-Rolph
  1990   Haiti: State Against Nation. New York: Monthly
          Review Press.
  1991   Anthropology and the Savage Slot: The Poetics and
          Politics of Otherness. *In* Recapturing Anthropology:
          Working in the Present. R. Fox, ed., pp. 17–44. Sante
          Fe: School of American Research.

Turner, Terence
  1992   What is Anthropology that Multiculturalist Should
          Be Mindful of It. Paper Delivered at the 91st Annual
          Meetings of the American Anthropological Associa-
          tion, San Francisco.

Tutay, Filemon V.
  1971   Private Armies Legitimized! Philippine Free Press,
          January 23:8.

Tyler, Stephen
    1986   Post Modern Ethnography: From Document of the
            Occult to Occult Document. *In* Writing Culture: The
            Poetics and Politics of Ethnography. J. Clifford and G.
            Marcus, eds., pp. 122–140. Berkeley: University of
            California Press.

University of the West Indies Development Mission
    1969   The Development Problem in St. Vincent. Kingston,
            Jamaica: Institute of Social and Economic Research,
            University of the West Indies.

U.S. Immigration and Naturalization Service
    1970   Annual Report, 1970, Washington, DC: U.S.
            Government Printing Office.
    1990   1989 Statistical Yearbook of the Immigration and
            Naturalization Service, Washington, DC: U.S.
            Government Printing Office.

U.S. News and World Report
    1984   Asian Americans: Are they making the grade? U.S.
            News and World Report. April 2:41–47.

Vail, Leroy (Ed.)
    1989   The Creation of Tribalism in Southern Africa.
            Berkeley: University of California Press.

Van Binsbergen, Wim
    1981   The Unit of Study and the Interpretation of Ethnicity.
            Journal of South African Studies 8(1):51–81.

Vassady, Bella
    1982   'The Homeland Cause' as a Stimulant to Ethnic
            Unity: The Hungarian American Response to
            Karolyi's 1914 Tour. Journal of American Ethnic
            History 2(1):39–64.

Verdery, Katherine
    1991   National Ideology under Socialism: Identities and
            Cultural Politics in Ceausescu's Romania. Berkeley:
            University of California Press.

Wakeman Jr., Frederic
    1988   Transnational and Comparative Research. Items
            42(4):85–88.

Wallerstein, Immanuel
   1974   The Modern World System. New York: Academic
          Press.
   1979   The Capitalist World Economy. Cambridge, MA:
          Cambridge University Press.
Williams, Brackette
   1989   A Class Act: Anthropology and the Race to Nation
          across Ethnic Terrain. 18:401–444. Palo Alto: Annual
          Reviews.
   1991   Stains on My Name, War in My Veins: Guyana and
          the Politics of Cultural Struggle. Durham, NC: Duke
          University Press.
Williams, Eric
   1964   [1944] Capitalism and Slavery. Chapel Hill:
          University of North Carolina Press.
Williams, Raymond
   1977   Marxism and Literature. Oxford: Oxford University
          Press.
Wilson, Peter
   1973   Crab Antics: The Social Anthropology of English-
          Speaking Negro Societies of the Caribbean. New
          Haven: Yale University.
Wilson, William Julius
   1987   The Truly Disadvantaged: The Inner City, the
          Underclass, and Public Policy. Chicago: University of
          Chicago Press.
Wiltshire, Rosina
   1992   Implications of Transnational Migration for
          Nationalism: The Caribbean Example. In Towards a
          Transnational Perspective on Migration: Race, Class,
          Ethnicity, and Nationalism Reconsidered. N. Glick
          Schiller, L. Basch, and C. Blanc-Szanton, eds., pp. 175–
          187. New York: New York Academy of Sciences.
Wiltshire, Rosina, Linda Basch, Winston Wiltshire, and Joyce Toney
   1990   Caribbean Transnational Migrant Networks: Implica-
          tions for Donor Societies. Ottawa, Canada: Interna-
          tional Development Research Centre.
Wiltshire, Winston
   1984   The Economic Impact of Caribbean Emigration on
          Labour Donor Societies: Grenada and St. Vincent.

Unpublished manuscript. New York: Research Institute for the Study of Man.

Wingfield, Roland, and Vernon Parenton
1965   Class Structure and Class Conflict in Haitian Society.
Social Forces 43(3):338–347.

Winkler, Karen
1990   Proponents of 'Multicultural' Humanities Research
Call for a Critical Look at Its Achievements. The
Chronicle of Higher Education. November 28:A5.

Wittke, Carl
1940   We Who Built America: The Saga of the Immigrant.
New York: Prentice Hall.

Woldemikael, Teklemariam
1989   Becoming Black American: Haitians and American
Institutions in Evanston, Illinois. New York: AMS
Press.

Wolf, Eric
1982   Europe and the People Without History. Berkeley:
University of California Press.
1988   Inventing Society. American Ethnologist 15:752.

Wood, Charles, and Terrance McCoy
1985   Migration, Remittances and Development: A Study of
Caribbean Cane Cutters in Florida. International
Migration Review 19(9):251–277.

Woodson, Drexel
1990   Tout Mounn Se Mounn, Men Tout Mounn Pap
Menm: Microlevel Sociocultural Aspects of Land
Tenure in a Northern Haitian Locality. PhD
dissertation. Department of Anthropology, University
of Chicago.

World Bank
1981   Memorandum on the Haitian Economy. May 13.
Latin American and Caribbean Regional Office.

Worsley, Peter
1984   The Three Worlds. Chicago: University of Chicago
Press.

Wurfel, David
1988   Filipino Politics. Development and Decay. Quezon
City: Ateneo de Manila Press.

Yanagisako, Sylvia Junko, and Jane Fishburne Collier
    1987   Toward a Unified Analysis of Gender and Kinship.
            In Gender and Kinship: Essays Toward a Unified
            Analysis. J. F. Collier and S. J. Yanagisako, eds.,
            pp. 14–50. Stanford: Stanford University Press.

Zolberg, Aristide
    1983   International Migrations in Political Perspective. *In*
            Global Trends in Migration. M. Kritz, C. Keely, and
            S. Tomasi, eds., pp. 3–27. New York: Center for
            Migration Studies.

Index